HEIDEGGER AND THE
PHILOSOPHY OF MIND

FREDERICK A. OLAFSON

HEIDEGGER AND THE PHILOSOPHY OF MIND

Yale University Press
New Haven and London

Designed by Nancy Ovedovitz and set in Baskerville type by
Rainsford Type. Printed in the United States of America by
BookCrafters, Inc., Chelsea, Michigan.

Library of Congress Cataloging-in-Publication Data

Olafson, Frederick A.
  Heidegger and the philosophy of mind.
  Bibliography: p.
  Includes index.
  1. Heidegger, Martin, 1889–1976. I. Title.
B3279.H49O37 1987   111'.092'4   86–11180
ISBN 0–300–03727–9 (alk. paper)

The paper in this book meets the guidelines for permanence and
durability of the Committee on Production Guidelines for Book
Longevity of the Council on Library Resources.

10 9 8 7 6 5 4 3 2 1

For
Allie
with love

CONTENTS

Acknowledgments, ix

Abbreviations, xi

Introduction, xiii

PART I · EXISTENCE AS THE GROUND OF PRESENCE

Chapter One
The Critique of the Cartesian Tradition, 3

Chapter Two
The World as Presence, 28

Chapter Three
Existence and *Dasein*, 52

Chapter Four
Time and Temporality, 75

Chapter Five
Feeling, Understanding, and Discourse, 102

Chapter Six
The Concept of Being, 134

PART II · PRESENCE AS THE GROUND OF EXISTENCE

Chapter Seven
The Turning, 153

Chapter Eight
Being as Presence in the Later Writings, 161

Chapter Nine
Being as the History of Being, 194

Chapter Ten
The Interdependence of Existence and Presence, 225

Conclusion, 247

Notes, 261

Index, 289

ACKNOWLEDGMENTS

I wish to thank the National Endowment for the Humanities for the Independent Research Fellowship awarded to me for the year 1978, during which work on this book was begun, and the University of California at San Diego for a sabbatical leave in the spring of 1982, which made it possible to write a first draft. I want to thank the Committee on Research of my university for the grants it has made in support of the typing of this book. I am also indebted to Celia Shugart for her careful work in preparing the manuscript and to Jean van Altena for many valuable editorial suggestions.

ABBREVIATIONS

A lmost all references are to Heidegger's published writings and lectures. In the list below, the dates given after each volume are the date of original publication or, in the case of lectures, the semester in which they were presented, and then the date of publication in the *Gesamtausgabe*. All references are to the German editions cited; but in the case of *Being and Time* and other previously published works that have now been republished in the *Gesamtausgabe*, the page references are to the original German editions. These page numbers can be found in the margins of the *Gesamtausgabe*, as well as in the English translations of *Being and Time* and some other works by Heidegger.

All translations except those of passages from *Being and Time* are my own. In the list below, the availability of English translations of entire works is noted. Where only portions of a work have been translated this is indicated by an asterisk (*). More detailed information about such partial translations can be found in M. Sass, ed., *Martin Heidegger: Bibliography and Glossary* (Bowling Green, Ohio: Bowling Green State University Press, 1982).

WORKS BY HEIDEGGER PUBLISHED IN THE GESAMTAUSGABE (Frankfurt am Main: Klostermann, 1975–)

I. Previously published works
SZ   *Sein und Zeit* (1927/1977). English translation by J. MacQuarrie and E. Robinson, *Being and Time* (New York: Harper and Row, 1962).
H   *Holzwege** (1935–46/1978).
W   *Wegmarken** (1919–58/1976).

II. Lectures
PGZ   *Prolegomena zur Geschichte des Zeitbegriffs* (1925/1979), vol. 20.
L   *Logik: Die Frage nach der Wahrheit* (1925–26/1976), vol. 21. English translation by M. Heim, *The Metaphysical Foundations of Logic* (Bloomington: Indiana University Press, 1984).
GP   *Die Grundprobleme der Phänomenologie* (1927/1975), vol. 24. English translation by A. Hofstadter, *The Basic Problems of Phenomenology* (Bloomington: Indiana University Press, 1982).

MAL   *Metaphysische Anfangsgründe der Logik im Ausgang von Leibniz* (1928/1978), vol. 26.

GM   *Die Grundbegriffe der Metaphysik: Welt-Endlichkeit-Einsamkeit* (1929–30/ 1983), vol. 29/30.

VWF   *Vom Wesen der menschlichen Freiheit. Einleitung in die Philosophie* (1930/ 1982), vol. 31.

HPG   *Hegels Phänomenologie des Geistes* (1930–31/1980), vol. 32.

A   *Aristoteles: Metaphysik IX* (1931/1981), vol. 33.

EM   *Einführung in die Metaphysik* (1935/1983), vol. 40. English translation by R. Manheim, *Introduction to Metaphysics* (New Haven: Yale University Press, 1959).

FD   *Die Frage nach dem Ding. Zu Kants Lehre von den transzendentalen Grundsätzen* (1935–36/1984), vol. 41. English translation by W. B. Bantin and V. Deutsch, *What Is A Thing?* (Chicago: Regnery, 1968).

GF   *Grundfragen der Philosophie. Ausgewählte "Probleme" der Logik* (1937–38/ 1984), vol. 45.

GB   *Grundbegriffe* (1941/1981), vol. 51.

P   *Parmenides* (1942–43/1982), vol. 53.

HAD   *Heraklit. 1. Der Anfang des abendländischen Denkens* (1943/1979).

Other published works by Heidegger

KPM   *Kant und das Problem der Metaphysik* (2d ed., Frankfurt am Main: Klostermann, 1951). English translation by J. S. Churchill, *Kant and the Problem of Metaphysics* (Bloomington: Indiana University Press, 1962).

VA   *Vorträge und Aufsätze** (Pfullingen: Neske, 1954).

ID   *Identität und Differenz* (Pfullingen: Neske, 1957). English translation by J. Stambaugh, *Identity and Difference* (New York: Harper and Row, 1969).

SG   *Der Satz vom Grunde* (Pfullingen: Neske, 1957).

G   *Gelassenheit* (Pfullingen: Neske, 1959). English translation by J. Anderson and E. H. Freund, *Discourse on Thinking* (New York: Harper and Row, 1966).

US   *Unterwegs zur Sprache** (Pfullingen: Neske, 1959).

N   *Nietzsche,* 2 vols.* (Pfullingen: Neske, 1961).

ZSD   *Zur Sache des Denkens** (Tübingen: Niemeyer, 1969).

INTRODUCTION

The status of the thought of Martin Heidegger within contemporary philosophy remains highly controversial. Since the appearance of *Being and Time* in 1927, Heidegger has been widely recognized as a thinker of great originality and power and as one of the two or three seminal philosophical minds of this century. This estimate of Heidegger's achievement has been mostly widely held on the Continent, but even there, there have been other sharply divergent and sometimes quite hostile judgments of his work. Elsewhere, especially in the English-speaking world, familiarity with his thought remained limited to a tiny minority within the philosophical community until the English translation of *Being and Time* appeared in 1962. Since then, the number of those who have some acquaintance with Heidegger's thought has increased considerably, but ignorance is still the norm among philosophers in this country. As a result, there has been little real understanding of what Heidegger in fact represents as a philosopher or of the sense in which he may be said to propose new options for philosophical thought in its dealings with a variety of traditional problems.

This book seeks to change this situation; and in this effort it is guided by two convictions. One is that Heidegger's thought is of the first importance and that for just that reason it needs to be set forth for a general philosophical audience in as clear and rigorous a manner as possible. The other, which may be more controversial, is that the philosophical interest of that thought is most evident when it is approached through the set of issues that make up the philosophy of mind. The justification for this judgment and for the interpretation of Heidegger's philosophy as a whole on which it rests is complex, and it cannot be convincingly presented in advance of the argumentation of the book itself. It is possible, however, even at the outset, to draw attention to the fundamental importance in *Being and Time* of the concept of the subject and, more specifically, of its ontological status. Much of what Heidegger has to say about this takes the form of a critique of Descartes, Kant, and Husserl; and the point he makes again and again is that these philosophers either interpreted the ontological status of the subject in terms of an inappropriate model or left it indeterminate. As a result, modern philosophy has failed to produce a satisfactory "ontological interpretation of the being of consciousness."[1] There can be no doubt that in *Being and Time* Heidegger undertook to supply just such an interpretation of the being of consciousness and thus of the subject. His critique of the implicit ontology associated with these concepts by philosophers like Kant and Husserl proved to be so radical, however, that virtually all the philosophical terminology they had employed for characterizing the subject had to be scrapped and replaced by a new construction of a fundamentally different kind. It is well known that the concept of consciousness was itself a casualty of this reconstruction. It is my contention, however, that it is of great importance for an understanding of Heidegger's thought that it begins with a critique of dominant traditions in the philosophy of mind. I will also argue that this choice of a point of departure had a decisive role in determining the direction his thought subsequently took, both in *Being and Time* and thereafter.

This brief statement of the way I propose to approach Heidegger's philosophy may well give rise to misunderstandings. There may be those, for example, who will take the fact that Heidegger's thought is being associated with the philosophy of mind as reflecting a belief on my part that Heidegger himself propounds a philosophy of mind. Since the term "mind" itself is by no means philosophically neutral and in fact carries quite substantial implications with respect to the matters with which it deals, any such supposition would clearly beg a number of important questions. This would be all the more serious because it is just these implications, as well as the philosophical tradition from which they derive, that Heidegger rejects and attempts to replace by a very different philosophical construction of his own. It must be stated at the outset, accordingly, that I have no intention of imputing a philosophy of mind to Heidegger. I use the term only to refer to the range of topics within philosophy on which Heidegger's critique bears most directly and thus to the proximate locus of the new concepts for which it clears the ground. This much, at least, in the way of an overlap or continuity between Heidegger's own thought and prior modes of philosophizing is plainly presupposed by his own mode of argumentation and is therefore properly assumed by anyone who wishes to retrace the path of that thought.

There is another challenge that may be made to such an undertaking as this. It may be asked *which* Heidegger I am addressing myself to—the Heidegger of *Being and Time* or the Heidegger of the writings which from the mid-thirties onward modified the principal theses and characteristic emphases of that work in what appear to be quite fundamental respects. There has been a great deal of controversy about the way in which the *Kehre*—the turning—through which Heidegger's thought passed is to be understood. There is even a question as to whether in its later phases his thought remained philosophical in any clear sense, since he abandoned much of his own earlier vocabulary, as well as the traditional philosophical terminology which it had been designed to replace. He also declared that the effort of thought he had made in *Being and Time* had been compromised by the use it made of the language of metaphysics which he subsequently abandoned. This might be taken to mean that his earlier thought was partially contaminated by its contact with the very philosophical tradition that it had attempted to supplant. If so, it would seem to follow that any attempt to show the bearing of the principal theses of *Being and Time* on issues in the philosophy of mind can only foster the same kind of confusion and thus block an understanding of just how radically incommensurate Heidegger's mature thought is with the preoccupations of what we call philosophy at the present time. It may thus look as though, if one goes to the earlier writings for what they have to say on topics relating to the philosophy of mind, it will turn out that all this has been superseded by Heidegger's revisions of his own thought. On the other hand, if one goes directly to the later writings, in the hope of finding something that is at least definitively Heideggerian, it may prove difficult, if not impossible, to find anything that is clearly relevant to philosophical issues as they are currently understood.

What I have just sketched is an extreme view of the discontinuity between the earlier and later phases of Heidegger's thought; and in appraising such a view, it is important to bear in mind that Heidegger continued to insist on the foundational character of *Being and Time* for any understanding of his thought.[2] That is an admonition which this book will heed; and although its primary purpose is not to propose a general interpretation of Heidegger's thought in all its phases, it will defend a view with respect to the character of the relationship between the principal phases through which it passed. This will be in some measure a unitarian theory of his philosophical evolution because I argue that there were very substantial continuities over time and through the *Kehre*, as well as the differences to which so much attention has been given. The distinctive feature of the kind of unitarian interpretation that I favor is that, instead of basing myself on the later writings and interpreting *Being and Time* from that later standpoint, I begin with the theses of that book and then show how they are carried forward and at the same time recast in significant ways that reflect difficulties arising out of their original formulations. The central place in any such effort of interpretation must, of course, be assigned to the concept of being which dominated the later writings in such an emphatic way. This concept is certainly not absent from *Being and Time*, but, in the portions of that book which were actually published, it had not yet assumed the central position that Heidegger evidently intended it to have and which it actually assumed in his later writings, although in a way that called into question how much of the preparatory groundwork of *Being and Time* could be retained. I will argue that the concept of being in Heidegger's later writings has been seriously misunderstood through a failure to pay enough attention to the way in which it is introduced in *Being and Time*, and that expectations that abstract from the very special use Heidegger there proposes for this concept can mislead us with respect to both the import of what the later writings have to say about being and the relationship in which these writings stand to *Being and Time*.

The argument that I will make on this point will draw very extensively on Heidegger's lectures from the period of *Being and Time* and thereafter which have been published as part of the complete edition of his works that has been appearing in the course of the last decade.[3] These lectures give us a much clearer view of Heidegger's development as a philosopher than we get from *Being and Time* or indeed from any of his subsequent works. In part, this is because in them Heidegger was developing the themes of his own thought in a more overt contact with the thought of other philosophers than he did in *Being and Time*, and the terminology he uses is often much closer to traditional philosophical concepts like, for example, that of intentionality than it typically is in his published works. We are thus in a much better position to understand the continuities between Heidegger's thought and that of influential predecessors like Husserl and also to identify the points at which the rupture came and the philosophical motivation for it. What is most valuable in the lectures from the period of *Being and Time*, however, is the new light they cast on the concept of being as such that Heidegger was working out at this time, but which was only briefly and somewhat enigmatically adumbrated in the published portions of that work. In the lectures this concept is developed much more fully and in a way that demonstrates just how closely it is linked to the concept of *Dasein*—that is, the kind of entity that human beings prove to be on Heidegger's analysis in *Being and Time*. At the same time, this concept of being as such establishes a very clear connection between Heidegger's thought in its earlier and its later phases, since in very important respects it remains unchanged through the *Kehre* that has been supposed to separate the latter quite radically from the former. It becomes evident, in fact, that what distinguishes the later Heidegger from the earlier is not so much an abandonment of the concept of *Dasein* in favor of a new concept of being as such, as has often been thought. It is rather a new way of conceiving the relationship in which these two elements in the position developed in *Being and Time* and in the lectures of that period stand to one another.

It is the two different ways in which this relationship was successively conceived by Heidegger that provide the organizing principle for this book. The first part, entitled "Existence as the Ground of Presence," is devoted to an account of what I take to be the principal theses defended by Heidegger in the period of *Being and Time* with respect to the kind of entity that we are and that can alone be properly said to exist in the special Heideggerian sense of that term. These entities for which the generic characterization is *Dasein* are (extensionally) the same entities that are usually described as "human beings," and they are conventionally distinguished as such by reference to their possession of rationality and the various "mental" powers it comprises. It is this characterization of what is distinctive of these entities that is to be replaced by one in terms of the new concept of existence. That concept is ontological in a double sense: first, because it expresses what is distinctive of a certain kind of entity, and second, because the special character of that entity turns out to be such as to involve a reference to its own being as well as to the being of other entities. The chapters that make up the first part of the book are primarily designed to explain this concept of existence as the concept that defines the mode of being of a certain kind of entity. In *Being and Time* Heidegger argues that because it is this entity that asks the question "What is being?" in its unrestricted and completely general form, we must understand the kind of entity it is before we can answer that question. Accordingly, in most of *Being and Time* and in the first part of this book as well, the emphasis is pervasively upon the characterization of a certain kind of entity, and questions about being in a broader sense are provisionally set aside. The final chapter of the first part, however, is devoted to a review of the passages in *Being and Time* that deal explicitly with the concept of being as such, and an attempt is made to determine in just what sense that work remained incomplete or defective from the standpoint of the general theory of being that Heidegger was trying to construct.

The second part of this book is entitled "Presence as the Ground of Existence." "Presence" is the term that Heidegger uses to express the fundamental character of being as such; and this title signifies the reversed relationship of being as such to human existence. Since it is in his later thought that the concept of being as presence is most fully developed, it is the texts and lectures of the later period that serve as the basis for the account given here. It is of great importance, however, to understand that this concept of presence that explicates the concept of being is not new in the later writings. It is used extensively in *Being and Time*, where it is closely linked with the concepts of existence and *Dasein*. This connection between presence and existence is central to the justification for viewing the later philosophy of Heidegger as continuous with the early writings that deal with the ontology of the subject. My procedure in this section is to begin with a short account, in chapter 7, of the *Kehre* itself and of the quite different kinds of considerations that appear to have motivated it. I then approach the later writings with a view to determining how they go beyond *Being and Time* toward a theory of being as such and to what degree that theory still conforms to the stipulations laid down in *Being and Time* as the way the concept of being is to be understood. By contrast to many accounts of the *Kehre* as a radical transformation of Heidegger's thought, my account shows that the concept of being as presence in the later writings maintains the principal distinctive features of the concept sketched in *Being and Time*. What does change quite profoundly in the later writings is Heidegger's conception of the relationship between existence and presence; and if that relationship remains one of interdependence as set forth in *Being and Time*, the terms of that interdependence are extensively revised. Chapter 8 reviews these elements of continuity and change in the concept of being as presence and also points to some difficulties that arise for Heidegger in his effort to transfer so much of what had previously been attributed to existence as the mode of being of *Dasein* to being as presence without abandoning the strict interdependence of the two that is the most distinctive feature of his philosophy in all its stages of development. Chapter 9 then presents an account of the concept of a "history of being" as it was developed in Heidegger's later period. It is in this concept that Heidegger's new understanding of the relationship between existence and presence finds its most emphatic and often paradoxical expression. The second part of the book closes with a critical appraisal of all the major aspects of the movement beyond *Being and Time*.

In this connection I must touch on a number of terminological issues that will be of considerable importance in what follows. It will be a major thesis of this book that Heidegger's distinctive use of the concept of being must not be identified with any familiar interpretation of the verb "to be," although it is very closely linked to such uses in ways that I will describe. It is equally clear, however, that Heidegger continued to make use of these familiar senses of that verb and its various nominalizations. One very important issue in *Being and Time* has to do with distinguishing different kinds of entities from one another; and this is described as a question about their being or mode of being. At the same time, Heidegger separates questions of this kind from questions as to whether there are in fact (or have been or will be) entities of these various kinds; and this too is a question about their being. Normally, these two kinds of question would be distinguished by saying that the former concern being understood as essence, and the latter, being as existence. Although Heidegger recognizes this distinction, he has reasons of his own for not making use of it for purposes of expounding his own position. He also deliberately violates it by using the term "existence" to characterize the mode of being—what would ordinarily be called the essence—of one kind of entity. All this makes exposition of his position in any language other than his own quite difficult. At the same time, I am convinced that his own usage in this regard—especially his multivalent use of "being"— has been responsible for a good deal of avoidable confusion on the part of his readers. Accordingly, I have taken some liberties in the use I make of these and related terms in this book; and I have done so in the interest of a greater degree of clarity with respect to what is most important and most original in Heidegger's thought. I have continued to use "exist- ence," for example, in its wider and familiar sense, as well as in the narrower Heideggerian one. I also prefer to speak of the kind of entity that something is rather than of its being when it is being as essence that is in question; and if the term "being" proves to be unavoidable in these contexts, I associate it with the other way of speaking so as to clarify its meaning. I have also tried to avoid altogether the use—possible in En- glish but not in German—of "being" as a synonym for "entity." All this is designed to reserve the term "being" for its most distinctive use in Heidegger's writings to the degree possible. Because in that distinctive use it means something like "presence," I also often use the phrase "being as presence" to signal the special character of the concept that is being invoked. Although I have done my best to make the contexts in which they occur clarify the use I make of each of these terms, some unclarities and inconsistencies of usage on my part undoubtedly remain. On bal- ance, however, I am convinced that the usages I have adopted are pref- erable to the introduction of all sorts of neologisms and special orthographical conventions that too often simply become new obstacles in the way of understanding.

What has been said up to this point may lead the reader to conclude that this book is an exercise in Heidegger interpretation and that, as such, it is addressed primarily, if not exclusively, to philosophers already familiar with Heidegger's philosophy. Such is not the case, however. For, although it is certainly not an "Introduction to Heidegger," it does ad- dress itself to the general philosophical community and claims to have something important to say to it. What that is, is summed up in the Conclusion, which places Heidegger's thought in the context of the con- temporary philosophy of mind. Much of the latter has been quite self- consciously post-Cartesian and anti-Cartesian; and it has celebrated the demise of the Cartesian subject under a variety of auspices. It should, therefore, be of real interest to contemporary philosophers to encounter a position like Heidegger's which is inspired by an equally resolute rejection of the Cartesian theory of the subject, but on quite different grounds and with quite different results from any that are familiar to us from anti-Cartesian philosophies in our own recent past. Although I take issue with Heidegger on many points, I argue in the Conclusion and implicitly in the book as a whole that Heidegger's way of moving against and away from Descartes constitutes a significant and deeply conceived alternative to current positions in the philosophy of mind. To this I should add that my exposition is guided by my sense of the questions that his theses must raise in the minds of philosophers; and I have tried to interpret Heidegger in such a way as to show how his line of thought meets (or can be interpreted in such a way as to meet) such questions and objections. I have also tried to acknowledge the real difficulties that his thought encounters in both its main periods, and I have offered some suggestions as to how these difficulties might be dealt with more successfully than, as it sometimes appears, Heidegger himself did.

Finally, I must say something about the relationship between this book and the large critical literature that deals with Heidegger's philosophy. I have studied the principal contributions to that literature carefully and have learned much from them. At the same time, I have not felt satisfied that existing interpretations do justice to the power and originality of Heidegger's thought. For that, it seemed to me, it would be necessary to examine the concepts of existence and presence in much greater detail and, so to speak, more aggressively than has been customary in the literature. More specifically, the existing literature does not, as far as I have been able to determine, deal at all adequately with the continuity that characterizes Heidegger's very distinctive use of the concept of being both before and after the *Kehre*. An interpretation which, like mine, stresses that continuity and traces it to the relationship in which the concept of being stands to the concepts of existence and presence will necessarily be quite different from those interpretations that do not proceed in this manner. Whether it is also inconsistent with any or all of these is more difficult to determine, precisely because these writers have not addressed themselves to many of the issues that are of greatest importance for my interpretation. It would not have been easy, therefore, to develop my argument in a continuing exchange with other interpreters; and the idea of a polemic in which I would contrast my views with indeterminately different alternatives had little appeal to me. I therefore decided to develop my own line of thought about Heidegger as lucidly and as cogently as I could without offering comparisons between my views and those of others. This decision was also motivated by the fact that for all the new Heidegger texts on which my interpretation relies so heavily, there is as yet hardly any literature of critical commentary. In any case, what my book seeks to do, precisely through this "skew" relationship in which it stands to much or most of what has been written about Heidegger, is to introduce a new set of questions in terms of which his thought can be interrogated. The richness of that thought is such that those who study it can only benefit from the availability of new perspectives on it.

PART I
**EXISTENCE AS THE
GROUND OF PRESENCE**

CHAPTER ONE • THE CRITIQUE OF THE CARTESIAN TRADITION

No major philosophical thinker of this century has had as extensive or as profound a knowledge of the Western philosophical tradition as Heidegger. Every step in the development of his own philosophical position appears to have been taken in the context of close critical study of the thinkers and the texts that had defined the issues with which he was dealing. In approaching his thought from the side of the philosophy of mind, it is important, therefore, to come to terms, first, with his interpretations and appraisals of some of the principal lines of thought that have given the concept of mind the position it occupies within Western philosophy. In this chapter I will give an account of Heidegger's treatment of Descartes, with whom the modern philosophy of mind begins, and of Husserl, his teacher, from whom he took much but whom he also subjected to searching criticism. In this way I hope to give a sense of Heidegger's relationship to the Cartesian tradition as represented both by its founder and by a twentieth-century philosopher—Husserl— who attempted to move beyond the Cartesian philosophy of mind but, in Heidegger's judgment, did not really succeed in doing so. This procedure of discussing the Cartesian tradition in terms of these terminal points in its evolution necessarily omits much that is of great importance for purposes of understanding Heidegger's relationship to modern philosophy. Most notably, he devoted much of his life to the study of Kant; but the complexity and ambivalence of his attitude to Kant's critical philosophy are too considerable to permit an adequate account of it here. At various points in the following chapters, there will be occasion, however, to discuss one or another aspect of this relationship to Kant as it becomes relevant to the progress of my argument.

What has been said might appear to suggest that it is only the modern philosophy of mind that Heidegger is concerned with. That is far from being the case. Heidegger insists strongly on the rootedness of modern Western philosophy in Greek thought and in the medieval tradition that transmitted the fruits of that thought to the modern world. In chapter

9 a brief account will be given of the distinctive achievement of Greek thought as Heidegger understands it and also of the way that achievement was denatured in the philosophies of Plato and Aristotle. In Heidegger's view, it was as a result of the loss of the insights achieved by the earliest Greek philosophers—Parmenides, Heraclitus, and Anaximander—that the concept of the subject eventually emerged in its modern form. For the most part, however, Heidegger's claim that modern subjectivism has its origin in Greek philosophy was developed in the period following *Being and Time*. In that work, subjectivism is identified with the Cartesian tradition; and it is therefore appropriate to begin this account of the first phase of his thought with his critique of Descartes.

I

Before turning to that critique, it is important to take note of another dimension of philosophical issues generally that is repeatedly emphasized by Heidegger himself. It is his view that, because in philosophy we are dealing much of the time with the kind of entity that we ourselves are, we must already have a certain implicit understanding of the matters that philosophy seeks to raise to the level of explicit conceptual formulation.[1] Indeed, one could say that it is just this implicit understanding that philosophy attempts to bring to appropriate expression. This may make it sound as though Heidegger were a philosopher of common sense; and there is in fact an element of truth in such a view, at least insofar as it supplies a salutary corrective to the fashionable view of him as a mystagogue. For most purposes, however, the implicit understanding that he postulates would have to be contrasted with common sense insofar as the latter takes the form of explicitly avowed opinions on various matters—opinions that reflect what Heidegger calls the "average understanding" that we share with our fellow men. Common sense so understood systematically misrepresents our nature and situation as human beings; and in so doing, it also violates the deeper implicit understanding that we have of ourselves, but that we also, according to Heidegger, do not really want to acknowledge having. The supposed reasons for this unwillingness need not occupy us here. The important point is that there is a complex and deeply motivated conflict between what we tacitly understand about ourselves and what we affirm in the way of "commonsense" views as what "everyone" knows. It is also Heidegger's contention that at the same time as we hold these commonsense views we continue to rely on this deeper understanding, and that to the extent that this is true our lives are a careful balancing-off against one another of these two quite different sets of understandings. Such a balance has to be carefully managed, because otherwise we would be brought up short before the fact that we are trying to have things both ways.

These considerations are especially relevant at the outset of an inquiry into the philosophy of mind, because there is reason to think, so Heidegger tells us, that philosophy itself is deeply implicated in the peculiar symbiosis of these quite different modes of self-understanding. Officially, philosophers have almost always been highly critical of common sense, which they often demote to the status of mere *doxa*. This critical stance does not, of course, guarantee that philosophy has not taken up into itself much in the way of "average understanding" that it should have scrutinized more carefully. Certainly there has been an extensive interpenetration of commonsense and philosophical notions that relate in one way or another to the "mind"; and it would not be easy to say whether the origin of many of our everyday locutions for talking about the mind lies in common sense or philosophy. To take just one example, the contrast between the "inner" and the "outer" which plays such an important role in our talking and thinking about the mind is common to both common sense and philosophy; and it is even maintaining itself in the midst of the current scientific effort to apply computer-based models to the task of conceptualizing the operations of the central nervous system. Although this idea of a contrast between the inner and the outer has become deeply entrenched as a master-metaphor for interpreting the relationships to one another of the private and the public and of the mental and the physical, the credentials that validate its employment are obscure, to say the least, and have never been properly examined with the care they deserve by the philosophies that make use of this contrast. Even in advance of such scrutiny, there is good reason to doubt whether this metaphor of the inner and the outer really represents the terms in which we operatively understand ourselves, and to wonder whether it is not rather an essentially derivative formation that issues from what Heidegger calls the "average understanding" and is put into canonical form by philosophy.

II

The intense interest that Descartes's philosophy continues to command is due in good part to the fact that it accomplished just this task. Descartes's own primary goal appears to have been to define and realize a form of knowledge that would be absolutely indubitable; and this project was of great significance for the developing self-interpretation of the mathematical sciences of nature. His method, as everyone knows, was to ask what could be doubted as a way of determining what could not be doubted. It turned out that all our beliefs about states of affairs and events in nature, and even the existence of nature itself, as well as of our own bodies and past histories, *could* be doubted and therefore had to be provisionally set aside until some secure foundation could be found for such beliefs. The final residue of this search proved to be the thought itself in which this question about what can and cannot be doubted was formulated. Descartes claimed that the proposition "I think" cannot be doubted; and he argued that, even before I have found a way of justifying my former belief in the existence of nature and of my body and my past history, I am entitled to infer that I exist simply as a thinking being. Such a conception of the self is obviously abstract in the extreme, since it excludes almost everything that, as we ordinarily suppose, makes up our natural being as persons. Nevertheless, the achievement of such a conception of the self must be recognized as a remarkable achievement, whatever its ultimate tenability proves to be; and it has rightly been regarded as presaging the development in the modern period of a purely epistemic form of selfhood that claims the right to treat everything, including its own natural and historical existence in the world, as an object of knowledge. That enterprise of pan-objectification assumes great significance in Heidegger's later philosophy.

The focus of the critique of Descartes in *Being and Time* is another aspect of his treatment of the self. Descartes had declared that the kind of being that was to be assigned to the epistemically conceived self of the *cogito* was that of substance; and it is this properly ontological classification that Heidegger calls into question.[2] The concept of substance is a philosophical rendering of the more familiar commonsense concept of a "thing," or *res*. According to Heidegger, the primary application of that concept is not to the mind or the self, but to familiar objects of experience like chairs and tables, mountains and trees. He views Descartes's decision to treat the thinking self as a substance as an uncritical transfer of a standard bit of ontological apparatus that he had inherited from the ancient world via late scholastic philosophers like Suarez. The effect of this transfer is to classify the self or mind, for ontological purposes, as a substance, or what Heidegger ironically refers to as a "spiritual thing."[3] It is the propriety of this assimilation of the thinking self to the only status—that of a substance—that Descartes believed to be available that Heidegger challenges.

This transfer of the concept of substance to the self is usually thought to be problematic because of the immaterial character of the entity so constituted and the puzzles relating to the character of the interaction between a material substance—the body—and its immaterial partner—the mind. But these puzzles are not the only problematic feature of Descartes's readaptation of the concept of substance; and for Heidegger it is not the most important one. He is concerned to show, instead, how this readaptation is effected and with what implications.[4] In its more familiar application to objects other than the thinking self, the concept of substance involves a distinction between the attributes of the thing in question and that in which they inhere—*substantia* as that which "stands beneath" them. An apple, for example, is red, round, hard, and sweet— these are its attributes—but all of these are attributes of *one* thing as well. Because substance as that in which these properties inhere is not itself susceptible of being perceived and described, whereas its attributes *can* be readily seen, felt, and so on, there has long been a feeling that there is something mysterious about it; but the contrast between the plurality of attributes and the singleness of that to which they belong remains fundamental to the concept of a substance. When the latter is transferred to the thinking self, it is accordingly preserved, although in a new way. To the attributes of the standard substance or thing, there now correspond the representations or ideas of the things that the self perceives or otherwise thinks about; and to the mysterious nucleus in which those properties were supposed to inhere, there corresponds that in which these representations are contained. It is rather as though substance in the picture we ordinarily form of it had been turned inside out or, better still, outside in. Indeed, this is not a bad way of understanding the change that has taken place, since to the attribute that a thing like an apple displays to general view, there now corresponds a representation *within* the new kind of substance, but with this difference, that the representation is accessible only to the view from within and cannot be perceived from without at all. Perhaps one might add that another consequence of this readaptation of the concept of substance is a change in the status of that which holds the attributes together as the attributes of one thing. From being inaccessible to experience and thus putatively mysterious, it has become something that is usually thought to be intimately familiar to each of us—that is, the act of the mind itself which, like a ray of light, plays on the representations of "external" objects that are hung, so to speak, on the inner walls of the mind.

It was as a result of this new way of understanding thought as the inner functioning of a substance or subject (*subjectum*) that the old relationship between subject and object came to be reversed. In Descartes's own writings this terminological reversal is not complete, and the old use of the term "objective" to characterize not some entity in the world— that is, what had been called the subject—but something in the mind, still maintains itself. Otherwise, all the elements of the new ontology are in place. The world, according to Descartes, is an aggregate made up of substances of the two kinds he had distinguished—material and spiritual—and this distinction also corresponds more or less to the one between substances of the old kind and the new, although the attributes that the former were allowed to have have been reduced to those connected with spatiality or extension. Since there can be only one space, of which all other spaces are parts, it follows that, strictly speaking, there can be only one substance of the first kind. As a result, the variety of qualitatively differentiated objects like apples and trees that are recognized in the commonsense view of nature, as contrasted with the geometrical-scientific conception, must go by the board. For the sake of convenience, however, we may speak in terms of the plurality of substances, both mental and material, that the commonsense view accepts and ask, as Heidegger does, how they are in the world together. Since the soul is not material in nature, it cannot have location in space in the way that material objects do; and it is only by reason of its contingent and quite mysterious linkage with a particular body that it is *in* the spatiotemporal world at all. The focus of Heidegger's interest is not, however, the difficulty of understanding how an immaterial substance can be linked with a material substance. It is rather the fact that as a result of understanding the self as a mental substance, its way of being in the world comes to be interpreted in terms of knowledge. "Knowledge" here is to be understood as "the way the soul or consciousness acts," and it is through this inner action that the soul achieves knowledge of an external world—that is, of the existence of things that are supposed to be outside it when it is understood as a mental substance.[5] Since the picture of the self that goes with this conceptualization limits its certain and direct apprehensions to its own internal states, it must reckon with the possibility that an external world does not exist. Only if there can be shown to be some kind of connection between what is in it and what is outside, can there be an inference from the one to the other that would establish the existence of an external world. It is quite unclear, of course, how an inner landscape that has been conceptually constituted as it was by Descartes, can afford any basis for such an inference. This has not kept philosophers who accept his picture from demanding a proof of the existence of the external world and from speaking as though this demand emanated from a self that, in the absence of a secure principle of inference, would remain limited to an apprehension of its own internal states.

For Heidegger, it is not the failure of philosophers to produce such a proof that is the "scandal of philosophy," as Kant thought; the scandal is rather that such proofs are still demanded.[6] It would be more appropriate to ask *why* this is so and why we persist in trying to maintain the picture of ourselves requiring that knowledge be a "transcending" of an inner domain toward an external world that is putatively independent of it. This picture is one of two entities of a single type—substance—existing side by side (*Neben-einander*). "Side by side" cannot, of course, have its literal meaning in this use, because one of the two substances does not have spatial location in the way the other does and can be said to have it at all only by virtue of its unclarified association with the other. Nevertheless, the adoption of the concept of a nonstandard substance— a mental substance—expresses precisely a determination *not* to be deterred by anomalies of this kind. What primarily characterizes substances that are thought of in this way is their self-sufficiency.[7] The soul is supposed to be able to apprehend itself inwardly with perfect adequacy without any thought of a world that is outside it; and once the existence of that world has been established, its relation to the soul can be accounted for by a psychophysical theory of sensation in a way that preserves the logical and ontological independence of the one substance from the other. Similarly, the mind is spoken of as standing in a relation to the world, and this implies that the mind is conceivable apart from this relation. As such, it is what Heidegger calls a "worldless subject"— that is, a subject that is not "sure of its world" and accordingly conceives itself, at least initially, in a way that abstracts from this problematic relation to the world.[8]

It needs to be emphasized that the notions of representation and sensation are intimately bound up with the conception of a "worldless subject."[9] These notions designate states or acts of a mind understood as apprehending itself from within. As such, they are properly described in the same manner as the mind itself—that is, in a way that isolates them from the existence of that of which they are representations. This treatment of them is imposed by the general model of mind that has been adopted, but it falsifies the phenomenological facts. As Heidegger observes, "We never 'first' hear a noise or a complex of sounds but rather the creaking wagon, the motorcycle."[10] Sensations, accordingly, are not the first objects that the self is conversant with, nor does it have to "give shape to the swirl of sensations to provide a springboard from which it (the subject) leaps off and finally arrives at a 'world.' "[11] Descriptions of experience as a mosaic of sensations or sense-data are, accordingly, very artificial constructions which may have some limited justification in a particular context of inquiry, but can never be validly generalized into an ontology of sense-data. For Heidegger, it follows, there are no intervening entities like sense-data out of which a world could be constructed or on the basis of which its existence could be inferred. As he explains in a remarkable passage, it is the whole picture of which such concepts form a part that is fundamentally mistaken.

> When *Dasein* directs itself towards something and grasps it, it does not somehow first get out of an inner sphere in which it has been proximally encapsulated, but its primary kind of being is that it is always 'outside' alongside entities which it encounters and which belong to a world already discovered.

Nor is any inner sphere abandoned when *Dasein* dwells alongside the entity to be known, and determines its character, but even in this 'Being-outside' alongside the object, *Dasein* is still 'inside,' if we understand this in the proper sense; that is, it is itself 'inside' as a Being-in-the-world that knows. And furthermore, the perceiving of what is known is not a process of returning with one's booty to the 'cabinet' of consciousness after one has gone out and grasped it; even in perceiving, retaining and preserving the *Dasein* that knows *remains outside* and does so as *Dasein*.[12]

The concept of *Dasein* invoked in this passage is, of course, Heidegger's own rendering of the subject in "the properly understood sense," as he puts it; and it will be explained in detail in chapter 3.[13]

By rejecting the concept of representation as the basis for a theory of knowledge or an ontology, Heidegger bypasses the whole approach to these matters that takes its rise from the fact of error and, in particular, of perceptual illusion. Since illusions occur in which there may be little or nothing to distinguish them from veridical perceptions, it has been argued that veridical and nonveridical experiences must have something in common, something that is the experience as such and that is prior to any determination of whether or not there really *is* something that conforms to it. The concept of a representation is just the concept of a given, an appearance that is neutral with respect to any question about what is really the case in the world. Originally, representations were thought to be domiciled within the mind as its inner states; but even when Hume's doubts about the mind as the container of these states had prevailed, and the mind itself had come to be defined as a construction out of such data of much the same kind as he supposed material objects to be, the idea persisted of experience as a mosaic of such neutral data. Supposedly it was only after various kinds of tests had been applied to these data to determine what kinds of predictions could reliably be based on them that definite assertions about what is the case in the world could be made; and these, of course, would be logically posterior to the apprehension of the individual data themselves. In fact, the very idea of such tests is a way of smuggling into this theory a distinction with which we are all conversant already, although, if the theory were to be believed, there is no way we could be. This is the distinction between what is really the case and what only seems to be the case; and there is good reason to think that we must be, tacitly, in possession of this distinction if we are to be able to introduce the concept of a sense-datum at all. For Heidegger, as later for Merleau-Ponty, our ability to use this distinction is fundamental in a way that cannot be captured or replaced by a phenomenalistic theory based on an ontology of sense-data.[14]

It is usual to refer to any philosophical affirmation of the existence of the commonsense world of natural objects as "naive realism"; and it might accordingly be thought that this term would accurately describe the position that Heidegger is defending. It is important, therefore, to take note of his explicit repudiation of any characterization of his philosophy as a form of realism.[15] Although he does not talk in terms of "naive" realism, the adjective "naive" would in his view undoubtedly compound the error involved in the use of the term "realism," since it implies that there is some relevant form of sophistication in our way of affirming the existence of the natural world to which, presumably, we ought to graduate from the naiveté of our original uncritical affirmation. "Critical" realism, unlike the naive kind, is sophisticated because it offers proofs, or at least arguments, in support of the claim it makes about the existence of the world. But it is just this idea of offering a proof that Heidegger utterly rejects; and because realism as a philosophical defense of the existence of an external world presupposes that such a proof is both required and possible, he wants no part of it. Such realism is itself caught up in the very assumptions that make it seem appropriate to speak of the world as external; and the apparently reassuring conclusions to which the realistic argument leads remain infected by the acceptance of these assumptions. In *Being and Time* Heidegger takes up one such case of a philosopher who argues for realism (and for a version of it that is critical in the most emphatic sense imaginable) and yet remains bound by assumptions that derive from the Cartesian theory of mind.[16] In his "Refutation of Idealism" Kant attempts to show that the mind's knowledge of its own existence is not logically prior to its knowledge of the existence of an external world, and that it is the latter that is prior to the former. This certainly appears to reverse the order of priority between the two kinds of knowledge that was established by Descartes. But this is not, in fact, the case, as Heidegger shows by reference to the way Kant's proof proceeds. That proof presupposes the contrast between what is "in me"—that is, the temporal succession of representations— and what is "outside me"; and Kant's claim is that temporal succession requires the existence not only of something permanent, but also of something permanent that is outside me. Thus, whatever the merits of the proof itself, it is premised on the very distinction which it claims to overturn. The picture it relies on is one of the existence side by side of two entities that are both assumed to be already present and in existence before the proof gets under way; and this fact must heavily undercut the claim of the argument itself to show that the mind can be apprehended as existing only on the basis of a logically prior apprehension of the existence of the external (and "permanent") object.

It is evident that for Heidegger the trouble with realistic theories is not that the proofs they offer are invalid, but that they are working with an unsatisfactory conceptualization of the mind as that from which the world is to be shown to be independent and to which it is supposedly external.[17] In order for realism to make sense, it must have a *locus standi*, a place from which it (or the thought in which it is formulated) can consider the question of whether the world exists; and this is true whether its conclusions turn out to be positive or negative. That place would have to be in some sense outside the world, the existence of which is under consideration; and it would have to be identifiable by the inquirer who stands in it as being such a place outside of and independent of the world. For Heidegger, there clearly is no such place, and the whole enterprise of realism that was to be mounted from it must accordingly fall to the ground. But what may be even more significant is the fact that in ordinary situations we do not behave as though we were standing in any such extramundane place from which the existence of the world would have to be worked out in terms of argument and inference. We are in some sense already beyond the artificial construal of our situation that is imposed by this dualistic model. As Heidegger says, "The fact that motorcycles and cars are what we proximally hear is the phenomenal evidence that in every case . . . [we] already dwell alongside what is [ready-to-hand] within the world" and that "with such presuppositions [we] always come too late" because, as the entity that makes these presuppositions, we are always already in the world.[18] In other words, we are already operating on the very "presuppositions" about the world and our being in it that realism seeks to justify. Heidegger might have added that if we were not so operating, as for example when we correct a mistaken first impression without doubting that we are now in the presence of the object we at first misperceived, it is unlikely that we could even form the concept of an illusion on which so much of the realist argument depends if it is to get started at all. Since we do in fact proceed in this way and are astonished if someone tells us that we are being naive, it seems fair to infer that in some sense we already understand that this is what we do and that there is no sensible alternative to so doing. But if this is something we understand, it is certainly not something that we can readily formulate in response to a philosophical challenge; and so common sense is often talked into believing that it is really as naive as the philosopher claims it is. It is just this inarticulate understanding that a new ontology of the subject along the lines projected by Heidegger is designed to vindicate; and that ontology can, accordingly, be described as lifting to the level of concepts what we already understand in a pre-ontological way.

Although it seems clear that Heidegger's own ontological inquiries stand in this positive relationship to the pre-ontological understanding that he claims we have of ourselves as being in the world, he is unwilling to speak of that understanding as "knowledge." In part, this seems to reflect a reluctance to make any primary use of a concept that has figured so prominently in the Cartesian interpretation of the epistemic character of our relation to the world. At the same time, the locutions that Heidegger uses as substitutes for cognitive verbs—expressions like "dwelling alongside" and others—can prepare us to understand the new concepts that his reconstructed ontology of the subject will introduce. These concepts are designed to avoid an implication that is central to the modern, heavily Cartesian concept of knowledge. This implication emerges from the analysis of knowledge as true belief; and it consists in claiming that belief as such must always, in principle, be separate from the state of affairs that it affirms, since what it affirms may be false. In other words, although the use of the concept of knowledge locks a belief to the world by entailing the truth of what is believed, we must always be prepared to fall back on an alternative description as "belief" of the mental state we first called knowledge. But the effect of such a strategy is to push belief all the way back out of the world, with the result that the world has to be understood as being in principle other than and thus external to our mental state. It accordingly becomes more and more natural to conceive all these states, including those of belief, as being situated in the extramundane locus to which the Cartesian philosophy assigned them. It might be said that Heidegger is looking for a way to block this sequence of moves and to tie our mental state, whether we call it "knowledge" or "belief," to the world more securely than is possible as long as we make use of the paired concepts of knowledge and belief to characterize our relation to the world. (It must be understood that such a description as this of what Heidegger does is itself cast in the language of the very Cartesian theory he is attempting to replace.) This is not to say that distinctively epistemic concepts will have no place in Heidegger's own philosophical vocabulary. It does imply, however, that, when they are introduced, it will be in a way that makes them derivative from—Heidegger says "founded in"—a deeper stratum of concepts that is so constructed as to block the kind of decomposition of subject/world totalities that proceeds along the lines just described. In contrast to the Cartesian procedure of dealing with the external world via representations, which entails that all our knowledge-claims about that world might possibly be false, the idiom in which Heidegger expresses himself acknowledges the fact that we could not be in the world at all without "knowing" all sorts of things that are the case. Because it is grounded in a way of being in the world that is not mediated by representations, Heidegger's new concept of the subject is properly described as being ontological, rather than epistemological. When, in the course of the elaboration of that concept, he takes up knowledge itself, it, too, will be treated in this same ontological mode, as chapter 5 will show.

It is in the context of the kind of reconstructive effort that has just been described that we can begin to understand why Heidegger abandons the concept of consciousness (*Bewusstsein*).[19] This is the master concept of the "mental" in all its variations, as these are understood under the Cartesian dispensation, although it is perhaps not always grasped just how closely it is tied to the special assumptions of that scheme and to the distinctions of inner and outer on which it rests. The etymology of both the English word "consciousness" and the German word *Bewusstsein* can help us here. Both these words either derive from or are formed on the model of the Latin word *conscius*, which has the meaning "knowing with. . . ."[20] The original context for this word appears to have been legal, so that "knowing with" is knowing with someone else in a sense that involves complicity. There are also Latin uses of *conscius* in which this element of duality—one person knowing *with* another—has apparently been internalized. Someone may thus be described as *conscius sibi*; and the reflexive construction indicates a relationship in which that person stands to himself. Typically, this is a matter of knowing something about oneself, such as one's own guilt or innocence—that is, something that one may be able to know only about oneself. This is true of the earliest uses of the English word as well.[21] Such a concept is evidently designed to signify, not an awareness that we may have of any object whatever, but rather a special reflexive awareness that we have of ourselves. When the word "conscious" and its nominalization, "consciousness," came into general philosophical use, they were, in effect, preformed to express the kind of internal knowledge that the mind has of itself and of its own acts and states. Although a number of philosophers have continued to use this concept while disassociating it from its original connotations, it is by no means clear that they have been successful.

Considerations of this kind evidently led Heidegger to conclude that a concept like that of consciousness could not possibly serve as the instrument of the new ontology of the subject that he was constructing. It could not do so because it incorporated the central element in the Cartesian scheme: the detachability in principle of mental states and mental acts from the world that was their object. By virtue of its inner logic, consciousness is the very "worldless subject" of which *Being and Time* is a running critique. Nevertheless, it would be a mistake to infer that because he subjects the concept of consciousness to such a rigorous critique and effectively abandons its use, all connections between Heidegger's thought and that concept were severed. After all, it was Heidegger himself who called for an inquiry "into the being of consciousness, of the *res cogitans* itself" as "an inevitable prior task."[22] This is quite different from treating the concept of consciousness as though it were wholly incommensurate with, and out of any definable relationship to, the kind of inquiry that is being proposed and the concepts that were to issue from it. It turns out, in fact, that the concepts that replace that of consciousness in Heidegger's thought share certain characteristics with it, most notably those associated with the imagery of light and vision. This in no way diminishes the fundamental originality of the revisionary ontology of the subject that Heidegger proposes. It does raise a serious question, however, about the appropriateness to an understanding of Heidegger's philosophy of approaches that derive from currently popular notions of history and the history of thought as a discontinuous series of logically incommensurate paradigms.

III

The negative outcome of Heidegger's examination of the Cartesian position has the effect of returning philosophical thought about mind and subjectivity to what can only be called a pre-philosophical situation. This is because there have been no real alternatives in modern philosophy to the conception of the subject that was initiated by Descartes; and so there is no alternative, for anyone disillusioned with that philosopher, to a return to the pre-reflective situation which his philosophy and so many others that followed it have evidently misdescribed. That situation is one in which, to use the language of Edmund Husserl, "the natural attitude" sets the terms of the understanding we have of ourselves and of our mode of being in the world; and the natural attitude is really another name for the ordinary man's understanding of such matters as what it is that we perceive and the relation in which our perceiving stands to what we so perceive. The implication of a critique of Cartesian dualism like Heidegger's is that this understanding, which philosophers have been so quick to dismiss as mere *doxa*, really deserves a great deal more respect than it usually receives. This holds especially for what is perhaps most characteristic of the natural attitude—its lack of familiarity with the idea of a representation or, indeed, of any entity that intervenes between the perceiver and what he perceives. Instead, it takes its stand unquestioningly on the proposition that what is seen is the thing itself and not some proxy for it. Since the peremptory overriding of this understanding under the auspices of the representational theory of mind has come to grief, it behooves the philosopher to proceed more cautiously and to make an effort to grasp the import of this pre-philosophical affirmation more adequately before trying to revise or correct it.

The idea that philosophy must henceforth call into question all the traditional apparatus of philosophical description and proceed instead *zu den Sachen selbst* was vigorously advanced in the early years of this century by the phenomenologists and, above all, by Husserl. It is hardly surprising that Heidegger should have found their program of inquiry deeply congenial, or that he should have participated actively in the work of the phenomenological school.[23] The antipsychologistic line of thought initiated by Husserl in his *Logical Investigations* appealed strongly to Heidegger, as did the sharp distinction between the mental act, whether of perception, memory, or whatever, and the object to which it was directed. The term that Husserl, following his teacher, Brentano, used to express the distinctive character of mental acts as so directed upon objects was "intentionality." It is used only once in *Being and Time*, and its adjectival form only two or three times; but the lectures from that period show conclusively that Heidegger regarded intentionality as the central topic of phenomenology as he understood and practiced it.[24] Phenomenology is declared to be the analytical description of intentionality as the fundamental mode of relatedness in which objects of all kinds are present to us; and following Husserl, Heidegger explicitly identifies the notion of an act of perception or thought with that of an intentional relation to an object.[25] Of particular interest to Heidegger was the Husserlian distinction between what are called "empty intentions," in which the object is signified but is not itself "bodily present" (*leibhaftig da*), and those perceptual intentions in which "the perceived entity is there in person" (*leibhaftig*)."[26] Heidegger also places strong emphasis on the fact that this bodily presence is utterly different from the consciousness we have of a picture (*Bildbewusstsein*), although Cartesian theories of perception in fact treat it as though it were a matter of having images before the mind.[27] But even with all this enthusiasm for the phenomenological style of philosophy and its principal discovery—intentionality—Heidegger warns against the tendency to use the latter as a slogan and insists on the need for caution vis-à-vis interpretations that associate intentionality with traditional philosophical assumptions, especially of the Cartesian variety. He states that "as a rule of method for the first approach (*Erfassung*) to intentionality," one ought "not to labor over interpretations but simply hold on to that which shows itself, however slight it may be."[28] What he points to as the first significant element in intentionality is the fact that the *intentum*—the object that is intended—and the *intentio*—the intending of that object in a particular mode—belong together. At the same time, however, he adds that this reciprocity is obscure and stands in need of further analytical description.

The work of the philosopher thus requires more than simply noting the intentional character of our relation to objects; and it is equally clear that the new respect for the natural attitude does not make it the final word on all outstanding philosophical issues. In this Heidegger was in agreement with Husserl, but they were to disagree radically with respect to the way the concept of intentionality was to be further elaborated.

Husserl clearly viewed the natural attitude from the beginning in a different and notably less positive way than Heidegger did; and if he endorsed the idea of a more sustained description of the world of the natural attitude than he had given at the beginning of his *Ideas*, this remained a matter of secondary philosophical interest to him. The natural attitude is, after all, pre-philosophical and therefore pre-critical; and although the philosopher may need to characterize the natural attitude carefully, it is also something that he must leave behind him, not something that he can continue to espouse in the way the ordinary man does. Specifically, the unquestioning acceptance of the existence of the world, which defines the natural attitude, would, if not suspended, render the study of pure consciousness impossible. This naive acceptance on the part of the natural attitude was to be replaced by a far more sophisticated and critical posture of mind that Husserl characterizes as the "transcendental standpoint." That standpoint is reached through a series of "reductions"—operations performed on the natural attitude for the purpose of isolating the "pure" consciousness that is necessarily obscured as long as it is not clearly distinguished from the natural world and its processes in terms of which it is all too often interpreted and explained. These tasks of a properly transcendental phenomenology enjoyed an obvious and overwhelming priority in Husserl's eyes over any benefits that might derive from a more scrupulous rendering of the natural attitude as such.

There is a serious ambiguity in Husserl's account of the considerations that necessitate an abandonment of the natural attitude. At times it appears that these are epistemological in nature and have to do with the uncertainty of all the knowledge of the world and its existence that we naively suppose ourselves to have. This line of reasoning runs parallel to that of Descartes's methodological skepticism; and, like the latter, it seems to be motivated by the hope of reestablishing scientific knowledge on new and, this time, really secure foundations. At other times, Husserl insists that his intention is not to call into question the existence of the world in the way a skeptic would, but rather to detach himself from the movement of consciousness in which that existence is asserted. This is not because that assertion itself is really open to doubt, but because he wishes to understand and characterize in its full complexity the act of the mind in which the existence of the world is posited. For the natural attitude, the existence of the world is so unquestionable and so aboriginally familiar, that it seems to declare itself to the consciousness that confronts it without there being any need for the latter to do more than open its eyes and take in this patent, though momentous, fact. It is precisely this sense of the obviousness and naturalness of there being a world that Husserl wants to break; and he wants to do so because he is convinced that, as long as it maintains itself, there is no hope of our being able to understand just how *un*simple and *un*selfdeclaring the existence of the world really is.

The reduction that opens up the study of pure consciousness is a refraining from any affirmation of existence in regard to the countless objects of very many different kinds that we normally acknowledge as existing without any thought of doing otherwise. It is extremely important to understand, however, that when these existential affirmations are suspended, they are not expelled from consciousness altogether but remain there in "bracketed" form; and it is these bracketed affirmations that constitute the object of phenomenological descriptions and analysis. It also follows that when the whole object domain or world of the natural attitude is bracketed in this way, the existence of the person who is carrying out the reduction—his body and his life in just this time and place—is included in this suspension. For purposes of the phenomenological analysis of pure consciousness, what is called the "empirical ego" counts as just another object in the world that has to be bracketed in order to isolate the pure consciousness that is not itself any kind of object, but rather the absolute correlate of the world that has been suspended. Such a consciousness must be understood not in terms of a personal history, but simply in terms of its having a world of objects, among which is the empirical ego. When the existence of that world is affirmed in the way it normally is, it is as though its presence eclipsed the pure consciousness to which it appears and reduced it to the status of just another element within the totality that is the world. In other words, it is as though the transcendental ego were rendered invisible by the empirical ego whenever the latter enjoys its normal assurance of its own existence. For just this reason, it becomes necessary, according to Husserl, to suspend the existence of the world and thus of the empirical ego so that the transcendental ego to which the world appears as a world can emerge in full distinctness and be described as the pure consciousness that it really is but that we can never see it as being as long as we remain in the natural attitude. The residual question here, to which Heidegger was to draw attention, is what happens to the empirical ego in these circumstances when it has been left behind, so to speak, as one component of the world so that phenomenology can concentrate its attention on the transcendental ego.[29] If this abandonment of the empirical ego means that it is being consigned to scientific psychology and to its characteristic methods of conceptualization as the only appropriate way of giving an account of it, it is doubtful, Heidegger indicates, how adequate that account will prove to be. At any rate, he was clearly not prepared to turn over our finite, "empirical" existence to a nonphilosophical mode of treatment at the hands of a scientific psychology and to have philosophy devote itself exclusively to a phenomenology of pure transcendental consciousness.

In the account that Husserl then proceeds to give of it, pure consciousness is described as consisting of acts and meanings or, as he puts it, of noesis and noema. These acts—acts of thought, perception, memory, and so on—are the datable element of consciousness, and they are intentional in the sense that they are in every case directed to objects. They do not, however, simply register the presence of such objects in a passive way. Instead, they *constitute* those objects in the sense of articulating their formal structures by virtue of which true and false statements about these objects and their existence are possible. These formal or logical structures of the object are not internal to consciousness in the ways that an act of thought or a sense-datum is; and Husserl avoids any characterization of them that has the faintest psychological ring to it. In any case, when the reduction is carried out, what remains as the datum for phenomenological analysis is precisely these structures of meaning and, of course, the noetic acts in which they are deployed. In the program of research that Husserl outlined for phenomenology, these analyses of the work of constitutive intentionality were to be extended to every domain of objectivity, and from this enterprise the "world" would emerge as the total logical space within which all facts, and thus all objects of whatever kind, would be comprehended.

Many students of Husserl's philosophy have been puzzled by the fact that the suspension of the existence of the world which was carried out for methodological reasons seems never to have been lifted; and they have wondered whether this means that the world itself has been reduced permanently to the status of a meaning, with all the strong idealistic implications that that would carry with it. Husserl's statements bearing on this issue are extraordinarily varied and only dubiously consistent with one another. He says, for example, that it follows from his analyses that the existence of the world is relative to the existence of consciousness, and that the existence of the latter is absolute.[30] At the same time, he did not want the dependence relationship of the world to consciousness to be understood in terms of the *production* of the world by consciousness. But if Husserl clearly wanted to maintain a distinction between constitution and production, he does not seem to have understood how confusing many of his own statements on the subject are when it comes to assigning an idealistic or a nonidealistic interpretation to them. The result is that the ontological status of pure consciousness is left indeterminate; and it is just this fact on which Heidegger's critique of Husserl bases itself. If Husserl had lifted the suspension of the existence of the world, he would have had to acknowledge the "empirical ego" as existing—that is, as more than just a logical construction constituted by the transcendental ego; and in that event, he would have had to give an account of the *ontological* relationship between the one and the other. He never gives such an account; and as a result the status of consciousness as "absolute" on which he relies gives rise to all kinds of incongruous conjectures as to the import of this adjective.

This difficulty within Husserl's philosophy to which Heidegger draws attention has many facets. One of these, already noted, has to do with the unlikelihood that a naturalistic psychology, with its predominant interest in causal regularities, could give an adequate account of the empirical ego. Another, which assumes great importance in Heidegger's critique as well as in his own account of these matters, is the aspect of the self that Heidegger refers to as its *Vereinzelung*—that is, the individuation of consciousness and of its mode of being as the entity that performs the intentional acts through which the world is constituted.[31] Clearly, if the existence of the world is not being denied, and if the suspension of the affirmation of its existence is not to be permanent, it will be necessary for a philosophy of intentionality like Husserl's to give an account of the entity to which such acts are attributed. If the empirical ego has been conceptualized in the manner characteristic of a naturalistic psychology, however, it will hardly be possible to treat its transcendental and intentional functions as something simply added to it, something it *also* does. As will become clearer later, these functions are in principle not susceptible of being assigned to entities of the kind that natural science and scientific psychology recognize. The latter are entities that stand in complex causal relationships to one another but that are, like Descartes's substance which *nulla re indigeat ad existendum*, logically self-contained for purposes of determining what each of them is or is not. There is, in short, no way in which a meaningful identity between an empirical ego understood in such psychological terms and a transcendental ego describable only in terms of its intentional functions could be established. As a result, Husserl has two stories about consciousness, a transcendental story and an empirical story, and no ontological way of bringing them together.

In fairness to Husserl, it must be noted that later in his career he made an attempt to deal with the topic of intersubjectivity and thus with the individuation of consciousness. In his *Cartesian Meditations* he makes it clear that the other consciousnesses, which have been reduced to the status of the meaning "other consciousness" in the course of the transcendental reduction, must nevertheless not be identified with such meanings within my own solipsistically conceived consciousness.[32] They are, he declares, transcendent to first-personal consciousness, which can never incorporate them into itself or even gain direct access to them.

This use of the word "transcendent" is particularly interesting because it is the same word that Husserl uses to characterize a wide range of natural objects which are such that they cannot be experienced exhaustively at any one moment but always involve a "more"—another side, for example—to which experience must subsequently advance without, however, ever reaching completion. What is most striking in this is the fact that, while this transcendence of natural objects is transformed into what Husserl calls "transcendence-in-immanence"—transcendence as a meaning—through the phenomenological reduction, without its ever becoming clear when transcendence as such is to be restored, Husserl explicitly denies that the transcendence of other selves can ever be equated with their transcendence-in-immanence in my consciousness.[33] Thus, the transcendence he attributes to them is what might be called a "hard" transcendence, by contrast to the "soft" transcendence of natural objects. It follows that pure consciousness is irreducibly plural and individuated (*vereinzelt*), just as empirical consciousness is; and this plurality is in fact the premise on which Husserl's whole theory of intersubjectivity as a community of monads rests. But if Husserl was able to move this far in the direction of an acknowledgment of the essential plurality of consciousness, nothing that he says in the Fifth Meditation casts any light on the nature or, indeed, the possibility of the identity of a transcendental with an empirical ego. In this respect, his position remained to the end vulnerable to the objections that Heidegger directed against it.

It is interesting that Heidegger does not concern himself in his critique of Husserl with the possible idealistic implications of the phenomenological reduction and explicitly characterizes that operation in non-Cartesian and nonepistemological terms. In his view, the bracketing of the world that the reduction requires is not to be understood as implying that from this point onward phenomenology will have nothing to do with entities—that is, with what exists. Instead, "the phenomenological disconnecting of the positing of transcendent entities has exclusively the function of making (such) entities present in terms of their being."[34] But if Heidegger at first seems to make no difficulty about the phenomenological reduction so conceived, he clearly does not accept the eidetic reduction that follows upon it. This reduction eliminates the singularity (*Einmaligkeit*) of *my* consciousness, which survived the bracketing of transcendent entities, and replaces it with a "pure field of consciousness" that abstracts altogether from such matters as whether an intentional act is *my* act. "The stream of experience (*Erlebnisstrom*) becomes thereby a region of being that constitutes a sphere of absolute positing (*Position*) as Husserl says."[35] What Heidegger objects to is thus Husserl's way of conceiving the subject in terms of the immanence and absolute givenness of its reduced objects. The reason for his resistance on this point is stated in the form of a question.

> How is it at all possible that this sphere of absolute positing, pure conscious-ness, that is supposed to be separated by an abyss from every form of tran-scendence, is also at the same time joined with the unity of a real human being that also exists as a real object in the world? How is it possible that experiences constitute an absolute and pure region of being and simultane-ously occur in the transcendence of the world?[36]

Heidegger clearly believes that Husserl has no answer to these questions and that, as a result, the theory he gives us is not a theory of the being of consciousness—an ontology of consciousness—but rather a theory of consciousness as a distinctive "region that is to be viewed in an absolute, scientific manner."[37] This is comparable to the situation in mathematics in which it is possible, Heidegger says, to "delimit the mathematical field, the whole domain of that which is the object of mathematical consid-eration and interrogation," and even "to give a certain definition of the object of mathematics without necessarily ever posing the question of the mode of being of mathematical objects."[38] Similarly, it is possible to delimit the region of phenomenology as Husserl does by characterizing consciousness in terms of its immanence, its absolute givenness, its in-dependence of the existence of this world and its purity or ideality, without "inquiring as to the being of that which belongs in the region" so characterized.[39]

It has already been noted that Heidegger speaks of the phenome-nological reduction as "making entities present in their being." Another discussion of the same topic makes it clear that what this involves is making them present in their "perceivedness" (*Wahrgenommenheit*).[40] It is explained that perceivedness is not to be identified with either the mental act of perceiving (*intentio*) or the entity perceived (*intentum*), understood simply as *vorhanden*, or merely existing. Such identifications separate the perceiving from the perceived or the perceived from the perceiving and thereby yield a "subjective" or an "objective" understand-ing of perceivedness when what needs to be grasped is rather the way perception "addresses itself to something that is perceived and does so in such a way that the latter is understood as something perceived in its very perceivedness."[41] What this means is that in perceivedness both an act and an object are essentially involved, and that the act is a necessary condition for the perceived object's being perceived, just as the latter is for the act's being an act of perception. Heidegger then goes on to point out that the relational character itself of this relationship of act and object is what is meant by intentionality, which thus emerges as the central theme of phenomenological analysis. When the reduction makes entities "present in their being" and in their perceivedness, it thereby makes intentionality itself present as the structure of the ways in which the subject comports itself in its relation to objects. But when consciousness is treated as an unindividuated region of absolute givenness, as it is by Husserl, what is missed entirely is precisely the "being of the intentional," or, as Heidegger also puts it, the "being of the acts."[42] "Being" here means not just the *kind* of act that a specifically intentional act is, but how it exists—that is, the kind of entity of which it is an act. Having separated the empirical from the transcendental ego and turned the former over to scientific psychology, Husserl is unable to deal with the being of the latter's acts and can approach these acts only as something "placed before our regard, as grasped, as given," and "not as what is real here and now and mine but according to its essential content."[43] The net result of the reduction in its eidetic phase is thus to concentrate attention on the *What*, the essence of intentional acts and to disregard their existence and with it their individuation—the fact that "these acts are mine or those of some other individual human being."[44]

Heidegger views this whole distorted treatment of intentionality as deriving not from the inherent logic of phenomenology, but from the continuing influence on Husserl of an essentially Cartesian conception of the subject.[45] That influence was plainly at work in the thought of the first modern philosopher to propose intentionality as the distinctive feature of the mental, Franz Brentano. As Heidegger points out, Brentano was never able to make a clear distinction between the different senses of "intentional object" as the entity itself that is perceived or thought about and as the way in which it is perceived, thought about, or otherwise intended.[46] This was a distinction to which Husserl gave great emphasis; and it is ironic, therefore, that he, too, should have construed intentionality in what were, at least in Heidegger's view, essentially Cartesian terms. His relationship to Descartes was complex in that he both celebrated that philosopher as the discoverer of pure consciousness and deplored the *sum* that followed upon the *cogito* as marking a descent from the properly transcendental level. This sounds very much like the same error that Heidegger censured in Descartes; and this in turn might make it appear that the great new beginning in the philosophy of mind that is made by rejecting Descartes's ontology was initiated by Husserl rather than Heidegger. In Heidegger's view, however, Husserl's new beginning fails in spite of all his great achievements, and Husserl's phenomenology becomes, through its implicit espousal of the worldless subject, another variant of the basically Cartesian philosophy of immanence that he had himself seemed to condemn. Indeed, he uses the word "immanence" very frequently in speaking of consciousness; and he is

prepared to speak of both sense-data—"hyletic data," as he calls them—
and intentional acts as being *in* consciousness. As a result, the latter
begins to sound very much like a container of some kind. It is this feature
of Husserl's position to which Heidegger draws attention in his comments on the second volume of *Ideas*, where Husserl was apparently
attempting to incorporate some of Dilthey's psychology into his own
treatment of consciousness.[47] Here the distinctive feature of human
being is analyzed in terms of traditional categories of the physical as
such, the body, the soul, and spirit (mind)—that is, in terms of the old
conception of man as the *animal rationale* compounded out of these
different elements, all of which are conceived as substances. The defining
characteristic of *Geist*, or mind, is then taken to be its reflexivity, its self-
consciousness understood as "an *inspectio sui*, an inner consideration by
the self of itself as the 'I' of intentionality, the 'I' as the subject of the
cogitationes."[48]

The criticism that Heidegger directs against Husserl is thus twofold.
By leaving the ontological status of the transcendental ego indeterminate,
Husserl made it inevitable that he would relapse, as he in fact did, into
a substantializing Cartesian conception of its mode of being, since this
was the only conception that the philosophical tradition afforded him.
Even more seriously, he so disassociated the transcendental ego from
the empirical ego that there was no way in which the individuated existence of the subject could be understood. Against Husserl's consign-
ment of the natural attitude to a naturalistic psychology, Heidegger
argues that it is precisely in the natural attitude that "factual, real consciousness" is given before the phenomenological reduction and with it
the "being of the intentional." Thus, "the meaning of the reduction is
precisely to make no use of the reality of the intentional," because "the
reality of consciousness is disregarded."[49] It is accordingly in terms of
the natural attitude that the task of an analytical description of the being
of the intentional must be carried out, and this means that such a description must recognize and preserve both the unity of consciousness
with the body and its character as that which makes it possible for the
transcendent world that is supposedly "separated from it by an abyss to
become objective."[50] Only by remaining within the natural attitude is it
possible to prevent the eclipse of intentionality that occurs both when
the transcendental standpoint is adopted and the world is reduced to
the status of a meaning and when the natural attitude is left to empirical
psychology, to which the very concept of intentionality remains alien.
Only in the natural attitude is the existence of both the terms in the
intentional relation fully acknowledged. All this does not imply, however,
that the natural attitude is an infallible guide to the nature of intentionality, and Heidegger warns against another misconception of the latter

that springs precisely from "the implicit theories that arise out of the natural conception and interpretation of things."[51] On this view, "the intentional relation comes to the subject by virtue of the existence (*Vorhandensein*) of the object," so that "if there were no physical things the psychic subject would exist by itself in isolation without this intentional relation."[52] What the natural attitude is all too likely to assume is that the subject and the object exist, and that there is in addition a relation between them—the intentional relation. It thus fails to do justice to the fact that "the relational character of the relation [*Verhältnis*] is a determination of the subject."[53] What the natural attitude is unshakably right about, however, is the fact that the subject is an entity, a real particular, not merely a "region of being," and that the intentional relation is thus a relation between two real entities. It simply tends to miss the equally important fact that this same intentionality is precisely what distinguishes one of these entities—the subject—from the other—the object—and it is this distinction that phenomenological analysis will have to bring out by a deeper interpretation of the intentional relation as constitutive of the being of the subject. In this way phenomenology and ontology will turn out to be a single mode of inquiry.

All these points in Heidegger's critique of Husserl are underscored in his comments on the drafts of the article the latter prepared for the *Encyclopaedia Britannica*.[54] These comments are the more interesting because they show not only the points at which Heidegger breaks with Husserl, but also the continuing use by Heidegger of certain central Husserlian notions like that of constitution to characterize the subject understood as a particular entity. Heidegger agrees with Husserl that the transcendental constitution of the world cannot be effected by an entity of the same type as that world, but he points out that this fact does not by itself give an answer to the question about the ontological character of that which "forms the locus of the transcendental."[55] He goes on to state his own view that "transcendental constitution is a central possibility of the factual self," although not of the latter understood simply in the terms that apply to other entities in the world.[56] This distinction makes it plain that there is both a sense in which the transcendental ego of Husserl is "*the same as* the particular factual ego" and a sense in which the two are different from one another.[57] The former is the sense that gives us "the concrete totality of the human being," whereas what Heidegger calls "somatology" and "pure psychology," although they presuppose that totality, work with concepts of the human being that abstract from it.[58]

These references to the existent subject as that which constitutes its world suggest another line of continuity between Husserl and Heidegger. Heidegger speaks of Husserlian consciousness not only as "immanently and absolutely given being," but also as "that in which every possible other entity is constituted and really 'is' what it is."[59] It is because the being of all other entities is itself constituted *in* consciousness that Husserl holds that the being of consciousness is absolute and prior to all other forms of being. This absolute being of consciousness is unacceptable to Heidegger for the reasons that have already been reviewed. Moreover, he does not conceive the being of the existing subject as absolute, since he speaks of it as not just positing (*setzend*) but posited (*gesetzt*),—that is, as not *causa sui*.[60] Nevertheless, when he speaks of the way consciousness ought to be conceived and insists that it cannot be understood in terms of its What, its essence, he goes on to argue not only that it must be understood in terms of its That, its being in the sense of its existence, but also, in the form of a rhetorical question, that it is an entity whose "What is precisely to be and nothing but to be."[61] Such a suggestion, of course, subverts the What/That distinction on which Heidegger is building here, and it raises further questions as well, such as how an entity without the more familiar kind of What can be "the concrete totality of the human being." The relevant point here, however, is that this identification of an entity with its being in the sense of its existence is not without affinities to the Husserlian association of consciousness and being noted above. The differences are that Heidegger speaks of a particular entity, where Husserl speaks of an unindividuated region of being that is absolute in a way that no particular entity's being can be. Nevertheless, in Heidegger's view, it is just such a particular entity that, through its intentional modalities, constitutes the world as such; and Heidegger states that "the problem of being is universally related to that which constitutes and that which is constituted."[62] This sounds very much as though Heidegger were saying that this is the entity for which everything it posits "is"; and although such a claim differs from that of Husserl in that Heidegger says "for" where Husserl says "in," the relationship between "is" (and thus being) and constitution (and thus intentionality) is common to the two views. This linkage was to be of great importance for Heidegger's understanding of the concept of being in all the stages of his development.

The Husserlian terminology of intentionality and constitution soon disappeared from Heidegger's published writings. In *Being and Time* the words "intentionality" and "intentional" occur only in passages in which Heidegger discusses the views of Husserl and Scheler, although in his lectures at the time of the publication of that work he uses these words extensively and for his own philosophical purposes. (By contrast, words like "constitution" and "to constitute" still occur very frequently in *Being and Time*.) It thus looks very much as though in the case of intentionality Heidegger made a terminological decision like the one he made in the case of "consciousness" and abandoned the term on the grounds that the subjectivistic connotations it had taken on through its use by Husserl especially had made it unsuitable for employment in the very different context of Heidegger's own thought. He speaks in this connection of a misunderstanding of "the structure of directedness and of the *intentio*:

> This misinterpretation lies in a perverted subjectivization of intentionality. One posits an 'I', a subject and assigns intentional experiences to its so-called sphere. The 'I' here is something with a sphere that so to speak encapsulates its intentional experiences.... [But] the idea of a subject that has intentional experiences only in its sphere and is not yet outside that sphere but enclosed in its own capsule is a misbegotten concept.[63]

A reconstructed concept of the subject would make it clear that the structure of intentional acts "is not something that is immanent in the so-called subject and thus initially stands in need of transcendence."[64] In these lectures intentionality was still accepted in a positive sense as "the ontological condition of all transcendence"; but later this relationship was reversed, and transcendence—an existing subject's essential relatedness to the world—became an ontological condition for intentionality.[65] The term "intentionality" then largely disappears from Heidegger's writings and lectures and is replaced by "transcendence." A term with ontological implications that were at best indefinite was thus replaced by one that was explicitly integrated into Heidegger's ontology; but there can be no mistaking the fundamental indebtedness of his thought to the concept of intentionality as developed by Husserl.

CHAPTER TWO • **THE WORLD AS PRESENCE**

The primary task of phenomenology, Heidegger claims, is to give an account of "the being of the intentional," and this means of the mode of being of the entity—the subject—whose acts or ways of comporting itself (*Verhaltungen*) have an intentional structure. It is also understood that in this account the *intentio*—the act of intending—must not be separated from the *intentum*—the entity intended. It follows that this act must not be conceived as the act of a subject that is taken in abstraction from the world it intends. But how is this to be done? If the world is simply the aggregate of actual entities, and if as such it exists in itself, it seems to follow that if a subject exists (even one conceived in intentional terms), it will simply be another entity added to the aggregate. It is not apparent why an account of its distinctive structure would require that anything special be said about the other entities that additively make up the world. Even if we insist on the relational character of intentionality and thus on the world or some entity within the world as an essential term in that relation, it seems clear that the relation cannot be constitutive of the being—whether as essence or existence—of the world as Heidegger says it is in the case of the being of the subject. If it were, the world would once again be pulled into the orbit of the subject, and all the old Husserlian difficulties would return. Everything thus points to the conclusion that the world must be, at best, a silent partner in the intentional relation that supervenes on it. Nevertheless, when Heidegger turns to the task of constructing a positive account of the kind of entity that the subject is, he begins with an analysis not of the acts of the subject, but of the concept of the world. His reasons for so doing are complex and are linked to considerations deriving from the history of that concept, so it is to that history that we must first turn.

I

Heidegger reviews some of the main stages in the evolution of the concept of the world in *The Essence of Reasons*; and in the course of that review he attributes great significance to Kant's treatment of the concept.[1] For Kant, "world," like "soul" and "freedom," was one of a number of concepts by means of which pure reason formulates its metaphysical theses; in this use, it signifies simply the totality of entities that are and have been and will be actual. This is what Kant calls the "dogmatic" use of the concept, and it is the one that is probably still most widely accepted by philosophers who concern themselves with the concept of the world, as well as by those who just make use of it. It is dogmatic in the sense that the notion is just assumed to have a perfectly straightforward meaning and reference, so that it is unnecessary to inquire into such matters as who uses the concept, and how the user grounds it in his experience. In Heidegger's view, this dogmatic assurance is possible only because the world has been thought of primarily as *ens creatum* and thus in a tacit pairing with the concept of God as the entity that creates the world.[2] If so, the dogmatic use of the concept is dogmatic precisely in the sense that it presupposes a contrast between the world and something other than and outside the world; and this something else—God—is the standpoint to which the paradigmatic use of the term "world" is assigned. What Kant does, in effect, is to raise a question about the use of a concept that presupposes such a paradigm, by a finite being that is itself in and forms a part of the very world to which reference is being made. In its employment by such a being, there is a contrast between thought and intuition. This would not be the case for a being endowed, as God is supposed to be, with intellectual intuition; and it turns out that under these circumstances the truth-conditions for typical statements about the world are anything but straightforward and may indeed generate irresolvable contradictions. What Kant proposes is not that the concept be scrapped because of these difficulties stemming from its dogmatic employment, but rather that the true utility of the concept, as actually employed by a finite being and as it functions in relation to the experience of the latter, be recognized. This use of the concept as what Kant calls a "regulative idea" orders the objects of empirical knowledge, which are always causally and otherwise conditioned, in such a way as to incorporate them within a totality—the world—that is itself unconditioned. Since this regulative idea of "the world" is not one for which a counterpart in reality can be known to exist, it is more loosely linked to the experience of the things and events that it seeks to integrate into the world. Accordingly, there is a strong temptation to regard such an idea as purely subjective and to contrast it unfavorably with the objectivity of the dogmatic concept that Kant revised.

Like Kant, Heidegger is a critic of the dogmatic concept of the world; but if his critique was deeply influenced by Kant's, it follows quite different lines. For all his potentially subversive revisions of the Cartesian scheme, Kant remained, in Heidegger's view, a partisan of the worldless subject to the end. It is this conception of the subject that generates the transcendental picture of the self as only contingently related to the world; and it is this picture that also makes it possible for the finite human self to interpret its own relation to the world on the analogy of God's relation to the world. Although the human subject remains indefeasibly finite by comparison with God, since it cannot create the world, it could nevertheless claim to stand outside the world as God does, to the extent that it can make a distinction between itself and its body, and, through this purification of its self-concept, it can conceive itself as standing outside the system of objects—the world—to which that body belongs. Once this distinction has been made, the treatment of the world as the comprehensive system of objects tends to be of a homogenizing kind, since the assumption is that the world contains entities of a single ontological type, for which an appropriate mode of scientific conceptualization in terms of causal regularities is available.

There is a grave difficulty, however, that complicates the set of contrasts on which this concept of the world as the totality of objects is based. In its simplest terms, it is the fact that, although there may be only one infinite subject, there are many *finite* ones; and although philosophy has often done its best to treat this fact as having no great significance for its inquiries, this is manifestly not the case. Once it is fully acknowledged that in this world that has been conceptualized as a totality of objects there are entities that are, like ourselves, subjects and that use the concept of the world as we do but from a locus that, unlike ours, appears to be internal to that world itself, there are really only two alternatives. In practical terms these reduce to one unless we are willing to have recourse to solipsistic assumptions of a heroic kind that would restore the monological character of our first understanding of the world. Otherwise, we have no choice but to promote these other subjects to a status like our own and to view them as standing outside the world as a system of objects and to decree that the appearance of their being in the world is confined to their empirical selves as it is to ours. Even so, the very fact of the plurality of subjects thus recognized makes it impossible to maintain the kind of indeterminacy that characterized the ontological status of the transcendental subject as long as it was unique. It must now be acknowledged that these other subjects exist as distinct entities; and such acknowledgment, once made in the case of other subjects, can hardly be withheld in the case of the self. But then the original concept of the world as a totality of entities set over against a unique transcendental consciousness lies in ruins, for there is simply no way in which the world can be regarded as the totality of actual entities when an indefinitely large population of such entities has been conceded to stand outside the world. The only way to restore the claim to totality is to redefine the world as a larger system of some kind, comprising not only "nature"— that is, the original system of objects—but also all the entities that use the concept of world and thus stand outside the original system. In the process of forming this new concept, the user of the original concept will also have definitively lost any privileged or unique status of the kind it implicitly accorded itself at the outset. It will not be only one of an indefinitely large population of like beings who are distributed through a world that is still an all-inclusive system but can no longer be identified with nature.[3] About "the world" in this new and larger sense, nothing can be said to be obvious, especially not the sense in which human beings, as users of the concept "world," may be said to be in it. This much seems clear, however. The effort to separate the world and the subject along transcendental lines has broken down, and the new concept of the world is predicated on leaving *in* the world just what was placed outside it under the old dispensation. There is, accordingly, no reason to suppose that the new concept of the world will be classifiable as "objective" or "subjective," since the original version of the contrast underwriting such a distinction has broken down, and there is no way of telling in what form, if any, it may be reestablished.

It is evident from what has been said so far that the concept of the world that Heidegger presents must be a concept of this larger system that is neither objective nor subjective in the sense that goes with the dogmatic concept and its theological-transcendental appendages.[4] It will also turn out that, in Heidegger's view, the dogmatic concept is derivative from the concept of the world that he elaborates and for which he reserves the term. The prospect of such a demotion of the familiar concept of the world to a derivative status inevitably arouses dire apprehensions in its partisans, who typically fear that all the subjective bric-a-brac of secondary and tertiary qualities that, under the Cartesian dispensation, had been domiciled in the mind so as to keep it out of the world is about to be redistributed there. What the objector fears is that in such a world all qualities will be on an equal footing, and that no distinction at all will be possible between what is "objective" and what is "subjective," with disastrous consequences for critical and scientific thought. In fact, imputations of romantic *Schwärmerei* of this kind are peculiarly inappropriate to Heidegger's thought; and he is at pains, for example, to disassociate himself from those who, like Goethe, have tried to contest the Newtonian theory of color as a secondary and subjective quality.[5] The error involved in such construals of his philosophical intentions is the supposition that he is trying to prove that what has been classified as subjective, whether it be a feeling of pain or a quality like color, is really just as objective as, say, the metric properties of an object.

This completely misses the point, for it is this assumed distinction between the objective and the subjective that is being reinterpreted, not
special applications of it. The real reasons for Heidegger's reconstrual
of the concept of the world are not to be sought in some *parti pris* in
favor of secondary qualities or in any attitude of opposition to the kinds
of classification of properties that may prove to be useful for the purposes
of scientific inquiry.[6] The important thing to remember about such distinctions is that they are made for specific purposes that make it seem
advisable to abstract from the full range of qualitative differentiation
that characterizes things in the world, and that to absolutize them into
ontological distinctions by"decontextualizing" them is a risky business.

The characterization of Heidegger's concept of the world that I have
just offered is faulty in one important respect. It suggests that the greater
richness of that concept is due to the fact that the world as so understood
comprises more entities (and entities of different kinds) than those that
make up the world on the traditional interpretation. But this way of
putting things is unsatisfactory because it implicitly espouses the additive
conception of the way entities are together in the world—a conception
that is a hallmark of the old concept. The world in the sense in which
Heidegger understands it is not the final resultant of an accumulation
of entities that simply exist side by side with all their differences in an
unproblematic way. Such a conception implies that the world is still being
viewed from outside as by a *cosmotheoros*, and it misses what distinctively
characterizes the world as that which we are *in*. "We" here refers to
entities having the character of subjects; and it is the way of being *in* the
world of such entities that is at issue.[7] The central claim underlying
Heidegger's whole treatment of this matter is that to characterize the
way we are in the world is also to characterize the way the world is for
us; indeed, this is what distinguishes his concept of the world from that
of an aggregate of entities. What he is saying will be totally misunderstood, however, if it is assumed that this notion of "being for" signifies
merely "appearing to be" or "being thought to be." Such an assumption
would mean that whatever is so described would be detached from the
world and assigned the status of a belief or a meaning that resides in
the subject. As something other than a collection of entities, the world
is indeed such as to imply the existence of a subject; but this does not
make it a thought or concept of that subject. Instead, it is both a character
of the subject-entity as that for which other entities exist as such *and* a
character of those entities as entities that exist for a subject-entity.[8] So
understood, it is neither objective nor subjective; or, if one prefers, it is
both.

In what follows, I will attempt to make this Heideggerian concept of
the world as neither objective nor subjective more accessible and more

concrete and to show why it is not only our "first" or "primary" world, as Heidegger describes it, but also the continuing and indispensable presupposition of the conception of the world as a totality of entities. This will be done by taking up first the notion of "being in" as it applies to entities like ourselves when we are said to be *in* the world. Then there will be a detailed account of the characteristics of the world as that which we are in. These will turn out to be features of the world that are neglected in the traditional lists of categories but do not fit the picture of what is merely "subjective" or "in the mind" either. Attention will also be given to the way in which concepts of entities emerge that abstract from the existence of the world as that which these entities are in and to the way in which the concept of the world is then assimilated to that of a totality of such entities. Finally, some questions will be raised about the way Heidegger conceives the relationship between nature as the totality of such "deworlded" entities and the world as the quite different milieu in which our existence is embedded.

II

There is a sense of the word "in" that tends to control the terms in which we think about the way we are in the world.[9] It is the sense of spatial inclusion, the sense in which water is said to be in a glass and a garment in a closet; in just this sense, it is suggested, I am in the room and, like these other objects, in world-space, which is the ultimate container in which everything is assigned its place. But if being in the world is being situated in world-space, it follows that the fundamental mode of relatedness of all the entities that are in the world is that of spatial adjacency of some kind. Within this world-space all objects, including ourselves, exist side by side, as indeed appears to be the case in our ordinary perception of the scene within which we ourselves are placed. Lined up in this way, some objects are so close that they touch one another, as, for example, a chair touches a wall. I, too, as one of these objects, sometimes touch the wall; and in the one case, as in the other, the mode of adjacency is the same and derives from their placement in space which, on this view, is the mode of being in the world that all entities share.

In Heidegger's view, this assimilation of our mode of being in the world to the mode of spatial inclusion that characterizes such entities as chairs and walls is profoundly mistaken. It also illustrates a deep-seated tendency on our part to fail to grasp the full implications of the fact that what we are trying to characterize is the kind of entity that we ourselves are.[10] As a result of this failure, we offer as a primary account of one of the modalities of our being in the world—touch, say—what is really an account of the relationship between two entities that are both presupposed as existing in the world in the mode of spatial adjacency. The example of such a substitution that Heidegger gives is Descartes's account of hardness in terms of a relation between two material objects, the thing that is touched and the hand that touches it.[11] Descartes argues that if an object (or the particles of which it is composed) does not move when the hand that is in contact with it moves, it is hard; otherwise it is not. This account has the advantage of permitting an assimilation of one mode of sensation to a relationship between two extended entities—the hand and the object with which it comes into contact—and thus of providing a clear and distinct representation of the otherwise confused business of sensation. Descartes's primary account of the way we are in the world was given, of course, in terms of just the kind of knowledge that such representations yield. Nevertheless, his account of touch can serve as an example of a much more general tendency to avoid giving any primary description of the way we are in the world by substituting a description of a relation between two entities within the world—entities that are already assumed as existing and as "given," without our having to describe how we are in the world with just these entities.[12]

In spite of all these complexities, most people would probably agree that there is some important difference between the sense in which the chair can be said to touch the wall and the sense in which we are said to do so, or between the way chairs are in a room and the way we are. If pressed, they would be likely to say that in our own case, we *know* that we are touching the wall, whereas in the case of the chair, there is no such knowledge. The trouble with this essentially Cartesian answer, which has already been identified, is that it makes our being in the world a matter of mental representation and thus a matter about which we could in principle be mistaken. More relevant in this context, it fails to explain the difference between the two kinds of touching because it removes the whole matter to the level of thought and belief and thus makes it inevitable that both touch and perception generally will be equated with a certain modality of the existence side by side of two *res extensae*—two objects within the world—and that the character of perception as a way of being in the world and with *(bei)* such objects will be missed. The upshot is that the real basis for the distinction between the two kinds of touching is never stated, because it is assumed that the matter has been satisfactorily dealt with already, and that it requires no further attention. More significant, it is not stated because all along there was an implicit understanding of what the difference consists in—an understanding that was relied on without acknowledgment, with the result that we never distinguish between the official answer and this implicit understanding. The basis for the distinction is in fact obvious; but, like many obvious things that have always been right in front of us, it requires a special kind of attention if it is not to remain unavailable to conceptual thought.

What, then, is this "obvious" difference between the chair's touching the wall and my touching the wall? It is that in the latter case the wall is present not only in the sense of really existing, but also in the sense of being present to me as the one who touches it.[13] It is this presence that is completely lacking in the case of the chair. The chair and the wall can act causally on one another in various ways, but neither can be present to the other. Because of this, both are "worldless" entities.[14] An entity can be said to have a world, as distinct from merely being one item in an aggregate of spatially adjacent entities, only if other entities are present to it. An entity to which nothing can be present can be said to be in the world in the sense of spatial inclusion, of course, but it is not in the world in the strong sense that requires that it also *have* a world. In Heidegger's parlance, it is an entity *within* the world (*innerweltliches Seiendes*), not one that is *in* the world (*in der Welt*). Being *in* the world is thus something that characterizes one kind of entity and not another; it does so by reference to the way in which that kind of entity is related to other entities. The language of "relations" is not very satisfactory here, because it always suggests a contrast between what something *is* and the relations in which it stands to other entities; and it will turn out that it is its mode of relatedness to other entities that constitutes the kind of entity that a subject-entity is.[15] There is a further linguistic difficulty here in that, if the other term of this relation is referred to as "the world" in Heidegger's sense of the term, the statement will be redundant inasmuch as the world in this sense entails the very presence or givenness that is realized in this distinctive relation among entities. To avoid entanglement in these complexities, it is essential to remember that, although "the world" does not denote simply an aggregate of entities and must therefore be distinguished from its constituent entities, it *is* the presence of just those entities and thus the totality of what is so present. "Worldliness" (*Weltlichkeit*) is thus a distinguishing ontological feature of both the entity that is such that other entities can be present to it and, in a different way, of those entities as so present.

The use of the notion of presence to explain the difference between the two kinds of touching and thereby the difference between being in the world and being within the world clearly requires a good deal of explanation and justification. The remainder of this chapter will be devoted to an account of the more specific ways in which the world— nonredundantly, entities within the world—is present; but the more fundamental questions about what presence itself is will be discussed in the next chapter. At this point, it may be helpful, however, to say something about the connection between the concepts of presence and givenness. As Heidegger uses them, they are equivalent concepts; but while this fact may help a philosopher familiar with the concept of the given but not with that of presence to orient himself terminologically, it can also be very misleading. In the Anglo-American tradition, at least, what is "given" is a sense-datum or a *quale*, not a thing or an object, and the locus of such givenness is the mind, not the world. When the concept of the given is construed in this way, it is usually assumed that the demise of sense-data invalidates any philosophical construction based on that concept. Heidegger, on the other hand, rejects sense-data but retains the concept of the given, applying it to the world rather than to intra-mental entities.[16] Consistently with this line of thought, he argues that "everything that is to be given (*alles zu gebende*) is referred (*angewiesen*) to a 'for,' "—that is, to something for which that which is given is given.[17] Of course, this "for which" is itself an entity that is in the world in the special way that involves the world's being present to it. What all this amounts to is that in construing givenness and thus presence as the "forness" of one entity vis-à-vis another, Heidegger also disassociates the given from the notion of being a special entity of some kind and from the related notion of incorrigibility with which it has been so closely linked in the Anglo-American tradition. This is not because he thinks that the existence of the world can be doubted, but because he accepts the fact that error is always possible in our apprehensions of entities within the world. Some attention will accordingly be given to his treatment of error at the end of this chapter.

III

One way of approaching the task of further explicating the concept of presence is to ask how the world as the whole of what is present differs from the world as the aggregate of entities. This is, in the first instance, a question about how these two different kinds of totality differ from one another as totalities; but it is also, as we will see, a question about the entities that make up one and the other totalities. In the latter form, it is a question as to whether the entities that make up the totality of what is present have any character or characters that do not belong to the entities that make up the world understood simply as the totality of entities. The answers Heidegger gives to both these questions are clearly affirmative; but this does not mean that the totalities, as well as the entities that make them up, are numerically distinct, and that we now have two worlds or two sets of entities on our hands. Heidegger's position is that the one totality—nature—derives from and thus presupposes the other—the world, in his sense—through an operation that he calls "deworlding" (*Entweltlichung*), in which certain characters of the world are discounted, or "leveled off" (*nivelliert*), in such a way that what remains satisfies a criterion of pure objectivity which qualifies it as a constituent of nature.[18] This appears to mean that nature is something abstracted from the world—a conceptual excerpt that does not exist in its own right, but only as embedded within the world, although on occasion we ignore and even forget this embeddedness. There are difficulties with such a view, especially since it is Heidegger's contention that it is quite possible for there to be no world at all in his sense of the term, even though the entities that make up nature exist. These difficulties will be taken up at the end of the chapter. For now, it is just the character of the world qua world—the characters that are leveled off to produce the concept of nature—that needs to be identified.

In a general way, these characters belong to the class of what are usually called "relational properties"; moreover, they are relational properties of a special kind, in which one term in the relation is a human being or an entity sufficiently like a human being to be able to perceive and to make some use of the entity within the world that is the other term. For just this reason, it seems plausible to say that the relational property in question is something merely subjective, something that is "projected" on some entity within the world but that is really wholly extraneous to it and is not, therefore, "objectively" part of the world, in the non-Heideggerian sense of that term. One such relation is that implied by the fact that entities within the world have the character of being here or there, near or far. These terms are indexical in that they relativize the location of things so described to the location of the person who so describes them. This mode of description has limited utility when it comes to communicating with persons who are not necessarily all in one place. Accordingly, there has been an effort on the part of some philosophers of language to show that all such relativizing descriptions can be replaced, at least in principle, by others that can be used by an open class of inquirers, without the ambiguities that arise from the use of indexical terms. This undertaking also requires suppression of the indexical features of our temporal language—words like "now," which locate events in time by reference to the time of speaking—in favor of universally intelligible descriptions in terms of a neutral system of measurement. If such an elimination of indexical terms were shown to be possible in principle, then "indexical properties" would have been shown to be simply a kind of shadow thrown on the world by a feature of our language that is in no way indispensable. Under these circumstances we could be permitted to go on using indexical language, but with the understanding that, as indexical, it does not express anything about the world that cannot be expressed by the language of some objective metric.

Heidegger's treatment of these matters is not formulated in linguistic terms in the way the above account of the opposing view is; but one can devise an answer to the latter that makes the same point about the indexical character of the world that he makes in his own way. Once again, his position is not that of a root-and-branch condemnation of any and all substitutions of an exact metric for the "here" and the "there" of ordinary discourse. What he does want to assert is the priority of ordinary discourse in the sense of the indispensability of understanding of things in the world in indexical terms; he would, therefore, reject the thesis of the replaceability in principle of indexical by nonindexical descriptions.[19] What this comes down to in concrete terms is that, if some-one were to attempt such a substitution and were to give locations only in metric terms, he would be in a position like that of a mapmaker, who must rely on the ability of those who use his maps to identify some point on the map as the place where they are (and where they are *now*—another indexical). If they cannot do this, and if no place on the map and in the territory it covers is designatable as a "here," the map will be completely useless, because people trying to use it will not be able to orient themselves within the space it represents. "Here" and "there" are, of course, only one of the forms that such orientation takes and there are many others like right and left, up and down, and so on. Heidegger discusses Kant's treatment of the first of these, which is typical in that it accounts for the difference by means of "inner feelings."[20] He shows that Kant cannot make the distinction in these exclusively "subjective" terms but must bring in the "memory of objects" that were, for example, on the right or on the left side of the room that he imagines entering in darkness. In other words, unless the room has a right side and a left side, there is no way in which these predicates could somehow supervene on it as the result of some purely subjective, inner feelings. It is the light-switch that is here on the right and the couch that is over there on the left. Perhaps some of these indexical modes of self-orientation can be reduced to others; but there is no possibility of our doing without any of them or of treating them as subjective in a way that undercuts the fact that we are dealing with something that is within the world.

What has just been said should give at least some preliminary understanding of Heidegger's claim that it is space that is in the world, not the world that is in space.[21] Even so, the sense in which it is entities within the world that are themselves here or there is still not adequately specified; and in order to clarify that sense further it is necessary that another even more significant character of the world as a totality of presence be introduced into the discussion. To that end it first needs to be pointed out how important the conjunctive relation is to the other concept of the world as a totality of entities quite apart from any presence that may accrue to them—in other words, to a world understood as consisting of this apple and that chair and this house and so on. There is a marked tendency for these objects to be taken, at least initially, as distinct "items" and for everything else to be taken care of subsequently in terms of the "relations" in which these items stand to one another. Causal relationships—the ways in which one thing or kind of thing affects or is affected by another—are thus not of primary importance when it comes to saying what is in the world; and the same appears to hold for dispositional properties and relational properties in general. What dominates the picture underlying the dogmatic concept of the world is a certain side-by-sideness of its constituent entities; and the word used by Heidegger to describe entities understood in this way as distinct items is *vorhanden*.[22] This has no exact equivalent in English, although it has some of the flavor of our expression "on hand"—that is, as one item in the world inventory; so I will use the German word here. Heidegger introduces it in its nominalized form, *Vorhandenheit*, as a substitute for "existence" (*existentia*) as it applies to entities other than those he proposes to characterize in terms of *Dasein*—that is, human beings. This expedient is dictated by his decision to reserve the term "existence" for the latter. At the same time, however, the concept of *vorhanden* serves to characterize the mode of being of all entities other than *Dasein* and thus the kind of entity that these are. Their ontological type is that of substance, the self-contained thing or *res* that can be understood simply in terms of its own properties—its What—and is not linked in any essential way to any other entity. Heidegger's principal thesis with respect to entities of this kind is that their character as *vorhanden* is a privative state. As such, it is not primitive but derived, and derived via an operation performed on the contexts in which such entities are embedded. As embedded in these contexts, which will be shown to have a functional or instrumental as well as a causal character, he calls them *zuhanden*.[23] This means that they are in some way "at hand" and available for use, just as the lee side of a mountain can be used for shelter. To argue that the "at hand" character of things is somehow prior to their "on hand" character is, of course, to reverse the order of priority that is espoused by those who take the *vorhanden* to be both ontologically and epistemologically prior to the *zuhanden*. If the world itself has such a functional or instrumental character, moreover, the subjective-objective distinction that undergirds the dogmatic concept of the world will have broken down again, this time irremediably.

That things within the world are usually understood in instrumental and functional terms is clear enough. The vocabulary of everyday life is full of words that name things in ways that express the function they serve. "Chair," "table," "knife," "hammer"—these are all words that render that to which they refer as something *zuhanden*, something that is for a certain use. As such, the entities are properly called *pragmata*—the Greek word for things embedded in a context of use—rather than *res*. Although these examples are all of artifacts—things made to serve a certain purpose—iron ore and marble have the same instrumental character as lending themselves to a certain kind of use, and so does the wind that a sailor catches. There are also things that do not appear to be instrumental to anything at all, but to the extent that such things become obstacles in the way of those that are, they take on a counter-functional character and are thus drawn into the same context of potential use as those with a positive instrumental value. It must not be supposed, however, that having a functional character is primarily a matter of being named or described in a certain way. It is not in the context of naming but in that of use that what is *zuhanden* shows itself as such; and it typically does so unobtrusively in that the focus of attention is not on the *pragma* itself, but on the work to which it contributes. Simply looking at a hammer does not reveal its instrumental character, Heidegger insists. In fact, its identity as a hammer, its *An-sich-sein* as *zuhanden*, consists precisely in this unobtrusiveness, this *non*-emerging of the hammer as a distinct item of the kind that we would include in an inventory of that sector of the world.[24]

It is in the unobtrusiveness that is a condition of serving as an instrument that another feature of the *zuhanden* becomes operative. "A hammer," we can say, "is something to drive in nails with"; but in saying this, we have a strong tendency to envisage the hammer as one thing and the nails as another and to postulate a "relation" between the two. But this misrepresents the *zuhanden* character of the hammer and the nails and also our operative understanding of both. As something to hammer with, a hammer is already understood in the context of nails, boards, and so on, in which it is used; indeed, Heidegger says that it already refers to that context of use.[25] This is very different from the kind of reflective understanding that attributes a "dispositional property" to the hammer as a distinct "object" with a certain shape and composition. The notion of a dispositional property treats the instrumental character of the hammer or whatever as being somehow enclosed or encapsulated within that one object, and in so doing, it collapses the referential structure of the *zuhanden*, reducing it to the status of something that is merely *vorhanden*. Indeed, this may be said to be the characteristic function of the concept of a property, according to Heidegger.[26] This concept does not afford an ontologically neutral way of designating anything that can be said about something as has been generally assumed in the philosophical tradition. A property "belongs to" a thing, and it thus presupposes that the thing in question has been abstracted from the pragmatic context in which it was first encountered and now stands free as a separate entity. Since Aristotle, this "belonging to" has been construed as being present in and being contained within the thing in question; but this conception obscures, to say the least, the referential character of that which is now said to "possess" this property. It is rather as though one were to say that the "pointing" of an arrow on a direction-marker is a "property" of the arrow, meaning by "arrow" a certain pattern of lines.[27] Heidegger's point here, which is not unlike that made by Wittgenstein in his discussion of the pointing arrow, is that the moment the arrow is equated with what is merely *vorhanden*—a pattern of lines—it loses its pointing function. The same applies to the instrumental character of a tool like a hammer, which is itself a kind of pointing to nails and boards and so on. Once the hammer is treated as an object—as wood and steel in a certain configuration—it ceases to be the center of a referential context and closes upon itself.

Heidegger's way of summing up his conception of the *zuhanden* as a character of the world is to say that "it is not things but references *(Verweisungen)*" that have the primary function within the structure of the world understood in terms of presence.[28] Indeed, the world is itself a *Verweisungszusammenhang*—a referential context—and what we call "meanings" *(Bedeutungen)* are the articulations of that world which derive from the specific instrumental identities of the *pragmata* with which we deal. In this instrumentally articulated world, everything has its place, which is determined in the first instance not by the coordinates of world-space, but by where things, understood as *pragmata,* belong within the routines of use that define their position within the world as an actional space. But this characterization would still be deficient unless it were pointed out that this world is also a space of possibilities.[29] Things can be moved and burned and cut and dissolved in a great variety of ways and for a great variety of purposes; and their solubility and inflammability and so on are not "add-ons" to some understanding of their nuclear identity, but rather the primary character in terms of which they are understood in a context of use. The possibilities they represent are not mere logical possibilities, of course, nor are they reducible to causal possibilities, although they are closely linked to the latter. They can be explicated only in terms of their contrafactual import, which consists in the fact that if, for example, one were to place a log in a fire, it would ignite and burn. The log that is inflamm*able* is not assumed to be in the fire; nor is it being predicted that it ever will be or that it ever will burn. In this sense, what the description "inflammable" conveys need not be anything actual, either now or in the future. But Heidegger's point is precisely that it is not in terms of this kind of actuality that a book or a hammer or any other *pragma* is understood primarily.[30] The terms in which such entities are understood involve a reference to something that need not occur and may not ever do so, but is nevertheless constitutive of the kind of entity under consideration. To understand something as *zuhanden* and in terms of the references it carries to what may not be actual is to apprehend it as being itself constituted in a way that can be expressed only by using some such word as "can." The account of what that "can" involves will not be complete until all the elements in being-in-the-world have been presented and, specifically, until the way in which the "can" that applies to the entity that is in the world grounds the "can" that applies to entities within the world has been analyzed. By way of anticipation, however, it is possible to indicate in what a fundamental way the world we are in is a world in which things *can* and *may* happen, without our being capable even in principle of reducing these modal features to either our own ignorance or to some metaphysic of pure actuality from which possibility would be forever banished.

It will have been noted that in discussing both indexicality and in-strumentality as constitutive features of the world, I have frequently talked in terms of the way in which various things and situations would be described. This may lead some to conclude that Heidegger's theses about these matters should really be taken as theses about language and about the plurality of descriptive modes it affords; and this interpretation, in turn, might seem to authorize the further conclusion that there is no reason to think that this plurality must also be attributable to the world. Especially when a dichotomous treatment of language *and* the world is accepted, along the lines favored by the dogmatic concept of the world, it can seem quite easy and tempting to accept a generous pluralism of logical modes at the level of language, while continuing to assume that the world itself is cast in some single ontological mode that is tacitly supposed to be independent of language. It would follow from this that an instrumental or *zuhanden* character is projected on things that in themselves are really just so many *vorhanden* entities to which the patterns of functional relationships projected on them are quite extraneous. A tree might thus be seen as something one could hide behind or as something that might fall on power lines during a storm; but these would be subjective additions that reflect the particular interest that someone may take in the tree, not what the tree itself is. By contrast, Heidegger's view is that there is no such projection, because there is no prior experience of the things in question as merely *vorhanden*.[31] It is the understanding of the tree or the hammer in functional terms that is primary, and it is from this primary understanding that the conception of things as merely *vorhanden* is then derived for special purposes. The *res* that is substituted for the *pragma* in the course of that derivation is constituted in such a way as to *make* instrumentality extraneous to it; and as what is held to be objectively present, it imposes a subjective character on everything that had been "naively" associated with it but that does not fit the new conceptual definition. What the theory of instrumentality as a subjective addition really assumes is that this conceptual shift can in principle be made permanent; this would mean that there would no longer be any occasion for understanding things in the world as anything but "object-things" which various "subject-things" may *take* as serving their subjective needs.[32] Heidegger's position, by contrast, is that even when instrumentality has been suppressed by this kind of conceptual operation, it is not simply eliminated from the world but maintains itself quite as stubbornly as indexicality does under the auspices of a scientific metric.

The reasons why instrumentality cannot be eliminated are worth examining. Heidegger describes essentially two kinds of cases in which the instrumental character of things appears to give way to a neutral, "objective" reality. One is the case in which something we have been using— an automobile, perhaps—breaks down and can no longer be used in the usual way, since it has been reduced to a "heap of metal" for which there is no place in our routines of purposive activity. Nevertheless, it retains its instrumental character, although now in the negative mode.[33] It has become an obstacle or a nuisance—something to be moved out of the way, something we may regret having spent any money on. But its valence of instrumentality has not been removed altogether; it has been converted into its opposite. In the other case it is we ourselves who pass over into a "theoretical," and at least ostensibly noninstrumental, mode of observation that involves our *not* intervening in situations that interest us.[34] This contrasts with our usual "hands on" policy of intervening to make things go in a way that serves our interests. The reason for the shift is that it permits us to see *(theorein)* how things will go by themselves; but it can hardly be ascribed to disinterested curiosity. Even when the inquiry is under the aegis of "pure science," the restricted area in which we do not intervene is itself typically brought into being by means of massive instrumentation and controls on its margins. Then, too, once we have learned through this special kind of observation how things go "by themselves," we use this knowledge for scientific experimentation and the technological harnessing of natural processes—instrumental uses if ever there were such. Overall, it is impossible to extract any natural object or process from the world understood as the domain in which it carries a valence of instrumentality. As a thing in the world, it is embedded in a context of involvements *(Bewandtnisse)* that are teleological in character—what Heidegger calls the *Um-zu* structures of the world—and that can be transformed but not eliminated or replaced.[35] These involvements, which Heidegger also speaks of as "meanings" *(Bedeutungen)*, structure the world as the ways in which it works; they are emphatically not mental states that have somehow been "misplaced" in world-space. The fact that these prelinguistic meanings constitute the primary articulation of the world as the milieu of action does not, of course, mean that they are therefore also attributable to metric space or to the de-instrumentalized objects that derive from the world via the operation of deworlding *(Entweltlichung)*. As has already been pointed out, such de-instrumentalized objects were expressly designed so as to exclude any such instrumental character, which is relegated to the margins of the area cleared by the *Entweltlichung* from which such objects emerge.

Despite all warnings, it must appear to anyone who approaches these matters with the traditional distinction between the subjective and the objective in mind, that the concept of the world is becoming steadily more subjective as indexicality and instrumentality are declared to characterize it. For such a person the question must arise as to whether a world that is so characterized will not turn out to be plural, and whether there will not prove to be as many "worlds" as there are "subjects." It must therefore be made clear that this is not the case, and that Heidegger's concept of the world is such as to make that world single and common to all who are in it. This common or public character of the world may in fact be added to indexicality and instrumentality as a third defining feature of what Heidegger calls "worldliness."[36] The word "intersubjective," which is currently used for much the same purpose, could also be used here and indeed is so used by Heidegger himself in his early lectures.[37] It has the disadvantage, however, of suggesting a priority of the individual subject and the need to construct the public character of the world by means of relations—*inter*, between—among an indefinite multiplicity of such individual subjects. The commonness of the world is not such a construction for Heidegger.[38] If it were, the understanding that each has of the world as one and common would be something that supervenes on a still more primordial understanding of the world in which that commonness plays no role. That there is any such prior understanding is what Heidegger denies; he is therefore committed to the position that for each of us the common character of the world is as fundamental as its existence.

The singularity of the world as Heidegger conceives it is made clear by his use of the definite article with the term in *Being and Time* and by the fact that it is not used in the plural.[39] Possessive adjectives like "mine" or "his" qualify "world" in one or two places, but they do so in a way that makes it quite clear that the fact that the world is mine in no way conflicts with its being yours or his as well.[40] It is in what he says about the instrumental character of the various things-in-use with which the world is filled that this common character is most strongly emphasized. Things that lend themselves to a certain use do not refer uniquely to the use that a particular subject that is perceiving them at a particular time might make of them. Instead, they are things that "one" can use in certain ways and for certain purposes; these things and their utilities are thus understood as making up the *same* world that I and others like me are in.[41] In this sense, the world, understood as a "work-shop" *(Werk-statt)*, is regulated by criteria that are general in their import; it is therefore public in the sense of being accessible and available to all. The indexicality of the world is thus not a way of tying it to a unique inhabitant whose ways of identifying and locating things in the world would be usable only by him. Instead, it is understood that what is "here" for me is "there" for you and vice versa, and that there is a perfect reciprocity of reference in which neither party is privileged. No doubt such indexical modes of reference have a measure of inexactitude, and for special purposes they need to be supplemented by systems of coordinates that make more exact determinations possible. It does not follow, however, that what is inexact is subjective. The location of things in indexical terms has therefore a perfectly good claim to be recognized as "public."

Although the public, nonsubjective character of the world is asserted very clearly by Heidegger, it would not do to leave the impression that this publicity is without its hazards as regards entities that are in the world in the distinctive way described earlier in this chapter. It will turn out that the notion of "mine" applies to the being of such entities in a strong sense that, at the very least, puts difficulties in the way of establishing sharable criteria of equivalence applying to many such entities. It is also Heidegger's view that when such beings treat their own lives as though they were public in the same way that things within the world are, something has gone seriously wrong.[42] This fact, together with the linkage that he establishes between the concept of such entities and the concept of the world, may mislead us into supposing that this strong sense of mineness, with its possible implication of uniqueness, must be extended to the world as well, which would then become in each case "my world" in a sense that would be hard to reconcile with the singularity and commonness just described. At this stage, it is not really possible to show why such an inference is both unnecessary and unjustified in the light of what Heidegger himself says. For now, what is important is to grasp the fact that the world is common in a sense that carries no pejorative connotations at all.

IV

It has become clear that Heidegger's new way of construing the concept of the world necessitates a distinction between the world and the entities within it. This distinction can also be formulated as one between those entities and their presence as entities. However it is formulated, this distinction is of fundamental importance at all periods of Heidegger's thought; but it is as elusive as it is fundamental. An effort must therefore be made to clarify, if only in a preliminary way, the relationship between the terms of this distinction, so that the ontological status of the world and of presence can be properly understood. In this connection, some things appear to be relatively straightforward. For example, there could be no world unless there were entities within it; but these entities could, and presumably would, exist even if there were no subject-entity and thus no world, at least in Heidegger's sense.[43] But even if these propositions give no difficulty, other aspects of the relationship between entities and their presence as entities are not at all perspicuous. Many of these are rather sketchily dealt with by Heidegger, and so in this section I will suggest ways in which he might have met certain difficulties his position involves.

One of the difficulties has to do with the fact of error, both perceptual and judgmental, and its bearing on the way presence is to be conceived. It was pointed out earlier that the whole Cartesian philosophy of mind arises from reflection on occasions on which we have been mistaken in our beliefs about what is the case in the world. Since there are such occasions on which the world and our beliefs about it are at variance, it seemed to Descartes and to others that the only safe method of proceeding was to assume, at least initially, that we might always be mistaken in the way we know we sometimes are. This would be to assume in effect that the world is *never* present or given as it really is, and that our experiences must accordingly be analyzed first in terms of our own states of mind, and that it is on the basis of these that we will subsequently be able to make reliable inferences about what is the case in the world. Heidegger's reasons for rejecting this whole line of argument that generalizes the experience of error have already been set forth. The question now is whether, from his non-Cartesian standpoint that insists on the unchallengeable presence of the world, he can accommodate the errors of perception and judgment that unquestionably *do* occur. The question is how we could ever be mistaken if the world is present to us as Heidegger says it is. Is it not possible that taking veridical states of mind as one's paradigm-case can lead into philosophical difficulties as severe as those that have been shown to arise when it is the case of error that is generalized?

In chapter 1 a general indication of Heidegger's strategy for dealing with error was given, and that account must be developed somewhat further here. There is admittedly not a great deal to work with since the fact of error, though explicitly noted and commented on, was never a central theme of his thought.[44] This is certainly true of the kind of everyday perceptual illusions and mistakes of judgment on which the Cartesian argument was based; and the kinds of error with which Heidegger does occupy himself at length have more the character of self-deception and are located at the level of ontological understanding rather than of commonsense belief. There are passages in *Being and Time*, however, and more extensive ones in the lectures of the period that deal with ordinary cases of error; and together they make it clear that what Heidegger means by presence is not in the nature of an incorrigible immediacy but instead is such as to permit things and qualities to appear to exist although they do not in fact exist. Thus, in his discussion of the Greek term *phainomenon* at the beginning of *Being and Time*, he distinguishes a first sense in which a *phainomenon* is something that "shows itself" and a second in which it is that which "appears" other than it is.[45] Of these it is the former that is fundamental and the second that is derived, in that, if nothing showed itself as it is, then nothing could *appear* to be other than it is. A thing can appear other than it is in the absence of any kind of illusion only if it is something with which one is independently familiar and it appears in just this way in given circumstances; but if this is not understood, an illusion *(Schein)* can indeed result. But even when this happens, it is not as though we were thereby enclosed within a domain of mere appearances to which nothing real might correspond. There is typically a context for such an illusion that is not itself mere appearance, inasmuch as the object we misperceive—for example, the famous stick partly immersed in water that looks bent—is situated among other entities that show themselves unproblematically as what they are; and there is also our prior familiarity with the stick as it was before it was partly immersed in water. Even in the case of hallucinations, where it is not a question of a real entity looking as though it were other than it is, but of entities that do not exist at all appearing to exist, contact with the world is not lost.[46] In the case of someone who sees elephants in a room where there are in fact none, Heidegger acknowledges that he sees objects that do not exist and that these objects are only notionally *(vermeintlich)* given as existing. But he goes on to argue that perception can be illusory in this way only because it is constitutionally directed to objects that exist within the world and not to some internal state. It is not the existence of the object, however, that confers this directedness or intentionality on perception, as though the latter as an "isolated psychic subject" lacked such directedness and acquired it only when standing in a relation for which the existence of the other term is necessary.[47] Instead, the subject always has a world already, regardless of whether particular objects—elephants in Heidegger's example—really exist. This is to say that an illusion is possible only within the larger context of having a world that is not only not called into question by an aberrant experience, but must stand fast if that aberrancy itself is to be possible.

It seems clear that it is in some such way as this that the apparently conflicting statements that Heidegger makes about the relationship between presence and existence *(Vorhandenheit)* can be reconciled with one another. On the one hand, he insists that something can be given and thus be present although it does not exist, while, on the other, he argues that although "perceivedness" is not the same as existence, the existence of what is perceived is in some sense enclosed *(beschlossen)* within its perceivedness or presence.[48] This apparent contradiction can be resolved if it is understood that the independence of presence from existence is always local and presupposes a wider context in which presence and existence are not so disjoined. But if this way of interpreting what Heidegger says meets the difficulty to which the fact of error gives rise, there is still another aspect of the relation between presence and existence or between the world and the entities within it that remains problematic. This new difficulty arises because the entities that are within the world are not dependent for their existence on their presence—that is, on the existence of the world as a milieu of presence or on the existence of the kind of subject-entity that makes presence possible. Even if there were no such subject-entities and, therefore, no world, these entities would nevertheless exist; and so it is evident that being-within-the-world is in no way essential to them. As Heidegger puts it, the world is not a property of these entities but something that "happens with entities."[49] But once we have on our hands a distinction between entities that are within the world and those that are not, a number of difficult questions arise about the identity of the former with the latter—an identity that Heidegger clearly wants to assert, as we have already seen. For example, is it the case that, if there is a world, all entities are within that world; or will this be true only of those entities that can in some narrower sense be described as present or given? Again, since the world is not just the sum of all entities but a referential whole within which entities belong to functional contexts of various kinds, it seems that not belonging to a world cannot be just a matter of not being part of a certain totality but must involve the loss of the functional or instrumental character that entities have within a world. This makes it sound as though entities that are not part of the world will be merely *vorhanden* in the sense of being stripped of all their relational and dispositional characters; and Heidegger makes it clear that this is indeed the case.[50] But how does this conception of the *vorhanden* as independent of the world and thus of the *zuhanden* comport with Heidegger's insistent claim that the concept of the *vorhanden* is derivative from that of the *zuhanden* through the operation of deworlding? And if being embedded in a functional or instrumental matrix is inessential to entities conceived as *vorhanden*, how will it be possible to assert the identity of entities that are within the world with those that one day may not be?

To the first of these questions, a fairly definite answer can be given. If there is a world at all, then, according to Heidegger, all entities will be included within it, even though their existence may never come to be known and they are not, therefore, in any familiar sense given or present.[51] Heidegger's claim here rests on his conception of presence as including not only those entities that are being perceived at any given time but also those that have been perceived and may be perceived again, as well as those that have never been and may never be perceived but in principle could be perceived. This conception of presence as including absence in these various senses will be taken up in chapter 4 and will therefore be allowed simply to stand as Heidegger's position on the matter for the present. But to the question about the identity or nonidentity of the entities that are within the world with those that would exist if there were no world, there is no ready answer; nor is there any real evidence that Heidegger ever gave any attention to the *prima facie* conflict between his characterizations of the *vorhanden* as both independent of and derivative from the *zuhanden*. The issue here is a momentous one, since the *vorhanden* constitutes the ontological character of the nature that Heidegger counterposes to the world. The question is thus whether nature is to be understood simply as a kind of special enclave that is constituted within the encompassing matrix of the world, or whether it is genuinely independent and antecedent to the world understood in terms of presence. When Heidegger speaks of the *vorhanden* as that by virture of which there is anything *zuhanden* and identifies the *vorhanden* with "the soil, the earth, wind and water" as that which is "always already there," he is unquestionably invoking the conception of the *vorhanden* as independent of the world.[52] He does this most obviously when he speaks of entities as "entering the world" *(Welteingang)*; elsewhere he makes it clear that it is *vorhanden* entities that so enter the world.[53] But what then becomes of the thesis that the *zuhanden* is in no sense the product of a projection of meaning and utility on *vorhanden* entities that are given antecedently? What is it that "happens with" the *vorhanden* entities that enter the world if not some sort of incorporation into a matrix of meaning and purpose? One could concede that the *zuhanden* might still enjoy a certain limited priority insofar as it is always as already incorporated that we first encounter entities within our world; and to this it might be added that there can be no question of there being such a matrix of meaning and purpose before entities have entered it. Nevertheless, once the concept of an independent *vorhanden* has been admitted, there is no way in which one can avoid treating the *vorhanden* as a necessary condition for the *zuhanden* and the latter as thus a derivative, rather than a primary ontological, concept, as Heidegger evidently intended it to be. This is especially the case now that natural science, as the exposing of the *vorhanden* as a stratum of the unintelligible and of the meaningless *within* the world, has advanced as far as it has.[54]

It is arguable, I think, that with the conception of an independent *vorhanden* that enters the world, Heidegger is attempting to deal with a problem that usually arises for other philosophers at a different point. This problem is one that is typically formulated in terms of the relationship between the mind (or thought or language) and the world; but Heidegger rejects this mode of formulation because, he insists, "mind" and its cognates always carry with them a prior commitment to the world as the common milieu of those who perceive and think and speak. But even if the world is not rendered subjective by Heidegger's position on this point, the question must eventually arise as to how to deal with the fact that there is a stratum of the meaningless in this very world and that, however marginal its status may be within a meaning-dominated world, it is nevertheless a prior and necessary condition for the existence of such a world. This is a question of how the relationship between a meaningful and meaningless world is to be understood; and it looks very much as though Heidegger has two, incompatible answers to this question.

One of these says, in effect, that the meaningless—the *vorhanden*—enters the sphere of meaning and is there transformed into something meaningful; this sounds very much like the hypothesis of representationalism, according to which the external world enters the mind via sense-data, which then become embedded in structures of meaning and are *recognized* as sense-data, and hence as meaningless, only in the course of subsequent philosophical analysis. Such a view of the relationship of nature to the world also seems to presuppose an extramundane point of view that would permit one to see all meaning as confined to one domain and, over against the latter, the domain of the meaningless; and this is a point of view that no finite subject, as Heidegger conceives it, could really assume. The other answer, which seems to me to represent the distinctively Heideggerian position, may be said to take its stand within the situation of an entity that is finite in this special way; it does not, therefore, attempt to envisage the situation from a point of view that is in principle unavailable to it. In so abstaining, the Heidegger of this answer would not be taking a skeptical attitude in the matter of what would exist if there were no subject-entities; he makes it quite clear that the latter "reveal entities *(das Seiende)* precisely as that which they previously already were," independently of their being so revealed.[55] He has also argued that the notion of "the being-in-itself of things would be completely senseless without the existence of man; [but] this does not mean that things themselves are dependent upon man."[56] In other words, it is through the entity that is in the world that the independent existence of things is revealed, and revealed without any tacit reservation that makes that existence conditional on the existence of the entity that so reveals it. If one speaks of the *vorhanden* as "entering the world," however, one is speaking not as an entity that is in the world, but from a standpoint that takes in not just the world of such an entity but also what lies outside that world. Not only is that not a standpoint from which we can speak; there is not even any reason for interpreting that fact about ourselves in privative terms as though it were something that is in principle possible but has simply been denied to us. It would, after all, be a standpoint from which entities that are not part of the world as the milieu of presence would nevertheless be accessible, in the mode of thought if not of intuition; and this sounds very much as though these entities would be both present and not present to the thought or intuition of whatever entity it is that is supposed to occupy this standpoint. More generally, may there not be something incoherent about trying to say what an entity *is*—*vorhanden* or whatever—when that entity *ex hypothesi*, and not just contingently, lies outside the world that is understood as the totality of what is *in any way* present or given?[57] If the answer to this question is affirmative, as Heidegger's certainly appears to be, then it seems best to view these statements about the *vorhanden* "entering the world" as inconsistent with that answer and as aberrations from the main course of his thought.

CHAPTER THREE • **EXISTENCE AND** *DASEIN*

The account given in the preceding chapter of Heidegger's concept of the world in terms of the notion of presence is just one facet of the larger account of being-in-the-world. We must now look at the kind of entity that is in the world in the special Heideggerian sense—namely, the "existing subject," whose mode of being is the topic of *Being and Time*.[1] To learn, as we have, that it always and necessarily has a world is a major contribution to our understanding of its ontological status. It is equally necessary, however, that this understanding be further developed to show how the special character of that entity accounts for the fact that there *is* a world as a milieu of presence. For special reasons that will be explained later in this chapter, Heidegger uses the term "existence" to express what is distinctive of the mode of being of the entity that is in the world; and in this usage it will turn out that presence in all its different modes is grounded in the existence of the subject-entity and, more specifically, in its transcendence. This chapter will introduce these central concepts of Heidegger's philosophy; but the concept of temporality that is required to give them their full range of implication will be reserved for the chapter that follows.

I

In response to the question "What kind of entity is it that is in the world?", there is an almost irresistible temptation to give the kind of answer that would completely miss the line of thought that Heidegger is developing. What we are tempted to do is to take an inventory of the kinds of entity that are already familiar to us and to decide which of these is the one that could be said to be in the world in the way that we are and chairs and tables are not. One such entity is the mind as a "spiritual thing," but it has already been shown that it will not do for this purpose. The next move is often to conclude that all that is left is the body; but this body is typically the conceptual residue of the operation by which the mind came to be treated as a distinct entity.[2] As such, it is the body as physiological science conceives it, and this means that it is understood in terms of the same concepts that define the mode of being of the tables and chairs with which a contrast is to be made. Under these circumstances, it is often thought that the only remaining alternative is to try to reunite mind and body and to conceive the entity that is in the world not as one *or* the other but as the human being that is both. If we wish to understand how presence is grounded in the kind of entity that is in the world, it would accordingly be to the concept of a human being that we should turn.

There is a difficulty, however, with this conclusion that the object of Heidegger's inquiry is the concept of a human being. The conclusion is correct inasmuch as Heidegger makes it quite clear that the entity whose ontological character we are trying to define is the entity that each of us is; and we are—each of us—human beings. But it is mistaken if we suppose that the concept of a human being can give us any adequate insight into the way the entity that each of us is grounds presence. For although the concept of a human being and the concept of the entity that grounds presence are extensionally equivalent in the sense that they apply to the same entities, they are not intensionally equivalent because they take these entities in different ways.[3] The concept of a human being typically is the concept of a "rational animal," and this representation of what we are, although certainly not false, conceals, Heidegger says, "the phenomenal soil" from which it springs.[4] It does this because the ontological understanding that informs it is implicit and uncritical; the kind of entity that we are has been decided in advance and without any sense of alternative conceptions that need to be considered. More specifically, this concept of a human being invariably assumes, although without acknowledging the fact, the presence of entities and thus the existence of the world; and because it is not acknowledged, the fact that the concept of a human being is grounded in that presence and cannot itself ground it, is passed over in silence. What is required is a concept of ourselves in which what has thus been kept in the background of the concept of a human being is made central and explicit.

Any concept that replaces the concept of a human being will inevitably seem novel and esoteric and will appear to bypass much, if not all, of what we know about ourselves, since this knowledge has been formulated in terms of the concept of ourselves as human beings. One of the major tasks confronting the designer of such a concept would be to show how some (presumably large) portion of that knowledge can be accommodated in the new idiom it generates and why any remaining portion cannot. It must be admitted that this "naturalizing" of a new concept does not figure at all prominently in Heidegger's philosophical practice.[5] Instead, he emphasizes the radical differences between the new concept he is introducing and its predecessor; thus he declares that the entity that each of us is cannot be understood, as other kinds of entities are, in terms of *what* it is at all—that is, in terms of its "nature" or "properties."[6] Nevertheless, for all this stress on the unfamiliar and even "uncanny" (*unheimlich*) character of the new understanding of ourselves that is being offered, there is also a sense in which it is not unfamiliar at all; it is only at the level of conceptual thought that it represents a startling new departure.

There is a parallel here between what has already been carried out in the case of the dogmatic concept of the world and what is now proposed in the case of the traditional concept of the subject. In the former case, Heidegger argued that the concept of the world as the totality of entities is the product of a conceptual operation in the course of which a prior understanding of the world in terms of presence and its modalities is not only replaced, but is also almost totally obscured. By contrast, the concept of the world that Heidegger proposes reverses that operation and restores to the world certain dimensions that had been removed from it. Something very like this is now on the agenda for the concept of the subject. In other words, it will be shown that major features of the pre-conceptual understanding we have of ourselves have, in effect, been suppressed and thus find no adequate representation in the concept of the subject corresponding to the concept of the object that derives from the dogmatic concept of the world. This is the concept of the subject as the "subject-thing" or worldless subject that is prior to and independent of the existence of the world. It is Heidegger's contention that this concept misrepresents at the same time as it suppresses a prior understanding we have of ourselves, and it is his goal to bring these suppressed features of the latter understanding to the level of conceptual formulation. Just as it may have seemed to many that the world became far too "subjective" in the course of being restored to its authentic mode of being as presence, so it is likely that what emerges from Heidegger's parallel reconstruction of the subject will seem much too "worldly." In both cases, however, this critical reaction signifies mainly that the old conception of the contrast between the subjective and the objective is still being used as the standard of judgment, without any grasp of the fact that it is just this standard that is being called into question.

II

It seems appropriate to begin this inquiry into the understanding we have of ourselves as subjects by considering perception. Heidegger himself does not devote a great deal of attention to perception as a distinct mode of subjectivity, any more than he does to memory or imagination. He does make it clear, however, that perception, or *aisthesis*, is the primary form assumed by subjectivity in the ontological interpretation of it that he is proposing; and a great many of his examples invoke perceptual contexts, even though they are seldom identified as such through the use of the usual psychological vocabulary.[7] The differences between the picture of perception invoked by the latter and the conception that Heidegger proposes are profound; and a clear understanding of these differences is of great importance in trying to comprehend Heidegger's project as a whole. Certainly nothing could be more alien to a concept of perception based on the notion of presence than an interpretation of perception in terms of representations and beliefs (or, more recently, "information transfer"), all of which seem almost designed to avoid an acknowledgment of the fact of presence.[8] But even Heidegger cannot jettison words like "see" and "hear" and "touch," or even "perceive" (*wahrnehmen*) itself. Seeing, in fact, as well as a number of related notions like that of light, have a quite special place in Heidegger's account of perception; and in what follows vision will be treated as the paradigmatic case of perception unless another sense modality is specifically at issue. With all this emphasis on perception, it must not be forgotten that the concepts Heidegger is introducing are by no means confined to perceptual contexts, and in later chapters they will be shown to apply to what we describe, again using psychological concepts, as "memory" and "thought" and so on. Heidegger is quite insistent, however, on the foundational role of *aisthesis* in relation to all these and on the impossibility of any form of thought that abstracts from that grounding in what he is also not unwilling to call *Anschauen* (intuition).[9]

If on this basis we proceed to ask how perception and especially seeing are understood—pre-philosophically, that is, and pre-scientifically—it is not easy to answer. The "ineluctable modality of the visual" of which James Joyce speaks appears to be what everyone is familiar with but what no one can put into words.[10] It is not particularly difficult, of course, to give an account of seeing in terms of *what* is seen or the circumstances that affect the seeing itself and make it clear or unclear, partial or complete, and so on; but in all such accounts it is just *assumed* that we understand what seeing is. If one were to express a desire for a further account of what seeing itself is, it is likely that one would meet with responses such as "It's what you do with your eyes; you do have eyes, don't you?" But this way of settling the matter by reference to the organ that makes seeing possible turns out on closer examination to be itself a *petitio principii*.

There is at least one thing we can say about seeing without benefit of any special scientific or philosophical knowledge. This is that seeing, as well as other modalities of perception, are characterized by a certain asymmetry, which consists in the fact that when I see, for example, a stone, the stone does not see me.[11] The stone is present to me in the sense introduced in the last chapter, but I am not present to it. This is not because I am invisible to it, as I might be to another human being or animal that could otherwise see me; it is because the stone is an entity of a kind to which *nothing* can be present. But since this is so and it is I who see and not the stone, there must be something about me that brings it about that entities like this stone are present to me. We can thus say at least this much about presence, namely, that it must not be understood as a kind of medium in which entities are uniformly and symmetrically immersed and in which they are, so to speak, suspended side by side with one another. Instead, we must recognize that if there are entities *to* which others are present, then it must be something about the former that accounts for the fact that this is so.[12] To say this is to imply that presence has a directional, or vector, character, in that it runs from the entity in which it is grounded to the entities that are present. It also seems plain that the understanding it expresses is one that is very widely shared, if not universal. What is it then about the perceiver that can explain this asymmetry and that makes it possible for the perceived entity to be present to the perceiver?

One answer to this question is that in seeing we *do* something that *makes* entities present to us. This idea of seeing as an action of some kind comes through strongly in the notion of a look or regard that we can direct toward this or that entity within the world or that we can avert or terminate entirely, as when we close our eyes. Because it is understood as spanning the distance between the perceiver and the object seen and it is as though it originated with the former and terminated in the latter, this understanding of seeing is very different from the transmission theories that begin with the reflection of light by the object and end with a series of neural events in the brain. Presumably it is some such notion as this of the look as what makes things present that underlies the ancient explanations of vision as a kind of fire that emerges from the eye, as well as the later metaphors of vision as a ray of light playing over its objects.[13] Heidegger has typically been quite sarcastic in his reference to such theories; but on occasion he too speaks of perception in terms that suggest that it spans a gap—a "between"—in a way that no transmission or "image" theory can capture.[14] More concretely, he describes the perceiver—the entity that is in the world—predominantly in terms of verbs of action. These are not only not drawn from the traditional vocabulary of perception; they are also almost completely nonpsychological in character. "To uncover" (*entdecken*) and "to open" (*erschliessen*) are two such verbs among a number of others.[15] These are typically verbs that are already familiar to us in nonpsychological contexts—for example, in sentences like "He uncovered the armchair" and "He opened the door." Moreover, these established uses carry a strong implication of some sort of volitional control over the actions denoted by these verbs, which are such that we can either perform them or not; and this may raise a question about their suitability for purposes of rendering what is presumably, by virtue of its ontological character, an essential feature of the entity under examination. It is quite clear, however, that Heidegger recognizes the difference between the established, familiar use of these terms and the new one he is proposing. Ordinary actions of opening or uncovering are of the kind he calls "ontic" rather than "ontological," because they are not necessarily bound up with the mode of being of the entity designated as their subject, whereas the latter are.[16] Accordingly, his decision to use these and other verbs in *Being and Time* as one principal way of rendering the ontological character of entities that are in the world must be viewed as an effort to make words that usually serve ontic functions express an ontological meaning. In the later phase of his philosophical career, Heidegger stopped trying to make these words function in this way.[17] At this point, however, it is the adaptation of such concepts as that of "uncovering" to ontological uses that must be described.

In their ordinary usage, the verbs "to uncover" and "to open" might well be thought to signify no more than a certain rearrangement of things within the world: the removal of whatever it was that formerly covered the chair and the placing of the door against the wall. What such a construal would miss, however, is the fact that, as a result of these actions, something happens to what was formerly covered or closed. (In the case of the door, "closed" would apply to the adjacent room or whatever is on the other side of the door and not just to the door itself.) Moreover, what happens to these entities is clearly an event of a quite different order from the removal of the cover or the movement of the door. What happens is that the armchair and the room beyond the door come into an area of visibility and of perceptual access generally. They come into *view* and, as Heidegger puts it, following his construal of *phainesthai* and *phainomenon*, "show themselves." Sometimes this is described in language that is almost violent, as when Heidegger says that "entities are torn out of hiddenness," and that the *aistheton*, or perceptible entity, is "struck by openness" in being perceived.[18] The notion of openness invoked here is borrowed from the familiar use in which it connotes something's being visible along an unobstructed line of sight. We may be tempted to use this clue to interpret the notion of openness as it characterizes the perceptual object in an ontic sense involving principally the transparency of the medium in which the object is situated (and illuminated) as well as the absence of intervening nontransparent objects. Uncoveredness or openness would thus characterize perceptual situations in which light can be reflected from the surface of some object and reach the retina of someone who is then said to perceive that object. Since the perception that follows is typically thought of as something that occurs in the perceiver, all that could be said to happen to the thing that is situated in that transparent medium would be that it reflects light in a certain direction, thus initiating the physiological and psychological process in the course of which a representation of it turns up in the "perceptual field" of the person whose eye the light enters. But this is very different from what Heidegger has in mind when he speaks of uncovering and opening and the resultant opennesss of the thing seen. He, too, uses the concept of the *diaphanes*, the Greek word for "transparent"; but his account of it is rigorously independent of anything that has to do with the transmission of light.[19] A medium may be diaphanous in the sense of permitting the passage of light, but this fact, which certainly states a condition of the possibility of vision, does not by itself make intelligible the other element in dictionary definitions of transparency— namely, "permitting a clear view of the object that lies beyond the intervening medium."[20] It is this sense of the *diaphanes*, as that through which something shows itself, that Heidegger insists on taking at full strength, unattenuated by representational and dualistic interpretations; and it is this kind of openness that founds the conception of seeing and perception that he proposes.

It will have been noticed that in the preceding description of uncovering and opening, it is the perceived entities—the *aistheta*, as Heidegger often refers to them—that are said to show themselves to the perceiver. This fact must qualify what has been said about the asymmetry of perception and about its spanning the gap between the object and the perceiver in a manner that runs from the latter to the former. It is this fact about perception that finds expression in another verb that Heidegger uses for rendering its special character: *begegnen-lassen*, which can be roughly translated as "to let (something) meet or encounter."[21] He underscores the importance of this somewhat awkward compound by saying that for his ontological purposes "the only distinctive feature of seeing that is taken into account is the fact that it lets entities that are accessible to it encounter (*begegnen*) unconcealedly in themselves."[22] The way in which this expression is compounded out of familiar verbs signals the special character of the action it denotes. This action is one of "letting" something occur, and this occurrence has an implied subject that is distinct from that of the other component verb, "to let." In this use, "let" does not seem to have its usual meaning of "allow," as, for example, by not intervening to prevent something from taking place. It is true that we can control perception to some extent by such interventions, but when we do so, something else typically "encounters" which we have not in any comparable sense "allowed" to do so. "Letting" in this sense does not appear to denote any distinguishable action at all. All that it requires is that its subject exist as an entity capable of perception. Its existence as such is thus a necessary condition for the occurrence of the event that is denoted by *begegnen* (encounter), a familiar "ontic" verb that, like "uncover" and "open," is being adapted to an ontological use. Normally it functions as an active verb, as when we say that one person meets another; but in Heidegger's use it applies to any perceived entity, and it is what would ordinarily be described as "being encountered" that is said to "encounter." In this new use, it still takes a grammatical object, which could be construed as either direct or indirect, but either way, it is the entity that "lets" what "encounters" do so. "To encounter" in this sense is thus equivalent to "to be present for"; and what both expressions convey is that two entities stand in a relation to one another such that one—the entity that encounters— is there for the other, which in turn is such that it "lets" this happen. What is most noticeable in this relationship between the one that lets and the one that encounters is the mixture of activity and passivity in each. The "letting" of the former is understood as going from it to the latter, but so as to make it possible for a reciprocating "encountering" to go from the latter to the former, in a way that Heidegger was later to describe aptly as *von sich aus auf uns zu.*[23] The fact that entities show themselves to the entity that makes that showing possible is what Heidegger calls the "miracle" of perception. The entity that perceives "brings it about that, although it is related to an entity that exists on its own, it does not by virtue of this relationship take away the independence of that entity but rather makes it possible for itself as standing in that relationship to it to assure itself of the truth of that independence."[24]

This examination of the verbs that Heidegger uses to denote what the entity that is in the world "does" in grounding presence has thus led to a somewhat perplexing result. The "action" of uncovering and opening is one that we engage in just by virtue of existing as the kind of entity we are, and its "effect" on its object is not the one-sided and even aggressive one implied by some of Heidegger's language, but rather is that of making it possible for the latter to show itself to us. Neither this enabling "letting" nor the self-manifesting of entities within the world can properly be described as an action in any sense that would involve a volitional or causal character of any familiar type. What this suggests is that the whole hypothesis that the entity that is in the world grounds presence through something that it can be said to *do* is mistaken, and that the language of action and passion may not be at all suited to

expressing what is involved in the grounding of presence. If the ontological character of the entity that is in the world is what accounts for
presence, however, we must determine whether Heidegger can tell us
anything about that entity as an entity, anything that goes beyond what
it *does* to what it *is*.

III

We may begin with Heidegger's statement that if entities within the world
are open and, as he also says, "cleared," in the way that they are, this
can only be because there is an entity in the world that is itself essentially
open and cleared.[25] It is because such an entity is itself open that other
entities can be open to it. The question is then what it means for openness
to be constitutive of the being of an entity in an essential way, as contrasted with the derived way in which openness characterizes entities
within the world. The only entity that has ever been conceived in this
way is the soul, insofar as it has been held to be internally transparent
so that nothing could be present within it that was not given or known
to its constant *inspectio sui*.[26] A soul, of course, is not in the world in the
relevant sense, as Heidegger has shown, and its openness does not,
therefore, involve the openness or presence of entities other than itself,
but only the presence to it of its own representations or what Heidegger
was later to call "presence in the *representatio*."[27] The openness of an
entity that is in the world must, by contrast, be also and essentially an
openness to it of entities other than itself. It cannot, therefore, be a
substance, if by that we understand something that, as Descartes says,
"has no need of any (other) thing in order to exist (itself)."[28] The hold
of this picture of substances existing side by side independently of one
another is extremely powerful, and its effect is to impose the status of
a "relation" on whatever appears to go beyond the boundaries of any
particular entity. Even if one were disposed to say that such a relation
is internal in the case of a given entity and thus somehow constitutive
of it, the underlying concept would still be the substance concept with
only this difference, that one of the relations in which that substantial
entity stands to something else would have been assigned an exceptional
status. But this is not the course Heidegger takes. He abandons the
concept of substance completely for purposes of characterizing the entity
that is in the world; he must therefore show that there is an entity that
is not a thing but that is not any less a particular entity.[29]

The concept used by Heidegger to characterize the mode of being of
such an entity is that of existence (*Existenz*). Both the noun "existence"
and the verb "to exist" have been used repeatedly in these pages in the
ordinary sense in which "to exist" is a version of the verb "to be"as it

functions in such sentences as "There is a fireplace in the bedroom," or "There are no longer any speakers of Cornish." This concept of existence is generally thought to be completely neutral and noncommital with respect to anything having to do with the relationship in which the entity in question stands to the entity that formulates such propositions about it. In his lectures, however, Heidegger argues that the concept of existence is not really as devoid of such implications as this "logical" interpretation would lead us to suppose.[30] More specifically, he suggest that its derivation from the Latin *existo* and the Greek *existeimi* gives it an original meaning of "to let or make stand on its own." This notion he in turn derives from that of the artifact, which is shaped by human hands and then "released" to stand by itself. Heidegger's thesis is thus that the ancient concept of existence was dominated by a metaphor of productive activity on the part of human beings, and that, in terms of this metaphor, whatever exists has to be thought of as something that this activity has shaped and left standing on its own. The Greeks, it is true, lacked a concept of the openness that makes possible the specifically human way of being in the world and of dealing with the instrumentalities in terms of which that world is constituted.[31] Nevertheless, Heidegger argues, there is a sense in which the understanding of existence that the Greeks did have connects it with the mode of being of the artificer and thus with the openness of the latter, although in the absence of an explicit concept, this understanding remained philosophically naive.[32] Because it was naive, it missed the fact that what really "stands out," or "ek-sists," in such productive activity is the fashioning entity itself. When an explicit concept of the latter as an ontologically distinct kind of entity is introduced, as it is by Heidegger, its special character can no longer be expressed in terms of a concept of the things that are supposed to be its products. It must be expressed instead through a reconstrual of existence itself as a "standing out" in the world through active involvement with the things of this world. Heidegger therefore confines the use of the verb "to exist" and the noun "existence" to entities of a single type, effectively to human beings. "To exist always means: to comport oneself, in the midst of entities, in relation to entities—to entities that are not of the *Dasein*-type and to those that are, including oneself."[33] Existence so understood is the peculiar mode of being of *Dasein* and does not apply to other kinds of entities.[34]

Existence is thus the mode of being of the entity that is open in the sense of standing out in the world; and, consistently with this terminological decision, Heidegger uses the word *Vorhandenheit*, rather than *Existenz*, to refer to what would usually be called the existence of entities that are not open in this way. The wider import of these terminological decisions will be considered in chapter 6, as well as the question of whether there may not be a sense of "existence" that is applicable to entities of both kinds. (That this may be the case is suggested by the fact that in Heidegger's usage both *Existenz* and *Vorhandenheit* appear to contrast one kind of entity with another and thus to have more to do with essence than existence in the ordinary sense.) For the present, however, it is this new concept of existence that needs to be further explicated; and for this purpose it will be helpful to turn to the other form in which Heidegger uses the concept of existence: the concept of *Dasein*. Here again Heidegger appropriates a German word that means "existence" in a very broad sense that is not confined to any one kind of entity, and he uses it as a name for the kind of entity that exists in his special sense of that term. *Dasein*, which is compounded out of the adverb of place, *da* (there), and *sein* (the verb "to be"), has the grammatical peculiarity that it does not take the plural. When it is used as the generic name for a kind of entity, this presents no difficulty. There are, however, indefinitely many entities of this type—as many, at least, as there are human beings—and a difficulty does arise in referring to these either individually or collectively. That Heidegger intends this concept to have a plural use, in spite of this grammatical obstacle, is clear from the various devices he adopts to get around it. For example, he pluralizes the participial form of *Dasein* in *Being and Time*, as in the phrase *die Mitdaseienden*.[35] In his lectures he also implicitly quantifies *Dasein* by using the indefinite article to form the expression *ein Dasein*, and he does the same with "being-in-the-world" (*ein In-der-Welt-sein*). He also uses phrases like *das jeweilige Dasein* (the *Dasein* in question at any particular time), *dieses bestimmte Dasein* (this determinate *Dasein*), and *das je eigene Dasein* (the *Dasein* that is in each case one's own) to refer to a particular *Dasein*.[36] This matter of the plurality that characterizes *Dasein* is not just a grammatical issue, but a philosophical one as well, since Heidegger contends that it is an entity that is both particular and finite that grounds presence and thus the world. It is therefore important to determine whether the plurality of *Dasein* has some essential role to play in the grounding and, if so, what the relation between the plurality of *Dasein* and the singleness and commonness of the world is. For now, though, it is enough to have established that the word *Dasein* is used by Heidegger not only as a generic term but as a way of referring to particular entities of that kind.

In attempting to understand what kind of entity *Dasein* is, it will be useful to examine two variations on the concept that Heidegger expresses by saying that *Dasein* is both "the being of the There" and "the There of being."[37] Both these locutions characterize the kind of entity that *Dasein* is by reference to the fact that it is the entity for which entities are *there*; but they do so in different ways. The first, *Dasein* as the being of the There, says that when *Dasein* exists (and there is no necessity that it should), it does so as a kind of place—the kind best described as a "clearing" (*Lichtung*), in which entities present themselves as entities.[38] If there were no such entity and hence no such clearing, the entities that would otherwise have presented themselves would not do so; but they would not therefore cease to exist.[39] When *Dasein* does exist, however, one can say that there is a "There is," and what this expresses is the fact that there is a place—a "There," or clearing—in which entities show themselves as entities. This is what the second phrase—*Dasein* as the There of being—signifies; and it is extremely important to note the connection thus made between the concept of being and that of entities showing themselves *as* entities. *Dasein* is the entity for which entities other than itself are *there*, not only (and indeed not necessarily) in the sense of the spatial adjacency that permits ostension, but also in the sense of declaring their character as entities to it. There is thus an essential link between *Dasein* and being when the latter is understood as entities showing themselves as entities; and Heidegger is willing to say that for this reason "being is grounded in an entity, namely *Dasein*."[40]

In all these formulations it is clear that the adverb "there," which figures regularly in existential assertions to the effect that "There is a such-and-such," retains something of its original indexical meaning. It is normally used in such assertions without any sense of its carrying such a meaning; and this in turn tends to encourage the idea that all existential assertions could, and perhaps should ideally, be made in such a way as not to be traceable even in principle to either the person or the locus from which they have been made. Pushed to the extreme, this require-ment would yield a kind of transcendental, or acosmic, status for the maker of such claims. Against this tendency, Heidegger's use of the "there" suggests that every ostensibly neutral "There is" must ultimately involve an "is there," and thus a linkage with the existence of the entity for which the thing in question is there. The very idea of such a nexus is quite unacceptable to many philosophers, who interpret it to mean that the existence of the entity referred to in the "There is" statement has been tied to the existence of *Dasein* and thereby rendered "subjec-tive." This reaction has already been shown to be due, at least in part, to an assumption that the word "for," as it is used in such phrases as "be there for," has some sort of contextual implication of "for me but perhaps not for you," as is often the case in ordinary usage. But the implication it carries in Heidegger's usage is rather "for me and in prin-ciple for anyone." Underlying this mistaken assumption is the idea that if the "There is" were accorded any sort of ontological status in its own right and were not simply subsumed under the entity whose existence it declares, then its status would have to be that of *another* entity, and one that would somehow capture or encapsulate the original entity.

What this neglects is the possibility that what the "There is" represents, beyond the existence of the entity that is there, is indeed another entity, but not one that would somehow transform the former into one of its inner states. In such a contrasting picture, what the "There is" would express would be both the being-in-itself of the entity in question and the supervenient "fact" of its being there *for* the entity—*Dasein*—that is itself essentially open to the being-in-itself of entities other than itself. In other words, in expressing existence in the familiar, neutral sense, it would express presence, and in expressing presence, it would express existence.

Such then, in broad terms, is Heidegger's characterization of the kind of entity that *Dasein* is. We may now ask what this adds to the earlier description in terms of what *Dasein* does. One thing seems clear in this regard, namely that the central element in both these characterizations is the concept of presence. The preceding account of the openness of *Dasein* should have made it a good deal clearer what presence is; even so, this openness has itself had to be explicated in terms of presence, with the result that we do not appear to have gone beyond the latter concept to some more fundamental ground of presence. Thus our understanding of existence as the mode of being of *Dasein* is still dependent on the notion of presence; and to the extent that this is so, the stated intention of this chapter—to exhibit existence as the ground of presence—has not been carried out. But if *Dasein* must still be understood in terms of presence, rather than the other way around, the concept of *Dasein* is not really distinct from the concept of the world with which we began; and to say that *Dasein* exists is simply to say that there is a world in the Heideggerian sense, but without our being able to show that it is the existence of *Dasein* that "lets the world happen."[41] One could assert, of course, that if there were no *Dasein* and hence no openness, then there would be no presence of entities and no world; and this undoubtedly represents Heidegger's position. But such an assertion does not provide any insight into why one could not just as validly turn it around and say that, if there were not any presence of entities, there would not be any *Dasein*. If *Dasein* makes a world happen, rather than the other way around, it should be possible to point to something that validates the one claim but not the other; but that is what has not yet turned up. When *Dasein* does exist, moreover, its openness must also and necessarily exist, and thus there is no way in which *Dasein* could somehow withdraw its openness in order to determine what would then happen to the presence of entities. All things considered, it looks as though the thesis that existence is the ground of presence still lacks a convincing justification.

IV

If there is a positive conclusion to be drawn from the previous two sections, it is that the concepts of what *Dasein* does and what it is pass over into one another, and that the contrast between the two may be ill-adapted to the special character of this kind of entity. If that is indeed the case, then it would make sense to look for a unitary concept in which both of these approaches to *Dasein* are combined. Such a concept is arguably that of *Selbstheit*, which Heidegger introduces in the course of his account of *Dasein*, and which certainly appears to amplify significantly what he has said about both the uncovering function of *Dasein* and its own intrinsic openness.[42] The obvious English rendering of *Selbstheit* is "selfhood," but this carries too psychological a connotation. I shall therefore translate it as "selfness." At the same time, it must be recognized that in declaring *Dasein* to be in some sense a self Heidegger is also unavoidably invoking a whole host of associated notions like those of unity, reflexivity, agency, and corporeality that attach to the familiar concept of the self. A question then arises as to what these notions, as well as that of the self as such, amount to when they have to be accommodated to the ontological mode of understanding on which Heidegger insists.

In introducing this concept of selfness, it will be useful to expand somewhat the account given in the last chapter of the indexicality and instrumentality of the world and to do so in a way that will show how these are grounded in the active and practical character of *Dasein*. According to Heidegger, *Dasein* is not only an entity that makes use of the instrumentalities that present themselves in the world; it also constitutes the end or *Worumwillen*—the "for-the-sake-of-which"—that makes it possible for entities within the world to have the instrumental and thus teleological character that is theirs as *zuhanden*.[43] What this means is that *Dasein* is able to act with a view to bringing about something that is not yet the case, and that, in every such action and in every use that it makes of some instrumentality at its disposal, *Dasein* acts out of an understanding of the prospective contribution that its action will make to something that in one way or another matters to it. This is not to say that it is motivated by a narrow egoism in which only what benefits a given individual really counts.[44] Heidegger places no such restriction on the end that is to be served by what we try to do. Nevertheless, in every case, it will be something that makes a difference to someone that is capable of understanding the instrumental and causal connections it involves. It is, moreover, as the *Worumwillen* of its own actions that *Dasein* is disclosed to itself; and what this means is that it is disclosed not as some inner domain to which it can gain access only by turning away from the world, but rather as that world itself, understood as the locus of its actions and its future.[45]

It is this way of "being to (or toward) oneself" (*zu sich sein*) that is fundamental to what Heidegger calls selfness.[46] What it comes to is that, insofar as what may happen in the world is understood by *Dasein* as a possibility, it exists as sustaining a relation to that possibility. This is not a neutral, detached contemplation of possibilities just as possibilities; they are understood instead as outcomes that may depend to some degree on what the person who envisages them *does*. They are also possibilities in which a particular *Dasein* has some sort of stake so that it is engaged for one possibility and against another. Thus *Dasein* acts for the sake of the realization of certain possibilities rather than others, and in so acting it realizes its identity as the entity to which these outcomes matter. They have, in fact, been *chosen*, and this is a choice of both one's world and oneself. The world that has been described up to this point as a totality of presence is now to be understood as "the totality of entities in the totality of their possibilities, and the latter are themselves essentially related to human existence taken in terms of its final purpose."[47] The world is also said to have as its fundamental character the *Umwillen*, the "for-the-sake-of," and, most important, "the world as that toward which *Dasein* transcends, is primarily determined through this *Umwillen*."[48] As such it necessarily implies a "will" in the sense of the freedom in which alone the world can be understood in terms of possibilities; and *Dasein* is to be understood as being "to" or "toward" itself in the mode of possibility and choice.[49]

It is the status of these possibilities that is crucial to any ontological revision of our understanding of the self. The usual thing is to treat them either in mentalistic terms, as the thoughts that the self entertains as an adjunct to its commerce with actual entities, or as having some sort of subsistence that makes them, on the one hand, independent of the self while, on the other, denying them the full-blown existence of actual entities. Heidegger clearly rejects both these ways of assigning an ontological status to possibility.[50] He also insists that, for his purposes, possibility is not to be understood as merely *logical* possibility—that is, as whatever does not involve an internal contradiction. It is possibility rather as what one *can* do; and although he offers no analysis of what such "agent possibility" involves, it is quite certain that he views it as primordial and not derivative from any form of causal possibility that would in turn derive from causal laws. (For Heidegger, logical possibility appears to be merely a pale remnant of the richer kind of possibility involved in agency.) Once the concept of possibility that he is presupposing has been specified in this way, it becomes evident that possibilities require the existence of an agent.[51] The picture of a self that simply *finds* possibilities that exist or subsist independently of it is thus unacceptable; and for it we must substitute a picture of a self that generates these possibilities by virtue of its active orientation in the world. Heidegger's way of expressing this new understanding is to say that *Dasein is* its possibilities.[52] This is not because the latter are to be understood as its inner dispositions or properties; they are rather the context that *Dasein* constitutes for the entities it uncovers. The notion of the world is thus not that of a static presence of entities that have been uncovered in their actuality and in relation to which any element of possibility would be a discrete, further increment. It is a presence within which such entities are understood *ab initio* in the context of what can be done with or to or about them—that is, within a matrix of possibilities generated by *Dasein*.

The concept of transcendence, which was first introduced in chapter 1 as Heidegger's replacement for the concept of intentionality, explicitly incorporates these elements of possibility and choice into the characterization of *Dasein* as a self.[53] Once again, this is a concept that presupposes the temporality of *Dasein*, of which an account has yet to be given. It must be introduced here in a preliminary way, however, if the implications of the foregoing discussion for the question to which this chapter is addressed are to emerge at all clearly. Heidegger tells us that there are several concepts of transcendence, and he is at pains to distinguish the ontological concept that he is introducing from both the theological and the epistemological versions of transcendence.[54] In the epistemological version, "transcendence" is the polar term for "immanence," which has been used to designate the character of the subject in Descartes's and Husserl's philosophies insofar as it can know only its own internal states. Transcendence would thus seem to be the characteristic of a subject that is not limited in this way. It breaks out of and beyond the "sphere of immanence" in which it is confined by the Cartesian (and Husserlian) conceptualization and spans the gap that separates it from its object. To say of *Dasein*, as Heidegger does, that it is "the being of the Between" is thus to declare that the subject is never so confined, and that it operates *ab initio* beyond the limits of any such sphere of immanence.[55] But clearly, if transcendence is introduced this way, it will remain linked to the concept of immanence as that which is transcended. In that event, there would have to *be* a sphere of immanence, so that something could be transcended; and Heidegger is naturally unwilling to accept this, since it would link his position with the very positions he has so emphatically rejected.

In expounding his own concept of transcendence, Heidegger begins with several distinctions.[56] That which is transcended is distinguished from that which transcends it, and both are distinguished from that toward which (*Woraufhin*) this transcendence—which is described as an *Überschreiten* (a striding-beyond)—moves. That which transcends is, of course, *Dasein*; but what it transcends is not some sort of partition between subject and object. It is rather, Heidegger claims, entities as such. This may make it sound as though Heidegger were replacing an epistemological concept of transcendence by a theological, rather than an ontological, alternative, but that is not the case. For what lies beyond entities is not God, but the world; and Heidegger says that it is toward the world that *Dasein* transcends entities. We already know that what is distinctive of *Dasein* as an entity is that it is that for which entities are there and that, as the totality of the entities that are so present, the world is essential to *Dasein*. But the world is not itself an entity; it is "the appearing of entities *as entities*" to *Dasein*, their "standing over against *Dasein* as entities and their being apprehensible (*erfassbar*) as so standing over against it."[57] But what precisely is involved in entities showing themselves as entities? One clue is supplied by Heidegger's claim that non-human animals do not see entities as entities; and in conventional philosophical terminology this difference might be attributed to the fact that the vision of animals is not informed by the categorical distinctions at work in human perception.[58] To see something *as an entity* would thus be to see it as existing, rather than not existing, and in terms of a contrast with what does not exist. This contrast has further ramifications as, for example, between what exists now but did not exist in the past and between what does not exist now but may exist in the future. If animals do not see entities as entities, it is presumably because they are not able to deploy such distinctions, or, if one prefers, because these structural contrasts do not "show themselves" to them. But human beings, unlike animals, perceive entities as such because they can make or register these contrasts; and it is for just this reason that they have a world as animals do not.[59] Animals, Heidegger says, have "access" (*Zugang*) to entities, but not to entities as entities and thus not to the world as the matrix of ontological contrasts just described; and what *we* are able to do in our capacity as *Dasein* is to transcend entities toward their being as entities and thus toward the world which, very significantly, is also described as "being" as such.[60] But this transcendence must also be understood in terms of a contrast, not only between what is and what is not the case, but between what is or is not the case and what might *possibly* be the case. In the next chapter, transcendence so understood will be shown to have an explicitly temporal character that is central to Heidegger's account of it. It should already be clear, however, in what sense "transcending entities" is a movement toward their being as entities and thus toward the world as the totality of possibilities that come into view when an entity is understood as an entity and in terms of the contrasts between what is and is not the case that go with the notion itself of an entity.

It must be apparent from what has been said so far that the concept of transcendence is at bottom a further elaboration of Heidegger's concept of existence as it was set forth earlier in this chapter. But if so, what has been said about transcendence can help us to understand the sense— so elusive up to this point—in which existence may be said to ground presence. Existence as the mode of being of *Dasein* has been described as an uncovering of entities; but with the introduction of the concept of transcendence, that uncovering has been shown to be by no means limited to actual entities. There is also an uncovering of possibilities; and though the sense in which such possibilities can be described as modes of presence has not yet been clarified, there cannot be much doubt that the uncovering of possibilities—especially since they are possibilities of action—has a transitive and asymmetrical character that is, to say the least, less evident in the case of the uncovering of actual entities. In the case of possibilities, it seems much more acceptable to say that *Dasein makes* them present in some stronger sense than it was possible to assign to the "let" of "to let-encounter" (*begegnen-lassen*) in the preceding analyses. When to this we add the fact that certain of these possibilities are *chosen* by *Dasein*, and that it is these chosen possibilities that implicitly order the world in which actual entities are uncovered as the *Worumwillen* of that world, the grounding function of existence in relation to presence emerges even more strongly.[61] This does not mean that actual entities are made present by *Dasein* in a sense that would imply a thoroughgoing control by *Dasein* over what will and what will not be uncovered or indeed exist. That human beings do not have that power has been clear for a very long time; and it is not Heidegger's philosophical intention to call that fact into question. What it does mean is that the presence of actual entities always has a context of possibility and choice, and one in which choice figures not only as a partial determinant of what will actually be the case (and be uncovered as such), but also as defining the practical meaning of the state of the world that does result. The claim Heidegger is thus making is that existence grounds presence, because it is only in the context of the uncovering of possibility in the mode of choice and of action that actual entities can be present to us at all. As the discussion of instrumentality showed, these entities are by no means understood originally in terms of a pure actuality that is independent of possibility. Our understanding of them reflects at every point the uses to which they can be put, as well as the contrasts they present to what might have been the case. Like so many other concepts for which similar claims are made, the concept of actuality (*Wirklichkeit*) that ostensibly prescinds from this medium of possibility in which our original understanding moves is, in

Heidegger's view, a subsequent derivation and presupposes the richer concept of the world in which possibilities of action occupy the central place.[62]

There is another way of approaching the difficulty that has hampered the treatment of existence as the ground of presence. This difficulty arose not just because an unexamined concept of actual entities as what is present was allowed to dominate the discussion, but also because the whole examination of what *Dasein* does and is was carried out in the present tense, without any recognition of the limiting implications of this fact. As a result, presence as such was identified with the present in the temporal sense of that word. It is only with the introduction of the concept of transcendence that it becomes possible to move beyond this assumption; but an alternative to it cannot be fully developed until it has been shown, through an analysis of temporality, that presence is not a matter of the present alone, and that the present tense stands in a complex relationship to the future and the past that is of fundamental importance for a full understanding of presence. That analysis is the task of the next chapter.

V

In the preceding account of the kind of entity that *Dasein* is, the singularity of the world and the plurality of *Dasein* have been strongly emphasized. Attention has also been drawn to the difficulty of explicating this notion of the plurality of *Dasein* in terms of the presence of entities alone. This difficulty is due to the fact that the presence of entities as entities is most naturally thought of as unitary and single and so does not offer any clues to the individuated character of the entities for which what is present is present. It was only with the introduction of the concepts of selfness and transcendence, therefore, that it became possible to understand not only how the uncovering function of *Dasein* takes on an active and transitive character, but also why the *Dasein* that effects this uncovering has to be understood as plural. The reason is that although transcendence belongs to *Dasein* as such, the choices that are centrally involved in transcendence are made by *Dasein* as individuated and particular.[63] But this, in turn, raises the question of how such a grounding of presence and of the world by many such entities can be reconciled with the singularity of the world that is thus grounded. When the notion of the world is tied to possibility and choice, it begins to look as though each *Dasein* would ground its own presence and its own world. Since this would run flatly counter to Heidegger's repeated insistence on the commonness of the world, it is necessary to try to determine how the positions he has taken can be reconciled with one another. The question that must be addressed here is whether Heidegger's strong emphasis on possibility and choice, and thus on what may differ from one *Dasein* to another, rules out any element of convergence and, as it might be called, cooperation in "building the world," or whether presence can be regarded as in some sense a collective act or achievement.[64]

The discussion in chapter 2 of the public character of various things in use certainly seemed to indicate that the orientation of each *Dasein* vis-à-vis such objects is not only convergent with that of others, but is essentially so. But Heidegger nowhere elaborates on this kind of convergence and commonness in a way that would demonstrate its compatibility with the choice-like character of transcendence. Here, as elsewhere, it is difficult not to feel that the grammar of the word *Dasein*— its use as a singular generic name—has tended to obscure the need for a closer analysis of what is involved in the plurality and particularity of the entities that bear this name. Even so, this failure is puzzling, since Heidegger does not simply accept this plurality as a fact and then proceed, as so many philosophers have done, to ignore it in his characterization of individual *Dasein*. Instead, he holds a strong theory of *Mitsein*, as constituting an essential ontological determination of *Dasein* as such. He has no patience with the view that a bridge has to be constructed by means of empathy "from the subject that is first given by itself to the other subject that is at first quite shut off (from it)" and he equates this view with the claim that the subject is somehow prior to its contact with an "external" world.[65] Instead, "being to others is an autonomous irreducible relationship of being and it is, as *Mitsein*, already existent with the being of *Dasein*."[66] The "being-together" of such entities cannot be understood "additively," as though it were just the result of factual existence of a number of such subjects"; and in his infrequent remarks about actual social formations like generations, Heidegger makes it quite clear that their "destiny" and thus their history cannot be understood as "composed out of individual destinies."[67] He even pushes the account of *Mitsein* to the point of speaking of the world as a *Mitwelt*—a world that is not only the same for all, but one in which each *Dasein* is there for others and "encounters" them.[68] He emphasizes the specifically social character of this *Mitdasein*, as when he declares, in a statement that must surprise those who view him as an individualist, that *Dasein* is "essentially for the sake of others."[69] This thesis, which serves to introduce a brief account of the alternative ways in which we can care for and about others, appears to mean that at the very least there is no way in which the life of an individual *Dasein* can be understood as a purely private economy of ends and means in which others figure only in an instrumental relationship to the purely individual ends projected by that *Dasein* for itself.

Unfortunately, this theory of *Mitsein* was not developed in the works that followed *Being and Time*; and the fact that it was not is a significant indicator of the course that Heidegger's later thought was to take. Even in *Being and Time* there are statements that are hard to reconcile with the view of *Mitsein* just presented. There is, for example, the statement that "the expression *Dasein* shows plainly that 'in the first instance' this entity is unrelated to others," although "it can still be with others afterwards."[70] This view of *Mitsein* as somehow secondary appears to have played a more considerable role in Heidegger's subsequent thought than the positive conception outlined above. Even in *Being and Time* the conception of my death as the "ownmost possibility" in terms of which I choose myself strongly reinforces that essentially nonsocial tendency in Heidegger's thought.[71] Whatever the reason, the theory of *Mitsein* is not developed, either in *Being and Time* or later, in a way that contributes to the definition of the relationship in which one *Dasein* stands to another in grounding the *same* world.[72] Because Heidegger fails to give an account of the mediating role of plurality in the relationship between *Dasein* and world, the definition of that relationship remains unstable in certain crucial respects. For one thing, the concept of the world tends to pass completely over into the orbit of *Dasein*—a *Dasein* that remains indeterminate with respect to its particularity vis-à-vis its plurality—and since this plainly goes against the grain of Heidegger's concept of the world, he is forced to compensate for this drift with statements to the effect that "the existing things that we call 'human beings' are possible in their being only because there is (*es gibt*) a world."[73] What is peculiar about this statement is the fact that Heidegger's use of the term "the world" makes it a tautology; and yet it is produced here in a way that suggests that it is something more than that. Of course, it is also a tautology to say, as Heidegger does, that "the world is essentially relative to human existence," and the two statements are in fact simply two formulations of the same fact, namely, that *Dasein* and the world define one another.[74] But in the first statement it is as though the presumption of human beings and thus of *Dasein* were being pulled up sharply and were being reminded of a dependence that runs from man to world, all this in a rhetorical context that hardly permits this dependence to be equated with the one that runs the other way. This kind of admonition was to become more and more frequent in Heidegger's later writings, but with this difference, that the dependence is there interpreted as a dependence of man on being, rather than man on world. Perhaps the difference is not so great, however, if we recall that the world has already been equated with being.[75] It is clear that the relationship between these two terms is in need of close analysis, and that the instability that has been noted in the relationship of the concepts of *Dasein* and the world to one another must affect the wider thesis that existence as the mode of being of *Dasein* is the ground of presence.

Under these circumstances, the task of the interpreter is to determine whether there is not a way of understanding Heidegger's position that would get around these difficulties. For such an effort of interpretation there are in fact some promising points of departure in the Heideggerian texts themselves. For example, when Heidegger tells us that "entities are always open as a totality," this does not mean, as might be thought, that every entity must be uncovered if any entity is uncovered, or at any rate not that they must all be uncovered in the same sense.[76] Heidegger qualifies his thesis that the world is open as a whole by adding that this is so even though "the whole is not also expressly grasped in its specific connections." What this means is that whenever entities within the world are uncovered, there will also be that which is *not* uncovered (*unentdeckt*) or, as Heidegger also puts it, "hidden" (*verborgen*) or covered over (*verdeckt*).[77] Sometimes what is not uncovered is simply the completely unknown, that of which no one has any inkling. Sometimes it will be something that is known, but imperfectly so and in a way that involves mistaken notions about its nature. Such mistakes may be innocent ones that can be corrected in the course of further inquiry, or they may be motivated by preconceptions in which we have some sort of stake that makes us reluctant to accept correction. Finally, these motives may be so deeply entrenched that we exert ourselves to maintain what we would otherwise acknowledge to be false. In this last case, about which he has a great deal to say, Heidegger speaks of something being not just covered over but "buried" (*verschüttet*).[78] All these gradations in the contrast between the uncovered and the not uncovered are of secondary importance. What is primary is that the contrast itself is one that is internal to the concept of the world. What is still covered over must not be identified with something that lies altogether outside the world—that is, that stands in no relation at all to *Dasein*. Although not disclosed as yet (and perhaps not destined ever to be disclosed), what is described as "covered over" is thereby understood—negatively—by reference to uncovering and presence and thus belongs to the very world in which it does not show itself.

These considerations suggest a way in which one might begin to differentiate between *Dasein* as plural and the world as singular, while not repudiating the essential link between them. *Dasein* would be in each case (*jeweilig*) a clearing (*Lichtung*) and a clearing of the world as a whole; but it would be differentiated from others in that the contrast between the uncovered and the not uncovered would be different in each case. Two people may see the same thing, for example, but from different angles; hence the aspects of the thing that are not uncovered for the one will differ from those that are not uncovered for the other. Again, some entities will remain completely not uncovered for one person but not for another; and so on. To a considerable degree, these differences would be functions of the practical orientations of the people in question—what they are doing, what they are interested in, and so on—and in this way choice would be involved in the constitution of the clearing that each *Dasein* is, just as it is in the grounding of presence as such. It follows that the clearing that each *Dasein* is would in one sense be particular, as *Dasein* itself is; and this particularity would contrast with the universality of the world. At the same time, it is important to see that this element of particularity does not mean that there are *many* clearings in any sense that would imply that there are many worlds. The entities that are uncovered by one *Dasein* are either the same as those uncovered by others, or they belong to a single interconnected totality with them; hence the clearing that each *Dasein* is will always be the same as those of others because they are clearings of the same world, although the distinction between what is uncovered and what is not uncovered can never be exactly the same for one *Dasein* as for another. Moreover, this fact about *Dasein*—that each *Dasein* is an uncovering of the same world that others uncover—is one that forms part of the understanding it has of itself. For the clearing that is thus common, it seems best to retain the term "presence," which in any case does not lend itself to pluralization. This unitary presence, however, must be understood as mediated by just the complex set of relationships among particular *Dasein*s that has been described, as well as by the shifting contrasts between the uncovered and the not uncovered that they involve. The world as a milieu of presence is thus, as Heidegger says, "essentially relative to human existence"; but this relativity must be understood in a twofold manner: first, as it most often is by Heidegger himself, by reference to *Dasein* generically, as the fact that there is any such entity at all; and second, by reference to the plurality of such entities as the multiple uncoverings that jointly uncover the same entities.

CHAPTER FOUR • **TIME AND TEMPORALITY**

I t is unusual for the topic of time to be assigned a prominent role in discussions contributing to the philosophy of mind. Being "in time" or "temporal" is assumed to be something that minds share with most, if not all, other kinds of entities; hence it is not a matter of special importance when the nature of mind is under consideration. In the case of *Dasein* as conceived by Heidegger, however, it is quite different. The concept of *Dasein* has been shown to be linked with that of the world and thus with the presence of the entities that are within the world; and since entities within the world are also in time, one would expect that, as the ground of the world, *Dasein* must also in some way be the ground of time. This proves to be the case. *Dasein* is shown by Heidegger to be temporal in a quite special sense that is prior to what he calls the "vulgar" conception of time as world-time. In the course of the preceding discussion, it has already become apparent that the *Zeitlichkeit* of *Dasein*—its temporality—is centrally involved in its existence and its transcendence, and thus in the grounding of the presence of entities as entities. The task of this chapter is to develop the hints that have been thrown out with respect to the role of time in these matters and to present an account of Heidegger's conception of time as temporality. To this end, I will begin with familiar ways of understanding time and world-time and then show both how world-time excludes and yet, at a deeper level, also requires—and indeed presupposes—temporality in Heidegger's special sense of that term. I will offer a characterization of temporality in its own right and then extend it into an account of how temporality is involved in the understanding of entities as entities and thus of being as such. Thanks to the recently published lectures that deal with temporality and the understanding of being, it is now possible to go beyond the position set forth in *Being and Time* and to present at least the gist of what Heidegger evidently intended to expound in the third section of part 1 entitled "Time and Being."[1]

The bulk of the discussion of temporality in *Being and Time* is concerned with temporality as a central element in the ontological constitution of *Dasein* as one kind of entity. The context for this discussion is provided by the question of how that entity can be a whole.[2] This question arises out of the account of transcendence as the movement of *Dasein* toward its possibilities, its always being "out ahead of itself" (*Sich-vor-weg-sein*) in such a way that at every moment of its life there is something unresolved and incomplete about it.[3] But if *Dasein* is necessarily always in an incomplete state in which something remains to be settled, it cannot be a whole in any sense that implies completeness or the realization of some definite character that would set a seal on its life. But this difficulty arises only when *Dasein* is understood in terms of its existence, and not as a *vorhanden* entity that is just what it is at each moment in its career and is thus no more or less complete or a whole at any particular moment. As a *vorhanden* entity, *Dasein* would form a whole simply as the entity that fills a certain spatial and temporal "envelope," as what Whitehead called a "space-time slab"; on this view, unfulfilled intentions and "work in progress" of whatever kind would have to be accommodated, perhaps in truncated form, within the actuality demarcated by birth and death. If *Dasein* is understood in terms of existence, however, death is a rupture of the continuity in the life of an entity that has always projected itself on some possibility and hence some future; Heidegger's question, therefore, is whether any form of wholeness that recognizes and accepts death on these terms is possible.

These matters relating to the special character of the wholeness that characteristically belongs to *Dasein* will not be taken up here. What is important for the purposes of this discussion is not so much the special character of the ending that is a human death, but rather the way the future and the past qualify the kind of present that *Dasein* has and become constitutive elements of the presence to *Dasein* of entities as entities.[4] Temporality understood as the unity of these different "dimensions" of time is at once the structure of a certain kind of entity (and thus of existence as its mode of being) and a necessary condition for the presence of entities as entities. The treatment of time and temporality in the period of *Being and Time* is thus marked by the same contrast between existence and presence that has been so important in the discussion up to this point; and some of the same tensions that have characterized this contrast will come into play in its application to time and temporality as well.

I

There is a close parallelism between Heidegger's discussions of the world and of time in their relation to *Dasein*. In both cases, there are established commonsense and philosophical views of the way *Dasein* may be said to be "in" the one and the other; and, as he did in the case of the world, Heidegger subjects this conventional wisdom about time to a stringent critique.[5] His aim in the first case was to show, against a transcendental line of argument, that *Dasein* is necessarily *in* the world and that it is in it in a distinctive way that we are constitutionally liable to miss or distort. Similarly, in the case of time, he rejects the traditional philosophical assumption that it is possible for us, at least at the highest level of intellectual activity, to extract ourselves from our position in time and the limitations it carries with it.[6] We are, therefore, in his view, temporal entities in a radical and insurmountable way. At the same time, we are not *in time* in the same way as entities like natural objects or our own artifacts are. One might have expected that Heidegger would reserve the preeminent sense of "being in time" for *Dasein*, as he did the corresponding sense of "being in the world." He did not do so, however, and, in fact, he rarely speaks of *Dasein* as being in time. This may be because being in time, in the case of *Dasein*, is really not distinct from being in the world, so that a second, parallel locution of this type would be likely to cause confusion. But not being *in* time is most emphatically not to be understood as being outside time; so the real point is to bring out the difference between the way of being in time of *Dasein*, if one chooses to speak that way, and that of other kinds of entities. In order to exhibit this difference clearly, it will be useful to begin by examining some traditional views about the relationship of *Dasein* to time, especially since these views have always stood in the way of an adequate understanding of the temporal character of *Dasein*. As in the case of the world, Heidegger holds that we have an unarticulated understanding of our own temporality that is very different from the views, both commonsense and philosophical, that we profess; and once again, it is this implicit understanding that he wants to bring to the level of conceptual formulation.

The distinction between what is in time and what is not has been deeply entrenched in the Western philosophical tradition since Plato. That distinction treats what is not in time as superior, both intrinsically and for purposes of knowledge, to what is in time. This Platonic conception of knowledge as directed ultimately to what is timeless became the model for the Christian idea of God's mind and knowledge. God himself was taken to be outside time, so his knowledge was in no way qualified by a temporal position. Instead, he knew everything, including things in time, in a timeless manner. In Heidegger's view, this conception of God's knowledge became, in the modern period, the model for understanding human knowledge.[7] By reason of its foundation in sensibility, human knowledge was not, of course, outside and independent of time in the way that God's was. As endowed with the faculty of reason, however, human beings were able to apprehend necessary truths and in that sense had access to a mode of understanding that is independent of temporal considerations. The perfection of human knowledge was thus conceived as a progressive approximation to a rational insight that effectively abstracts from our original situation, in which what we know always bears the mark of where we are ourselves placed in time.

It need hardly be said that Heidegger opposes this whole tradition of thought which, in effect, takes the knowing subject out of time in a manner very similar to the way it took it out of space. What he objects to is not so much the implied otherworldliness of such a view of the subject, as the underlying conception of the time from which that subject is supposed to have been extracted. This is the conception of world-time, of time as the time of processes and events in the world; and it must be understood that the "world" of this world-time is the world understood as the totality of entities, not the world as Heidegger understands it in terms of the *presence* of entities.[8] *Dasein* is certainly not in that world as an entity side by side with other entities; nor is it in world-time if that means assimilation to the status of the entities that occupy positions within the kind of sequence that it involves. In the former case, this is because *Dasein* is the entity that *has* a world, as trees and rivers do not; and in the latter case it is because *Dasein has* time in a sense that finds no application to such entities as those just cited although they are most certainly *in* time. More generally, Heidegger's procedure in the case of both the vulgar concept of the world and the corresponding concept of world-time is to point out features of the world and of time that are not only not acknowledged in the vulgar concept, but are in fact irreconcilable with it. This strategy is to show that these concepts are derivative from and dependent on another kind of time, the time of *Dasein* itself, which he calls "temporality." This derivative status is something that the vulgar concept of world-time not only does not recognize, but also—paradoxically—tries to hide by means of a distinction between objective and subjective time, along lines very similar to those followed by the kind of dualism that wants to evade the need for a concept of the world as that which we are in.[9] In both cases, there is an attempt to accommodate deviant features of the world and of time by assigning to them a special status that is, however, of the same ontological type as the guiding concepts of the world and of time and thus avoids the need for more fundamental revisions in that scheme. This procedure gives rise to paradoxes in the case of time, as in the case of the world, where the postulation of a mental substance containing representations rendered the reality of the external world problematic. In the case of time, it will be shown that there is a corresponding paradox that has to do with the uniquely privileged status accorded the present, as against other temporal modalities.

Heidegger regards Aristotle's account of time as the classical exposition of time as world-time and uses it extensively for the purpose of demonstrating the derivative character of world-time.[10] According to Aristotle, time is a feature of movement—*kineseos ti*—although Heidegger insists that this movement need not be understood as spatial, and that the concept of world-time is not identical with the spatialization of time, as Bergson supposed. Aristotle further characterizes time as "the number of movement in respect of the before and after," and this notion associates time with counting, although not necessarily with clocks, whether of the ancient Greek or the modern kind. This counting can just as well be (and, of course, originally was) the marking of the successive positions of the sun as it makes its way across the sky. What we say in effect is "Now it is here," "Now it is here," "Now it is here"; and in each case the Now is a different moment and Here a different place. Together, all those positions or points would form a line; but the Nows in terms of which those positions are counted also make up a series, which is itself treated as something that exists. This entity is identified with time as such and is thus a kind of container within which movement and change take place. All entities that move in the sense of changing from one state to another are accordingly in time. The character of time considered in this way is thus dominated by the essential role of the Now in its constitution; and its internal articulation into tenses must be understood in terms of variations on the Now, which is, Aristotle says, both the same in all its occurrences and different.[11]

Although Aristotle conceives time in this way as world-time, he also maintains that it has an essential connection with the soul as that which alone is able to count. In this respect, as in others, Heidegger views Aristotle as implicitly testifying to a richer conception of time than the one he actually formulates. Subsequent thought about time, although moving in the track laid down by Aristotle, has typically been more deficient than he was in any sense of what the concept of world-time left out; this was especially the case when attempts were made to supplement the account of objective time with one of subjective time. Such conceptions invariably reproduced the fundamental features of world-time as a series of Nows, with the sole difference that the entities that were supposed to be in subjective time were thoughts and other such denizens of the mind. Other modifications of the theory of world-time took the form of a sharpened definition of the Now as a point-instant; and where Aristotle had conceived it as having a certain thickness, modern thought from Descartes onward has emphasized the atomicity of each instant and thus reinforced the logical isolation of every present from every other present.[12] It has been recognized, of course, that such a view of the Now or present makes it difficult to do justice to the continuity of time; but, for the most part, attempts to deal with this question have been psychological in nature and have taken the form of speculation about a "sense of passage" in which that continuity would somehow be captured. Because such speculation rests on an acceptance of the conception of objective or world-time, whatever it produces in the way of a sense of passage can hardly be more than a subjective nuance within the experience of time. It cannot, therefore, call into question the adequacy of the wider theory of time that it presupposes.

If the theory of world-time does not necessarily involve a spatialization of time, it does amount to a reification of it in the sense of treating it as an entity, or *res*, that is *vorhanden*.[13] Such reification reaches its climax in the theory of the world as a four-dimensional continuum of which one dimension is time. For the purposes of discourse about the world so conceived, the use of a modified, all-purpose present tense is often recommended; and this surely tends to confirm Heidegger's thesis about the way the Now and the present govern our understanding of world-time, even in this ultimate scientific version. The inherent instability of our understanding of the Now is such that, while what is identical in all Nows (to use Aristotle's contrast) yields a conception such as this, what is different continues to assert itself in a way that generates radical skepticism about the very possibility of the access to all the points in world-time that is implicitly assumed in the conception of the world as a four-dimensional continuum. This kind of skepticism is best known through a famous puzzle proposed by Bertrand Russell; and although the issues it raises have not been dealt with explicitly by Heidegger, they serve to throw light on the point he is making in his critique of world-time, and especially on the priority assigned to the present in such a conception of time.[14] Russell imagines a people that has a full set of memories of a normally extensive past, although this people actually came into being with these memories only a few minutes ago. The past they "remember" thus never really existed. The example is intended to show that no one can be sure that he is not in a similar position and that his "memories" do not systematically misrepresent the past without his being able to detect this fact in any way. The root of the difficulty is that all these memories are themselves rigorously "present," since they, like everything else, must occupy a position in world-time, that is, in some Now or present. Insofar as they are in a present within world-time, these memories are simply *vorhanden* and hence in no way necessarily linked to the other, earlier presents of which they purport to be "memories." It thus seems to follow that the so-called memories of this newly created people and those of another people who really did exist at the time when what the former remembers is supposed to have taken place would be epistemically equivalent.

What strikes one about the example, however, is that Russell does not press his skepticism to the point of calling into question the reality of a single "objective" past. It is assumed not only that there was a past, but also that it was of a certain character which the "memories" of the newly created people misrepresent. Russell has a perfect right to make such a stipulation; but if he does so, its status within the world of the story he tells must be explained. For example, if some other human being was in existence at the time when this strange new people was created, then that person would presumably have memories that would approximate much more closely to the truth about the past than do the false "memories" of the latter. In that case, he might be able to convince these new beings that, by ordinary standards of evidence, their beliefs about the past are false or, at least, very different from the memory-beliefs they have about the period *since* they came into being. No supposition of this kind is included in the story as Russell tells it, and so the falsity of the "memories" of the newly created people is not presented as being even susceptible of being established within the world of the story. As a result, the example clearly takes on a transcendental character, in that it involves the postulation of a state of affairs by someone who is outside this or any similar state. From this undefined position, he is able to entertain as meaningful the idea of a total contrast between what someone "remembers" and what was in fact the case, and to do so in a way that is itself apparently not open to doubts of the kind being shown to be valid with respect to the "memories" in the story. Examples like this are peculiar, in that they take advantage of the locationlessness of the subject implied in them so as to be able to postulate the state of affairs involving the contrast in question, while avoiding any application of it to one's own case; and one may suspect that this is the real point of the whole exercise. For if such application were made the contrast on which the skeptical implication of the example depends would be wiped out, since then no one could be assumed to have any more access to the "real" past than the newly created people have. If even this much were accepted by the formulator of the example, and he were then to say no more than that it is *possible* that everyone's memories, including his own, are false, we would want to know, first, how he could give meaning to the concept of the past as such if all his memories were just so many present states of his consciousness; and, second, how he could even describe that present and the "memories" it contains in a way that does not implicitly violate the absolute logical and ontological distinction between past and present that has been established by the theory of world-time.

The difficulties that arise out of the very formulation of a case like this are indicative of the incoherence of the theory of world-time to which Heidegger wants to draw attention. At the deepest level, the trouble with this theory is that it cannot provide a satisfactory account of what it calls "subjective time" and so cannot give an account of itself as a theory of time. It masks this difficulty by an oscillation between the understanding of time that someone who is in time can have and an understanding of time that involves a transcendental and thus, ultimately, a nontemporal position. The one who is in time is held to know the past (and the future) through representations; but because these representations are always themselves present, it is not clear how they can ever reach out of that present and why they do not simply collapse into that present in such a way as not to carry a reference to anything outside it. But this is not allowed to happen; and it is avoided by implicitly postulating a transcendental position from which there is unquestioned referential access to all points in time and from which it is evident that the representations contained in the present of someone in time are, indeed, representations, however imperfect, of a past that lies outside that present. For someone who is *in* time, the references to other times contained in these representations could not even be identified as such; but by adopting a transcendental standpoint, this difficulty is simply not allowed to arise. What is never explained, however, is how the referential power of this transcendental position and of its tenseless present is established in such a way as to make it invulnerable to the skeptical doubts that stem from the presentness of all the representations of those who are placed *within* world-time. To all appearances, this standpoint is simply assumed to be available so as to make up for the limitations that the theory of world-time imposes on the representational activity of those who occupy positions in it and thus secure against skeptical doubts the referential capacity that we are nevertheless so sure we possess. But even if that capacity—what Heidegger calls our "transcendence"—is safeguarded by a strategy of this kind, it cannot explain how the theory of world-time can be held by a subject that is *not* in a transcendental position with respect to time—that is, by an ordinary human being who is finite in the sense of being located at a particular point in time. Thus there is a pressing need for a reconstruction of that theory which will ensure that it does not undercut the ability of its adherents to formulate and hold it. A first step in such a reconstruction would quite naturally be a reexamination of the assumptions about the character of the present, the Now, on which that theory is based.

II

In undertaking an analysis of the Now, Heidegger proceeds in a way that is closely similar to his earlier treatment of the spatiality of *Dasein*.

In the latter case, the notion of the There proved to be of decisive importance. "Now," like "there," is an indexical term, and as such, it dates the events in the world to which it applies by reference to the time at which it is used, and so to the person who uses it. As we saw in the earlier discussion, this indexicality is often held to be a limiting and inconvenient feature of our terminology of temporal reference, something to be eliminated in favor of an objective time metric. By contrast, Heidegger holds that clock-time, which is a kind of quintessence of world-time, itself depends on a Now that has not been stripped of its indexical force as it is by the theory of world-time. The notion of a replacement of the Now and of the indexical features of the language of time generally by a system of temporal distinctions that abstracts from the kind of dating that the Now effects must, accordingly, be an illusion. This means that with respect to the question as to whether the distinctions between past, present, and future can be eliminated in favor of a nonindexical distinction between events in time as "earlier than" and "later than" other such events, Heidegger would come down strongly on the negative side.[15] The status of any such conception of an objective time understood in terms of the latter distinction remains problematic in Heidegger's thought, even when temporality has been fully acknowledged; it will accordingly be discussed at the end of this chapter.

The Now itself is to be characterized in a phenomenologically adequate manner that abstracts from any *parti pris* in favor of an objective time. The need for such a prior characterization arises out of a paradox that is produced by the assimilation of the Now within the theory of world-time to the status of the entities it qualifies.[16] So conceived, the Now serves as the name of the moment in which these entities are present, and, like them, it passes away. The result of this assimilation of the Now to something *vorhanden* is that, as so reified, all Nows will themselves be in time in the sense that they come along and then pass away. One can thus say that a certain (former) Now is no longer, and that another is not yet; and in saying this, we are manifestly dating these Nows. But the time in which Nows come along and pass away is not the time that they constitute as a tenseless series of Nows; and the Now in which a former Now is no longer and a prospective Now is not yet is not a Now in the sense of being just another member of that series. As such a series of Nows, world-time is tenselessly *vorhanden* as a kind of container within which events are ordered in relation to one another and are, to use Aristotle's phrase, "encompassed" (*periexesthai*) so as to form a continuous series (*synexeia*). But what such a conception can never explain is how there can be a Now that is in any way different from any other, a Now that is privileged in that it marks where we are. If the series of Nows that makes up world-time is tenselessly *vorhanden*, then there is an almost irresistible temptation to explain what is distinctive about the Now that is *now* by postulating a kind of movement of the subject along the temporal dimension of the world. But if we do that, then we must recognize that the kind of time in which we are "at" a certain Now, rather than another, is not the time in which all such Nows form a dimension of a *vorhanden* world. The theory of temporality might be described, in fact, as an account of that second kind of time, in which an entity—the entity that each of us is—is at a certain point in a reified world-time. This way of putting things would have the serious disadvantage, however, of underwriting the priority of such a world-time to temporality, which is, in Heidegger's view, the "original time" from which world-time derives. It is necessary, therefore, to describe temporality in a way that does not presuppose world-time as that with which temporality is to be contrasted.

All these caveats notwithstanding, the theory of world-time does offer important clues for a positive account of temporality. This is because the principal features of world-time can be viewed as so many reified counterparts of the mode of being temporal of the entity that constructs this theory and that is able to have such a representation of time only *because* of its distinctive temporality. World-time is "framed" (*gespannt*), for example, in the sense that it is made up of segments or stretches; it "runs" from one point to another (and, of course, beyond as well).[17] As such a framed segment or stretch, world-time is conceived as somehow existing on its own; but this conception, which is problematic enough by itself, also fails to make clear how time could be *manifest* as such a span or stretch. But if it is not possible for world-time so understood to be *for* an entity whose present is always just one moment, or Now, what must the present be so that other times can be *for* it and *for* the entity whose present it is? One answer to this question would be to postulate a direct quasi-perceptual intuition of past and future events. But this typically requires that these past and future events have some sort of reality so that they can be the objects of such an intuition—a requirement that is met, for example, by the conception of the world as a four-dimensional continuum. This is not the line that Heidegger takes.[18] He does not think of the past as being somehow stored up or of the future as being already in place so as to be able to serve as that which this intuition would be an intuition of. He takes his stand on the common-sense position that the past is what is no longer the case and the future in what is not yet; and he shows no disposition to transform these negatives into some paradoxical form of actuality.

The alternative Heidegger proposes is to stop thinking of the Now as a self-contained moment and to bring out instead the internal complexity of the Now as that in which the world is present. Instead of being a term in a series, such a Now frames time in such a way as to set up a contrast with something past or something future. Every Now is a "Now when such-and-such is the case"; it thus carries a contrast with a time when such-and-such was not or will not be the case.[19] Such a span of time cannot be equated with a part of the series of Nows that is world-time, because then the question would arise as to how this part of the series came to be isolated from the series as a whole. Since it does not do this on its own, the Now in which it is picked out must be understood as setting up the contrast with a Then and thereby spanning the interval so constituted. But in so doing, it also, as Heidegger puts it, "dates itself."[20] Another way of putting this is to say that, in the Now, time is stretched (erstreckt) in such a way that it holds on to what has been and awaits something that is to come. The former is thus taken as that which is no longer, the latter as what is not yet; and what is now the case is present in the strong Heideggerian sense of that term as what once was not and later will (or may) no longer be the case. If what is now the case were simply replaced in the next moment by something else, then in each of these moments what is the case would be a Now without a contrasting Then, a present without a past or a future. But there is a future only if what is not yet the case is something other than just a state of the world that is located, for some transcendental and nontemporal observer, further along the time dimension. The future and the past are thus not simply indices of the location in time of a particular subject in the way that the present, or Now, is supposed to be; they are also the horizons onto which that Now opens.

It was noted in the last chapter that there is a strong tendency to assume a special linkage between presence as such and the present as that which the present tense expresses. It is that assumption that is being called into question by the concept of temporality that Heidegger proposes; and the effect of this line of thought is to associate time as temporality more closely with the uncovering and opening functions of Dasein as the entity that *has* a world. There is no present, it has now begun to appear, without a contrast between what is now the case and what was and what will be the case. But what is no longer or not yet the case is clearly what is *absent* in the sense of that term corresponding to the sense of "present" as what is now the case. If so, we have acquired a sense of "present" that contrasts with "absent" and another that must include it; and the wider concept of presence must accordingly be construed in such a way as to make a place within it for both the narrower concept of the present and the corresponding concept of the absent.[21] That absence should be a mode of presence seems at first an unrewarding kind of paradox. But if we consider the way in which we talk and think about the past and the future, as well as the present, the matter takes on a quite different aspect. For we do not act as though there were some fundamental difference in epistemic status between the present on the one hand and the past and the future on the other. We habitually refer to past and future events as standing in an unproblematic continuity with what is going on in the present, and without any sense that, in so doing, we are violating some distinction in status between the present and the other "dimensions" of time that affects the availability of the latter for purposes of our commerce with them. It may be that just this sense of a referential access to past and future that is—at least in principle—unproblematic gives some plausibility to the theory of a world-time in which all the states of the world are contained in a tenseless *Nunc Stans*. The whole point of the latter theory, however, is to assimilate both the present and the absent to a tenseless present, and not to leave any place for temporality as our having a world in which the distinction of the present and the absent retains its full original meaning.

The established ways in which we account for the undeniable role of the past and the future in our experience typically fail to do justice to the implication in one another of present, past, and future as structures of the world. It is common, for example, to assign our relation to the past to "memory" and to account for the latter by means of a theory of the kind of mental functioning it involves. It is important to understand, therefore, that Heidegger is not putting forward either a theory of memory or a modification of such a theory of the kind proposed by Bergson, since he holds that such theories are inevitably informed by the very assumptions about the objective and subjective aspects of time that he rejects.[22] This is because memory is typically construed in terms of episodic acts in the course of which we reach out of the present and back into the past so as to recapture something from our earlier life. The facts that are so recovered may also be thought of as having been "stored" after their actuality had lapsed and, as so stored, continuing on with us through each of the successive presents in which we live. (It may, of course, be more or less easy to retrieve them from storage.) In both these versions, our conception of memory presupposes the privileged character of the present, since it is only through an occasional sortie into the past (or a trip to our mental library) that we are portrayed as leaving a life and a world that are otherwise unimpeachably "present." What this misses, of course, is the way this supposedly present world bears a burden of pastness that is not at all a mere external supplement that a helpful memory is constantly adding to an otherwise rigorously present state of affairs. The identities in terms of which we understand and deal with the things and places and artifacts in our world are not construed on the basis of such a rigorous distinction between present reality and added information about the past. This is the typewriter I bought in Cambridge more than ten years ago, and Valley Forge is the place where the Continental Army wintered in 1778. If we are to be thought of as carrying our pasts with us, the place where we "store" them is the world, not our heads. We move and act and live within a world that is instinct with pastness; and although it is true that we do on occasion suddenly recollect things that we had forgotten, that recollection itself occurs within a world that is itself historical—that is, a world in which what happens (*geschehen*) happens in a present that has a past and a future.[23]

Similar observations could be made about the future as a dimension of the presence of the world. There is a strong tendency to interpret our relationship to the future in terms of "predictions"; and in the classical problem of induction we are represented as making such predictions on the basis of evidence drawn from the past and present observations, which may well have no applicability at all, if Hume is right, to the future course of events. The past at least "has been" and is therefore determinate, whereas in the case of the future, it is not even clear whether the law of the excluded middle properly applies to it. The effect of these ways of thinking about the future is to distract our attention from the way in which things—"present" things—are what they are in an essential linkage with what will or may happen in the future. This is most evident in the case of artifacts designed to serve purposes like damming the water in a stream to insure an adequate water supply next summer or to prevent a flood like the one that occurred last year. The discussion of *Zuhandenheit* in chapter 2 has shown how unnatural it is to treat such artifacts as though they were decomposable into purely physical objects and the thoughts that supervene upon the latter and connect them with future outcomes and past events. If such entities were compounded in this way out of these disparate elements, and the future and the past were merely meanings that we attach to what is itself simply present, it would follow that, if we were to refrain from deploying these meanings, we could capture the world in terms of pure presence. But the future is not some gratuitous addition that thought contributes to what is already solidly given; it is that to which we are already committed by virtue of the presence of the entities that we now perceive. We are, of course, liable to error with respect to the future as well as the past; and when we are mistaken, another identification of some entity will have to be substituted for the one we originally espoused. But the new identity will prove to be like the first in that it too mortgages the future— the future course of our "experience" and the future course of events— as did the first.

What this thesis of the essentially temporal character of the world amounts to can be best shown in terms of the interlocking character of the system of tenses we use. It may at first look as if the present, past, and future tenses serve to state facts about the world that are fully independent of each other and thus conform to the picture implicit in

the theory of world-time. For one thing, the perfect tense very conspicuously violates the logically segmented character of world-time by virtue
of which each Now is fully independent of every other Now. If I say
"That statue has been there since 1940," I am saying something about
the present state of the world that is true only if its past state was such
as to include this statue's standing on this spot. The future perfect tense
illustrates the point even more perspicuously. If we say "The statue will
have been there for fifty years in 1990," we describe its future state by
reference to what will be the case during a period of time leading up to
it—a time that will be past in 1990 but is future, at least in part, in
relation to the time of this utterance. More generally, and independently
of the use of the perfect tense, whatever is past is the past of a particular
present, and the same holds for the future. Thus the present state of
the world is always implicitly involved in references to past and future
times; and every "It was" is thus implicitly an "It is now the case that it
was." Similarly, every present, every "It is" is implicitly an "It will be the
case that it was." Each tensed statement thus carries with it other temporal
perspectives on the fact that it states; and there can be no pure present
that is not embedded in this set of contrasts. The point here is not that
we have to make use of this complicated set of perspectival contrasts in
all the temporal references we make. If we like, we can assign each event
we are concerned with to some point in a single time metric, thereby
suppressing much of the linguistic evidence of its changing relationships
to the reference point—ourselves—in relation to which they are successively future, present, and past. But even as we reform our representation of the temporal order by eliminating its indexical features, any
reference we make to that order would presuppose our ability to understand it in terms of the Now and the contrasts set up by the Now. It
is thus evident that the logically segmented time-order that we substitute
for the more complex perspectival structure of our own temporality can
at best conceal the latter and cannot dispense with it.

A philosophical theory of temporality like Heidegger's is hard to imagine except in the setting provided by just such attempts to reform and
simplify our understanding of time. This is because the *concept* of temporality is first disengaged from a pre-conceptual understanding of time
when it comes to be identified, as it is by Heidegger, as that which is left
out by a theory of world-time. To some extent, even the language in
which this new understanding of temporality finds expression bears the
mark of the contrast with the logical segmentation of world-time that is
transcended by temporality. But this does not alter the fact that what is
central here is the claim that temporality is prior to the ordering laid
down in the concept of world-time, even though the *concept* of world-
time came first and thus influenced the idiom in which temporality itself

is rendered. The point is similar to the one made earlier about the relation in which the concept of transcendence stands to that of immanence. In both cases, it is important to understand that these new Heideggerian concepts do not presuppose, in the one case, the segmentation of time or, in the other, a sphere of immanence, so that they can break out of the limits these would impose. Heidegger's claim is rather that the earlier concepts represent a distorted understanding of the matters that his account gets right. Although these distortions may have provided the occasion for Heidegger's new analysis and thus have influenced the language in which the latter is couched, his philosophical intention is to present something that is in principle independent of and prior to the distorted understandings that are the occasion for his own philosophical effort.

III

The account of temporality that has been given up to this point has been shaped largely by the relationship in which it stands to world-time—the world-time that leaves no place for it and yet presupposes it. It has become apparent that temporality cannot appropriately be thought of as a dimension of some super-entity—the world as *vorhanden*—and must instead by understood in a way that assimilates it much more closely to presence and to the uncovering and opening functions of *Dasein* in which presence is grounded. Temporality is in fact a necessary condition for the presence of entities as entities, Heidegger claims, and as such it is an essential element in the ontological constitution of *Dasein*.

We are so accustomed to thinking of ourselves as being in time that the notion that there is something special about our *way* of being in time may be hard to assimilate. The account that has just been given of the temporal character of the world, as well as what was said in a preliminary way about the transcendence of *Dasein* in the last chapter, indicates in general terms what this special way is. But these indications must now be expanded into a much fuller and more explicit characterization of *Dasein* as an entity that *has* time. As a first approach to such a characterization, we should note that the temporality that distinguishes our way of being in time is understood by Heidegger as "temporalization"— a nominalized form of an active and often reflexive verb "to temporalize (oneself)."[24] *Dasein* is sometimes the explicit grammatical subject of that verb; but even when it is not, and "temporality" or "the world" replace it, it is always the implicit subject. As in the case of verbs like "to uncover" and "to open," which express the way of being in the world of *Dasein*, there is a question about what makes the use of an active verb appropriate as a description of the special temporal character of *Dasein* and its grounding of the world-time in which we ordinarily think of ourselves as being situated in pretty much the same way as everything else. The verb "to temporalize (oneself)," unlike "to uncover" or "to open," is not drawn from ordinary language, so it is not necessary, as it was in the case of those verbs, to explain how its philosophical use differs from its ordinary use. What is the same in the two cases, however, is the suggestion carried by all these verbs of something like an action, and thus of the possibility of withholding the "actions" they denote. In the case of "uncovering" and "opening," such implications proved to be rather misleading; and it was only after a somewhat circuitous argument that a notion of spontaneity that *was* applicable to the "uncoveredness" of *Dasein* was isolated. That notion was introduced with the notion of transcendence; and it was pointed out that a full account of that notion would require an account of the temporal structure of *Dasein* and especially of its futurity. But just when that account is about to be offered, it looks as though the same problem is back again, since it has turned out that the temporality of *Dasein* is a matter of its "temporalizing itself," and we cannot without circularity explain the actional character of *this* notion in the way we explained that of the prior ones. What we require at this point is thus an account of the temporalization of *Dasein* that explicates the kind of action it involves and does so in an independent way that can then serve as the basis for understanding the agency involved in uncovering, since this has turned out to depend on transcendence and hence on temporality.

The first thing that must be made clear about temporalization is that it is not an action in any sense that would imply that we choose to engage in it or have any alternative to doing so. Not only does temporalization not denote any ontic action of the kind discussed in connection with uncovering and opening; it does not denote any higher-level "mental" action like a decision to use the concepts of past, present, and future either. The idea of such a decision is not, of course, very plausible; but if past, present, and future were thought of primarily as concepts that we make use of, then it would be possible, at least in principle, to imagine our *not* doing so and to speak of our actual use of them as involving an implicit decision. For Heidegger, they are not concepts at all, although we can form concepts *of* them.[25] They are ontological dimensions of presence that are grounded in the temporality of *Dasein*. If there is to be any prospect of understanding this temporality as temporalization in a way that preserves some sort of action character for the latter, we must not look for some action that we could identify as temporalization. Instead, we must try to understand *all* actions in a way that would place them within the primordial temporality of *Dasein* out of which they issue, instead of in the world-time in which they are ontically understood. To put the same point somewhat differently, even though the conditions of our existence are such that there is no way to avoid dealing with time, it may nevertheless be the case that the temporality of our actions itself has an action-character at the deepest level.

That this is what Heidegger wants to assert becomes clear in his analysis of the "moment" (*Augenblick*) as the configuration of temporality in which the active character of *Dasein* is not obscured by a false assimilation to world-time.[26] In the moment, *Dasein* does not *await* the future, but projects it as that which it has chosen and is acting to bring about. As explained in the last chapter, the future that has been chosen is at once a state of the world and a state of the self; and it has the status of a possibility to which *Dasein* has committed itself. This is the characteristic posture of *Dasein* as an agent. It is not an estimation of probabilities; nor does it understand the future event to which it has committed itself in a detached third-personal way as something that either will or will not occur, depending on the conjuncture of circumstances in the world. In the moment, there is thus realized a unity of an anticipated future and a present understood as a movement toward that future; and it appears to be Heidegger's claim that this unity is possible only for an entity that chooses its own future from among a set of possibilities. If there were no such choice and no action designed to realize what has been chosen, the relation in which *Dasein* would stand to the sequence of events would be completely that of a spectator, and it is questionable whether the temporality of such a spectator would permit the kind of "having a future" that characterizes *Dasein*.[27] If world-time is treated as always already laid out or in place, then this distinction becomes simply a distinction between different ways in which a segment of that time is filled—namely, by a prediction or an intention. But if temporality is prior to and a necessary condition for world-time as a modality of presence, as Heidegger claims, then a question arises as to whether it is even possible to have a future otherwise than in the mode of choice and intention and action, if what we are talking about is the temporality of a finite being and not some *cosmotheoros* who inhabits a tenseless present.

It is widely assumed that one could have a future in a purely theoretical or representational mode that would include even one's own future actions and without its making any difference that they were one's own actions. In fact, this theoretical stance is widely held to be the fundamental character of the relationship in which we stand to our future. Once again, however, it looks as if this way of conceiving our having a future depends on our trying to place ourselves at a standpoint that, in fact, we can never occupy. Every projection of our own future actions unavoidably has a conditional character—"If I were to do so-and-so rather than such-and-such"—and the only way we can remove that condition is by deciding what we are going to do and envisaging our future in the light of the intention so formed. But this way of having a future is a way of having it as what we are about to do or bring about. The linkage here among the notions of the future, possibility, and choice is clearly a very close one.[28] There are, of course, plenty of things going on in the world that we can control only marginally, if at all, but the future course of which we can project with a high degree of accuracy; and this way of having a future in the theoretical mode of a spectator may be thought to be quite independent of any special character that agency confers on our relation to future events. But, in fact, there is no way in which these two ways of having a future can exist side by side with a separate sphere assigned to each, since the impact of our agency on the future course of events is indeterminate, even if it always remains tiny. Under these circumstances, in which it appears that we must choose one of these conceptions of the future as the framework within which the other will be interpreted, Heidegger comes down strongly in favor of the future understood as that which is to be brought about. This is not to deny—and he certainly does not—that it is possible to isolate sequences of events within the world toward which we can adopt a purely spectatorial attitude and the future course of which we can await without any intention of intervening in it.[29] But he insists that when we do this, we do so as entities that are in principle capable of such anticipatory intervention, even if only in the mode of imagining some action that is in fact beyond our powers. These sequences of events thus take place within a world for which the future is always the locus of possibility; and it is in this sense that the future of *Dasein*, as the entity that is conversant with possibility, enjoys a priority over any future that is envisaged in a purely predictive way. It should also be pointed out that we try, nevertheless, to extend this way of looking at things to ourselves and to our own lives; but Heidegger holds that, in doing so, the most we can accomplish is to obscure the fact that we are always also choosing or, in his language, projecting a future in a way that cannot itself be objectified by being reduced to the content of a mental episode occurring *now*.[30] The clear implication is that having a future in a predictive-spectatorial mode is parasitic on having a future as an agent, and that it is in its capacity as an agent that *Dasein* has a future. The primary mode of transcendence and hence of temporal ecstasis is that of choice and action; thus temporalization is not something we do in the sense of some special action, but something that we are always "doing," inasmuch as our understanding of ourselves and of our situation is always one of some possible action. In other words, in choosing and in acting we are always temporalizing ourselves by committing ourselves to a particular future;

and the action-character of temporalization is in the first instance that of having a future in the mode of choice.

In his lectures on logic in 1925–26, Heidegger discussed the Kantian treatment of time in some detail and with special attention to the combination of spontaneity and receptivity involved in temporality.[31] Spontaneity was viewed by Kant as belonging to thought, as distinct from sensation; and pure thought uncontaminated by sensation was supposed to be nontemporal in character. Time, understood as the form of the inner sense, had to be associated with pure thought through schemata if thought was to make contact with objects in the world; and through this combination the spontaneity of pure thought was tempered by the receptivity that sensation necessarily involves. Heidegger viewed this doctrine of temporal schematism as Kant's closest approach to an insight into the fundamentally temporal character of *all* human thought and experience; but it was limited by the assumption that in-itself thought is independent of time.[32] In Kantian language, this accommodation of pure thought to the conditions for a knowledge of objects on the part of an entity endowed with sensibility rather than the intellectual intuition of God is described as "self-affection" (*Selbstaffektion*).[33] Pure thought, in other words, acts on itself in such a way as to make it possible for it to be affected by—in the sense of receiving representations of—time as the infinite given magnitude within which alone, as an a priori form of sensibility, any object can be given to it. In Heideggerian language, which prescinds from the assumption of an originally nontemporal "I think" as the quintessential subject, this self-affection is characterized as "letting oneself be given" something, a "letting something encounter" (*begegnen-lassen*), and a "letting something stand over against oneself" (*gegenste-henlassen*).[34] This letting-encounter with which we are already familiar from the discussion of uncovering is described as being "in advance" (*vorgängig*) of the actual encountering of the something that encounters; and this means that when something encounters, it does so as that which was "looked to," and so anticipated, in a prior prospective reference to (*Hinblicknahme*) the future course of events.[35] Since, for Heidegger, there can be no subject without a world, there can be no subject in the absence of such a letting-encounter. It follows that in the existentially conceived subject, there can be no spontaneity without the receptivity implicit in any letting-encounter, although the prefix verb "to let" still asserts an element of agency even in this passivity. The doubts expressed earlier as to whether the agency signified by that use of "let" was more than window dressing can now be seen to have been met by the argument set forth in connection with the concept of temporalization.

There is another passage in which Heidegger draws on Kantian language in a way that may be taken as summing up his own position with respect to the active character of temporalization and thus of temporality.[36] He observes that a union of spontaneity and receptivity in the subject along the lines described above does not imply that human beings "create time," as would be the case if they were endowed with the *intuitus originarius* of God. But although we are not capable of such a pure spontaneity, we are endowed with an *intuitus derivativus*, which Heidegger characterizes as "the *intuitus originarius* of a created entity."[37] What this seems to amount to in Heideggerian terms is a contrast between an entity for which temporality would be somehow optional and one for which it is, so to speak, compulsory, but in a way that preserves a certain analogy to the freedom of the former and thus justifies the (qualified) use of the same description for the latter. The difference is that God is supposed to create time from outside time, whereas human beings make time "be" as a mode of presence—that is to say, as a unity of past, present, and future. This is also the unity of *their* being, so it is proper to say, as Heidegger does, that the subject or, in Kantian terms, the "I think" *is* time as the realization of just this unity.[38] It is time in the sense that it stretches itself out by holding on to its past and anticipating its future; and, as Heidegger says, a present (*Gegenwart*) that is ecstatic and transcendent in this way is "a mode in which time is temporal (*zeitlich*)."[39] He also remarks that what shows itself in such making present (*Gegenwärtigung*) "is time."[40] One could thus say that *Dasein* lets time show itself as world-time by *being* time as temporality; and if this is the case, it follows that "all propositions about time . . . have, as expressed propositions, the character of an indication: they only indicate *Dasein* while as uttered propositions they mean in the first instance something *vorhanden*."[41] Thus, "in the expectation (*Gewärtigung*) of an event," for example, "our own *Dasein* is always concurrently expected"; and more generally, "every way of construing the Now is a saying (*Sagen*)" in which *Dasein* understands itself in a temporal context that reflects the choice it has made of itself.[42]

It is also in the lectures from the period of *Being and Time* that Heidegger formulates his conception of the way in which time as temporality makes possible the presence of entities as entities—that is, their being.[43] What this means is that it is possible to understand *that* an entity exists and *what* that entity is as so existing only because the temporality of the entity that understands projects the existence of the entity in question beyond any immediate givenness, anticipating it as it will be and holding on to it as it has been. In this sense, temporality is a necessary condition for letting an entity encounter (*begegnen-lassen*). Heidegger expresses this by saying that any present perception is "ecstatic" in that it stands outside itself, or transcends itself temporally in such a way as to "let that for which it is open, encounter in the light of its horizon."[44] More specifically, "there can be an understanding of being in intentional perception because the temporalization of ecstasis as such, i.e. making-present as such (*Gegenwärtigung*), understands that which it makes present, as present (*Anwesendes*) in its horizon, i.e. out of presence (*Praesenz*)."[45] Thus, things *are* for us, they are manifest as entities, they stand on their own with just the characteristics they have, only to the degree that they can be for us in absence as well as in the present; and it is only as understood in terms of both presence and absence that they can be uncovered. Both presence in the primordial sense of that term and the temporality that corresponds to it thus involve an essential element of negation in the sense of a contrast with what is *now* the case; and Heidegger acknowledges an indebtedness to Hegel for this insight into the connection between being and nonbeing.[46]

These are passages of great significance for the understanding of Heidegger's philosophical project in *Being and Time*; and their full meaning, as well as some of the ambiguities implicit in the interpretation of being they propose, will be taken up in chapter 6. What can be said here is that, in Heidegger's eyes, temporality constitutes an essential structure of the There as the clearing within which entities can show themselves as entities. In other words, it is in terms of the ecstatic character of temporality, the horizon of past and future in which every present is embedded, that the various essential permutations of the concept of being like actuality and possibility and nonbeing are to be understood.[47] Although most of the preceding discussion has dealt with the ecstatic dimension of presence in terms of the future, the same kind of analysis must apply to the past as well. Having a past is not, of course, decisional in the way that having a future is; but it is from what I am in the mode of having been that the possibilities in terms of which my future is understood and chosen derive.[48] It is the unity of the three temporal ecstases that alone can constitute the domain within which *Dasein* can comport itself in relation to entities within the world, to itself, and to others like itself. This reference to others as participating in the same kind of temporal openness as oneself is of special importance, because it carries forward the conception of the commonness of the world to the world as past and future, as well as present. On this point, Heidegger is especially emphatic, as when he declares that "the Now and every [other] time determination that is expressed is *publicly accessible* for everyone in being-with-one-another."[49] "The 'Now when . . .' and 'then, when . . .' that are expressed and construed in daily being-with-one-another are fundamentally understood even though they are unambiguously dated only with certain limits"; and "the time that each *Dasein* expresses and construes is, therefore, as such already made public on the basis of its ecstatic being-in-the-world."[50] This publicness has the drawback that it may assimilate the temporality of each *Dasein* to the world-time within which we locate one another as well as *vorhanden* entities. When this happens, there is a strong tendency for the future, especially, to be understood as something we *await* (*Gewärtigen*), as though it were not already present to us in the mode of transcendence and choice that has already been described. Nevertheless, it would be a mistake to suppose that the publicness of time should be understood in a one-sidedly negative way; and Heidegger makes it clear that, as in the case of the world, this commonness is an essential feature of temporality, not merely what he calls a "deficient mode." As such, it is temporality as a common structure of *Dasein* that underlies and makes possible clock-time; and it is we, as Heidegger says, that "give time to watches by saying 'Now.'"[51] It could equally well be said that we give time to the sky as our first "clock" by setting up the temporal contrasts—the spans—in terms of which the changes in the position of the sun can be "counted."

It is perhaps not altogether surprising, in light of the complexities that were pointed out in connection with Heidegger's doctrine of the single and public character of the world, that this strong assertion of the public character of time as generated by temporality should be crossed by another, contrasting line of thought. It becomes apparent that, although temporality effects a public and common ordering of world-time, Heidegger also wants to say that the "moment" (*Augenblick*) as the authentic modality of the present and of making present is realized only by individual *Dasein*.[52] Because authentic temporality involves a decision and a project that an individual *Dasein* can make only for itself and by itself, it is never in the first instance shared or public. It is, instead, the temporality of *Dasein* as *vereinzelt*—that is, as single and individuated and thus prior to and independent of the structures of world-time.[53] It is this individual *Dasein* that is the true bearer of authentic temporality; and from this it seems to follow that this individual *Dasein* must also be the ground of world-time. None of this negates the public character of temporality in its positive aspect, as discussed above, but it does appear to make that public character derivative from, rather than a constitutive element within, authentic temporality. If it is indeed the case that "being-with-one-another as a mode of authentic existence must be determined primarily out of the resoluteness (*Entschlossenheit*) of the single individual (*des Einzelnen*)," then the public character of temporality would seem to accrue to it as a kind of supplementary increment.[54] But this is a picture of *Mitsein* that Heidegger elsewhere energetically repudiates.[55] Such an independent constitution of world-time would seem to run the danger of being private in a sense that would render a subsequent constitution of a common world-time highly problematic. If Heidegger seems to be calling into question the possibility of a shared world-time that is an expression of authentic temporality, and to be doing so against his own best inspiration, this would seem to be another indication of a conflicting disposition that leads him to view what is public as necessarily inauthentic.

This conflict surfaces very clearly in the quite different attitudes Heidegger evinces in different contexts to the fact that *Dasein* understands itself out of its world. At one time, this fact about *Dasein* is presented as having nothing to do with authenticity and as deriving from the transcendence of *Dasein*.[56] At another, understanding ourselves out of things is equated with "projecting one's own potentiality-for-being (*Seinkönnen*) upon what is feasible, urgent, unavoidable, and advisable in the matters with which we busy ourselves from day to day."[57] What is detrimental about the latter way of understanding ourselves out of the world is that things may take over the direction of our "potentiality-for-being" so as to leave us awaiting outcomes in a way that is the opposite of authentic temporality. This does not happen because other people have succeeded in imposing their authentic understanding of themselves out of their world on us, but because neither we nor they have been able to achieve an authentic mode of temporality, with the result that we are both in some sense lived by our world.[58] The question raised by all this is whether there is a way in which *Dasein* can understand itself out of its world, when that world and its time are common and shared, without thereby lapsing into an inauthentic and "worldly" form of temporality. It is not clear, for all the emphasis he places on being-with-one-another, that Heidegger has an unambiguous answer to that question.

IV

In the course of this chapter the world-time with which we began has been shown to presuppose temporality as that which makes possible the manifestness, or presence, of world-time. Temporality has been shown to be a self-temporalizing of *Dasein* as the entity that *has* a future and a past, as well as a present. This line of argument inevitably raises the question as to whether, in Heidegger's view, there would be no time if there were no *Dasein*. It is already quite clear that he defends a similar position with respect to the world, maintaining that if there were no *Dasein*, there would be no world. But he makes a distinction between the world as such and the entities that are within the world; and he says that the existence of entities is not dependent on the existence of *Dasein*, even if that of the world is. In the case of time and temporality, there is no parallel distinction. The entities within the world that are independent of *Dasein* are described as being "timeless" (*zeitlos*), just as they are "worldless" (*weltlos*); but "timeless" here means not that they are not in time, but that they are entities *for* which there is no time as there is no world.[59] They are also described as *innerzeitig* ("within-time-ish"), a term that corresponds to *innerweltlich* ("within-the-world-ish"), the term that Heidegger used to describe their state in the world. What both descriptions convey is that these entities are encompassed by or contained in something—the world or time, as the case may be—that does not exist *for* them. The milieu within which they are situated is peculiarly that of the entity—*Dasein*—for which entities are present as entities and for which these entities are also present as "having been" and "about to be." These structures of pastness and futurity (as well as of presentness understood as being bound up with them) properly belong only to *Dasein*, since the chair I sit in, for example, does not have a past as I do. But the only way *I* can have a past and a future is by having a world that is past and future as well as present; and the pastness and futurity of that world accrue, so to speak, to the entities within it. But if their participation in my temporality is understood as something wholly extraneous to their character as entities, then it follows that if there were no *Dasein*, these entities would not only be "timeless" as they are when there is a *Dasein*; they would not be in time either, for there would be no time for them to be in. What is more, Heidegger embraces this conclusion explicitly and denies that there can be any "nature-time" (*Naturzeit*)—that is, any time other than that of the world and so of *Dasein*.[60]

It is not clear just how this claim is to be taken. Taken at face value, it would seem to imply that the entities that survive the demise of *Dasein* and its world could not change from one state to another, because there would be no time for them to change in; but one can hardly suppose that this is what Heidegger intends to say. Admittedly, he betrays a noticeable tendency to assume that temporality—the "original time" of *Dasein*—is time itself; and such a claim goes far beyond the thesis that we are able to *have* time only because we are temporal in a sense that cannot be explicated in terms of the world-time we have.[61] Other locutions that he uses, however, suggest a quite different picture, as, for example, in the passage already noted that describes the "I think" as a modality of time in which "time becomes temporal." Similarly, the statement that "what shows itself in making-present is time" certainly seems to suggest that time has some status other than as constituted by temporality, and that it is this independent time that comes to presence in the temporality of *Dasein*. We also have Heidegger's explicit statement that *Dasein* does not create time; and since this statement is made in the context of comparison with God, who, in Christian theology, is supposed to do just that, one must assume that *Dasein* creates time in neither an ontic nor an ontological sense.[62] It thus appears that Heidegger *could* hold that there is a "nature-time" that is independent of *Dasein*, and that this time is to be understood in terms of a sequence of events (*Nachein-ander*) that are ordered as earlier and later but do not have the character of past, present, and future. Nor would this imply that it is as so ordered that time is first given to *Dasein*, or that past, present, and future are "subjective" additions that *Dasein* projects on the pure time-order. Temporality would still be primordial in the sense that time as a *Nacheinander* could only *be for* an entity that is characterized by transcendence and thus by temporality as well. In the light of these considerations, one may even surmise that in saying that there is no "nature-time," Heidegger does not intend to deny that change and relationships of "earlier" and "later" are independent of the world and of *Dasein*. It may be that he is simply not prepared to call such a *Nacheinander* "time" because he re-serves the term for the world-time that presupposes the distinction among past, present, and future.[63]

If that is not the case, however, and Heidegger's statement that there is no "nature-time" must be taken literally, there is reason to think that he would face difficulties very similar to those that arose in connection with the relationship between the *zuhanden* and the *vorhanden*. In both cases it would look as though he were trying to have things both ways. In the one instance, he does so by making what is in effect an existence-statement about the *vorhanden* that falls outside the world, despite the fact that the world has been expressly designated as the milieu within which all such statements as modes of uncovering and presence must fall. That the corresponding statement in the case of the temporality/ nature-time pairing is negative—"There is no nature-time"—does not alter the fact that here too Heidegger would be transporting a "There is" outside the setting—the world—within which it must, by his own principles, be encompassed. What is central here is the way in which the finiteness of *Dasein*, which Heidegger so emphatically asserts, is to be understood. It would be paradoxical to claim that this finiteness is such as to make it impossible for *Dasein* to refer to any time before (or after) there is any *Dasein*. What it surely does entail, however, is the impossibility of making such references without thereby incorporating such times into the world of *Dasein* and thus into a time that is past and future as well as present. To speak as though this were not the case, or to assert that outside that world there is a *vorhanden* and that there is not any time, is to say that we have a double perspective on the world—one as an entity that is in it and another as one who can see it in relation to what lies outside it. In the first case we would then have to go on to speak of the external *vorhanden* as entering the world; in the second, of time as coming into being with that world. Moreover, if Heidegger seems to be com-mitting himself to just these notions on occasion, it is surely better to rely on those statements of his that do not involve him in the difficulties that such notions generate. Perhaps it would be best to argue that if *Dasein* ever exists at all, then its world must comprise all times, including those that precede as well as those that follow the existence of *Dasein* itself.

If this suggestion were adopted, the concept of the world would be modified in that what is contrasted with it would be different. In the formulations that Heidegger gives us, the contrasting term is entities that are *vorhanden* and not in time; within the world these same entities become *zuhanden*, if only in the deficient mode, and in that world they are also "in time" although themselves time-less in the sense of not *having* time. In the modification I am proposing, the world would extend backward and forward in time to whatever entities exist when *Dasein* does not, but it would be understood that it does so as the perspective that a *Dasein* which does exist has during the period of its existence. This means that this world would be informed by both the temporality and the instrumentality that are essential to the mode of being in the world of *Dasein*, even though large tracts of it would contain no entities of the *Dasein* type. What could be contrasted with the world so understood would be not a stripped-down version of the entities that make up that world—that is, the same entities minus world-time and *Zuhandenheit*— but rather a domain without any finite centers of orientation at all. This domain would not be a Kantian thing-in-itself, which, after all, is something that finite "minds" are supposed to be acted on by and which they attempt to "know," although they must always fail in that attempt. It is rather something that we can think of only in contrafactual terms of a particularly paradoxical kind, since what is involved is the supposition that no entity like ourselves—the entity that is entertaining this thought— has ever existed or ever will. Insofar as we are willing to use the word "world" to describe what is thus supposed, it would be a world with no There at all, and certainly no contrasting Here, no Now and no Then. Whether any concept we have can really be said to apply to such a "world" is problematic in the extreme; and the status of anything that, as it were, lies outside the range of both presence as such and the conceptualization that presupposes presence must be equally so.[64] What confronts us here is the radical disparity between the mode of being of *Dasein* and that of things, between things as present and things as independent of presence and the world. This is something we rarely even think of, because we implicitly believe that presence is the natural domicile of things. But when we are compelled to acknowledge not only that there may one day be no *Dasein* as perhaps there once was none, but also that there might never have been any *Dasein* at all, we are forced to try to separate the mode of being of things from that of presence and to postulate a status for them that would be the contrasting term to the world as the milieu of presence. The best index of what Heidegger means by the finitude of *Dasein* may be the fact that this effort encounters overwhelming difficulties, whether it takes the form of a bifocal theory of the in-itself like the one just described or that of a denial that any such independent reality exists.[65]

CHAPTER FIVE • **FEELING, UNDERSTANDING, AND DISCOURSE**

The foundations of Heidegger's "ontological interpretation of the being of consciousness" are now in place. The concept of the subject has been progressively revised in such a way that its being-in-the-world and its temporality are now understood to be essential to it, and all vestiges of a domain of immanence have disappeared. With the latter has gone the contrast between the "inside" and the "outside"; instead of being understood as a "spiritual thing" incongruously set down in a spatial milieu which it knows only through its representations of it, the subject has become *Dasein*, the There of being, and as such a necessary condition for the presence of that external world about which, in its earlier incarnations, it entertained such persistent doubts. It is time, therefore, for this new ontological conceptualization of the subject to be put to work so as to determine its capacity for accommodating some of the more specific modalities of what has been interpreted traditionally as "mental" activity.

The title of this chapter contains three major rubrics under which our everyday understanding of ourselves is organized, rubrics that also receive a good deal of attention from Heidegger. These correspond to the three distinctive and essential characters of *Dasein* singled out by Heidegger in *Being and Time* as its *existentialia*—a term that he prefers to "categories" because the latter properly applies, he claims, not to *Dasein* but to entities of the *vorhanden* type.[1] These three *existentialia* go by the German names of *Befindlichkeit*, *Verstehen*, and *Rede*, of which only the last can be rendered in English—as "discourse"—in a relatively unproblematic way. Of *Befindlichkeit*, one can say in a preliminary way that it is Heidegger's term for that whole subdomain of the subject's life that is ordinarily thought of as "feeling"; as the traditionally most "subjective" element within subjectivity, it thus presents a special challenge to a theory like Heidegger's. The difficulty about *Verstehen* is not one of translation as such, since "understanding" renders Heidegger's use of the German word quite satisfactorily. It is rather that our associations with the kind of knowledge to which the term *Verstehen* has referred in recent German philosophy are likely to prove misleading. This use must therefore be sharply contrasted with Heidegger's use, which is also the key to his whole way of interpreting the "cognitive" aspects of subjectivity.

This chapter will be devoted to an account of how each of these three *existentialia* are incorporated into the wider theory of *Dasein*. In the preceding chapters, in which the concepts of *Dasein* and existence were introduced, some use was made of the kinds of considerations that underlie Heidegger's treatment of both *Befindlichkeit* and *Verstehen*, especially the latter; and there have also been a few preliminary observations on Heidegger's concept of language. The account given in this chapter will accordingly emphasize the specifically ontological character of each of these functions of *Dasein*, since this is what defines the transformation through which our more familiar notions of feeling, knowing, and language pass in the course of Heidegger's revision of them. More specifically, it will show that this ontological character can be understood only when the central importance of action, as well as of the correlative notion of possibility, for all the functions of *Dasein*, has been grasped. One of the principal implications of Heidegger's concept of existence is that what exists in this sense—*Dasein*—does not exist and also act, but that its action, as well as the "undergoing" or "passion" that is the inevitable counterpart of action, is precisely what makes it the kind of entity it is. Accordingly, there is no dimension of *Dasein*'s being that is prior to action and the kind of understanding it involves, any more than there is any locus outside the world or outside time that *Dasein* can be said to occupy. If there were such a place or such a dimension of *Dasein*'s being, then it might be possible to look out from it on human action and to describe it in terms of concepts that would be in some sense independent of the circumstances that characterize the situation of an actual agent—for example, being able to do certain things and not others, uncertainty about outcomes and preferring certain outcomes to others. It is even arguable that, at least in philosophy, we typically think about action in a way that subtly distances the thinker from the circumstances of action, just as the same transcendental tendency of thought has been shown to distance him from the world and from time. Heidegger's philosophy as a whole is in direct opposition to any such tendency; and this opposition is symbolized by his claim that the most general characterization that can be given of *Dasein* is one in terms of *Sorge* (care).[2] This, of course, is an ontological, not a psychological characterization; and its import is not a claim that life is a burden, but that there is no way we can understand ourselves and our world except in terms of alternative possible outcomes, and no way either in which these possibilities can be disconnected from what we can and cannot do so that our relation to them would be that of spectators for whom, in principle, nothing would "mat-ter." The true meaning of "care" as Heidegger uses it resides in just this unavoidable modality of our lives in which we must act and therefore choose among possibilities that are *our* possibilities, but without possess-ing or even being able to postulate any form of knowledge or being in which either these possibilities or the choices we make among them would be absorbed into the actual in a way that would relieve us of our re-sponsibility and freedom. In examining what Heidegger has to say about feeling, understanding, and discourse, it will be important to keep in mind that all three must be understood as ways of having a world in which possibilities are not reduced to actualities, whether as thoughts or as dispositional properties or whatever, and that it is within such a world that we must be understood as acting and, in the context of such action, feeling and understanding and speaking.

I

Heidegger tells us that in the philosophical tradition, "emotions and feelings come under the rubric of psychic phenomena, where they func-tion for the most part as a third class of such phenomena after repre-sentation and volition." As such "they sink to the status of accompanying phenomena" and have not been thought to deserve much attention in their own right.[3] This low, tertiary status is also what is accorded them in the Lockean classification of the kinds of qualities that things on oc-casion, at least, seem to possess. There are the primary qualities of size and shape, for which external counterparts are claimed that actually have them. Then there are the secondary qualitites like color and smell for which such counterparts are claimed by common sense but which do not really have them. Finally, there are inner states of a third kind—Santayana calls them "tertiary qualities"—for which, it is said, only victims of the pathetic fallacy claim any external counterparts and which, in any case, do not correspond to anything outside the mind. These are thus the most radically inward of all our mental states. Because the principal business of the mind has been held to be knowledge, feelings and emo-tions have often been viewed as so much subjective "noise" that must be discounted if the true signals reaching us from the "objective" world are to be identified correctly.

In the phenomenological tradition, the epistemic status of feelings and emotions was somewhat more favorably evaluated; but, at least in the case of Husserl, this was done in such a way as to ratify the standing presumption in favor of theoretical reason among the different forms of mental life. For the purposes of Husserl's phenomenological inquiry, there could be no doubt about the preeminence of cognition or about the judgment as the primary vehicle of our cognitive apprehensions. As he points out, for every mode of mental life that is not prima facie propositional or judgmental in character—for example, our feelings of love or anger—it is always possible to effect a conversion to the judgmental mode. This is done by making explicit the "thesis"—the claim about the object to which the feeling is directed—that is implicit, Husserl assures us, in every intentional act. "Thus, the valuing consciousness constitutes an 'axiological' objectivity that is novel over against the world of mere things, an entity of a new region," and, more generally, "every act-consciousness that is carried out in a non-doxic manner is in this way potentially objectifying (although) the doxic cogito alone does the actual objectifying."[4] What this means is that forms of intentionality that are not explicitly judgmental are to be regarded as convertible into others that are; and accordingly, it is to the latter that Husserl's phenomenological analyses are primarily devoted. In this respect, of course, Husserl was simply translating into phenomenological terms a prejudice in favor of theoretical and cognitive modes of consciousness that had established itself within Western philosophy at a much earlier time.

It is already evident that Heidegger does not accept this way of treating forms of consciousness that are prima facie nontheoretical. This is implicit in the fact that, instead of viewing the *zuhanden* as derivative from the *vorhanden* via an addition of a value-property to the latter as the general ontological type, Heidegger treats the *vorhanden* as derivative from the *zuhanden*. In general, the idea of authenticating some function of *Dasein* by postulating a property corresponding to it does not appeal to Heidegger; and in the case of feelings and emotions, as with other matters, his method is rather to call into question the whole scheme within which such an expedient seems to be required. Superficially, his account of *Befindlichkeit* may seem to resemble a judgmental theory of the emotions, since he certainly builds on their intentional character. Feelings and emotions are intentional in that they express something; and to the extent that they do, they cannot be viewed simply as self-contained, occurrent states of the self, comparable to a sensation or a sensory *quale* like a color patch. It has often been pointed out that we are pleased, for example, that we passed an examination or received a gift; in such cases our pleasure is intrinsically *about* something in a way that a sensory *quale* cannot be. This intentional form of analysis can clearly be extended to a great many feelings and emotions, and Heidegger presents such interpretations of two of these—fear and anxiety.[5] By itself, however, this intentional construal of feelings and emotions would only very partially realize the conception of *Befindlichkeit* he proposes, as long as what they express is not interpreted within the context of existence as the mode of being of *Dasein*. What is of greatest importance in this connection is the fact that the world in which *Dasein* exists is not an objective world in the sense of the totality of entities that are actual. It is a pre-objective world in which possibilities have not been reduced to one or another kind of actuality; and it is the world as a "space" of possibilities that *Befindlichkeit* uncovers in its own distinctive way.

The word *Befindlichkeit* itself combines in a uniquely happy way, for which there is no equivalent in English, the notions of location—of finding oneself somewhere—and of being in a certain state—whether of well-being or its opposite or somewhere in between. But this state is quite emphatically not to be interpreted as a "state of mind," as the translators of *Being and Time* have rendered it, since this would tend to reestablish the very picture of the mind as a receptacle of inner states, among them feelings, that Heidegger is most concerned to avoid. The "place" in which one finds oneself when in a certain state is not the mind, but the world, since it is in the world that things have happened and are happening that affect us, by either blocking or facilitating our efforts to bring about certain outcomes and avoid others. Beyond saying that there is no justification for regarding these projects of ours as egoistic in character simply because they are necessarily ours, Heidegger does not offer any explanation of why outcomes in the world in general matter to us; nor does he appear to think that any such explanation is required, or that he must advance a general theory of human motivation.[6] Instead, he simply takes his stand on the fact that we understand ourselves and our world in terms of possible outcomes that we can to some degree control, outcomes that affect us according to their positive or negative effects on our concerns and undertakings. As we move through the world, we register how things are going for us. People threaten or support us; our bodies fail or sustain us; and all these circumstances may be both anticipated as possibilities about which we can still try to do something or registered as achieved fact that may or may not leave some margin of continuing uncertainty regarding the outcome that concerns us. Whatever the case may be, it is through feeling that we take in the way things are for us and more generally "how we are and how we are faring."[7] The force of the notion of *Befindlichkeit* is that it interprets the work of feeling as an uncovering, a disclosure of where we are in the space of possibilities and actualities that is our world. In the feeling of fear, for example, something in the world is uncovered, not in objective terms as possessing such and such properties and such and such a location, but as about to do me harm unless I take countermeasures. Such an uncovering presupposes a rich context of projects, preferences, empirical likelihoods, capacities, incapacities, and vulnerabilities; but the import for me and my well-being of this whole complex "involvement" (*Bewandtnis*) registers with me, or "encounters" primordially, in the medium of feel-ing.[8] Feeling, understood in terms of *Befindlichkeit*, is thus properly viewed as a primary modality of being-in-the-world, a primordial way in which we have a world in the unimpoverished sense of that term.

Once again, it is important to emphasize that what is uncovered in the modality of feeling is indivisibly a state of the self and a state of the world.[9] This is not because feelings of various kinds have been magically infused into things. The point is rather that because *Dasein* has not been sealed off from the world by conferring on it the status of a mental substance, the state of the world that it uncovers in terms of its relevant possibilities and actualities is its own state. *Dasein*'s being an entity for which things matter or make a difference is the ground of the world's being in a favorable or unfavorable configuration, for there is no way in which the concerns of the self can be separated by a distinction of reason from the world in which they are deployed. This is why it is not justifiable to treat as purely subjective either specific emotions like fear or anger which, after all, refer to the things and situations in the world that are usually said to cause them, or the more diffuse states of feeling that we call "moods" (*Stimmungen*).[10] Moods like depression or boredom are often thought to be even more exclusively states of the self and even more independent of the kinds of worldly situations and occasions to which fear and anger point. But even moods do not lack an intentional or referential character. If I am depressed, for example, this mood, which may be of brief or long duration, expresses how things are for me at that time; and how things are for me can hardly be isolated from how things are going for me in the world or from how they have gone or are expected to go. Even in the case of anxiety (*Angst*), which Hei-degger regards as in some sense the fundamental mode of *Befindlichkeit*, the world remains a constitutive element in the form of uncovering that characterizes this mood, even though the practical network of entities within the world "collapses into itself," as he puts it, and "the world has the character of complete meaninglessness."[11] This sounds as though in anxiety *Dasein* would be uncovering only itself to itself, and as though a splitting off of the self from the world were realized in this mood. In fact, however, it is in anxiety that the world is most authentically un-covered *as* the world; and this is possible precisely because it is grasped not just in the standing configurations that constitute its "public inter-pretedness," but in terms of possibilities that are the possibilities of *Dasein* as free and individual (*vereinzelt*) and responsible for itself.[12] This is to say that the world is grasped in its deepest identity with *Dasein*, since the choice of self that *Dasein* makes is also a choice of the world it is to be in. In this choice, *Dasein* is indeed alone—*solus ipse*, as Heidegger puts it—and it is this aloneness and the uncanniness that goes with it that we experience in anxiety and that we typically turn away from in a kind of flight back to the familiar public interpretedness of the world.[13] It is important to remember, however, that "this existential 'solipsism' does not transfer an isolated subject-thing into the innocuous emptiness in which it would exist without a world; much rather, it brings *Dasein* before its world as world and thus itself before itself as being-in-the-world and it does so in fact in a quite extreme sense."[14]

It should now be clear why Heidegger speaks of *Befindlichkeit* in ontological, rather than epistemological, terms. In the light of what has been said about feeling as a way of registering how one is doing (*wie einem ist*), it might not seem inappropriate to describe *Befindlichkeit* as a form of knowledge. The considerations that speak against any such description derive in the first instance from the implications associated with the traditional concept of knowledge and, more specifically, from the ontological assumptions on which it rests. These were examined in chapter 1 and are such as to make knowledge something that goes on inside a mental substance that in principle could exist with all its inner functions even if the entities to which the latter refer did not exist at all. If this picture is rejected and the subject, properly understood, is seen as the entity that grounds the presence of the world, then the knowledge that was formerly interpreted as the inner act of a distinct substance must be reinterpreted as just this uncovering function itself that has now taken the place of substance as the mode of being of the subject. Once again, however, Heidegger appears to have judged that the term "knowledge" itself was too heavily compromised by its established associations to be suitable to the new conceptualization he offers. The place that he *does* make for the concept of knowledge will be described later in this chapter. The relevant implication of his decision at this juncture is that *Befindlichkeit* (and, as we shall see, understanding and discourse as well) must be spoken of in ontological terms—that is, as what we *are*, rather than as our knowledge of what we are, under penalty of being assimilated to the ontological model that invariably goes with the predominance of the concept of knowledge in Heidegger's judgment.

There is another consideration that speaks in favor of this ontological idiom as a way of rendering the character of *Befindlichkeit*; and this one does not depend on any terminological decisions that may or may not command general acceptance. It has to do with the role of choice, and thus of action, in the uncovering, or letting encounter, that is the mode of being of *Dasein*. *Dasein* chooses itself and, in so doing, chooses its world; it cannot therefore properly understand itself as standing in the relation of a spectator to the world and to its own actions as comprised within the world. Although our powers may be insignificant by comparison with the other determinants of the character of the world that we uncover, even the tiniest degree of efficacy on the part of our actions is enough to make it the case that the state of the world comes to us as something that we, in however modest a degree, bring about. We can, of course, *know* the world as what is so brought about, but there is, to say the very least, a significant difference between what is known in the mode of bringing it about and what is known without any such role in making it the case. What we know in the former way is bound up with our own choices and actions; and these are more properly described as what we are than what we know. Because our feelings and emotions are those of persons whose choices and actions implicate them in the bringing about of the present state of the world and also set the practical context within which that state is understood, they are themselves informed by the same transcendence as our choices and actions. It is, therefore, proper that they should be described in the first instance as modalities of our being—of what we are, rather than as cognitive apprehensions of a state of the world that is treated as being independent of our own being in the world and of our role as agents. In this sense, the choice of the ontological idiom for characterizing *Befindlichkeit* is a way of acknowledging the actional character of transcendence as it informs our feelings and emotions and as the latter consequently express and enact what we are as individual human beings.

There is a difficulty here about this ontological mode of statement as it applies to feelings and emotions. The question is simply whether these feelings are susceptible of error. If they were spoken of in epistemic terms, this would certainly be the case. But if viewing them as knowledge or as knowledge-claims is deprecated, as it is by Heidegger, and if instead we are encouraged to understand them ontologically as modalities of our own being, does it follow that we always are as we feel we are, that we are always faring just as well or just as badly as our feelings say that we are? The claim that what our feelings tell us about ourselves can never be mistaken or even misleading may not at first blush seem to have much to recommend it; yet the notion of a discrepancy between the way we feel and the way we are also presents difficulties. There are circumstances in which such a gap plainly exists, of course, as when someone is in a happy mood although he is, without knowing it, mortally ill. In such a case, however, it is the superior "knowledge" of the person who sets up the example that also provides the other term in the contrast with the way the person in question "finds himself." The real question is whether this contrast is possible in cases in which there is no such undisclosed knowledge; and here the answer is not so clear. At any rate, we cannot in such cases simply invoke some independent criterion of well-being as a standard against which to measure the "accuracy" of a person's feelings about the state he is in. Then, too, determining what those feelings are may not be easy; in this connection it is of great interest that Heidegger states explicitly that we may be in a mood without in the ordinary sense "knowing" that we are.[15] We may, for example, deny without hypocrisy that we are in *any* mood, when in fact we are; and such moods may have great power over us precisely because they are not acknowledged. Such moods would ordinarily be called "unconscious"; but such a description would hardly be acceptable to Heidegger, if only because its linkage with the concept of the conscious. But if there are moods that are not acknowledged or are refused recognition, then the question about a possible disparity between the deliverance of *Befindlichkeit* and how things actually stand for us takes on a rather different aspect. It is at least possible that in a mode of uncovering that is prior to and largely independent of our explicit acknowledgments, whether to others or ourselves, we always register how things are with us—even when we respond to what is so disclosed by denying the existence of the mood in which the disclosure occurs. At the very least, it would appear that the state we are in and the feelings we have move very much closer to one another when thought of in this way than they do in more conventional interpretations of the affective life. This also suggests that the kind of inauthentic feelings that are at variance not only with the "realities" of our situation but also with our own deeper sense of that situation in the mode of *Befindlichkeit* provide a rich field of phenomenological analysis. Whether such inquiries would reveal any affinity between Heideggerian phenomenology and psychoanalytic thought is a further, potentially interesting question.

The other question that may arise in regard to this theory of *Befindlichkeit* concerns feelings that resist assimilation to the intentional model described above. Among these, the feeling of pain is usually regarded as the most recalcitrant case. There is no discussion of pain and pleasure in Heidegger's writings, and only a few references to the somatic or physiological basis of feeling.[16] He remarks that the fact that anxiety is "physiologically conditioned" constitutes an "ontological problem," but the precise nature of this problem is not defined, and no attempt is made to deal with it beyond laying down the general principle that "physiological release (*Auslösung*) of anxiety becomes possible only because *Dasein* is anxious in the depths of its being."[17] To defend Heidegger's line of thought on this point would require an argument showing how pain, for example, can be understood as a mode of uncovering, rather than simply as a datum offered to our awareness. What pain so understood would uncover would be how we are with specific reference to our bodies. A pain in a certain part of the body would register the injury that we have suffered there; hence there would not be an injury as a state of the body *and* a pain caused by that injury, but rather the pain would be the original mode in which that injury is uncovered by us. The prospects for such a mode of analysis, for which Aristotle's treatment of pleasure could in many respects provide a model, are necessarily unclear; but this would seem to be a good way of trying to adapt Heidegger's thought to the understanding of matters with which it has all too rarely been brought into close contact.

II

Befindlichkeit, Heidegger tells us, is never without its *Verstehen* and this means that we never uncover how we are except in the context of a practical field that we in some measure understand.[18] If, for example, we did not understand that something detrimental might happen to us as a result of something else, or if we did not understand at all how to go about trying to prevent or bring about outcomes that are detrimental or beneficial, *Befindlichkeit* could not be the specific, possibility-oriented kind of uncovering it has been shown to be. This may make it sound as though "understanding" were simply another word for knowledge (*Erkennen*), and more specifically for the knowledge of the world that makes it possible to give a sense to the notion of things being one way or another for us. But such a straightforward equation of understanding with knowledge would be misleading. This is not because there is no connection between understanding and knowledge, nor because Heidegger repudiates the concept of knowledge altogether. The reason is rather that, in Heidegger's view, understanding is the prior and more fundamental notion, which must be grasped in an adequate way before the concept of knowledge can be properly formulated.[19] It must be grasped, moreover, in ontological terms, as was the concept of *Befindlichkeit*. If we were to neglect this ontological dimension of understanding and allow the implicit philosophical prepossessions that have been associated with the concept of knowledge to dictate the way we construe it, not only would we miss its true character, but the way in which knowledge emerges from understanding would also be fatally obscured. In this section, accordingly, an attempt will be made to set forth the authentic ontological character of understanding and then to show how the concept of knowledge derives from it.

But first it is necessary to clear up the confusion alluded to at the beginning of this chapter between Heidegger's use of the term *Verstehen* and its use in the hermeneutical tradition from Schleiermacher to Dilthey and beyond. In that tradition, the word "understanding" has denoted the kind of knowledge we have of other human beings, of their mental life and the characteristic products of that life, most especially those that fall under the rubric of culture: texts, works of arts, and so on. Broadly speaking, Heidegger's relationship to Dilthey was a positive one; but his use of the term *Verstehen* has nothing to do with the divination of the mental state out of which some expressive act or product has issued.[20] Such a conception would not only make understanding a subspecies of knowledge without any prior clarification of the ontological status of knowledge as such; that subspecies would itself be one conceived in terms of minds and their contents, and as such would represent a distorted ontological thesis, rather than a legitimate demarcation of a special province of knowledge. "Understanding" as Heidegger uses the term is not confined to cultural entities or human beings; it is understanding of the world in the broadest possible sense. As such, it presupposes the existence of other entities like ourselves in the mode of *Mitsein*, but these other *Dasein*s are understood, as we ourselves are, out of the common world that we all share.[21] The only thing that connects these two very different uses of the word "understanding" is that both are contrasted with knowledge as *Erkennen*, and especially with the regularities of sequence on which such knowledge has typically been supposed to turn. Both uses involve a purposive/teleological character that goes beyond mere regularity of sequence; but, as the account of the *zuhanden* in chapter 2 showed, Heidegger's way of formulating this kind of purposiveness is explicitly nonpsychological and thus stands in marked contrast to that of Dilthey.

Although understanding is not a subspecies of knowledge, there is a kind of knowledge that has a clear affinity with it. This is the "knowing-how" that is contrasted with "knowing-that" by philosophers who are interested in some of the same things as Heidegger but do not want to abandon altogether the language of knowledge. The distinction between knowing how and knowing that derives from the fact that the latter is explicitly propositional and uses language as its vehicle, whereas the former is a skill that one may have without being able to formulate any propositions or truth-claims about the matter in question. Even when there is a need to express what we know in this way in some explicit propositional form, this may prove difficult and the propositional rendering of our "know-how" may prove very imperfect. We know how to swim or drive a car or cook a meal in a way that is hard to describe precisely because this knowledge is so intimately part of us, laid down as it seems in our hands and eyes and in our bodies generally, rather than in speech or writing.[22] But if this insistence on the distinctive character of the implicit and the tacit as something more than a blurred version of propositional knowledge moves in the direction of a conception of understanding like that of Heidegger, it can do so only within the limits prescribed by the concept of knowledge itself, of which knowing how remains a special case. This means that it is typically accom-

modated to the ontological assumptions—themselves usually implicit—
that go with the prevailing philosophical models of knowledge. The
result is that the more radical implications of this paradigm shift remain
largely undeveloped, and the ontological apparatus that is already in
place remains undisturbed.[23]

Heidegger's way of proceeding is very different. Building on the
earlier analyses of the *zuhanden*, he develops the sense of *Verstehen* that
signifies a being able and thus a "can" that belongs to the entity—ourselves—that is said to understand. This "can" is interpreted as a *Seinkönnen*, a potentiality for being that is peculiar to *Dasein* and not merely
another "dispositional property" of the kind that we freely attribute to
all kinds of entities.[24] If this "can" were a notion that applied to *Dasein*
in just the way that it applies to every other kind of entity, it would
probably have to be interpreted as an implicit conditional; what a person
can do would be what he would do *if* something were the case that is
not actually the case. On such a view, there would be no categorical
"can," no capability that a person has, just as he is, without any reference
to some modification that his condition might undergo. By itself, without
reference to such a change, that present condition would have to be
described in terms of "is" rather than "can." It would be actual through
and through; and this actuality would be transcended in possibility only
if the situation became different from what it is. Since, after such a
transition, the situation would once again be pure actuality, it appears
that such possibilities would always involve only a notional contrast between one actual situation and another and never be something predi-
cable of an actual situation independently of such a comparison. Against
this line of reasoning, it is Heidegger's contention that there are some
entities—human beings understood as *Dasein*—that must be described
in terms of possibility, in the sense of what they *can* do, and that every
effort to reduce the being of these entities to the actuality of the "is" or
the "will" that is just a transposed "is" must fail. He does not offer an
analysis of the "can" as such, but he is plainly committed to an unconditional "can," which he would presumably call "existential" rather than
"categorical," since he associates the terminology of categories with the
mode of being of the *vorhanden*.

This existential "can" of *Dasein* is what corresponds to, and in fact
grounds, the possibility that was shown in chapter 2 to be such a pervasive
feature of the world. It is thus another principal modality in which
existence as the mode of being of *Dasein* effects the presence of entities
to itself. The account of the instrumental character of entities within the
world has already shown what their primary mode of presence is; what
can now be added to that account is that the "can" that applies to these
entities—entities that *can* be moved, *can* be eaten, *can* be burned—derives

from the "can" of *Dasein*.[25] It is *Dasein* as the entity to which this primordial "can" belongs that uncovers entities in the world as entities that can be moved, eaten, and so on, just as it is *Dasein* as endowed with *Befindlichkeit* that uncovers the fact that they can or cannot be so moved as something that matters. More specifically, Heidegger seems to be saying that the way such entities are individuated is a function of the kind of understanding we have of them in terms of what we *can* do. This is to say that the lines of cleavage that run through the world and divide it up into distinct (though not logically isolated) units are constituted by the different forms assumed by the "can" of *Dasein*. Something is distinct from something else if we can separate the one from the other for the purposes of action—that is, for the purposes of something we can do to or about it. Even at the level of the organization of our perceptual field into discrete objects, the fact that something—a chair or a stone—moves (and thus can be moved) as a unit assumes a decisive importance. Eventually we may come to view this primary pragmatic organization of our world into unit-entities as being naive and parochial, and as reflecting a mode of conceptualization that remains much too closely tied to our practical interests. But in adopting a more sophisticated ontology that perhaps relativizes the unit-entities with which we deal to the language we use, we will hardly have overcome the linkage between the conceptual ordering of our world and the "can" of human existence—that is, the range and calibration of the kind of agency over which we dispose. We will simply have gained an insight into this linkage that we then express in a relativizing manner as though we were implicitly contrasting all the orderings we use to either an independent order that is absolute and perhaps inaccessible or to the absence of any prior order at all, which we may conceive to be the final truth of the matter. What Heidegger, by contrast, has tried to convey is that the world in which we are is indefeasibly a world of *pragmata*, and that, although new, more sophisticated *pragmata* corresponding to higher levels of agency on our part may be substituted for old ones, this cannot be interpreted as undercutting the ontology of *pragmata* in principle in favor of an ontology of mere things.

There is another dimension of the "can" of *Dasein* that is not developed by Heidegger, but that seems to follow so directly from what he says that it must at least be indicated briefly. It has to do with causality, and specifically with the contrafactual character that causal laws are generally recognized as having. In other words, causal laws state not only what actually happens when certain conditions obtain, but also what would happen *if* these conditions were to obtain. If the regularities expressed in such laws were confined to the actual sequences of events that have taken place, are taking place, and will take place, it can be argued that a distinction between causally connected events and equally regular, but causally unconnected sequences could not emerge. In practice, this difficulty is overcome by interpreting the future segment of the domain of events to which a causal law applies in terms of possibility; but it is important that this be done in such a way as not to obscure the issue of its contrafactuality. If the future is regarded, for example, as simply an incremental set of actual events, it will follow that, even in the larger set of events produced by the accession of that new increment, the distinction between a true causal regularity and a chance association of events might fail to emerge. It thus appears that a strong notion of events that are not and may never be actual must be introduced in order to spell out the import of causal laws; and this is to say that the notion of causality itself requires a concept of possibility and of possible events. The question then arises as to how this notion of possibility is to be interpreted when the only real instances of a causal law we can point to are actual instances. It has been suggested by G. H. von Wright that our ability to understand the contrafactuality of causal laws is bound up with our ability to initiate a sequence of events that would not otherwise have taken place.[26] If in circumstances in which there is no reason to suppose that x will occur, we act so as to bring about x, and y then follows, von Wright argues that we have a form of contrafactuality that is not itself causal— that is, it is not itself an instantiation of a causal law—but one that nevertheless grounds the contrafactuality of causal laws by supplying the element of possibility in whose absence the latter would amount to no more than a regular concomitance. What this means in Heideggerian terms is that only entities that, like ourselves, can understand a state of affairs as possible and can act to bring it about when it would not otherwise occur, can understand the world in terms of causal laws. This does not imply that such causal laws are "subjective," if by that we mean that their truth or falsity would not be common and public. Nor does it mean that these laws become operative only when they are discovered; Newton's laws, Heidegger states, exhibit the entities to which they refer "as they already were before (their being discovered)" and "to uncover in this way is the mode of being of 'truth.' "[27] What it does mean is that entities within the world can present themselves as characterized by causal regularities only to an entity that can act and thereby initiate change that would otherwise not occur. An assertion of a causal law thus implies that there are such entities and indeed identifies the maker of the assertion as such an entity.

These considerations should help us to explain why understanding, like *Befindlichkeit*, must be conceived in ontological, rather than epistemic, terms. Through the analysis of understanding as *Seinkönnen*, *Dasein* has been shown to be in the world in the mode of setting up an agency-based ordering of the entities around it. Its primordial "can" is differentiated, of course, by reference to varying situations and projects; and the specific configuration of possibility and impossibility with which we have to contend changes accordingly. But in every case, it is the world as such a network of possibilities that we "understand." Now, if we were to speak of such understanding as "knowledge," we would be, at the least, in danger of implying that we are merely the spectators of a state of affairs that owes nothing to us or to the kind of entity that we are. If Heidegger's analysis, which on this point is very close to the thought of John Dewey, is correct, the ordering of our world is inseparable from our being in it; thus it would be disingenuous, to say the least, to construe understanding in terms not of what we are but of what we know and of what is thus, by implication, fully independent of anything that pertains to us or our mode of being.[28] The difficulty here stems from the fact that if this notion of independence is taken in an ontic sense, as it usually is, or if the distinction between the ontic and the ontological is simply elided, all these rigid distinctions between what the object is in itself and whatever role we play in the process of coming to know it may be perfectly appropriate. We certainly do not make it the case, in any ontic sense, that a spark can be produced by striking a piece of flint; and it is our recognition of this that makes it seem natural to conceive understanding as a form of knowledge. After all, we can misunderstand such matters or understand them incorrectly; and this entails that what is eventually understood correctly must be something that has been what it is all along, even as we were slowly groping our way toward it, and that it is only something that enjoys this kind of independence of us that we can properly be said to know. But, as Heidegger's point about Newton demonstrates, this kind of "retroactive" truth *does* characterize understanding as he conceives it, and the independence—in this sense—of what is known is therefore not at issue. What prevailing conceptions of this independence miss, however, is the distinction between the generic worldliness of the world by virtue of which entities have the kind of instrumental character that derives from the "can" of *Dasein* and the particular dispositions of such entities, which are often such as to defeat our purposes and which we are certainly not in a position either to control or to predict perfectly. This distinction between the ontological and the ontic applies to understanding as it does to all functions of *Dasein*; and accordingly, we are liable to make mistakes about the orderings of the world on which we depend in the course of our projects. What is equally important, however, is that when we get things right, the world to which they belong is a matrix of possibilities and as such derivative from the mode of being of *Dasein*. Understanding as an ontological modality of the uncovering of entities within that world is thus the constituting of the "space" within which both truth and falsity become possible; and to the extent that this is so, it is itself a mode of being and not just an ontologically indeterminate mode of knowledge.

The line of thought that has been presented so far remains incomplete without the conception of interpretation (*Auslegung*) that Heidegger associates with his theory of understanding.[29] "Interpretation," as he uses the term, presupposes understanding as a primary, meaningful articulation of the world; and it develops and extends this understanding. Whereas understanding may remain implicit and tacit, interpretation is described as being explicit; and this means in the first instance that what Heidegger calls the "as-structure" of the entities that have been understood is in one way or another singled out for attention.[30] In other words, what something is taken as being in a certain form of understanding— "a table, a door, a wagon, a bridge"—is made explicit; and it is this "as" that constitutes the meaning in terms of which what that entity is and what possibilities it presents is anticipated (*Vorgriff*).[31] This way of making the distinction between understanding and interpretation, in terms of a contrast between what is implicit and what is explicit, does not by itself enable one to determine what degree of explicitness interpretation requires. Matters are not made any clearer by the fact that understanding and interpretation are both, in principle, prior to any kind of linguistic expression, although the latter serves the purposes of both. Perhaps the point of the distinction is not so much to designate some point at which understanding passes over into interpretation as to draw attention to the contrast between the implicit and the explicit as such. This is clearly a distinction of the greatest importance, and it marks the point at which understanding becomes reflexive and raises its own themes to the level of explicit attention and the further elaboration that such attention permits. Just where that point is situated depends entirely on the context and the character of the interest that is at work in it. There need be no single, standard cutoff point at which understanding becomes interpretation. Normally, for example, a golf-swing would belong to the implicit know-how of the player, who would be attending explicitly to such matters as the wind direction, the lay of the land, and so forth. But it is quite possible—and these days it has become very common—for such implicit elements in our performance in a sport or elsewhere to be subjected to close attention and for an effort to be made in a quite explicit way to correct or improve what we had previously executed in a quite unselfconscious manner. And even when we do become aware of elements of our competence on which we have been relying, there will presumably be others that remain implicit; and it may be that the complexity of understanding (and thus of our various forms of competence) is such that it is not possible even in principle to transform understanding wholly and without residue into interpretation by listing everything that goes to make up that understanding. If so, it may also be that in this conception of understanding as a tacit, and thus normally unexamined, mode of "being-with" the things we understand, we have a further clue to the kind of role that might be assigned to the "unconscious" in Heidegger's philosophy.

In the account given earlier of the ontological character of *Befindlichkeit*, considerable emphasis was placed on the connection between the possibilities that constitute the practical field within which we fare well or badly and the choices and actions by which we make ourselves what we are. In choosing among these possibilities, we are choosing ourselves; and the feelings and emotions that register how things are for us subsequently are therefore to be thought of in the first instance not as a modality of knowledge, but as continuous with and expressive of the character that we give our lives by these choices. Because the tendency to construe understanding as a form of knowledge is a good deal stronger than the corresponding tendency in the case of *Befindlichkeit*, it may seem problematic whether such an argument for an ontological mode of characterization can apply to understanding. This doubt is reinforced by the consideration that understanding is preeminently common and shared in a way that makes it unclear how a choice-character could attach to what is so understood about the world. It is clear, nevertheless, that Heidegger construes understanding in such a way that the same line of thought that was developed with respect to *Befindlichkeit* is applicable to it. Understanding, accordingly, always has the character of a project (*Entwurf*), and what this means is that it is always bound up with the possibilities to which *Dasein* has committed itself.[32] The word "project" may suggest a deliberate plan, something that is worked out *in foro interno* and then carried out in the world; but this interpretation would greatly narrow the scope of what Heidegger has in mind. There are, to be sure, such explicit and reflective projects, but they always supervene on a prior situation in which we were already "projecting ourselves" upon certain possibilities and thereby understanding ourselves and our world in terms of these possibilities as the implicit goals of our action. Within the context of such a project, the world articulates itself in certain ways, and the entities within it take on a significance (*Bedeutsamkeit*) and a meaning (*Sinn*) that derive ultimately from the possibility upon which we have projected ourselves. This significance is the as-character that interpretation elaborates; but interpretation "is never a presupposition-less grasping of something given," nor is it a matter of "throwing a 'meaning' over something that is just given."[33] What interpretation articulates is not a meaning that it first introduces, but the actual entity in question itself as it has been antecedently taken by *Dasein* and situated within the

referential totality of its projects and so of its world. In this sense, "interpretation has always already decided either finally or with reservations
in favor of a certain way of conceiving" what it has to deal with.[34]

This prior "decision" on which interpretation rests is one that is made
in understanding itself as the projecting of an entity on a "for-the-sake-
of" (*Worumwillen*); and this is so even when there seems to be no real
leeway for interpretation, and the entity in question simply "stands there"
before us as what it is—for example, a chair or a door. Such "decisions"
appear to have been made for us by our society or our culture, insofar
as it is proper to speak of them as decisions at all when there is no
significant alternative to this pre-established mode of understanding. In
such contexts we are in effect "lived by" the public understandings that
preside over our world by predefining the entities that are in it; and
Heidegger indicates that it is inevitable that much of our life should be
governed by such anonymous understandings.[35] As a general style of
personal existence, however, this pre-decided mode of understanding
of what entities are to be taken as being would conceal the real decisions
that may be involved in such determinations by assimilating them to the
status of "fact," of what "everyone" knows. Such decisions can arise in
connection with the humblest objects of everyday life, as when we have
to decide whether a broken toy is a piece of junk or a precious memento
of childhood. The point is not so much that its being the one is incompatible with its being the other, but that these different characterizations
of what it is have differing implications for action among which we have
to choose. In the sense that it always in principle involves such determinations and choices as these, understanding is choice-like, no matter
how many of these choices seem to have been made in advance for us.
And if it is choice-like, it expresses what we are, instead of being merely
a neutral apprehension of something that is fixed independently of anything that we do or are. Understanding should therefore be spoken of
in a way that reflects these facts, and that is what the ontological mode
of characterization on which Heidegger insists is designed to do.

A good deal of attention has been given in this chapter to Heidegger's
reasons for *not* characterizing *Befindlichkeit* and *Verstehen* as forms of
knowledge. At times it seems almost as though Heidegger's prejudice
against the concept of knowledge on the grounds of its philosophical
associations is so strong as to preclude the possibility of his assigning any
positive role at all to any thing that goes by this name. This is especially
true of what he calls "theoretical knowledge," the kind of knowledge
that seeks to satisfy the criteria that would qualify it as "scientific." It
may even seem unclear whether this negative attitude merely expresses
a reaction to the implicitly philosophical self-characterization of theoretical knowledge or science or whether it amounts to a repudiation in

principle of such methods of inquiry, quite apart from the account of themselves that they offer. To make the latter assumption would be to discount in advance the value of anything Heidegger has to say about science; and this would be a loss, since much of what he says has real merit. His view of science and technology will be taken up in part II; for now it may be noted that characterization of modern scientific methods of inquiry in *Being and Time* is not only far from being completely negative, but significantly amplifies the general account of understanding and interpretation that has just been reviewed.[36]

It has been shown that understanding and interpretation reflect at every point the active nature of the being—*Dasein*—that deploys them. Consequently, the ordering of the world that they effect is one that presupposes the possibilities of action and the decisions that characteristically belong to *Dasein*; and it is Heidegger's claim that in the world of *Dasein*, this interplay of decision and fact is fundamental and uneliminable. Indeed, in *Being and Time*, he goes so far as to declare that the great strength of modern post-Galilean science is its prior determination, or thematizing, of the kind of object with which it is concerned.[37] But if there is no way in which we can somehow divest ourselves of the projects and, in general, of the pragmatic interest in outcomes that have been shown to play a constitutive role in understanding, it is possible and sometimes quite necessary to hold back in the sense of not intervening in the course of the world, at least provisionally, so as to be able to see what takes place, as it were, without us. In the natural sciences especially, such holding back regularly occurs when an experiment is under way and the test conditions have been established. If at that point the experimenter were to try to play an active role and *make* the predicted result ensue, no one would think that he had established anything. Having put the question to nature, he must let nature answer; and he must hope that his question was well formulated so that the answer, when it comes, will not be inherently ambiguous. The same kind of holding back and just watching to see what will happen can be observed in ordinary life as well, although it may be that here the ethical constraints against covert intervention to help bring about the desired outcome are less well developed than they are in the natural sciences. In all such contexts, it is necessary to find a way of describing the events that we are observing which does not subtly prejudge the outcome; and this means describing the objects and situations involved in a way that maximally abstracts from the pragmatic context in which they are embedded. When this kind of description is pressed to the limit, as it is in the exact sciences, we arrive at the concept of "nature" as what is totally "meaningless," since the context of the world as the matrix of meaning has been discounted as far as possible.[38] It is the carefully contrived outcome of this process of description and observation that constitutes theoretical or scientific knowledge.

What is objectionable in all this is not the attempt to avoid doing anything that would turn the question we pose to nature into a covert answer as well. It is rather a supposition that is often associated with these procedures—the supposition, namely, that it is possible and, from the standpoint of theoretical knowledge, necessary to treat the larger context within which we take up this posture of merely waiting and watching as though it could be reduced to the merely *vorhanden* in just the same way as the natural processes that are observed within that context. Such a generalization of the theoretical attitude would mean that it is possible in principle for us to become spectators in relation to the very actions and procedures by which we set up the situation within which we subsequently confine our role to that of spectators.[39] That would require, of course, that in doing so we not bring into being a new pragmatic context—a new "praxis," as Heidegger puts it—that would in turn have to be reduced, thereby generating an infinite regress that could be avoided only by a preemptive judgment in favor of the *vorhanden* as the only admissible ontology for use in talking about anything, including our own decisions and actions. The ideological character of such a resolution is glaringly evident; but it is just this ideology that often becomes an unquestioned premise of what is offered as theoretical/scientific knowledge. It is this associated dogma that is objectionable to Heidegger and that explains his negative attitude toward theoretical knowledge or, more properly, toward the unique, exclusive status assigned to it by much modern thought. Such a treatment obscures the interdependence of knowledge and praxis; and if that does not always, or necessarily, produce grave consequences in the natural sciences, it may well do so in other areas of inquiry. What is obscured is what happens *before* the point at which we suspend intervention in order to see what happens, and especially all the decisions made in the course of determining what that point should be. To treat such matters, either implicitly or explicitly, as being of the same order as the matters under investigation and, as such, as governed by the same, ultimately cognitive or technical considerations is to justify their not being subjected to the kind of examination that is appropriate to any element within a system of human praxis. Since such a mode of treatment must be enforced in the face of differences that it is impossible to remain wholly oblivious to, it is the kind of ideology that also preeminently satisfies the criteria for what Heidegger calls "inauthenticity."

The general conclusion to which this consideration of Heidegger's treatment of theoretical knowledge points can best be gathered from what he says about the hermeneutic circle.[40] The latter is most familiar in the context of textual interpretation, in which assumptions about the overall character of a text—for example, that it is a letter or a speech or whatever—guide the interpretation of specific passages but can also be revoked and replaced by another general description in the light of passages that cannot be reconciled with the first assumption. Heidegger's version of this circle is one in which theoretical knowledge, generally, rests on background understandings that are those of our "common knowledge of human beings and the world."[41] Any dependence of this sort is typically regarded as a serious flaw in such knowledge, and great efforts are made to eliminate it so that history, for example, may eventually become "as independent of the standpoint of the observer as natural science supposedly is."[42] When theoretical knowledge is treated as though it had somehow spun free from the existential and pragmatic context of understanding and expressed facts that no longer presuppose that context as a condition of their intelligibility, the hermeneutic link between such knowledge and understanding is broken. Whether a tendency to such an absolutization of science is itself merely an interpretation that is separable from the substantive knowledge it comprises is not, perhaps, a question that is as easy to answer as is sometimes assumed; indeed, it is one about which Heidegger may have held different views at different times. *Being and Time* does not appear to present any grounds for supposing that there cannot be a science that acknowledges the continuing need to situate the kind of knowledge it produces within the ontological conditions of being in the world and thus of understanding. A science so conceived would itself be a modality of human existence; nor would it have to abandon the claim to be true in as strong a sense as can reasonably be required or incur any unwelcome relativization to particular historical or social circumstances. What it would not claim is that its domain—nature—is coextensive with the world or that it can, out of its own conceptual resources, explain the other modalities of existence on which it depends as conditions of the possibility of there being a world from which nature can be disengaged by the procedures already described.

III

The preceding discussion of understanding and interpretation has already implied at several points that *Dasein* makes use of language in the exercise of these functions. Just because the latter are so readily construed as linguistic in character, it is important to emphasize that in Heidegger's view they cannot simply be subsumed under linguistic activity; and in this connection, the largely tacit character of much of our knowing how, as distinct from our knowing that, offers confirmation of

Heidegger's point. But now that that point has been made, it is time to consider the positive role of language in Heidegger's account of understanding and interpretation and, more generally, of being-in-the-world. The use of the word "positive" may be somewhat misleading here since a considerable part of what Heidegger has to say about language in *Being and Time* concerns the multiple ways in which language and discourse lend themselves to inauthentic modes of personal existence and, as in the case of the philosophical concept of truth, suggest a profoundly misleading model of truth as the correspondence of a judgment to a state of affairs. Nevertheless, discourse, together with understanding and *Befindlichkeit*, is one of the fundamental ontological features of *Dasein* and as such, must receive close attention.[43]

There is also a special reason, growing out of the contemporary philosophical situation, why Heidegger's treatment of language deserves scrutiny. Much current philosophy characterizes itself as "linguistic," and it focuses its inquiries on the specifically logical structure of the concepts that are deployed in the different modes of language use. As a result of this intense concentration on the linguistic/logical articulation of what are sometimes called our "conceptual instruments," the traditional issues of metaphysics are frequently dealt with only to the extent that they lend themselves to formulation as issues about the kind of language we use or should ideally use. This has often meant that ontological issues are treated as being linguistic, in the sense of having to do with the kinds of entities that a given language permits us to refer to. It can even be argued that language has replaced the Cartesian *cogito* as the subject that is set over against the world and that constitutes the distinctive concern of philosophy, while science is assigned responsibility for the world. (One peculiarity of such a subject is that it is nonindividual and nonpersonal; in these respects, it has certain points of resemblance to Heidegger's later conception of language, as will be shown in chapter 8.) But whatever advantages this mode of philosophizing can claim, there can be little doubt that it has some quite significant disadvantages. One of these is that we become so accustomed to treating language as a quasi-transcendental correlate of the world that we forget that it is very much *in* the world. More specifically, through an effective separation of language from its users and their distinctive mode of being in the world, all questions about the ontological status of language itself may be elided and even never raised at all. Thus it is not at all uncommon to find linguistic philosophers holding that there is no difficulty or incongruity in combining a purely psychological and even physicalistic theory of the "verbal behavior" of human beings as language-users with a very abstruse conception of language as the medium within which the logical articulation of our conceptual schemes—our most general maps of reality—takes place. Accordingly, ontological issues are treated as having to do with the kinds of concepts that are to be admitted to a language, but language and language use are not seen as raising any interesting ontological issues at all. It is precisely this ontologically unproblematic status of language itself that Heidegger challenges.[44] If he is right, we would have to recognize that the "existence" of language is not compatible with all ontologies and that, in treating language as a given, we are presupposing (and thus failing to lift up into explicit philosophical scrutiny) much that has important implications for the kind of ontology that we are to adopt.

It has been shown in earlier chapters that assigning the subject a transcendental status, either explicitly or implicitly, results in a high degree of ontological indeterminacy, since it becomes unclear what entity *in* the world can be identified with that subject, even though some such identity continues to be presupposed. Something very similar seems to occur when this transcendental subject is conceived in linguistic terms. The psychological character of older theories of the subject then yields to the logical properties and functions of language; and it is in terms of the latter that the business of cognition and, generally, of reason is analyzed.[45] It is thus sentences that imply and expressions that refer; and the exploration of these logical powers of words goes forward as a distinct form of inquiry, to which it has even been suggested that the name "linguistic phenomenology" might be given. It is consistent with such a description that a strict line of demarcation is drawn between this logical characterization of language and both its psychological and its phonetic and physiological aspects. This distinction in turn supports the claim to independence from empirical considerations that is made for the conceptual truths that are supposed to issue from the former kind of inquiry. But, as typically happens in transcendental contexts, it never becomes clear how the only entities that the empirical study of language can turn up—sounds and inscriptions—can possibly have the specifically logical powers or discharge the specifically logical functions that the theory would assign to them. The situation is the more difficult inasmuch as such theories typically have no recourse to a "mind" whose "acts" might somehow mediate—whether successfully or not is another question—the radical disparity between an empirical description of the entities out of which language is constituted and the logical functions which some entities, after all, must carry out. But because the postulate of the independence of logical properties of language is so strongly held, this unmediated contrast is not perceived as an ontological problem. It may even be treated in linguistic terms itself and declared to consist simply in the difference between two kinds of "story" told from the standpoint of different kinds of interests, both of which are perfectly legitimate and the discrepancy between which need raise no perplexing ontological questions.

The notion that logical distinctions need not raise any ontological issues is one that is quite naturally associated with an insistence that the concept of the world must be understood in such a way as to deny it any logical or propositional characteristics of the kind that would accrue to it, for example, if it were an aggregate of facts rather than things. Although Heidegger also understands the world as a totality of entities rather than facts, it is a totality of *present* entities; and it is accordingly impossible on his view to draw this kind of distinction between the world, on the one hand, and significance (*Bedeutsamkeit*) and the as-structure of entities, on the other. The articulation that characterizes the world by virtue of the instrumentality of *zuhanden* entities is not itself propositional; but it supplies the indispensable basis for interpretation and assertion, and thus for the eventual emergence, under the influence of theoretical interests, of "facts" or "states of affairs" that are the worldly counterparts of the logical structures of assertion. It is hardly surprising that Heidegger should reject the conception of philosophy that builds on this distinction between the world and the logical; but he does more than simply reject it. He also tries to understand and interpret it in terms of what he regards as the deepest tendencies at work in the course of the history of Western philosophy. Chapter 9 will present these analyses. Here, in connection with Heidegger's treatment of language, it will suffice to point out that both logic and the conception of philosophy as logic rest on a certain understanding of the *logos* itself (and thus of the word and speech), of which "logic" is supposed to be the science. This understanding is one that assimilates words to the status of things—whether these are mental or physical things makes little difference—and thereby renders what comes to be thought of as their "relationship" to the world an insoluble puzzle.

That this is the case can be shown by a consideration of the semantic aspect of language—the aspect in which words have meaning and, by virtue of that meaning, stand for things in the world.[46] That words stand for things is the implicit understanding on which all thinking about language, whether sophisticated or naive, proceeds; but precisely because this presupposition is so fundamental, we are unlikely to spend much time or effort trying to define the character of the relationship between language and world. When we do turn to this relationship, it is likely that we will try to interpret it in terms of some model made available to us by the standard, usually quite uncritically espoused ontology of the subject. This is what happens when the language-world relationship is treated as being mediated by mental representations along the lines laid down in the two-substance ontology discussed in chapter 1. In light of the perplexing isolation from the world of the entities called "representations," there was never any possibility that they could effect the mediation of the word-world relationship that is required when words are initially conceived as *vorhanden*—that is, as objects of a particular kind. These difficulties have contributed to a disposition—widespread at the present time—to interpret that relationship in terms of a special concept of reference that dispenses altogether with any subjective or, for that matter, cognitive form of mediation.[47] On this view, not all words are to be interpreted as standing for something in the world, but those that do are said to "refer" to something. Thus, if I say that the cat is on the mat, the expression "the cat" purports to stand for something in the world. The central thesis of this theory is the claim that such an expression refers just in case there is a cat on the mat. The existence of the object in question is thus the only condition that must be satisfied; and to speak of the semantic aspect of language is simply to invoke this condition. The relationship of language to the world is thus simply a matter of its being the case that a certain expression occurs in some use of language *and* its also being the case that the object denoted by that expression exists. In effect, the referring expression and the object to which it refers are treated as entities that are side by side within the world in a way that makes it very hard to see in what sense the former can refer to the latter. Certainly the expression—the word-thing—that is said to do the referring is not described in any way that implies that either the word itself or anything connected with the production of that word *has* a world, as distinct from merely occurring within the world. To all intents and purposes, it is as self-contained and as little in need of any other entity in order to be just the entity that it is as is the object to which it is said to refer or, for that matter, any other entity that happens to be within the world. When words and sentences are treated this way, there is nothing to betray the fact that there is a world for them to be "about." All traces of asymmetry in the relationship between word and object have disappeared; and as a result, there is no sense in which the latter could be said to exist *for* the former or *for* the entity that utters it.

Such an absolutization of reference is not only profoundly mysterious; it is also made possible only through an artificially maintained obliviousness to other elements in such situations, most notably the role of the persons who declare that an expression in fact refers to something. Whether they acknowledge it or not, there is a conspicuous difference between their assertion of the fact that an expression used by someone else successfully refers and that prior act of reference as they conceive it. On their view, the latter is simply a speech-act on the part of the individual in question; as such, it stands by itself and leaves completely open the question of whether the entity referred to in fact exists. If someone else then says that the first act refers successfully and that the entity in question exists, this assertion can hardly be regarded by the person who makes it as simply a "world-less" item of reality that now stands side by side with the "referring" expression of the first speaker and the object to which it supposedly referred, and that remains as closed in its own mode of being to both the one and the other as they are, on this mode of conceptualization, to one another. It is surely implicit in any statement about a prior reference that the expression in question and the object it denotes exist *for* the person who is making the statement and that their doing so is intimately bound up with the making of that statement. The latter must therefore share the mode of being of the person who makes it as the kind of entity that *has* a world. But if this holds for the expressions that refer to the first act of reference and its object, why should it not also hold for that first reference and indeed *all* references? Once again one suspects that, as in the case of the Russell paradox, there is a tendency for the person who acts as umpire for other people's references to slide without acknowledgment into a transcendental role—that is, into the position of a subject for which the world is tenselessly and exhaustively given. Once such a perspective is available, it becomes possible to demote the other person's references (and even one's own) to the status assigned to them by this conception of reference, because there is built into the theory itself just such a transcendental perspective on the world, and because, as an adherent of the theory, one thus gets back what was sacrificed by the application of the theory to oneself as well as others. What one gets back is the status of being a perspective on the world, not just an entity or an event within it, and one gets it back purified of all the susceptibility to error that is its unavoidable accompaniment in the nontranscendental form that was sacrificed. Admittedly, this transcendental perspective is available only in principle; and it cannot be invoked to settle specific questions of truth and falsity. Even so, it would appear that the adherents of this theory are more than satisfied with the exchange and, in their private reflections on these matters, do not insist unduly on this limitation.

If what has been said so far seems to suggest that Heidegger's treatment of language can have nothing in common with contemporary linguistic philosophy, that would misrepresent the true state of affairs. There have, after all, been significant divisions within linguistic philosophy itself, and disagreements about the importance of the pragmatic dimension of language—the relationship in which it stands to its user—have been especially notable. In the eyes of those who first worked out the idea of a rigorously linguistic philosophy, the pragmatic aspect of

language was of interest only to empirical psychology. Since it was assumed that the language of interest to a philosopher must be a perfected
language of science, the pragmatic features that characterize actual language use were viewed as candidates for elimination. It was regarded
as axiomatic that such a language must be able to describe its object in
a manner that is wholly independent of everything that has to do with
the situation and special characteristics of those who construct the description; what is said about it must be detachable in principle from both
the saying of it and the sayer. Against this view, there developed, mainly
under Wittgensteinian auspices, a disposition to question the distinction
between what is said and the saying of it and to treat the speech-act itself
and the circumstances in which it is performed as important features of
language as the object of philosophical analysis. From this standpoint,
the abstraction of what is said from the context of its being said by
someone, although it may have a certain limited kind of usefulness, gives
a profoundly false picture of language to the extent that, as typically
happens, the fact and the character of that act of abstraction are not
included in it. Consistent with this interest in the pragmatic dimension
of language, this approach to language puts great emphasis on the variety
of language uses and what it calls "language-games" and resists all attempts to discount this variety in favor of some standardized model of
fact-stating discourse of the kind best exemplified in the exact sciences.

With all this, Heidegger may be said to be in agreement, although
his own enunciation of comparable antireductionistic theses predates
those of Anglo-American linguistic philosophy by many years. In *Being
and Time* this attitude is already quite explicit:

> Between interpretation that is still completely enveloped in concernful un-
> derstanding and the extreme counter-instance of a theoretical assertion about
> something present-at-hand, there are many intermediate steps. Assertions
> about occurrences in the surrounding world (*Umwelt*), descriptions of what
> is ready-to-hand, "situation reports," the noting and ascertaining of the facts
> of a case, the description of a state of affairs, the narration of something that
> has taken place. These "sentences" do not admit of reduction to theoretical
> statements without an essential perversion of their meaning.[48]

The emphasis here falls equally on the irreducible variety of language
uses and the act-character that attaches to all of them. It is hardly surprising, therefore, that Heidegger holds discourse to be the act that
founds language, which is therefore essentially bound to the speaker
and qualified by the situation of the latter in a way that cannot be suppressed or eliminated.[49] When it comes to the terms in which that situation is to be conceived, however, a gap opens up between current
speech-act theory and the Heideggerian philosophy of language, a gap

that is almost as wide as that between the latter and the earlier positivistic philosophy of language. For the speech-act theorist, the situation presupposed by a speech-act such as that of promising is one that can be described by familiar empirical means and comprises such facts as that the parties to the promise have certain kinds of knowledge and certain intentions. It seems fair to say that sets of conditions like these are, at least in intention, ontologically neutral, in that they do not specify what kind of entity the speaker is or must be. Heidegger's account of discourse, by contrast, is much more general in character, and it is explicitly ontological in its account of the situation that discourse presupposes. That situation is quite simply the one rendered by the phrase "being-in-the-world." What needs explaining here is why discourse presupposes and requires a speaker that is an entity of the *Dasein* type, to whom a world is disclosed, and also why it is that language is possible only when there is a disclosure of the world and how language as discourse is itself a modality of that disclosure.

Heidegger distinguishes four features that characterize speech.[50] Speech is about something; it says something about that something; it communicates what it says; and it manifests (*bekundet*) the state of the speaker. Of these, the first two are of primary importance in the uncovering function of discourse; and of these the "aboutness" feature of speech—its *Worüber*—must be taken up first. It has already been shown that this "aboutness" cannot be explained simply in terms of the coexistence of the entity in question and the word for it as used in some speech-act—which, by the way, need not be of the fact-stating type. That entity must not only exist; it must also be present to the speaker in one of the modalities of presence that have been described in earlier chapters. It has also been established that it can be present only because it has been uncovered (*enthüllt*); but it is not so uncovered in a primary way by discourse itself.[51] Typically, the entity about which we say something is one with which we have a prior familiarity in contexts of perception and use, so a pre-linguistic meaning is already involved in our relationship to it. It is something to lift or burn or break in half, and it has already been disclosed to us as such. But if discourse is not the primary mode of uncovering an entity, it may, nevertheless, as the discourse of the entity—*Dasein*—that does so uncover it, be said to appropriate that uncovering; it thus has the character of an *apophansis*, a showing forth (*Aufzeigung*) of what it is about.[52] In other words, it is not as though words came first and meanings were then attached to them; rather, there are pre-linguistic meanings for entities that have been uncovered, and to these meanings words are then attached. But in appropriating this uncovering of an entity, discourse also makes its own contribution to it. It does so by effecting an explicit articulation of the entity that has been uncovered. In declarative discourse, this articulation takes the form of predication, as when we say "The chalk is too hard." Such articulation itself presupposes a context of use—in this case, my writing with the chalk—in which the entity in question serves a purpose (its *Worumwillen*) that in some sense lies beyond its physical limits. Heidegger uses the Platonic concept of *diairesis* to characterize this "dividing" of an entity by the introduction of a distinction between the entity as such and the predicate that expresses its way of functioning.[53] But at the same time that discourse divides the entity in this way, it also unites it with itself in a synthesis corresponding to the *diairesis* already effected. The resulting proposition thus expresses not just a logical unity—a collocation of concepts—but an articulated uncovering of the status of the entity in question as an entity within the world of *Dasein*.

It is the copula—the *is* of predication—that, in Heidegger's view, expresses this ontological function of speech as the articulating showing forth of the entity that it is about.[54] Instead of being simply a device for connecting two concepts with one another, the verb "to be" expresses the uncoveredness of the entity about which the statement in which the "is" appears is made. Thus what it expresses is not just the existence of that entity in the ordinary sense of that term, although it does that too, but also its presence. "The 'is' gives itself as an expression of being," Heidegger tells us; and it is thus evident once again that he equates being with the presence of an entity—that is, its status as uncovered.[55] Saying that something is something does not *make* it the case that the entity in question is uncovered, since that is brought about by *Dasein* as such, independently of any linguistic powers it possesses. Nevertheless, if the "is" itself and discourse in general do not have a performative character, they can be said to express the performative character of the *Dasein* that enunciates that "is" and that has already by its existence brought about the presence that is being declared. As Heidegger puts it, "In an assertion about something the understanding of being must necessarily express itself in which the *Dasein* that asserts— that is, shows forth—already exists as such."[56] The full complexity of Heidegger's use of the notion of being here will be explored in the next chapter. What is already clear, however, is that language as discourse is ontological in a double sense: first, in that it is constitutive of the being of *Dasein* as the entity whose existence effects presence, and, second, as expressing the understanding that *Dasein* has of the being of the entities that it uncovers. It is also becoming clear that the distinctive Heideggerian concept of being will not be identifiable with either of the uses to which the term was put in the preceding sentence, but will involve both in an essential way.

A clue to the form that this concept of being will assume is offered by what Heidegger says about the close affinity between being and truth in the context of this same discussion of speech as an existential of *Dasein*.[57] It has traditionally been supposed that the primary application of the concept of truth is precisely to assertions—that is, to something that is said. Since for Heidegger, assertions are not uncovering in a primary way, we may guess that they are not for him the primary bearers of truth either. What is "true" in the primary sense is the entity—*Dasein*—whose existence is a necessary condition for the uncoveredness of entities; and, in a secondary and derived sense, "true" applies to those entities themselves as so uncovered.[58] In this secondary sense, therefore, being true is simply being uncovered, and Heidegger goes so far as to say that the "is" is always also an "is true."[59] This will surprise many; but it should be understood that it does not mean that every assertion is true in the sense of being "suited to its subject matter" (*sachangemessen*).[60] "Being true," as Heidegger uses the term, is rather to be understood as being in a domain in which truth and falsity in their usual senses are the two possibilities in terms of which one's commerce with the world is defined.[61] That domain, of course, is the one that *Dasein* constitutes as the entity that realizes the presence of entities. It follows that if there were no *Dasein*, there would be no truth, but this means that there would be no falsity either; so it is inappropriate to interpret Heidegger's concept of truth as "relativistic." He is not saying that when *Dasein* exists and there is, accordingly, such a thing as truth, things are as they are rather than some other way, because they are made so by being uncovered.[62] If there were no *Dasein*, things might be just as we have supposed them to be; but it would not be true or false that they are so.[63] Because of this linkage between truth and *Dasein*, Heidegger is prepared to say that "truth exists" in the same sense of "exist" that applies to *Dasein*; and he speaks of truth in the same way that he speaks of *Dasein* as being "between subject and object in their usual superficial senses."[64] Heidegger has thus worked out a sense of "true" that is both quite different from the usual sense and a necessary condition for use of the latter; and this may lead us to expect that he will do something similar in the case of "being." We are strengthened in that expectation by the fact that he extends the same usage of "exist" to being itself and is willing to say that "being exists."[65]

The reference to conventional theories of truth offers an opportunity to notice a special liability that attaches to language generally as in some sense the product of discourse (*die Hinausgesprochenheit der Rede*).[66] The guiding consideration here is that, although speech is not uncovering in a primary way, it becomes, upon being uttered, a principal modality of uncovering for its hearers, who will often not have had any "original experience" of the entities to which it refers. The assertion itself which, as Heidegger says, "preserves the uncoveredness" of the entity that it is about has itself the mode of being of the *zuhanden*; and this is to say that its being is derivative from that of *Dasein*, which is, in a primary sense, uncovering.[67] What happens is that, in spite of this derivative status and in spite of the fact that assertion is not uncovering in a primary way, it displaces *Dasein* in this function and appropriates to itself the latter's mode of being toward the entities that have been uncovered. Thus it comes to be understood as having in its own right a relation (*Bezug*) to the entity that is uncovered, a relation that is treated as one between two entities both of which are within the world. This, of course, is the relation of agreement or correspondence in terms of which truth comes to be interpreted; and with this conception of truth as a relation that simply holds or is *vorhanden* between two entities within the world, the mode of being of *Dasein* as uncovering is assimilated to that of these entities and the relation in which they are held to stand to one another. It is in this way that discourse as what is said (*das Geredete*) takes on a kind of anonymous and public mode of being, thereby lending itself to an interpretation of the uncovering function that obscures the special ontological character of *Dasein*.[68] The paradoxical consequence of this assimilation of the mode of being of language to that of word-things is that language, which is dependent on the uncoveredness of entities, becomes a principal modality of the obscuration of that very uncoveredness.

It has already been noted that for Heidegger discourse and language are essentially communicative. That communication is a function of the *Mitsein* that also characterizes the way of being in the world of *Dasein*. As Heidegger puts it, "that a *Dasein* by expressing itself communicates (itself) to others means that by showing something forth in an assertion it shares with the other *Dasein*s the same understanding relationship (*Verhältnis*) to the entity about which the assertion is made."[69] It is in keeping with this emphasis on communication that he should treat "hearing" as "constitutive for speech" and "listening to" as "the existential openness of *Dasein* as *Mitsein* for the other."[70] At the same time, however, it is just these communicative modalities of *Dasein*'s being that are most susceptible to the kind of distortion that results from the reification of language just described. What happens, it seems, is that "what is said" displaces the entities that speech uncovers, so that communication ceases to "impart the primary ontological relationship to these entities."[71] It becomes mere talk (*das Gerede*) in which "things are so because one says so." The result is "to pervert the act of uncovering into an act of closing off," because mere talk systematically avoids going back to the ground of what is talked about.[72] The reason for this perversion of language is not wholly clear; but Heidegger connects it with the acceptance for purposes of communication of what he calls the "average intelligibility." This presumably includes the kind of accommodation to intersubjective criteria of reference and identification that is a necessary condition for shared understanding; but in light of his strong affirmation of the commonness that characterizes our being with one another in the world, he can hardly mean that this is in itself objectionable. Perhaps it would be better to say that such accommodation is hazardous, since it can take on a life of its own and evolve in the way Heidegger describes. This is an important point because, if what Heidegger says about average intelligibility is not interpreted in a way that makes it compatible with his conception of commonness, it would follow that all forms of social life are doomed to inauthenticity. It is true that Heidegger holds that in poetry a modality of language in which the world can become "visible for those who are blind" is preserved.[73] But poetry is not a solitary activity; and if it does not accept the conditions laid down by the average intelligibility, this is not because it abandons commonness or *Mitsein* in favor of a wholly private mode of access to the world. Whether Heidegger thinks that the language of our public life can ever be poetic in this sense, or that this has ever been the case, even in ancient Greece, is unfortunately quite unclear.

CHAPTER SIX • THE CONCEPT OF BEING

The account of Heidegger's ontology of the subject is now complete in its essentials. It may well be asked, however, how this is possible when the text on which this account is principally based—*Being and Time*—is notoriously incomplete. What we have is only about one-third of the projected work, since Heidegger intended to add a section entitled "Time and Being" to the two sections of part I that were published; and the projected part II was to contain sections on Kant, Descartes, and Aristotle that together would have constituted a "phenomenological destruction of the history of ontology."[1] Because these projected sections were never added, it has been widely thought that the book itself remains a fragment; and if it is that, then any claim that its line of argument is essentially complete must be suspect. More specifically, it is generally held that the position developed in the portions of *Being and Time* that we have can hardly be complete, because the concept of being as such is not characterized in those portions, although it is the goal of Heidegger's inquiry in that book. In the light of all this, the claim advanced in the first sentence of this chapter must seem to invite a prompt and crushing refutation.

But, strong as this argument for the incomplete and therefore indeterminate status of the position that Heidegger develops in *Being and Time* may seem, there are weighty considerations that speak against it. First, major studies of the themes of what was to have been part II were published independently by Heidegger, most notably in his *Kant and the Problem of Metaphysics*. Moreover, with the publication of his lectures from the period of *Being and Time*, especially *The Basic Problems of Phenomenology*, the line of thought that he evidently intended to follow in the section on "Time and Being" has been set forth; it is also possible to gather, from these lectures and others, how he understood the concept of being as such. At various points in the preceding chapters, attention has been drawn to features of this emerging account of being; and special emphasis has been placed on the account of temporality as a necessary condition for the understanding of being that is presented in *The Basic*

Problems of Phenomenology, where, it should be noted, the account of Aristotle's theory of time clearly anticipates the treatment of it that was planned for part II of *Being and Time*.[2] It is time now to pull together all these observations so as to define the special character of this concept of being and to show what its relationship is to the ontological conception of the subject as *Dasein* that has been set forth in earlier chapters. To this end it will be useful to begin with an examination of what Heidegger tells us about being as such in *Being and Time*, especially in the opening sections in which the central importance of the question of being is set forth.

I

The opening words of *Being and Time* are a quotation from Plato's *Sophist*; they speak of what is meant by the word "being" (*on*) and raise the question of whether this is really understood.[3] Heidegger adds that this question has fallen into neglect since the time of the Greeks, and that it is his intention to revive it and to ask once again what the "meaning of being" (*der Sinn von Sein*) really is. We have, he says, a certain understanding of being that is manifested in our use of the verb "to be"; but this understanding is of a "vague" and "average" kind, and it is the task of the philosopher to raise it to the level of an explicit concept. Heidegger then proceeds to review a number of objections that are typically made to such an attempt, such as the claim that being is the most general concept there is and must therefore be indefinable, since there is no further concept in terms of which it might be defined. But the assumption on which these objections rest—that is, that being is a *summum genus*—is itself unexamined and in need of careful scrutiny. It must not, therefore, be allowed to block an inquiry into the meaning of the term "being" itself.

In the discussion that follows, Heidegger makes three principal claims about the meaning of "being": first, that being is always "the being of entities" and "that which determines entities as entities";[4] second, that being itself is not an entity; and third, that an inquiry into the meaning of being must take a certain kind of entity as its point of departure and as a clue to what being as such is.[5] Whether these three claims can be reconciled with one another and together be made to yield a single, univocal meaning of being may well be questioned. The first links the concepts of being and entity to one another by making being that which "determines entities as entities"; and this would naturally be taken to mean that being is a property of entities, presumably an essential one. But the second claim calls any such inference into question, since Heidegger makes it clear not only that being is not itself an entity, but also that it is not a property or an attribute of entities. The sense in which being is always the being *of* entities is thus rendered problematic. The third claim makes this emphatic contrast between being and entities ambiguous, however, by postulating a special affinity of some kind between being as such and one kind of entity. Overall, it looks very much as if Heidegger wants to distinguish the concept of being very sharply from that of an entity and yet at the same time to associate these concepts with one another. This might well be possible if the term "being" were assigned two senses—one in which it is closely linked to the concept of entity in some more or less familiar way, and another in which it is not so linked. Heidegger certainly does not say that this is what he is doing; but it may well turn out that this is the only way in which his readers can construe all the things he says so as to make them consistent with one another.

To begin with his first thesis, it is important to see that the notion of "determining entities as entities" is itself ambiguous. It would be natural to take it to mean that being is that which makes entities entities, as would be the case if being were an essential property of entities. If Heidegger does not regard being in the sense in which he is interested as a property of entities, however, it is unlikely that he would construe "determining entities as entities" this way. That expression could alternatively be taken to mean something like "assigning the character of entities to entities." The difference between these two construals is that in the first, being must *always* characterize entities if they are to be entities at all, whereas in the second, being is associated not with making entities entities, but rather with something like *taking* them as entities. This last conception obviously has a close affinity with the notion that we have already encountered of entities showing themselves *as* entities; so there may be an antecedent probability that this is the way Heidegger understands the phrase "determining entities as entities." If that is the case, then the thesis that being is the being of entities would have to be similarly construed. This means that being would not be a property or attribute that entities always and necessarily possess, but rather that, since being is a matter of entities being determined or showing themselves as entities, there can be no being without entities. But this, unlike the first construal, would not rule out the possibility that there could be entities without being.

If we understand the first thesis in some such way as this, then a great deal of what Heidegger says by way of explicating it falls into place as his way of distinguishing the sense of being in which he is interested. As we have already seen, he is strongly opposed to a conception of being as a genus—a *summum genus*, of course—and this is precisely the conception that is implied by the claim that being is a property of entities.[6]

Any such attempt to interpret being as a property of entities, either in terms of some conception of essence or in terms of existence as a "real predicate," must come up against the fact that Heidegger rejects the distinction between being as essence and being as existence as logically posterior to the meaning of being he is attempting to articulate. Being cannot be identified with the What of essence that contrasts with the That of existence, nor the other way around; it "lies in the fact that something is *and* in its being as it is" (emphasis added).[7] With these approaches to being declared irrelevant to Heidegger's inquiry, it is evident that the ontology he is attempting to construct will not be general in the sense of distilling a universal concept of being from regional forms of being—that is, from the many different kinds of entities, such as numbers, persons, theoretical objects, sense-data, and material objects—that are said to exist. There is, it is true, a brief discussion in the introduction to *Being and Time* of the relevance of ontological issues to foundational questions in mathematics and biology and other domains of inquiry; but there is nothing to indicate that Heidegger has any real interest in the full range of entities that a general ontology of the kind I am characterizing here would have to take into consideration.[8] Instead, he begins part I of *Being and Time* with the undefended assertion that "any entity is either a 'who' or a 'what'," thus vastly simplifying the full complexity with which a general ontology in the stipulated sense would have to deal by bringing together under the rubric of the "What" a great many different types of entity.[9] He then proceeds to concentrate on the second kind of entity, the one that has the character of the Who; and the sense of being in general that is supposed to be common to the Who and the What receives no attention, although it is surely being in this sense that makes any and all entities just that—entities. Most readers of *Being and Time* have probably assumed that being as such is this being that is common to all kinds of entities, but in this they are mistaken.[10] The discussion of the second and third claims cited above will show that this cannot be the case, because the concept of being that emerges from *Being and Time* is not the concept of being as that which makes entities entities.

According to Heidegger's second thesis, being itself is not an entity. This means, in the first instance, that it is not to be understood as a kind of super-entity like God, an entity whose essence includes and entails its existence and that confers being on lesser entities for which this is not the case. This way of interpreting being has long been established in the Christian tradition, but its confusion of being with an exceptional or unique entity is profoundly mistaken nonetheless. Being is not, in other words, *any* sort of particular; it is not susceptible of plurality and is characterized rather by unity and singularity.[11] At the same time, it is not an *abstract* entity, as these contrasts with particularity and plurality might lead one to think. Because such abstract entities, in the Platonic formulation, are outside time, they are not subject to change and can therefore be constantly present to the appropriate form of rational intuition as the changing objects of the senses cannot; but this, too, in Heidegger's eyes, is just another way of trying to postulate a super-entity and not a satisfactory way of characterizing being as such. Permanence or timelessness does not suffice to transform any entity into being as such; and, as has become evident in preceding chapters, the latter as Heidegger conceives it is not in fact atemporal at all.

Ordinarily, to say of something that it is not an entity would be to say that it does not exist at all because, other than entities, there would be nothing left for it to be. In Heidegger's terminology, however, that conclusion does not quite follow. There is a precedent in *Being and Time* itself for this notion of something that is not an entity but does not, therefore, simply not exist. This is true of the world, which, Heidegger tells us, contains entities but is not itself an entity, as we saw in chapter 2. Since the worldliness of the world is to be understood in terms of the presence of these entities, the one real clue we have to what is involved in existing otherwise than as an entity is one contained in the notion of presence. If being *exists*, as the world does, and, like the world, is not an entity, and if "being," in Heidegger's special sense of the term, is to be understood in terms of presence, then it is evident that the concepts of being and the world (or the worldliness of the world) are very closely related to one another. In a way, this is a paradoxical conclusion, because, if valid, it is puzzling, to say the least, that the concept of being to which the whole inquiry in *Being and Time* is directed should prove to coincide with the concept—that of the world—with which part I begins. Of this, more will be said later in this chapter. What needs to be pointed out here is that if being and the world are one, then being, like the world, will be dependent on the existence of *Dasein*, which is itself an entity. Not only will it make sense to say "Being exists," but it will also be true that being exists only if *Dasein* does. *Dasein*, of course, is an entity of a very special kind; but there is still the question of whether it is so special and so different from other entities that being can stand in such a relation of dependence to it without thereby taking on some of the characteristics of entities and, most notably, particularity and plurality.

Heidegger's third claim about being as such appears to be a resultant of the two preceding claims. This is the claim that, although being is not itself an entity, an inquiry into the meaning of being must take a certain kind of entity as both its point of departure and its clue to the nature of being as such. What exactly is entailed in making this sort of use of one kind of entity is by no means clear; and Heidegger gives no independent reason for supposing that this might be the right way to pursue this inquiry. As it turns out, the kind of entity that is declared to be uniquely suitable for serving in this capacity is the entity that is itself able to ask the question "What is the meaning of being?" Since we ourselves are the entities that ask that question, it is our mode of being in the sense of the kind of entities that we are that is to be the subject of the preliminary inquiry that will lead to Heidegger's answer to the question of being. Is it because we already have a certain understanding of being without which we could not ask the question of being that we have been chosen for this purpose? If that is the case, there is still no explanation of why this procedure is appropriate in the case of an inquiry into being, for it is obviously not the one we employ when we are inquiring into other matters of which we have some understanding that we want to refine conceptually—for example, the nature of motion. Since the analysis of *Dasein* as our own mode of being effectively takes up the whole of *Being and Time* as we have it, the presumption about being as the ultimate goal of this inquiry that guides this methodological decision on Heidegger's part is surely of the greatest importance, and yet one can hardly claim that it has been clarified at all, much less adequately.

It is only in Heidegger's further elaboration of the relationship between being and *Dasein* that the underlying reasons for the claim that a concept of being can be reached only through the analysis of *Dasein* as one kind of entity begin to emerge. If being were an attribute of entities, it would follow that, like the other attributes of entities, it would be something to which understanding or knowledge would address itself but which would obtain even in the absence of any such understanding. But that is not the way in which Heidegger speaks of being. He says, for example, that his inquiry into being is not intended to be "deep" (*tiefsinnig*) in the sense of trying to puzzle out "what stands behind being."[12] Instead, his inquiry "asks about being itself insofar as it enters into the intelligibility of *Dasein*." There are other statements to the same effect, such as that "being ... is dependent upon the understanding of being," and that "being 'is' only in the understanding of those entities to whose being something like an understanding of being belongs."[13] What is even more remarkable is that, as the concept of being becomes increasingly tied to that of understanding and of the entity that understands—*Dasein*—it is also being detached from the concept of entities (*Seiendes*). "Entities *are*, quite independently of the experience in which they are disclosed, the acquaintance in which they are discovered and the grasping in which their nature is ascertained."[14] This statement is part of an explicit contrast with being, which is then declared, in a sentence that has already been quoted, to be "only in the understanding of those entities to whose being something like an understanding of being belongs." Ordinarily, the concepts of being and of entity—both of them nominalizations of the verb "to be"—are linked with one another in such a way that anything that *is*—any entity—would also be said to have being as that by virtue of which it is an entity at all. What Heidegger is doing in linking his concept of being to understanding and hence to *Dasein* is breaking its linkage with the concept of entity. The result is expressed in the following passage: "Of course only as long as *Dasein is* (that is, only as long as an understanding of Being is ontically possible), 'is there' Being. When *Dasein* does not exist, 'independence' 'is' not either, nor 'is' the 'in-itself.'...*In such a case* it cannot be said that entities are, nor can it be said that they are not... Being (not entities) is dependent upon the understanding of Being."[15]

It will be apparent that this characterization of being has strong affinities with others, already cited, that construe being in terms of the presence or self-manifesting of entities as entities. That this is a revisionary use of the concept of being seems beyond dispute, although it does not follow that it is without philosophical precedents. It does appear, however, that even if this construal of the concept of being proves to be justifiable, those who, like Heidegger, use it in this way must use it in an implicit pairing with a concept of being that is *not* tied to understanding or to *Dasein* and is in fact applicable to anything that can be described as an entity. After all, if entities show themselves as entities, they are showing themselves precisely as something that *is*; and even if we insist with Heidegger that their presence be characterized as "being" in a special sense of that term, it in no way follows that the first "is" must be contingent on, much less identical with, the second "is" of presence. This is what Heidegger's statement above appears to require; but elsewhere he seems just as plainly to be making use of the verb "to be" in a way that would be outlawed if the implied interdiction on its use were taken seriously. In one passage, which has already been cited, Heidegger states that "entities *are*, quite independently of the experience in which they are disclosed," since it can hardly be supposed that the concept of being is separable from the verb "to be." Equally significant and even more explicit is a passage in which, in the course of his discussion of Newton's laws, Heidegger states that even if these laws were neither true nor false before Newton discovered them, this does not mean "that before him there were no such entities as have been uncovered and pointed out by those laws."[16] In other passages he makes a sharp distinction between questions about *Dasein*'s existence as its characteristic mode of being and the question of whether there are any such entities or not; and the latter question manifestly invokes a sense of existence that is the same as the one contained in the reference to the physical entities with which Newton's laws are concerned.[17] The conclusion to which all this points is that, in practice, Heidegger himself recognizes a connection between the concept of "entity" and that of "is" and thus of being as that concept is ordinarily understood. It also follows that when he speaks of being as such in his special sense of the term, we ought to understand this to mean "the presence to or being for *Dasein* of entities as that which is or exists." This is to say that there are *two* concepts of being—one familiar and the other new, at least as a concept— at work in typical Heideggerian uses of this term. The first is pretty much taken for granted; the second is the one on which he focuses attention, and for which the term itself is officially reserved.

II

Because Heidegger's concept of being is a revisionary concept, it must not be identified with any prior concept associated with the term; and yet it is predicated on just such a prior use, in which "being" and "entity" and the verb "to be" are all indissolubly linked to one another. In attempting to characterize this new concept further, we must rely less on contrasts with prior uses and more on positive affinities with other concepts to which Heidegger draws attention. Of these, none is more important than the relationship between being and truth, which Heidegger strongly emphasizes but unfortunately does not develop very far. In a passage that is especially significant because it mediates the relationship of being and truth through the concept of *Dasein*, Heidegger seems almost to equate being with truth. "Being (not entities) is something which 'there is' only in so far as truth is. And truth *is* insofar and so long as *Dasein* is. Being and truth 'are' equiprimordially."[18] The question that must accordingly be asked is just what this affinity, if not identity, of being with truth really amounts to.

In a lecture series devoted to "the question about truth," Heidegger examined in detail the Aristotelian conception of being as truth which appears to have strongly influenced his own thinking on this point.[19] This discussion, which builds on an analysis of the *logos* as assertion along the lines of the account given in the last chapter, centers on the issue of how it is possible for an assertion to be false; and it does so in the interest of an understanding of how an assertion can be true. The details of Heidegger's interpretation of Aristotle are too complex to go into here. What emerges from it is the point that, according to Heidegger, the possibility of falsehood depends on our being "in touch" with the world, at least in the mode of the simple presence of something that may as yet be unidentified.[20] When we perceive this something *as* an object of some definite sort, this identification involves a complex network of temporal references. These go forward to possible events that could be expected if, to use Heidegger's example, the thing encountered in the forest is indeed a doe and back to our first encounter with it when it proves to be just a bush. The structure of these temporal references—what Heidegger calls their "phenomenological chronology"—is essential to the possibility of both falsity and truth. A present that lacked such a referential structure and the comparisons and contrasts that it makes possible would not be susceptible of being true or of containing an assertion that could be true in any sense that applies to all these temporally distinct "experiences." Similarly, the form of presence that would go with such a mutilated present would have been deprived of just those dimensions of possibility that are needed in order to qualify it as the presence of just this or that entity. The structure of the temporal references that are necessary for the truth (or falsity) of an assertion are thus the same as those in terms of which the presence of the entity about which the assertion is made constitutes itself. It is these shared structures of temporality that, in Heidegger's view, justify treating truth as "the most authentic" sense of being when the latter is understood as presence.[21]

These considerations should make it possible to understand a little more clearly the organization of *Being and Time* and the movement from the analysis of *Dasein* to time as temporality and then to being as such on which that organization turns. This sequence is discussed in the same series of lectures, although in somewhat more Kantian terminology.[22] There it is a question of how the "I think" is related to time, and this question is asked against the background of the Kantian assumption that the "I think" is nontemporal in character and that its thoughts receive a temporal interpretation only through the schemata of the transcendental imagination. This fiction is maintained to some degree in *Being and Time* itself; for it begins with an analysis of *Dasein*—the existing subject and thus the "I think"—in which the element of temporality remains largely implicit. The primary characteristic of the "I think" is spontaneity; and in the Kantian scheme the defect of this pure spontaneity is that it cannot by itself produce substantive knowledge. Translation of the forms of judgment of the nontemporal "I think" into temporal schemata makes it possible for the latter to *receive* the content that it must have if it is to achieve real knowledge. Spontaneity thus has to be counterbalanced by receptivity, which turns out to be essentially bound up with time. Heidegger also interprets time in terms of receptivity; but, unlike Kant, he wants to show that the linkage of spontaneity and receptivity—of the "I think" and time—characterizes the "I think" as such and is not just a necessary condition for the achievement of nonanalytic knowledge by the "I think." Not only does he want to deny that the "I think" is outside time in the Kantian sense; he also wants to deny that it is *in* time in the manner of an object like a planet or a streetcar. For the "I think" *is* time in the mode of temporality; and it is as a consequence of this that it is characterized by receptivity. When the implications of this receptivity are understood, they must substantially qualify our first understanding of *Dasein* which, as we have noted, is largely in terms of its spontaneity.

It is, nevertheless, true that the second section of part I of *Being and Time*, "*Dasein* and Temporality," does not convey any strong sense of the modification that the concept of *Dasein* undergoes with the explicit introduction of temporality. Instead, it is as though temporality were being assimilated to the spontaneity of the functions of *Dasein* described in part I. It may be that the rhetorical momentum of the first section of part I was too strong to permit the treatment of time to serve as the hinge of Heidegger's argument that it was to have been through its position in the plan of part I as a whole. If so, this is presumably because Heidegger's primary concern in the second section is to explore the sense in which *Dasein* can be said to form a whole and more specifically a transtemporal whole.[23] Thus the emphasis is still on the active being of *Dasein* deploying itself in the form of temporality, rather than on time as "a source of knowledge," as Heidegger calls it. It is only at the very end of *Being and Time* that he asks, in the form of a rhetorical question, whether time may not be "the horizon of being"; but he gives a rather extended account of how this horizon is constituted in his lectures *The Basic Problems of Phenomenology*. Similarly, in the earlier lectures on truth, he states that "time is the condition of the possibility that there is (*es gibt*) something like being."[24] In the same text he straightforwardly identifies the being of entities with "the presence of what exists" (*des Vorhandenen*).[25] If in *Being and Time* temporality is characterized for the most part in terms of "project" and "ecstasis," and thus in a way that strongly emphasizes the spontaneity of the "I think," it is here made clear that this spontaneity is associated with an equally fundamental receptivity. This receptivity is described as a *Voraus sich geben lassen des Worauf*—that is, as letting oneself be given in advance that to which one's project refers; and the self is said "to posit itself as such that something can 'encounter' it on the basis of this self-modification."[26] The language Heidegger uses here is once again a peculiar mixture of active and passive; and if the active element in the conception of a *Sichgebenlassen*—that is, the *-lassen* part—represents the condition inherent in the being of the self that permits it to be acted on (*affiziert*), the fact remains that it *is* acted on in this distinctive manner. Time as the *Wie*—the mode—of this *Sichgebenlassen* is accordingly "the most original and universal form of givenness (*Gebbarkeit*)"; and it is this givenness that yields the sense in which time is "the horizon of being."[27] As such, it is in some sense consubstantial with the "I think"—not as something *vorhanden*, but as something that is itself "unthematic" in the sense that it "lets something be seen by, as it were, constantly withdrawing and vanishing."[28]

On the strength of all this, it seems very likely that if the third section of part I of *Being and Time* had been written, it would have developed the account of temporality along the lines sketched out in the lectures— that is, in a way that does justice to its essential mediating role in relation to truth as *aletheia* or uncoveredness and to being as the presence of entities. In that case, a conception of being as such would have emerged as the encompassing milieu of presence that *Dasein* both clears, through the complex structure of its own temporality, and dwells in as a zone of openness. The distinguishing feature of that milieu would be that in it entities are embedded in a referential context in which they *are* in the sense of being *for* a plurality of existing subjects. It would thus be essentially a domain of truth, not because it would be populated by assertions or propositions, but because it would realize the conditions of temporal coherence and convergent referentiality without which neither propositional truth nor being as the presence of entities would be possible. Such a conception would, in fact, be that of a world in the special Heideggerian sense as amplified by his account of temporality. The articulation of such a conception of being would, in one sense, have been continuous with the analysis of *Dasein* with which *Being and Time* begins, just as the analysis of temporality was. In another sense, however, it would have involved a "turning" inasmuch as being, as a unitary and common milieu of presence, must necessarily enjoy a certain independence, if not from *Dasein* as such, then at least from any particular *Dasein*. There would therefore be a sense in which being, even when conceived in terms of presence, would remain distinct from *Dasein*; and in order to do justice to this fact, it would be necessary to adopt a perspective that would be significantly different from that of any particular *Dasein*. Even though this kind of turning was central to Heidegger's conception of *Being and Time* from the outset, there proved to be serious difficulties in the way of any such reorientation of the account of *Dasein*. These difficulties derived from the way in which Heidegger had developed some major concepts of which he made use, and they must now be briefly characterized.

III

The concepts of being and truth, as well as those of world and temporality, are very closely linked in *Being and Time* to the concept of *Dasein*. It has already been pointed out that Heidegger goes so far as to use the verb "to exist," which expresses the mode of being of *Dasein*, to express the mode of being of both being as such and truth. He drives home the point by declaring that both being and truth are finite, just as *Dasein* is.[29] What this means in the first instance is that there is nothing eternal or necessary about either being or truth. It is quite possible that there should not be any being or any truth; and if there were no *Dasein*, this would indeed be the case. In other words, there is no necessity that there be a milieu of presence and of truth; and the milieu that now exists may come to an end. The reason for this is that presence is grounded in existence as the mode of being of *Dasein*; and being and truth exist—in both Heidegger's sense of that term and the familiar one—only because *Dasein* does. If there were no entities of the *Dasein* type, then there would be no being either.

If the concept of being is linked as closely as this with *Dasein*, how can it avoid being simply identical with *Dasein*? This is not to suggest that the entities that are within the world of *Dasein* must be identical with it, but rather that their presence as entities would have to be re-garded as equivalent to the existence of *Dasein*; and since being has been equated with that presence, being would have to be equated with *Dasein*. *Dasein*, of course, is an entity, and being is not an entity; but then the fact that the world is not an entity did not keep "worldliness" from being an existential character of *Dasein*. Why then should something compa-rable not hold in the case of being as the *Seiend-heit*—the being-ness—of entities, especially when we have Heidegger's own explicit statement that it does? The only basis on which one could resist this equivalence of being with *Dasein* is the distinction between *Dasein* as a generic concept and *Dasein* as the name of (many) particular entities. If being and *Dasein* were in fact equivalent notions, one would have to face the question of how being can be equated with *Dasein*, which is plural and particular, without thereby losing the singularity and commonness that characterize it? If it is to retain these features, being plainly cannot be identified with each individual *Dasein*. The alternative that would preserve these char-acteristics of being would be to say that being in Heidegger's sense is independent of each particular *Dasein*, although it is *not* independent of *Dasein* as such. Being as a milieu of presence does not, after all, begin to exist with the birth of a particular human being; and it survives the death not only of each one of us but cumulatively of all of us as long as we are replaced by others. There is a real question, however, as to whether in *Being and Time* Heidegger has developed the conceptual instruments that would be required to give an account along these lines of both the independence and the dependence of being in its relation to *Dasein*.

In this regard it is important to notice that neither *Being and Time* nor any of Heidegger's other writings or lectures of this period offer an analysis of the role of *Mitsein* in the constitution of being as presence that is in any way comparable to the account of the role of temporality in this same connection. The point of the latter account is that the presence of entities does not, as it were, simply declare itself to an undifferentiated and static awareness, and that the uncoveredness of entities is, instead, a function of a complex structure of temporal references in terms of which the being of the entity that uncovers must be understood. As a result of this analysis, the existing subject—*Dasein*—comes to be understood in terms of a set of temporal contrasts between "now" and "then" and between "already" and "not yet" that prove to have a constitutive function not only in relation to the kind of entity that *Dasein* itself is, but also in relation to the being as presence of the entities it uncovers. In the case of the contrasts between self and others, however, the promise of the strong theory of *Mitsein* to which Heidegger commits himself in *Being and Time* is simply not realized when being as such is under discussion. Although it is understood that it is an essential feature of *Dasein* that the entities it uncovers are, at least in principle, the same entities in the same world that other like entities uncover, and although Heidegger has indicated that the relationships among these uncoverings are not merely additive in character, there is no real account of the way in which *my* uncovering an entity as an entity depends on someone else's doing so as well. As a result, the uncovering of entities as entities by one *Dasein* comes to seem quite distinct from their uncovering by others, even though it is stipulated that each such *Dasein* understands that its uncovering is not unique and that the entities uncovered are the same from one case to another. At no point is there any definite indication of why uncovering *must* be joint and convergent, if that is indeed what Heidegger holds to be the case; it is therefore hard to see why the uncoveredness or presence in which entities show themselves as entities and as the same entities that others uncover must be single and common. In the absence of such an account, it might seem just as plausible to hold that in each case the uncoveredness belongs to the *Dasein* that realizes it, and that being as presence, like *Dasein*, is essentially plural in character. But such an assumption would miss entirely the dimension of being as presence in which it is independent of any particular *Dasein*; and if it can be said to do justice to the dependence of being on *Dasein* referred to above, it does so in far too drastic a way by, in effect, identifying the one with the other. In these circumstances, it would begin to look as though Heidegger's statement about the secondary ontological status of *Mitsein*, which at first appeared to contrast so sharply with his insistence on its essentiality, represents his real view of these matters.[30]

The alternative to such a view would be to understand being as a milieu of presence in a way that makes it essentially social and historical in character. As chapter 9 will show, Heidegger did, in his later period, develop a theory of the historical character of being; but that theory can hardly be described as social in any sense that turns on a strong conception of *Mitsein*. In *Being and Time* he sets forth a concept of the historicity of *Dasein* as part of his account of temporality; and at certain points that concept is characterized in a way that suggests what its social aspects might be, but without any elaboration.[31] In the account given in the lectures of the way in which temporality operates as a necessary condition for being as presence, there are no references to any role that a socially conceived historicity might play. It is not surprising, therefore, that no sense emerges from the writings of the early period of the way the commonness of being as a milieu of presence might be mediated by complex referential structures that are peculiar to *Mitsein* and that "decenter" uncovering and thus presence in a way comparable to that effected by temporality. If a theory that does justice to considerations of this kind having to do with *Mitsein* were to be developed, it would have to take into account such facts as that what I uncover as a hammer, say, has been previously used (and thus uncovered) as a hammer by others, and that it is normally from these others that I have learned what a hammer is and how to use one. Facts of this kind are certainly acknowledged by Heidegger; and he emphasizes that an instrument like a hammer is available for general use by an indefinite number of beings like me. In that sense there is nothing egocentric about uncovering as Heidegger conceives it. Nevertheless, he usually speaks of uncovering in a way that gives little or no prominence to the derivative character of most uncovering, with the result that it may sound as though a radical and original uncovering were effected on each occasion by an individual *Dasein*, unless, of course, it has relapsed into the unauthentic and anonymous mode of *das Man*. Hence the complex dependence of our uncovering on the uncoverings effected by others does not emerge at all distinctly in Heidegger's account. This could also be expressed by saying that, for the most part, what we uncover is a world that is already uncovered, already there as a world; and this must substantially qualify, although not in a negative or prejudicial way, any conception we may have formed of the spontaneity and independence of individual *Dasein* in its uncovering function. It should also be noted that to the extent that this dependence is acknowledged, there will be a tendency for the plurality of users of, say, a hammer to be thought of as standing in a somewhat more "passive" or receptive relationship to the single "prior" identity of the hammer that, as the matter is now understood, will always already have been uncovered as such. Such a picture is in marked contrast to the one that dominates the account given in *Being and Time*; and it would again be legitimate to expect any extension or amplification of the conception of *Dasein* in that book to do justice to the special kind of socially mediated "passivity" that it involves.

If these considerations have merit, then it would follow that in a theory of being as essentially involving *Mitsein*, there would have to be some modification of the conception of the agency of *Dasein*. In the discussions of the act-character of uncovering in preceding chapters, it was shown that the element of agency that such uncovering involves is, in the first instance, ontological rather than ontic in nature. This agency thus comprises the whole set of conditions having to do with possibility and temporality that is realized with the existence of *Dasein*, rather than just a particular isolable act like opening a door. But this distinction between the ontic and the ontological levels of agency must not be interpreted in such a way as to separate the ontic from the ontological or to obscure the fact that it is actual particular actions that carry the distinctive ontological character of *Dasein*'s agency.[32] But if that is the case, and if the choices among possibilities that these actions represent have the role in the uncovering of entities as entities that Heidegger attributes to them— the role, that is, in respect of being as such—and if, furthermore, being itself is to have a common, unitary character, then there must be a way in which such actions contribute to, or at least remain consistent with, that character. What I am suggesting is that, if the choices and the actions of one *Dasein* were not made in such a way as to relate them, at least in some minimal degree, to the choices and actions of other *Daseins*, it is hard to see how the specific uncovering they effect could be shared. If, for example, one person belongs to a faction that wishes to restore the monarchy, then the situations that are uncovered in the context of that choice will have the same meaning not only for members of that faction but also for those who oppose it, although in that case with all the signs changed, so that what is an opportunity for one group becomes a threat for the other. But if such a choice were one that had no social meaning, one that was made in complete abstraction from all contexts in which either opposition by or mutuality with others would be possible, how could it uncover anything that would be relevant to the choices of others and thus form part of the world we share with them? What all this comes down to is simply the proposition that, if being as a milieu of presence is indeed common, and if it is realized by us as active beings in our choices, then these actions themselves must have some convergent character, some character of shared or sharable intelligibility or they could not function in the manner that Heidegger describes.

Heidegger's characterization of existence as the mode of being of *Dasein* and of the choices in which it chooses itself and its world cannot be said to meet this requirement. Whatever he may have understood implicitly in the way of conditions defining the possibilities among which we choose and the choices themselves, he pays no attention to this dimension of choice and action. Moreover, such attention as is given to the more specific character of choice—in the account of resoluteness (*Entschlossenheit*), for example, or of death as one's "ownmost possibility"—markedly neglect its social character.[33] Since it is existence that grounds presence and thus being as a milieu of presence, it follows that this deficiency in the characterization of existence must pass over into the account of presence and being and render their common, unitary character at least somewhat problematic. If being is dependent on existence and thus on *Dasein*, but not on any particular *Dasein*, there must be a way of accounting for this distinctive dependence-cum-independence; and this means that existence itself must be conceived in such a way as to make such an accounting possible. But this will hardly be possible if the "we" of *Mitsein*, however emphatically espoused, remains at the level of mere acknowledgment and does not define the matrix within which the choices we make take on their common meaning. To the degree that existence is conceived in terms that do not acknowledge this dimension of choice, it can hardly be clear why being as presence is not straightforwardly dependent on individual *Dasein*. There will, accordingly, be a standing temptation to correct this incongruous feature of such a theory of existence by more drastic measures that assert the independence of being, but in a way that eliminates the possibility of accounting for its dependence and thus contravenes the deeper strategies of Heidegger's thought in a quite fundamental way.

It is hardly necessary to say that when Heidegger revised the position set forth in *Being and Time*, he did not do so along the lines that have been proposed here.[34] It may therefore be asked whether the analysis offered here, in which the commonness of presence guides the reconstruction of his thought, has any relevance, since there is no evidence that it conforms to Heidegger's own sense of what was wrong with his own first formulation. But is that really the case? There cannot be any real question that the relationship of being to *Dasein* is at the center of Heidegger's revision of the theses of *Being and Time*. It is also evident that his treatment of the agency of *Dasein* undergoes a profound change, a change that seems designed to safeguard in the most emphatic way possible the unity, singleness, and commonness of being as against the plurality of *Dasein* and in general to emphasize the independence of being vis-à-vis *Dasein*, although without quite denying a continuing element of dependence. There is also, as already indicated, a historical dimension to this revised theory of being, and with that history of being a conception of its social dimension is at least implicitly associated. All these new (or newly prominent) elements in Heidegger's thought are worked out in a way that is very different from the conception of *Mitsein* that was central to the sketch of a reconstruction just offered; but this does not alter the fact that Heidegger's reconstruction deals with the same themes and thus testifies to a similar sense of what was deficient and unsatisfactory in the position set forth in *Being and Time*. In following these themes through the thought of his later period, it may be helpful, therefore, to bear in mind the alternative revision proposed here and to compare the repercussions on the concept of the existing subject in Heidegger's prior account that are entailed by the one and the other.

PART II
**PRESENCE AS THE
GROUND OF EXISTENCE**

CHAPTER SEVEN • **THE TURNING**

There is general agreement that Heidegger's thought underwent significant change during the nineteen-thirties; and this view is supported by Heidegger's own willingness to speak in terms of a Heidegger I who preceded this "turning" and a Heidegger II who followed it.[1] With respect to the more specific character of this change, there is no comparable consensus; but there can be no doubt that it reflects difficulties he encountered in attempting to complete *Being and Time*. Since the parts of that work which were not published had to do with being as such, it has been assumed that the thought of the later period must be understood as Heidegger's attempt to give an account of being by means other than those that were used in *Being and Time* and that had on this view proved unequal to the task. At the same time, it has also been widely felt that the difficulties that Heidegger encountered in trying to complete *Being and Time* cannot by themselves account for the extent and character of the change that came over his thought; and there have accordingly been attempts to go beyond specifically philosophical considerations and to seek a fuller explanation of the "turning" (*die Kehre*) in his life and in his reactions to the events of his time. It is a common feature of most of these accounts, whether of the one kind or the other, that *Being and Time* and the specific strategy it deploys for dealing with being as such tend to be lost from view and to play a minimal role in the explanation that is offered of the subsequent course of Heidegger's thought.

It was indicated in the Introduction that a quite different way of interpreting the transition to Heidegger's later period would be followed in this book; and the task of part II is to make good on that promise. As a preliminary to that undertaking, this chapter will review briefly both the major lines of interpretation of the turning. Heidegger's own account of the reasons for his failure to complete *Being and Time* will be examined first; and then some of the more salient modifications of the position set forth in that work on which he does not directly comment will be taken up. I will also try to determine whether there is some deeper connection between the considerations brought forward by the two different approaches to the turning and to assess the relationship in which all of them—connected or not—stand to the problematic of *Being and Time* as analyzed in earlier chapters.

I

In his *Letter on Humanism* of 1947 Heidegger gave the following explanation of why *Being and Time* had remained incomplete: "The (third) section (of *Being and Time*, part I) was held back because thought fell short of an adequate utterance of this turning and did not reach its goal while availing itself of the language of metaphysics."[2] This explanation is significantly amplified by a longer statement in the course of the Nietzsche lectures of 1940. Heidegger says that his intentions in *Being and Time* have been completely misunderstood because man is still being understood as a subject and not as *Dasein* and thus not in terms of his reference (*Bezug*) to being. At the same time he accepts some responsibility for this misunderstanding because, he says, his own thought, which was trying to fight free from the metaphysical tradition, was thereby brought into close contact with it and thus ran the risk of becoming itself a new philosophy of subjectivity.[3]

Neither of these statements specifically identifies what it was in *Being and Time* that was metaphysical or subjectivistic in some objectionable way. As Heidegger came to understand the term, "metaphysics" denotes a specific feature of philosophical thought—the tendency, namely, to miss the distinction between being and entities and to consider the former only in terms of the latter. This is a tendency that he attributes to both ancient philosophy and modern Western philosophy. What makes Heidegger's first statement above puzzling is that in *Being and Time* he was already keenly aware of this distinction and of its importance.[4] How, then, can the effort of thought in *Being and Time* have failed by reason of its making use of "the language of metaphysics" in which this distinction is not observed? And how is this metaphysical tendency connected with the subjectivism that Heidegger also detects in *Being and Time*? After all, one of the classical forms that the misunderstanding of being as such has taken finds expression in the translation of *ousia* as "substance" which Heidegger explicitly rejects in *Being and Time*, as elsewhere.[5] He insists, moreover, on the harmful effects of the application of this concept of substance to the characterization of the mode of being of the mind—the subject—in the philosophy of Descartes. Altogether, it seems quite paradoxical that Heidegger should in effect accuse himself of implication in a form of subjectivism that he had so vigorously censured.

Nevertheless, there is a way of making sense of what Heidegger says about *Being and Time* and the ontological difference—his later term for the distinction between being and entities. In that work he had also interpreted the inadequacy of ancient ontology in terms of its tendency to treat all entities on the model of the *vorhanden*, or *res*, to the detriment of an undistorted understanding of the entity that is *Dasein*. This tendency to a false assimilation of the concept of *Dasein* to that of a thing or substance is also powerfully reinforced by a disposition in each of us to avoid any understanding of ourselves that makes the decisional character of our lives paramount and thus confronts us with a responsibility that each of us must bear alone. Throughout *Being and Time* Heidegger insists strongly on the radical difference between the one kind of entity—*Dasein*—and the *vorhanden* kind of entity—so strongly, in fact, that he appears to have little interest in the subdifferences among the very diverse entities within the latter category. This distinction between *Dasein* and entities within the world is itself ontological in nature, even though it has to do with entities rather than being as such, because it is the modes of being of these different kinds of entities that are being distinguished from one another. Because the concept of being as such was understood, in the period of *Being and Time*, in a way that makes it dependent on *Dasein* and thus on what is after all, for all its distinctiveness, an entity, it follows that an ontological understanding of entities of this kind carries with it an understanding of being as such. But this is what Heidegger was later to deny; so, when we find him declaring that in *Being and Time* he was still ensnarled in the language of metaphysics, the only plausible interpretation is that he had come to think that by associating being so closely with one kind of entity—*Dasein*—he had failed to do justice to the radical distinction between being and entities and had thus lapsed into the very metaphysics that he had ostensibly repudiated.

It must be emphasized that Heidegger nowhere spells this out in the way I have just done. What confirms this analysis, however, is the radically modified status of *Dasein* in the writings of the later period. The concept of *Dasein* does not disappear, at least at first; but its active character, which was of such fundamental importance in the account given of presence and being, is effectively eclipsed. Once again, there is no express acknowledgment by Heidegger of how different the account given of *Dasein* in the later writings is from the one in *Being and Time*. Nevertheless, the active aspect of *Dasein* is now associated not with the uncovering of entities as entities—that is, with being—but with the obscuration of being. This obscuration is declared to be the hallmark of the subjectivism that has made impossible any genuine understanding of being in modern philosophy. Here again the reader of *Being and Time* must be somewhat taken aback, since that book maintains a strong and continuing polemic against subjectivism. The subjectivism repudiated in *Being and Time* is essentially the Cartesian position which, by introducing the concepts of mental substance and representation, misses the phenomenon of the world altogether and substitutes for it the bogus concept of the "external world," which it then proceeds to belabor in such a futile way. Nowhere in *Being and Time* is there any suggestion that choice and action as functions of *Dasein* are in any way bound up with the subjectivism that Heidegger there condemns.[6] In the later philosophy, however, and especially in the reformulations of his case against Descartes in the lectures on Nietzsche and elsewhere, the gravamen of the charge against that philosopher shifts away from his reifying conceptualization of the mind to a quite different issue. Heidegger claims that Descartes's thought represents an attempt to achieve a kind of human self-sufficiency and security through a form of representional thought that seeks, in effect, to control being as such by accepting as real only what can be accommodated to its own schemata—in Descartes's language, to its own clear and distinct ideas. This kind of thought is further described as establishing the character of modern scientific and technological civilization, which Heidegger came to view as a kind of manic collective effort to control everything by subjecting it to human will and to the "values" it generates in its sovereignty over the earth.

The coincidence of this renewed and broadened polemic against modern subjectivism with the dropping of the active role of *Dasein* and, eventually, of the concept of *Dasein* itself made it appear that the whole approach to being as such through *Dasein*—the approach that characterized *Being and Time*—was implicated in the modern subjectivism that Heidegger so strenuously condemned. It is at just this point, however, that extraphilosophical considerations impinge most directly on the way the turning was effected by Heidegger. In the years immediately preceding the turning, Heidegger himself had espoused just such a hyperactivistic attitude as the one he subsequently condemned; and he even went so far as to associate that attitude with the philosophical theses of *Being and Time*.[7] Among other things, he declared Prometheus to have been the first philosopher and thereby identified philosophy itself as the supreme form of a human praxis that was to subsume the life of the individual in the collective self-assertion of the people and the state to which he belonged.[8] Whether this way of bringing the leading concepts of *Being and Time* to bear on the social and political realities of the time was in any way required by the underlying logic of the position it develops is a matter about which there has been much discussion. What must not be underestimated in this connection is Heidegger's own lack of prior experience in dealing with political and social themes, not to mention actual experience of the political world. Much of what he said and wrote during the period of his rectorship strikes one as the kind of thing that a rural conservative of somewhat nationalistic bent might say if he commanded the idiom of *Being and Time* as his means for expressing himself, in a moment of national crisis, about matters to which he had not previously devoted much, if any, thought. In any case, it is impossible not to understand the pervasive quietism that soon replaced this Promethean stance as Heidegger's reaction to the exaggerated voluntarism of this brief episode in his own intellectual career.[9] One must also wonder whether, like many such reactions, it does not err in the opposite direction just as seriously as did the line of thought it seeks to correct. In these circumstances, it hardly seems justified to treat either Heidegger's voluntarism or his quietism as authoritative interpretations of what the theses of *Being and Time* amount to as applied to matters relating to society and collective action. Indeed, it seems more likely that this whole sequence of events had a seriously distorting influence on the development of his thought, since it appears to have caused him to move between options of thought, neither of which accurately reflects the state in which issues having to do with *Mitsein* and the commonness of being had been left by the movement of thought in *Being and Time*.

If such unavowed considerations of a personal nature did exert an influence over Heidegger's thought in the manner sketched above, it is important to see how they intersect with the properly philosophical reasons for the turning that Heidegger himself cites. If an entity—*Dasein*—had indeed assumed a role in *Being and Time* that was such as to render problematic the independence and unity of being as such, it would follow that some way would have to be found to scale down that role so as to reduce the threat it represented to the integrity of being as such. In practice, this could only mean that the agency of *Dasein* and, more specifically, of individual *Dasein*, and the significance of that agency for the clearing of entities as entities would have to be sharply curtailed. But this is a conclusion to which disillusionment with political action and a growing animus against the managerial tendencies of modern Western civilization might also point. It is not difficult to imagine how a confluence of these two lines of thought might take place, although one should certainly be careful about ratifying any assumption that the one entails the other. A similar caution is indicated with respect to Heidegger's enlarged conception of subjectivism, which in his later writings becomes so broad and inclusive a tendency that it encompasses all the familiar forms of human agency and can be effectively repudiated only by those who espouse a thoroughgoing quietism. Moreover, it is far from clear how the indefeasibly active character of human existence on which Heidegger insisted so strongly in the period of *Being and Time* could fail to have some role within the relationship of *Dasein* or man to being as such, as long as being is conceived in terms at all like those of *Being and Time*.

II

On the basis of the reasoning just offered, it might seem to follow that Heidegger's later writings would be devoid of interest to anyone who understands the unfinished task of *Being and Time* in the way that I proposed in the last chapter. But this is not the case. Although major elements in the problematic of that work were redefined without any real acknowledgment or justification, as, for example, in the dropping of the active character of *Dasein*, there is still a sense in which Heidegger, in his later writings, is dealing with the question of how being as a milieu of presence is to be conceived. The underlying assumption now, however, is that presence is somehow the ground of existence, rather than the other way around; and it can be argued that, in working from this new assumption, Heidegger is testing some of the limits of the independence and the dependence of being vis-à-vis *Dasein*. That he was at least tempted to declare that independence to be complete and unqualified is something that the later texts show rather plainly; but they also show that, in the end, he was not willing to take that step.[10] What is most significant in all this is the fact that he is still working with the same concept of being as presence as he was in the period of *Being and Time* and is not reaching beyond *Dasein* to some notion of being that could not even be adumbrated within the universe of discourse of the earlier work. What *has* changed is the understanding of the relationship between existence and presence; and it must be said that the change is a change in the right direction. It is certainly unfortunate that this change was carried out, not in the form of an openly avowed reappraisal of an earlier stand, but under the confusing circumstances of a personal commitment that subsequently had to be reversed and of a polemic against the modern world that often seems extraneous to the philosophical questions at issue. Nevertheless, the direction chosen was the right one, because what needed to be explored at the end of *Being and Time* was precisely the sense in which being as presence could be said to be independent of *Dasein*, and that is indeed what Heidegger undertakes to do in his later writings. Although the idea of a dialectic was not one that ever had any appeal for him, it may even be the case that his exploration of the two ways of understanding the relationship of existence to presence can contribute to the emergence of a more adequate view that builds on the insights into the errors and excesses of these two hypotheses that were gained in the course of these explorations.

It is a sign of the underlying continuity of Heidegger's thought through the turning that the later writings do not at any point introduce a *new* concept of being as such—that is, one that is at variance with the conception sketched in *Being and Time*. In fact, it would not be inaccurate to say that the concept itself and the considerations that dictate how it is to be construed are presupposed by Heidegger in these writings, instead of constituting their principal expository task. That being is presence is simply assumed, without any real supporting argument; and it is assumed in much the same way as it was in the passages in *Being and Time* that were reviewed in the preceding chapter.[11] What Heidegger appears to be most concerned about in his later writings is not validating this assumption so much as establishing that being so conceived is in some vitally important sense prior to and independent of human beings and characterizing the way in which this priority and independence are obscured. What this means in practice is that Heidegger is committed to denying that existence as the mode of being of human beings is the ground of presence and thus of being; and he must do this while making use of essentially the same concept of being as presence that he presupposed in *Being and Time*. But if being as presence is to be the ground of existence, rather than the other way around, it is evident that the status of the concept of *Dasein* will have to be redefined in such a way as to reflect the fact that it is no longer its openness, to the extent that this survives at all, that accounts for the uncoveredness of entities. Since *Dasein* was declared in *Being and Time* to *be* its openness, and this openness was inherently an uncovering of entities, a preempting of its function in this regard necessarily entails its effective demise; and this is surely the reason why, in the later writings, the term *Dasein* gradually drops out of use except when the theses of *Being and Time* are under discussion. When this happens, it is typically replaced by the term *Mensch*—"man," or "human being"—and this, of course, is the very term of reference to ourselves that *Dasein* was originally designed to replace. Moreover, it is a fact of great importance that the "man" that so replaces *Dasein* in many instances appears to be the unreconstructed concept that Heidegger had subjected to such damning criticism. The significance of this paradoxical reversion to a seemingly invalidated concept for an appraisal of Heidegger's enlarged conception of modern subjectivism will be taken up in the next chapter.

In the course of the examination of texts from the later period in the chapters that follow, it will also be important to pay close attention to the conceptual strains and displacements produced by assigning priority to being as presence over existence. The locus of one such displacement has been identified in the remarks just made about the concepts of *Dasein* and "man"; and it will be of interest to determine the full range of the consequences of this shift. But the relationship of being as such to entities is also of great importance in the scheme set forth in *Being and Time*, where they are declared to be independent of both *Dasein* and being. It will therefore be necessary to determine how the relationship between being and entities is affected if the relationship between being and *Dasein* comes to be conceived in different terms. If both entities and being as such prove to be somehow independent of *Dasein* or man, then it would seem likely that the relationship between being and entities would become much closer than it was in *Being and Time*; and in that case, the need to distinguish, as in chapter 6, between being as always and necessarily characterizing entities and being as supervening on entities might no longer be so strongly felt. In that case, however, Heidegger would be confronted once again with the difference between being as what makes entities entities and being as what makes entities present as entities; and the question would be whether he is prepared to say that entities are always and necessarily present inasmuch as they are always associated with being. If that were the case and *Dasein* were still understood to exist contingently, then presence would no longer depend on *Dasein*. At the same time, however, it would not be clear how entities could be distinguished from being as the milieu of presence, since all entities would necessarily be present. In many ways this would seem to be an incongruous state of affairs. The only alternative would be to say that although being and entities are both independent of *Dasein* or man, entities are also independent of being. Such an independence would be very difficult to conceive, however, especially in light of the close conceptual linkage that is usually taken to obtain between entities and being. One thing, at least, is clear in all this, and that is that, quite generally, as being becomes independent of man understood as *Dasein*, it moves toward a closer association with entities. What is by no means clear is how close an association with the latter or how complete a separation from the former is really feasible. On these matters there may well be unresolved tensions in Heidegger's later thought to which careful attention should be given.

CHAPTER EIGHT • BEING AS PRESENCE IN THE LATER WRITINGS

The Essence of Truth (1930) is probably the first essay in which some of the characteristic preoccupations and emphases of Heidegger's later thought begin to emerge. The first substantial account of the concept of being as such is offered in the lectures of 1935, which were later published as the *Introduction to Metaphysics*. The lectures on Nietzsche from the late thirties, and especially those given in 1940, develop the same line of thought still further; and the lectures on Parmenides from 1942 are an especially rich source. Heidegger's principal commentary on the relationship between *Being and Time* and his later thought is the *Letter on Humanism* (1947); but there are important passages in the introduction and afterword that he added to *What is Metaphysics?* in the forties. His last major statement about being is the seminar on "Time and Being" in 1962. Together, these texts, as well as a few others to which I shall refer in passing, form the basis for the account of the treatment of the concept of being in Heidegger's later writings to be presented in this chapter. Its purpose is mainly to draw attention to features of the treatment of the concept of being in these texts that have an important bearing on the relationship of this concept to the one that emerges from *Being and Time*. I will show that there are tensions that may amount to incompatibilities between different features of the account of being that Heidegger gives; but a full critical appraisal will be reserved for chapter 10.

I

It is not immediately obvious just what it is that differentiates *The Essence of Truth* from its immediate predecessors, since the conception of truth it develops is much like that set forth in *Being and Time*. Nevertheless, there is a distinctive emphasis on the tendency of *Dasein* to become so absorbed in the routines of practical activity by means of which it secures itself that "entities as a totality" (*das Seiende im ganzen*) are obscured, and even the fact that this has happened is "forgotten."[1] This line of thought is not really new inasmuch as *Being and Time* repeatedly draws attention to the tendency to "jump over" and thus miss the distinctive status of the world as an ontological character of *Dasein* itself. In fact, the discussion of this tendency in *The Essence of Truth* seems to hark back to *Being and Time* quite explicitly by making use of the expression *das Seiende im ganzen*, which is a synonym for "the world," instead of *das Sein*—being—which became the favored expression in the later writings.[2] These clear affinities between this essay and the earlier work notwithstanding, there is nevertheless this difference: the "going-astray" (*Irre*) of *Dasein* is now being imputed not to some failure to understand itself in the proper ontological mode but precisely to its tendency to become too absorbed in itself. Heidegger says, for example, that *Dasein* begins "to take its measures" from its own practical concerns, oblivious to "the totality of entities," and that its existence thus becomes a kind of "insistence" in the sense of a concentration on "what is offered by entities which are open as though through and in themselves"—that is, independently of their belonging to the world that is in fact a necessary condition of this openness.[3] In other words, *Dasein*, of which the world is a necessary ontological character, can nevertheless become self-centered in a way that makes it oblivious to this feature of its own being; it then proceeds to treat entities as though their openness or accessibility required no explanation. This obliviousness, which is familiar from *Being and Time*, can be characterized as a kind of disequilibrium within being-in-the-world between the component of that totality that is properly described as a particular entity—*Dasein*—and that which is not such an entity—the world. But whereas in *Being and Time* the dependence of what is not an entity on what is an entity made it appear that any such disequilibrium could be rectified through an adequate ontological analysis of the mode of being of the latter, in *The Essence of Truth* that begins to seem problematic, and an independent account of what is not an entity and has somehow been "forgotten" seems needed.

In *The Essence of Truth* the need for such an account is only adumbrated, but in the *Introduction to Metaphysics* it is addressed directly. According to Heidegger, this work deals with "the openness (*Aufgeschlossenheit*) of that which the forgetfulness of being closes and hides."[4] What is forgotten is now described as "being," rather than "entities in their totality"; but in both works it is the tendency of *Dasein* to forget that is in question. There has, however, been a highly significant change with respect to *who* forgets. Typically it is now "man" that forgets being, not *Dasein*. In *Being and Time* and the other writings and lectures of that period, it was understood that these terms named the same entity, the difference being that *Dasein* captured its ontological character in a much more adequate way than did the concept of a human being. What happens in the *Introduction to Metaphysics* is that Heidegger not only uses the term *Mensch* ("man" or "human being") more frequently than *Dasein*, but he also opens up a conceptual gap between the two terms for which there is no precedent in *Being and Time*. He speaks, for example, of *Dasein* as being "thrown to me so that my self may be *Dasein*," of man as being "forced into such a *Dasein*," and also of a certain failure with respect to the openness of being as equivalent to "never entering *Dasein*."[5] These are ways of speaking that would be ruled out if *Mensch* and *Dasein* were extensionally equivalent terms, because they postulate the possibility that some entity that is a human being might not be a *Dasein*. It is also noteworthy that in being partially detached from the concept of "human being," the concept of *Dasein* is more closely associated with that of being, since "never entering *Dasein*" is equated with "stepping out of being."[6] There is still a distinction between the two insofar as *Dasein* is described as "the place (*Stätte*) of openness for (being)" and as "the breach into which the superior power of being breaks"; and these descriptions imply that in *Dasein* being as such somehow reaches beyond itself.[7] It is significant, however, that both being and *Dasein* are now spoken of as being granted to man, and one wonders whether under these circumstances *Dasein* should any longer be classified as an entity at all. It is clear, in any case, that it no longer names an entity that in and of itself realizes openness, but at most a relationship in which "man," conceived in some other way, can come to stand to being as an openness that is unique and independent of him.[8]

What is suggested by the new prominence of "man" and the association of *Dasein* with being as such is that the work of moving beyond the concept of man—the work that was done in *Being and Time* by replacing it with the concept of *Dasein* as the entity that realizes openness—has to be done again, but this time in a different way. It is consistent with this surmise that the terms used in speaking about man in this work and in other later writings are precisely those that were subjected to a devastating critique in *Being and Time*. Most notable among these is the concept of representation (*Vorstellen*), but the concept of the subject is used as well.[9] In the period of *Being and Time* this concept was treated as having an acceptable, as well as an unacceptable, sense, but it is now virtually identified with the latter. This means that the new line of argument that Heidegger is constructing will be directed against a concept of the subject that was shown to be invalid in *Being and Time*, but that this will no longer be replaced by a more satisfactory concept of the subject as it was there. Such a substitution unavoidably preserves the particularity and plurality associated with our ordinary understanding of what a human being is, as the earlier discussion of *Dasein* showed.

The new strategy is to use the inadequacies of the human subject—its incapacity to generate any genuine openness—as grounds for arguing that it must subordinate itself to a unitary form of openness that is somehow prior to and independent of it. What is paradoxical about this strategy is that it does not draw attention to the fact that it is this defective concept of a "human being" that is responsible for the inadequacies and limitations that are being attributed to the kind of subject it denotes. Under these circumstances, the adequate concept of the subject that had been worked out by Heidegger in *Being and Time*—the concept of *Dasein*—either drops out altogether or, as has been shown, passes over into a close association with the concept of the authentic openness for which the term "being" is reserved. This pairing of *Dasein* with being is never really stabilized in Heidegger's later writings, however, and so the concept of *Dasein* increasingly gives way to that of man. It will be shown, moreover, that, as this happens, Heidegger begins to treat the concept of "man" as though it had a double use—one in which it denotes a "subject" that merely "represents" entities to itself and another in which it signifies "the There, the clearing of being." In the latter sense, which is the one that Heidegger has in mind when he speaks of "man as man," the concept of *Dasein* lives on, despite the eclipse of the term; and in this new guise, it is attended by all the old puzzles about its relationship to being as such.

In any case, being, understood as an openness that the human subject by itself cannot generate, is now described in a way that strongly underscores its independence of the latter. We are told that it has nothing to do with the fact that "we observe entities." "We can only encounter (*antreffen*) [an entity] because it already *is*."[10] What the emphasis on "is" means here is that an entity must not only already exist in the ordinary sense if we are to observe it; it must also be already open or uncovered. This is confirmed by the distinction Heidegger makes between two senses of "to appear" (*erscheinen*).[11] The second of these is the sense in which "to appear" is to offer a surface or an aspect for a look or a regard; and it is emphasized that this sense presupposes another in which the entity appears independently of its being seen by an observer. In general, it is now evident that it is neither the thought nor the perception of a human subject that generates or gives access to the world or being; and this means that existence understood as the mode of being of the entity that thinks and perceives can no longer be held to ground the presence of entities as entities in any primary sense. For that, being itself as "a presence that arises and appears" (*ein aufgehend erscheinendes Anwesen*) is required, and this is being understood as a presence that is prior to and independent of any "subject," however distinctive its ontological character may be.[12] The language in which Heidegger conveys this supremacy of being over man is strongly figurative and portrays being as that which "overpowers" man by making him its "place of openness."[13] Being is also described as "ruling" or "holding sway" (*walten*).[14] This "holding sway" is itself necessarily and essentially an appearing (*Erscheinen*); and human thought has to be understood not as an independent determination by the criteria of logic of what is the case in the world, but as an apprehension (*Vernehmung*) that is responsive to and dependent on the being as presence that grounds it.[15] Everything in this account thus appears to reverse the asymmetry that characterized the relationship of existence to presence in *Being and Time* and to replace it with a maximally asymmetrical relationship of being as presence to existence.

At the same time, however, doubts arise about just how different this relationship really is from the prior one, given that being as presence is so closely tied to apprehension (*Vernehmung*). This sounds very much like the linkage of being to the understanding of being in *Being and Time*; and the latter, of course, carried the implication that if there were no understanding of being—no entity that could understand being—there would be no being. Is any such implication possible when the dominance of being over man is asserted in the emphatic terms that have just been noted? That it is indeed possible is suggested by the fact that in the course of his highly figurative description of being in its relationship to man, Heidegger states that being needs (*braucht*) a place of openness in order to appear.[16] This claim is amplified by the assertion that, although being overpowers man, the latter, in thinking and speaking, also performs an act of violence that is directed against being as that which overpowers him and yet is also in the interest of being as presence. The character of this act is further described as "a holding-open of entities as a totality" and as "a taking-over and completion of the stewardship of the rule of that which overpowers"—that is, being.[17] In his capacity as *Dasein*, man "takes over the knowing realization of appearing (*Erscheinen*) and thus acts as a steward for unhiddenness and protects it against hiddenness and concealment."[18] However unclear it may be, all this suggests some sort of dependence of being on man and some sort of capability in man for maintaining, if not originating, openness. Why this openness has to be maintained and protected is not really explained, but if the "need" of being is genuine, it can hardly be one that it meets itself by simply employing man for this purpose; and this is to say that being is not fully independent of that by which this need is met—namely, man. But to speak of "man" in this way is really to revert to the conception of him in terms of *Dasein*—that is, in terms of an openness that is *not* confined to the circle of its representations; and something like this often happens in Heidegger's later writings. On this occasion, however, Heidegger tries to safeguard the priority and supremacy of being by making the further claim that man is destroyed as a result of this paradoxical intervention that does violence to, and yet somehow succors, being as presence.[19]

The only real clue that Heidegger gives to the reasons why being *needs* a place of openness if it is itself a prior and independent openness or presence is found in a brief review of the history of the distortions to which the relationship of being and thought has been subjected. He speaks of truth or unhiddenness as "a space established for the appearing of entities" and states that because it "could not be maintained and preserved in its initial originality (*Ursprünglichkeit*) it collapsed."[20] This statement seems to mean that a milieu of presence that once existed somehow came to an end; but if that is understood to mean that entities no longer showed themselves as entities, then it presents serious difficulties. Certainly there is nothing to suggest that at any point in Western or any other history the disclosure of entities as entities within a framework of temporality and possibility came to an end. If anything of the sort *had* happened, the misconstrual of being in terms of entities, which Heidegger insists is the hallmark of Western metaphysics, could never have occurred, since entities would not have been accessible as entities. What this statement might more plausibly be taken to mean is that this fact that entities are present as entities was once understood but then ceased to be understood at some point in Western history, and that being itself as that presence was thereby eclipsed. Whether or not anything of the kind really took place is a matter that will be discussed in the next chapter. But if it is Heidegger's contention that this is what occurred, then there would be a straightforward way of interpreting his otherwise puzzling references to the openness of being as such. These references are puzzling because being itself simply *is* openness—that by virtue of which "entities first become and remain observable"—and so a reference to it as being itself open strikes one as redundant.[21] But if there is a distinction between that which is present and presence as that by virtue of which what is present is present, then it becomes possible to envisage a case in which entities are indeed present, but presence as such is forgotten or hidden—that is, is not itself present.

This is a point of very great importance for the interpretation of Heidegger's later thought generally, and especially of that aspect of it in which the priority and independence of being as such to any human subject appear to be so strongly asserted. If being as such can be hidden and inaccessible to man, then it certainly seems to follow that it must in some sense be separate and independent of him. But it now appears that there are two different senses in which being as such might be hidden: one in which the uncoveredness or presence of entities is unqualifiedly prior to the existence of any entities like *Dasein*, and another in which it need not be independent in this sense but may obtain without being recognized as what it is and thus remain in that sense hidden. The vital issue for the interpretation of the later theses about being as such is therefore whether the hiddenness of being as such and the independence that is thereby implied are to be understood in terms of the first or second of these senses. Accordingly, it is of prime interest that a great deal of textual evidence speaks in favor of the view that the distinctive concern of Heidegger's later writings is with the hiddenness/unhiddenness of being as understood in the second sense. The lectures on Nietzsche of 1940, for example, include an account of the relationship (*Bezug*) in which man stands to being that in its essentials is the same as that in the *Introduction to Metaphysics*. Man is described as the "refuge" (*Unterkunft*) of being; and it is explicitly denied that the distinction between being and entities is in any way attributable to any "act" or to any "distinction" that human beings make or, indeed, to the nature of man as such.[22] Once again, it is "man" that is described as being carried by the distinction between being and entities, and his relationship to entities as entities is declared to be possible only because he has been granted a relationship to being. What is of immediate interest, however, is the emphasis on the obscuration of being and the way in which this obscuration is described. Heidegger speaks of the "unthought unhiddenness of entities" as equivalent to "unthought being"; and this is further explicated as meaning that although "being itself is (*west*) as the unhiddenness in which entities are present, this unhiddenness itself remains hidden as what it is."[23] The claim that being is not "thought"—that is, not acknowledged as being—certainly seems to imply a reference to man as the entity that fails to make this acknowledgment, although in some passages this implication is avoided by speaking instead of the "staying-away" (*Ausbleiben*) of being.[24] But even when this idiom is adopted, the staying-away of being is described as something that is itself "left out," or omitted (*Auslassung*), and that which leaves it out is identified explicitly as human thought.[25] Heidegger also denies that, in staying-away, being "tarries somewhere apart," and he asserts that "in (this) staying-away (of being) there is a reference to something like a place" from which unhiddenness as such is absent.[26] Since this place is further described as "the essence of man," it is plainly equivalent to the notion of *Dasein*—the There of being—and the warning that this is not man for himself as a subject would hardly have been necessary had the concept of *Dasein* rather than that of man been used, since *Dasein* is quite definitely not such a subject.[27] The effect of all these qualifications of the original metaphor of staying-away is to associate the notion of the hiddenness of being as such very much more closely with human thought than seemed possible when being was said to "withdraw itself." This linkage to human thought is reaffirmed when Heidegger speaks of "a decisive step back that the human thought that has left being out can take out of this leaving-out."[28] The thought that takes this step back would "let being be (*wesen*) as being"; and in doing so, it would return to the domain that properly belongs to it—a domain that is significantly described as having been left to it by being "in the concealed form of the essence of man."[29] In this sense, an acknowledgment of being is also a form of self-understanding on the part of man as *Dasein*. This is underscored by Heidegger's statement toward the end of the Nietzsche lectures that being is characterized by what he calls *Subjektität*—something that involves its being determined by, and thus presumably linked to, the subject, but not a personal subject as would be implied, he claims, by the term *Subjectivität*.[30] Presumably, what differentiates a personal from a nonpersonal subject is agency and particularity; so the new equilibrium between man and being is one that requires not so much a radical independence of being from man, but a union of the two that is not disturbed by any "personal" element on the side of man. It is worth noting here that a subjectivity that is not personal could also be understood as one in which the manifold differences among particular subjects are not simply abolished but are in some sense neutralized through shared standards of equivalence and validity—that is to say through an operative "inter-subjectivity."

The pattern followed by the texts examined so far is one in which an emphatic assertion of the priority and independence of being as presence is followed by other formulations that appear to qualify that independence to the point where it might well be compatible with the position of *Being and Time*. It is hardly surprising, therefore, that the relationship between the theses about being in that work and the treatment of being in his later writings should have been a matter of concern to Heidegger, or that he should have commented on it on several occasions. The most extensive discussion of this kind is found in the *Letter on Humanism*—a work that is usually read for its repudiation of any suggestion of an affinity between Heidegger's thought and Sartre's existentialism.[31] What is a good deal more interesting, however, is the part of the discussion in which the concept of being is brought into a close, explicit relationship with the concept of *Dasein*. In *Being and Time*, *Dasein* had been declared to be *die Lichtung*—"the clearing"—and similarly in the *Letter on Humanism*, man is said to be "the There, that is, the clearing of being."[32] But being is also said to be "the clearing itself "; and other descriptions of being as "the giving-itself-into-the-open" (*das Sich-geben ins Offene*) and "the locality of the truth of being" (*die Ortschaft der Wahrheit des Seins*) associate being with the attributes of openness and place that attached to *Dasein* in *Being and Time*.[33] This openness of being is also said to be the Between within which there can be a relationship between subject and object, a characterization of being that runs parallel to the statement in *Being and Time* that *Dasein* is its own Between.[34] Significantly, both the earlier and the later statement occur in the context of a critique of the subject-object relation, for which a prior ontological foundation must be provided, Heidegger argues.

If *Dasein* is a clearing and man is also a clearing, and if being then proves to be a clearing as well, one may well wonder whether all these assertions are compatible with one another and whether the clearing in question is the same in each case. Man's being a clearing in the required sense is essentially connected with his being or—in the later writings— becoming *Dasein*; and if that is the case, then two of these clearings would be identical with each other. That would still leave the question of how the clearing that is *Dasein* is related to the clearing that is being as such; and here it is very difficult to reconcile what Heidegger says about being as the presence of entities as entities that is realized through their being cleared by *Dasein* with the later characterization of being as somehow prior and independent. After all, there are passages in *Being and Time* in which the dependence of being on *Dasein* is unambiguously asserted. In one such passage, it is stated that "only as long as *Dasein* is, is there (*gibt es*) being."[35] In the *Letter on Humanism* Heidegger reaffirms this statement; but he goes on to explicate it in a way that reverses the dependency relationship between being and *Dasein* instead of just expanding it so that it would run both ways.

> (The statement) means: only as long as the clearing of being occurs does being make itself over to man. But that the "there," the clearing as the truth of being itself occurs, is something that being itself "sends." This is the destiny of the clearing. The statement does not, however, mean that the *Dasein* of man in the traditional sense of *existentia* and conceived, as it has been in modern times, as the actuality of the *ego cogito*, is that entity by which being is first created.[36]

But if the dependence of being on *Dasein* is thus transformed into a dependence of *Dasein* on being, it is not at all clear whether it is really the *Dasein* of *Being and Time* that is being talked about. After all, the latter is hardly identifiable with any "traditional sense of *existentia*" and certainly not with the *ego cogito* as it has been conceived in modern times.[37] In this connection it is significant that the term "man" figures prominently in this passage, and that it is to "man" that being is described as making itself over. Heidegger's fear seems to be that man will be credited with "creating being"; and although it was not man, but a very untraditionally conceived *Dasein*, on which being was said to depend in *Being and Time*, he is evidently prepared to construe major theses of that work as though, in the absence of such an amplification, they would have carried just this implication. Thus, to his own question about the way in which the relationship between being and existence is to be understood, Heidegger lays it down that "being itself is the relationship insofar as it holds existence in its existential, that is, ecstatic essence to itself and gathers it to itself as the locus of the truth of being in the midst of entities."[38] The concept of "project" (*Entwurf*) that was so central to the active conception of *Dasein* in *Being and Time* is similarly reinterpreted in such statements as that "that which 'throws' in projecting is not man but being itself which sends man into the ek-sistence of *Dasein* as his essence."[39] Once again, the worry seems to be that "man" will be credited with some productive or creative function in relation to being, for Heidegger states that although "being clears itself for man in the ecstatic project, . . . this project does not create being."[40]

Since it is the notion of "creating being" that is the sticking point in this argument, it must be examined more closely to determine whether it is necessary to take such elaborate measures against it. It is clear, first of all, that in *Being and Time* there can be no question of man creating being. In the universe of discourse of that work, the very notion would be a conceptual muddle, for if any entity can be said to create being, it would have to be an entity that is conceptualized as *Dasein* and not as "man." But there is a further question as to whether in the terms of *Being and Time* even *Dasein* could be said to create being. It is true that "only as long as *Dasein* is, is there being"; and the notion of creation might be used simply to express this dependency relation. There are real disadvantages in using the word "creation" that way, however, because it invites confusion between the ontic and ontological senses of the agency of *Dasein*. It is ontic agency understood as what an entity does that is associated with the *ego cogito* and that is therefore objectionable to Heidegger; and it is ontic agency that would be involved in "creation." Taken to an extreme, the conception of ontic agency yields a kind of Nietzschean voluntarism in which the particular human will as a will to power enjoys a sovereignty over everything and over being as such. The *Dasein* of *Being and Time* was not the ground of its own being, however, and it had no choice at all about its own ontological character as an entity that uncovers entities as entities.[41] Since being is understood as the presence of entities that is realized by the constitutional openness of *Dasein*, it seems clear that to speak of *Dasein* as creating being presupposes that *Dasein* is prior to being as presence and then makes being be by creating it. But this view was never suggested or ratified by *Being and Time*, which did not, therefore, stand in need of revision on this score. There were conceptions of a Promethean human agency, however—among them the Nietzschean conception of the *Übermensch*—to which Heidegger was evidently attracted.[42] Although, for the reasons just cited, these ideas are not equivalent to a "creation" of being as presence by *Dasein*, it may well be that Heidegger felt they had come uncomfortably close to something like that, and that in order to avoid any such implication he had to scale back the agency of *Dasein* quite drastically. As a result, the intense polemic against "humanism" that fills the *Letter* is somewhat ambiguous as regards the position against which it is directed. In other words, it is not really clear whether Heidegger is saying that in its original formulations, as contrasted with the interpretations he now offers, *Being and Time* itself was implicated in the metaphysical errors he is censuring— the errors that lead to humanism and in general to the attempt to establish the sovereignty of man over the earth.

The more specific character of the priority of being to *Dasein* that Heidegger has in mind in the *Letter on Humanism* is somewhat clarified by what he says about the nature of the clearing that being is. Central to this account is the notion of the "look" (*Anblick*) in which things are revealed to us. Heidegger contends that this has always been misunderstood in the "metaphysical" tradition of Western philosophy, which typically construes the concept of clearing in terms of "that which is sighted (*das Gesichtete*) in the looking-at (*Hinsicht*) of categorial representation (*Vorstellen*) from the side of subjectivity."[43] This is to say that the concept of clearing is derivative from the concept of a look that originates in the subject who directs it on something that is thereby cleared. But if "the clearing itself is being," and if, it might be added, "being itself is the relationship" to a "subject," then this picture must be wrong.[44] For in the right picture, it is "the clearing itself that first grants the look or aspect (*Anblick*) out of which that which is present touches the human being that is present to it so that he can then touch being in apprehension (*Vernehmung*)."[45] In other words, it is not the looking as an act of the subject that gives rise to the look or aspect of the perceived object, but rather the latter that "draws the looking-at (*Hinsicht*) to it."[46] Aspects are thus not tied to subjects, but the other way around. Heidegger goes on to say that it is being—that is, the clearing—that is itself "the relationship that holds existence in its existential, that is, its ecstatic essence to itself and gathers it to itself as the locus of the truth of being in the midst of entities."[47] It thus appears that the transitive character of perception as a looking-at has been reassigned to the aspect itself and now runs from the aspect to the subject, rather than the other way around.

In connection with this discussion of how the notion of the look is to be understood, it is worth noting another treatment of it in which Heidegger's intentions emerge even more clearly. In his lectures on Parmenides in 1942, Heidegger developed further the contrast between a reflective experience of the look (*Anblick*) "as a subjective activity directed upon objects" and an experience of it as "the looking-at-one (*das ihn-Anblicken*) of the human being who comes toward one."[48] The latter experience of the look is the characteristically Greek one, according to Heidegger; and it differs from the former—which is the characteristically modern view—in that it is "the showing-itself in which the essence of the human being who meets one has gathered itself and in which the man who so meets is subsumed (*aufgeht*) in the double sense that his essence is assembled in the look as the sum of his existence and that this assembled and (yet) simple totality of his essence opens itself in the look."[49] In other words, the look is to be understood in terms of the aspect (*Anblick*) of the "object," rather than the mental act of the one who looks; but this very aspect is itself described as a look (*Blick*).[50] It is as though Heidegger were saying that all looking in the usual sense is really a matter of being looked at *by* the person whom we would ordinarily describe ourselves as looking at. Since a great deal of looking-at is not looking at other human beings but at things, this analysis must be adjusted, and this is where Heidegger introduces the Greek gods. He points out that Plato understood being itself as *eidos* and *idea*—that is, as "the aspect or look in which something gives itself, the 'face' (*Gesicht*) that 'a thing' or generally an entity 'makes.' "[51] "Being—*idea*—is that which shows itself in every entity and looks out of it," and this look—*thea*—of entities, which the look of human beings at most awaits, is identified with the gods (*theoi*) who are thereby themselves identified with being as presence.[52] It is the look of the god that presents (*dargiebt*) unhiddenness (*Unverborgenheit*), and "this looking that makes possible presence for the first time is therefore more original than the presence of things."[53]

It is not easy to say just how one is to understand this bold identification of being as *Unverborgenheit* with the look—the *thea*—of the gods. But one meaning is clear: namely that the clearing that is essential to all human seeing is not organized solely or principally by the directedness or intentionality of the *human* look. In other words, it is not as though that look were a shaft of light that illumines its object but leaves the source from which it issues—the eye or the mind—invisible. Instead, in a more adequate (and, according to Heidegger, more Greek) understanding of vision and the look, it would be grasped that that which looks and sees is itself also necessarily visible. This might be expressed in terms of the metaphor of light by saying that, in place of a beam of light, there is a diffracted and diffused illumination in which everything that looks is also, in principle, looked at. Translated into the language of the modern subject-object relationship, this would mean that when I look at an object, I am also looked at, if not by that object, since objects as such do not "look" at all, then from the place that the object occupies and, if not actually, then at least in the sense of being visible from that place.[54] It is presumably this visibility in principle as a necessary condition for looking that is expressed by Heidegger's interpretation of the Greek gods as "those who look into the unhidden" and as "the being that looks into entities."[55] The notion of a look that is always operative, as it were, and that is omnipresent as that of the gods may be presumed to be, is well suited to expressing the special character of a visual space that is subject to the conditions that have been described.

Fanciful as it may seem to the contemporary reader, this introduction of the notion of the look of the gods into the discussion of being as presence cannot fail to be of great interest to anyone who thinks that the common or public character of presence needs more attention. The first question that it raises is whether the fact that gods are thought of as persons does not make the understanding we have of their "look" very similar to the one we have of our own look before the latter is corrected so as to make the look as aspect prior to the look as act. Presumably the look of the gods is privileged and exceptional by comparison with the look of entities like man that can at most effect "presence in the *representatio*" and not authentic unhiddenness. If it were not, then we would be threatened by an infinite regress. But if it is privileged in this respect, does it not follow that this divine look is very like what the uncovering function of *Dasein*—not man—was originally supposed to be?[56] If that is the case, then Heidegger's whole analysis of presence would seem to revert to the standpoint of *Being and Time*, with the sole difference that another, more potent kind of entity—gods, rather than men—has been invoked, an entity whose look could effect the kind of general *Unverborgenheit* that the look of human beings apparently cannot. To this, Heidegger might reply that the gods are not really entities, and that it is not their personal and plural character that expresses the deepest apprehension of being on the part of the Greeks.[57] But then, what *is* it about this notion of the gods and their look that can help us to understand the notion of being and presence? It would not be very satisfactory to be told that, in order to understand what the gods do in this connection, we must *already* have an independent understanding of being. It is surely significant, moreover, that to make up for the deficiencies of the human look, Heidegger has had recourse to the notion of another *look* to account for the fact that the things *we* look at already have an aspect-character—a "face"—when we look at them. The claim that things have that character independently of our looking at them may also be one for which there is a sound basis. If so, however, it is not because everything is already the object of a divine regard, but because we are members of a community of "viewers" who are distributed through time and space in such numbers that we may well see what we see as something that has already been seen and as something that presents itself in a virtually infinite number of aspects to all possible points of view. Indeed, that kind of openness is something that no single look and no individual viewer can realize; and it does not seem out of line to suggest that the difference between the kind of visibility that such a community of viewers generates and that generated by a single, inevitably egocentric regard is one that might be figuratively expressed in terms of the disparity between men and gods and between the kinds of look that might be imagined to characterize the one and the other.

There was no significant further development of an interpretation of being as presence along these lines. However, Heidegger's last major treatment of these themes—the seminar on "Time and Being"—includes an interesting attempt to introduce a new concept—that of *Ereignis*, usually translated "event"—into the account of being as such.[58] The contours of this new concept are by no means well defined; but it appears, under all interpretations, to assign an event-character to being as presence and, thereby, to correct a tendency of which Heidegger himself takes note to confuse being as presence with something that is present.[59] This, of course, is an event of a very special—indeed unique—kind, and various efforts have been made to translate the term *Ereignis* in a way that would adequately convey this special character. Although no notable progress in further clarifying the notion of *Ereignis* as "appropriation" or whatever is likely here, it does seem worthwhile to indicate the direction in which the introduction of this notion moves the whole consideration of being as presence. Especially important in "Time and Being" are indications that Heidegger is disposed to move explicitly beyond the unsatisfactory options in which either being is created by man or man by being.

That being is to be understood as presence remains the basic postulate that it is throughout Heidegger's thought.

> Being by which every entity is marked as such means presence (*Anwesen*). Understood in reference to that which is present, presence shows itself as letting-be-present.... Letting-be-present shows what is peculiar to it through the fact that it brings into unhiddenness. Letting-be-present means: to dis-conceal (*entbergen*), to bring into the open. In dis-concealing there is a giving (*Geben*), the giving namely, that in letting-be-present gives presence, i.e. being.[60]

What is new in this account of being as presence is the claim that this presence which lets entities be present and in that sense "gives" them to us is itself given (*eine Gabe*) to man.[61] The latter is "addressed by presence" and is "himself in his own way present to everything absent and present."[62] He receives the " 'There is' (*es gibt*) as a gift as he grasps what appears in the letting-be-present."[63] Accordingly, "To think being in the distinctive sense requires that we let being as the ground of entities go in favor of the giving that is the hidden counterpart of dis-concealing, i.e. in favor of the "There is" (*es gibt*, literally "It gives"). As the gift of this "There is," being belongs in the giving. As a gift it is not pushed out of the giving. . . . Being *is* not. There is (*es gibt*) being as the discon-cealing of presence."[64] Being as presence thus has an iterated character. As a letting-be-present, it gives entities to man; and presence is itself given, again to man, in the absolutely unique and distinctive event that Heidegger calls *das Ereignis*.

The seminar "Time and Being" bears the same title as the third section of part I of *Being and Time* which was never published; and time is accordingly involved in Heidegger's account of the "giving" of being as presence. In certain respects the role of time in the seminar account is not very different from the one that Heidegger had worked out in the period of *Being and Time*. For example, he speaks of the gift to us of presence in its several modes as a *Reichen*, an extending or passing of presence to us; and this extending is temporal in a special sense, since presence is always in the modalities of past, present, and future, which also reach out to one another.[65] This gift of presence which is also a giving of itself is characterized by Heidegger as "the clearing of that which we call the time-space (*Zeitraum*), the open (*das Offene*), that clears itself in the passing on to one another of advent (*Ankunft*), pastness, and the present."[66] It is this openness alone that "allows our familiar space its possible extension." Presence as such a domain of openness is thus given by time, which Heidegger declares to be four-dimensional in the sense that its usual three dimensions—past, present, and future—are cleared for us by being held together *and* apart; and time's fourth dimension is this "*Reichen* (passing-on) that determines everything."[67] This is a giving which also withholds, however, because "it holds open the 'has-been' while refusing to let it become present," and it also "holds open the coming-on out of the future while in this coming it holds back the present."[68] But if all this sounds a good deal like the earlier conception of the temporal transcendence that makes possible being as the self-manifesting of entities as entities, there is also this noteworthy difference that Heidegger speaks here in terms of time, rather than temporality. As a result, the time that "extends" being as presence is not described in a way that ties it to temporality as an existential structure of *Dasein*; it is as though this "authentic time" (*eigentliche Zeit*), as Heidegger calls it, were now a kind of world-time, but without being reduced to a multiplicity of Nows as was the case in *Being and Time*.[69]

Being has thus been defined as presence, and time is "the domain of the extending (*Reichen*) of the clearing of a presence of several types."[70]

But now that time has been introduced explicitly into Heidegger's characterization of presence, the same question arises as in the case of presence as such: the question of the relationship of time to the soul or consciousness or, as Heidegger puts it, to man. Even though time is no longer identified with temporality, his answer is still that "without man there is no time," the same answer that he gave in *Being and Time*.[71] But what, he asks, does this "without man" mean? "Is man the giver of time or its receiver?" As in the case of being as presence, Heidegger's primary concern is to forestall any notion that "man is first man" and *then*, additionally, takes on a relation to time.[72] The truth, Heidegger believes, is rather that "man can only be man while he stands within the threefold extending of time"; and this, too, is the same view that he took of man vis-à-vis being. "Time is not the creature (*Gemächte*) of man nor is man the creature of time." Then—and this is most interesting—he says: "There is no making (*Machen*) here. . . . There is only a giving in the sense of that extending that clears the time-space."[73] These statements suggest a strict mutuality in the relationship of man to time with no priority on either side. Both the notion of a receiving and that of a giving of time by man would misconstrue that mutuality and are therefore unsuitable characterizations of the function of man or of *Dasein*.

This ruling out of both an active and a receptive role for man vis-à-vis time and, since time "extends" being, vis-à-vis being as well is perhaps the closest Heidegger comes to a recognition that both the active model he had used for characterizing *Dasein* in *Being and Time* and the receptive model he had used for man in his subsequent writings are unsatisfactory, and that an idiom that would in some sense be neutral is needed. More specifically, although both being and time must now be thought of as in some sense "given," Heidegger makes it quite clear that there is no point in trying to inquire further into this giving. Admittedly, there is a temptation to ask what the "it" is that "gives" being and time, but this is, he tells us, simply a misguided attempt to accommodate the absolute uniqueness of the event that is this giving to the ontological conventions of ordinary thought.[74] All we can really say is that this event occurs (*das Ereignis ereignet*). It is the event by virtue of which the Parmenidean *esti gar einai* holds true; and both express, at least for Heidegger, what might be called the supervenient character of being and time in respect of entities. But this supervenience vis-à-vis entities (*das Seiende*) is also understood by Heidegger in terms of the connotations of the word *eigen* that is a component of *Ereignis*. By virtue of this event, one entity or kind of entity (man or *Dasein*) is brought into its own, into what is proper to it. It thus appears that as "appropriation" this event carries an essential reference to man. Since this is also an event without which man could not be man and certainly could not be *Dasein*, it is clear that it, too, would have to be described as neither a giving nor a receiving by man, since both these notions imply that "man" as such is already in place, independently of the giving or the receiving in which he is supposed to play one role or the other.

It is true that great emphasis is placed on the fact that in "bringing man into his own," this event also withholds itself and thus "preserves its own (*Eigentum*)," with the consequence that the appropriation that the *Ereignis* effects is simultaneously an "expropriation" (*Enteignis*).[75] This withholding can be understood, however, as expressing what Heidegger spoke of in the Nietzsche lectures as an unhiddenness that is also unthought. What it amounts to is that man dwells within an openness that he does not understand as such; and this state of affairs is possible even though this openness—being as presence—does not obtain independently of man. What is implied is rather that, although "man belongs in the *Ereignis*" and does not stand outside it as one to whom something is given by something or someone else, he stands within it in a way that is characterized by a certain obliviousness on his part to his so belonging.[76] This obliviousness in turn is not really very different from the tendency originally attributed to *Dasein* to understand itself as one entity among others and to leap over the fact that, unlike other kinds of entities, it has a world. It is that world, as Heidegger points out in a very significant parallel to his similar statements about being, "through which entities become entities"; and it is that world as the milieu of presence that man is in that makes him man.[77] That there is such a world and that entities are within that world in the sense of manifesting themselves as entities to the entity for which they are manifest is an event that indeed deserves special recognition. At bottom, it is the same event that was previously expressed as the fact that *Dasein* is or exists at all (*dass überhaupt Dasein ist*).[78] But since the import of this event cannot be captured in terms of any particular *Dasein* or any actual population of such entities, it is necessary to find some way of speaking about it that transcends these limits but without separating it from man as such and without sacrificing its event-character to one of the conceptions that transform presence into something present. For all its obscurity, Heidegger's conception of *das Ereignis* seems designed to meet these requirements.

II

The discussion up to this point has shown a gap opening up between the concepts of being as presence and man, a gap that did not exist between being as presence and *Dasein*, as these were understood in the period of *Being and Time*. It has already been pointed out that, as this gap opens up, the concept of *Dasein* either drops out altogether or remains tied to that of being as presence, with the result that its linkage to the concept of man takes on a new element of contingency. At the same time, this new picture, in which presence is the ground of existence, is significantly qualified in various ways that make it appear that the old picture of existence grounding presence has not been rejected entirely. To the extent that the latter maintains itself as an element in Heidegger's thought, the term "man" begins to function in the way that *Dasein* did when there was an acknowledged extensional equivalence between the two; and locutions like "man as man" begin to make an appearance. What man would be otherwise than "as man" is not explained; but it is clear that the use of the locution "man as man" presupposes the availability of another concept for the entity that is called "man" insofar as it is *not* man. "Man" served as such a "fall-back" concept for *Dasein*; and if it begins to function like the latter, another concept will have to take its place and serve in its former capacity.[79]

Against the background of this account of the conceptual shifts produced by the new priority of presence over existence, a question arises about what happens to the relationship between the concept of being as presence and that of entities as a result of this change. The question here is whether being as presence can remain as independent of entities generally as it was when it was tied to the entity whose mode of being is existence—namely, *Dasein*—or whether the fact that both being as presence and entities are now independent of *Dasein* means that they will be more closely linked to one another. This is a matter about which Heidegger seems to have held different opinions; and there is a record of these shifts in the successive editions of the afterword to *What is Metaphysics?*. In that work, an initial assertion that "being presumably (*wohl*) obtains (*west*) without entities but an entity never without being" was later amended to read: "Being never obtains without entities (and) an entity never without being."[80] Whether this change really settles the question of interpretation is uncertain, however, and it may well be that, as in the case of the relationship between being and *Dasein*/man, Heidegger's treatment of the relationship of being to entities is too heavily qualified in too many unreconciled ways to be construable in one way or the other. As in that prior case, the solution to the problem is rendered more difficult by the almost complete disappearance of a concept that was of central importance in the original formulation of these relationships: the concept of world, which occurs in the later writings even less frequently than *Dasein*, to which it was logically linked.[81] Formerly, it was understood that entities could exist without a world, just as they could without being, because both "world" and "being" were tied to *Dasein*, which might very well not exist. But if being is not tied to *Dasein* and is not like "world" in this respect, to the degree that the latter concept survives at all, then it seems to follow that what exists independently of man (or of *Dasein* as originally conceived) is both entities and being as presence; and this would naturally be interpreted to mean "entities *as* present." Is there any possibility under this new dispensation, one is tempted to ask, of entities existing independently of both man and being as presence?

In this connection Heidegger's use of the Greek concept of *physis* becomes very relevant.[82] *Physis* was translated into Latin as *natura*, and from it we get our term "nature," which serves, among other things, as a way of referring to what would exist in the absence of human beings. Heidegger does not accept this translation, because in his view it misses the distinctive meaning of *physis* by assimilating it to an altogether different set of ideas related to birth. In his interpretation of the term *physis*, he goes so far as to equate it with *ousia*—that is, with being as the *Seiendheit des Seienden*; and as such it is described in terms very similar to those used for being: as "the holding sway that arises" (*das aufgehende Walten*) and "the standing-there-in-itself" (*das In-sich-dastehen*).[83] But what is most important in these characterizations and what contrasts most conspicuously with the concept of nature, is Heidegger's claim that "*physis* as a holding-sway that arises" is already an appearing (*Erscheinen*) as well.[84] "Appearing" as used here does not mean simply "offering a surface for a look," although this is a secondary meaning of the term that has been mistakenly taken as its primary meaning. The primary meaning of *Erscheinen* is declared to be "that which gathers itself and in its gatheredness brings itself to a stand and thus stands" (*das sich sammelnde und in der Gesammeltheit Sich-zum-Stand-bringen und so Stehen*).[85] What strikes one about this very obscure characterization is that it is hardly different from that given for *physis* itself, and that it does not seem to involve anything that would ordinarily be described as an appearing at all. Nevertheless, Heidegger unmistakably associates appearing in this sense with openness and thus with presence when he says that it is appearing in this sense that "tears space open."[86] As being (*ousia*), *physis* is also "that which is present (*anwest*) in unhiddenness" and that which "comes forth into unhiddenness"; thus it is utterly different from the mere *vorhanden* which had earlier been supposed to be that which existed independently of the world and which "entered the world" if a world existed.[87] Overall, since being is said to be that which distinguishes entities as such, it begins to look as though *physis* and entities must be identical, and as though entities, because of the character of *physis* as an appearing, will necessarily be present, and present in a sense that is related to, though evidently not dependent on, appearing *to* or being present *for* someone.

Not surprisingly, however, there is another side to this matter; and it has to do with Heidegger's use of the Greek notion of *lethe* and the cognate verb *lanthanesthai*.[88] These are often translated as "forgetting" and "to forget"; but although Heidegger concedes that these translations are correct, he insists that they miss what is most characteristic of the Greek way of understanding this forgetting. According to our way of understanding these matters something is forgotten or hidden if some "human subject in its subjective comportment has not noticed it" or has failed to hold on to it.[89] By contrast, the Greeks thought of what we call "being forgotten" as a kind of hiddenness, and of this hiddenness as something that surrounds what is hidden in such a way that "those who are present are as if cut off " from it.[90] The condition of being hidden— *lethe*—is thus "not a mode of comportment of the 'subject' but an 'objective' occurrence, something that takes place from the side of the entity itself."[91] This hiddenness is contrasted with that signified by the Greek word *pseudos*, which expresses a sort of distorted or erroneous appearance of the thing in question, which is thus not completely hidden. As the more radical mode of hiddenness, *lethe* is counterposed by Heidegger to *physis* as the going-up (*Aufgehen*) of entities into *a-letheia*, understood as *Unverborgenheit* or unhiddenness. According to this understanding, *lethe* seems to designate the status in which entities abide to the extent that they are not cleared (*gelichtet*). The question must therefore be how this state, which is also described as "the night" that "makes everything present vanish," is to be understood in relation to *physis* and *aletheia*.[92] In conformity with this metaphor, concealing and disconcealing are properly understood as "events" (*Ereignis*) that "come over entities and man" and "determine the mode (*Weise*) of (such) entities."[93]

This line of thought suggests that in the concept of *lethe* we have a radical contrast to *aletheia* and thus to presence and *physis* and to being as presence as well. If that is the case, it must follow that entities could exist even if being as presence and all its cognates did not. What Heidegger says in this connection is quite different, however. From the polarity of *lethe* and *aletheia* he draws the conclusion that both concealing (*Verbergung*) and disconcealing (*Entbergung*) are fundamental traits of being itself, which cannot be one-sidedly identified, therefore, with *aletheia* and *physis* but encompasses *lethe* as radical hiddenness as well.[94] Our concept of being must therefore include *lethe* as "that hiding which lets the past, the present, and the future fall away into the way of an absence that is itself absent."[95] This linkage of being with both *lethe* and *aletheia* would entail that being always *is*, but the being for which this status is assured is no longer identical with *aletheia* or presence; and it would not be the case that being as presence always is. Instead, there could be entities that are radically hidden and in no way present; and the effect of the extension of the concept of being to include *lethe* seems to be precisely to break the identification of being with presence, thereby allowing it to function as that which makes entities entities, whether or not they are ever present. The trouble is that Heidegger still seems to want to treat these two quite different senses of "being" as though they were somehow one and to make hiddenness and unhiddenness complementary to one another within a single concept of being.

This concept of being that includes both *lethe* and *aletheia* and makes them somehow complementary to one another is strikingly similar to Heidegger's argument during the period of *Being and Time* that linked presence and absence to one another in the understanding of being that the temporality of *Dasein* mediates.[96] The difference, of course, is that presence and absence were then understood to be bound up with the existence of *Dasein* for which absence is a mode of presence by virtue of its referential temporality. But at that time, the being or milieu of presence with which *Dasein* was necessarily associated was understood to be finite as *Dasein* itself was; and this meant that it, as well as the contrast between presence and absence that it constitutes, might well not exist at all. If that were the case, then the radical hiddenness that Heidegger calls *lethe* would descend on entities in a way that would no longer involve any complementary linkage with *aletheia* and presence. Against this, it might conceivably be argued that any question about a possible situation in which there would be no presence at all but in which there would still be entities is itself one that presupposes being as presence. What this means is that the entities that are imagined as surviving even if there were no being as presence are themselves present for the purposes of this question. Admittedly, they are present as prospectively nonpresent, but this is just the kind of nonpresence, or absence, that Heidegger originally includes within being as presence. To this it might be replied that while this may be so now, when presence still obtains, the nonpresence of the surviving entities will not presuppose presence when there is no presence at all. What this comes down to, at least within the context of Heidegger's earlier thought, is the question of what exactly is implied by the finiteness of *Dasein* and whether the correlative finiteness of being as presence is such as to preclude its having any range or extension beyond the limits of the actual existence of the entity or entities on which it depends.

This issue was touched on briefly in chapter 5, where it was suggested that the finiteness of *Dasein* should be construed in such a way as to allow its world to extend over periods of time in which there was no *Dasein* in existence. It cannot be said that in the period of *Being and Time* Heidegger sharply distinguishes between these alternative construals of finiteness; and it may even be that the lack of resolution on this point was another factor necessitating a broader treatment of being as presence than was possible within the limits of the original theory of *Dasein*. We have already seen that in his discussion of the status of Newton's laws, Heidegger states that "once entities are uncovered, they show themselves as precisely the entities that they already were beforehand"; and this certainly seems to extend the range of truth and thus of being as presence back in time to a point at which there may have been no *Dasein* and thus no presence in any actual form. By parity of reasoning it would follow that such entities show themselves now as the entities they would continue to be even if *Dasein* were no longer to exist. This means that there can be truth and presence with respect to situations in which there may be no *Dasein*; and the question thus becomes whether the truth and the presence which obtain now by virtue of our thought (and perhaps for as long as some thinker like us exists) but which also refer beyond our or anyone's actual existence are to be understood primarily in the light of the former or the latter facts about them. If they are understood in terms of the former, as it seems they are by Heidegger when he denies that there can be any truth if there is no *Dasein*, then both *Dasein* and being would remain finite in a radical sense; if in terms of the latter, as I have suggested they should, then *Dasein* would remain finite, but the truth and the being as presence with which it is conversant would not be so limited. All that can be said definitely about Heidegger's attitude toward these alternatives is that in his later writings he no longer speaks of being as finite as he did earlier. It is true that he does not speak of it as infinite either; but, following Heraclitus, he does suggest that being may be that which "never sinks" (*das Niemals-Untergehen*), and he also associates it with Anaximander's notion of the *apeiron* as that which transcends all limits.[97] Thus, it seems legitimate to conclude that the being of Heidegger's later period is at least nonfinite in character.

That Heidegger in his later period construes being in a way that makes it independent of the finiteness that characterizes *Dasein* does not by itself answer the question of how this nonfinite being as presence is to be understood in its relation to entities. Heidegger is quite emphatic that this relationship is one of difference; but it is not clear whether being is different from entities because it is that which makes them entities or because it is that which makes them present in the enlarged sense of that notion in which presence is no longer tied to *Dasein*.[98] What *is* clear is that it cannot differ from entities in *both* these ways without splitting into the two senses that correspond to the two differences: being as what makes entities entities and being as what makes entities present. Nevertheless, when Heidegger tries to combine these two senses in one, as he seems to want to do, his language betrays the difficulty. He says, for example, that "entities can be as entities only when they enter the cleared (*das Gelichtete*) of this clearing"—that is, of being; he thus identifies the character of entities as entities with their being cleared—that is, present—within the clearing of being.[99] The effect of this statement is to tie the concept of entities to that of the clearing they are described as entering; but then this linkage is qualified by the use of the phrase "as entities" which suggests that there is some way that entities can be otherwise than as entities. This possibility reopens the gap between being as such and whatever it is that is indeed an entity but must also be susceptible of being something else as well, given that it apparently *becomes* an entity when it enters the clearing of being as presence. One is reminded here of Heidegger's earlier use of the notion of entities as entities, according to which entities were uncovered as entities by *Dasein*; but in that use it was not a question of something that was not an entity actually becoming one, but rather of something that was an entity showing itself as such. A closer parallel is the split that took place between the concepts of "man" and *Dasein* when the latter came to be tied to that of being, rather than the other way around. In that case, however, there was already available a term for what the entity that becomes *Dasein* is insofar as it is not (yet) *Dasein*—namely "man." In the case of "entities" there is not only no such term already in place, but it is hard to think what such a term might be. The pressure to postulate one is indicative, however, of the strains produced by the effort to make one concept do two such disparate jobs.

In the brief discussion of these matters in chapter 5, a reference was made to Heidegger's essay on "The Origin of the Work of Art" and to the clue it may offer to the way the notion of what is not (yet) an entity might be interpreted. It arises in the context of a contrast between "the earth" and "the world" in which the latter is to be understood in terms not very different from those of *Being and Time* and the former as that which emerges into the unhiddenness that is constitutive of the world. The point is that, although it does so emerge, the earth is and remains other than and independent of any such emergence and the character that thereby accrues to it. "(A stone) proclaims its heaviness... but at the same time as it weighs upon us, it denies itself to any penetration into it. If we were to attempt such penetration, by splitting open the rock, it never then reveals in its pieces an inside that has been opened up. The stone has (instead) at once drawn back into the very heaviness (*das selbe Dumpfe*) of its weighing (*seines Lastens*) and the massiness of its pieces."[100] Heidegger goes on to conclude that "the earth appears, openly cleared as itself, only where it preserves and protects itself as that which is essentially inaccessible and withdraws before any disclosure and thus keeps itself permanently closed." Here, it seems, is a very plausible way of interpreting what Heidegger has said elsewhere about radical hiddenness as *lethe* and night; and although he does not connect this inaccessibility with the distinction between what is an entity and what is not, the notion of that which is in principle closed offers a contrast to that which emerges into clearedness that might well correspond to that distinction. It is certainly difficult, for example, to associate individuation and particularity in any normal sense that might be thought to characterize entities with what is closed in the sense Heidegger has in mind; and this may be the reason why Heidegger uses a term like "the earth" which is hardly susceptible of pluralization. For just this reason this term is well qualified to serve as the fallback term for "entities" when the concepts of the latter is linked to being as a clearing, as Heidegger seems to intend.

At the same time as he declares "earth" and "world" to be "essentially distinct," Heidegger wants to claim that they are "never separated," and if they are not, there must always be a clearing. It is not obvious, however, why this must be the case. If the inference is that there must be something open by contrast to which that which is closed is closed, it does not seem that such a purely conceptual linkage can sustain the weight of an ontological inference. More important, one might ask whether the contrast between the closed and the open and between *lethe* and *aletheia* really stands up once the notion of a clearing has been detached from the notion of a finite entity such as *Dasein* was supposed to be originally. When presence is associated with an entity that is not only finite but finite in a way that characterizes its modes of perceptual and other access to entities within the world, it is not difficult to give a sense to what is and must remain hidden from it, whether in the mode of lying beyond the limits of its range of perception or reference or in the mode of some inaccessible "interior" of entities that are accessible perceptually. It is difficult, however, to think of the look of the gods as having the situated character and resulting spatial orientation vis-à-vis other entities that go with this limitation in the human case. And if there *is* a presence of a nonfinite kind such as the look of the gods might be supposed to generate, why should there be any residual distinction between what is hidden and what is unhidden or present at all? Why should not entities be so saturated with presence that *nothing* could remain hidden or closed? This question takes on a special urgency when one considers what Heidegger has said about the gods as "the being that looks into entities" and about a primary appearing that "tears space open." This certainly makes it sound as if the presence so generated would be pervasive and unchanging. But if he now insists that the distinction between the hidden and the unhidden is maintained under all conditions, this can only mean that the look (*thea*) of the gods is itself finite, since otherwise nothing could lie outside it. In that case, the presence that is assignable to the look of the gods would have to be conceived as supervening on entities in a way very similar to the supervenience of an (explicitly finite) *Dasein* on these same entities. (The only other possibility is that the look of the gods, though not itself finite, could withdraw or render itself inoperative on certain occasions; but it is not clear where it could withdraw to or how its inoperativeness could be distinguished from finiteness in Heidegger's terms.) It thus looks very much as if a distinction between hiddenness and unhiddenness cannot be reconciled with a nonfinite conception of being as presence. Indeed, Heidegger's attempt to maintain the distinction under these circumstances strongly suggests that he is reverting to the notion of a finite entity for which entities are present only on the condition of their remaining absent or hidden as well. *Within* such a notion there would still be the possibility of a contrast between hiddenness and unhiddenness, not only with respect to entities, but also with respect to being itself, along the lines suggested earlier in this chapter. If being as presence is independent of any finite entity and is unlimited in the way that Heidegger is apparently inclined to suppose it is, however, the possibility of the first of these contrasts and perhaps the second as well becomes quite problematic.

III

In the record of his remarks to the seminar on "Time and Being" Heidegger is reported to have said that after the meaning of being had been clarified, the analysis of *Dasein* was to have been "repeated in a more original and completely different way."[101] Although "Time and Being" contains some indications of the way in which Heidegger might have gone about revising his theory of time, he did not ever carry out the broader task that he had thus outlined. It is clear, however, that one major goal of such a revision would have been to show that "the powers" that man has been thought of as possessing—among others, those of discourse, understanding, and mood (*Stimmung*) that were so fully characterized in *Being and Time*—are not really *human* powers at all, but rather powers by means of which "entities open themselves as such," powers that man can at most tame and direct.[102] It is thus evident that these are powers that are really transferred to man as *Dasein* from being as such; and it seems likely that it is in this aspect that Heidegger would have presented them in any systematic revision of his account of *Dasein*.

There is one part of this task that he may be said to have carried out, although not in the mode of an explicit revision of what he had said earlier about *Dasein*. That is the part that has to do with the "power" of language. A great deal of Heidegger's later writing is about language, and from it emerges a picture of language that at least seems very different from that offered in *Being and Time*.[103] This aspect of his later thought has probably been more widely influential than any other; and insofar as his treatment of being as such has had an effect on contemporary thought, it has been in the form given to it by his· account of language. It is thus especially important to examine this area in which Heidegger actually carries out something like a revision of the theory of *Dasein*, in order to determine just how sharply it breaks with his earlier account of language and whether it, too, is marked by the tension between a conception of being as independent of and being as dependent on *Dasein* or man.

The question that Heidegger raises again and again in his later discussions of language is whether we understand at all adequately what language is. We assume that we do and that language is a kind of datum with which everyone is familiar at the outset. The words for language in Western European languages show that the understanding we claim to have is one that associates language primarily with the production of speech (*stimmliche Verlautbarung*) by certain parts of our bodies and with the communication thereby achieved.[104] Understood this way as a certain form of human activity, language quite naturally comes to be thought of as something that we create; and it is this view of language that Heidegger wishes to discredit. Therefore, he must show that language has some status other than that of "the utteredness" (*Hinausgesprochenheit*) of discourse or speech that he declared it to be in *Being and Time*. This would appear to suggest that it is Heidegger's own earlier views of language that are being corrected, but this is true only up to a point. Not only are there the ambiguities about the "creative" character of *Dasein* in *Being and Time* that were noted earlier; there is also the fact that in certain respects the objectionable view of language that Heidegger is attacking is a naturalistic conception that he had himself rejected in that earlier work. Discourse, and thus derivatively language, was unambiguously described in *Being and Time* as a modality of the uncovering of entities as entities; and the whole strategy of the treatment of language was to show that at every point it is embedded in and presupposes existence as the mode of being of the entity—*Dasein*—that is itself conversant with being understood as the uncoveredness or presence of entities as entities. There is no reason to suppose that in his later writings on language Heidegger wants to repudiate these theses of *Being and Time* or to conflate them with crudely naturalistic conceptions of language. It looks, instead, as though he wants to revise the earlier notion of the *way* in which discourse and language are related to one another, but still within this general conception of the uncovering character of discourse and language.

This is suggested in the first instance by the fact that the term *Rede* (discourse) drops out of the later writings in favor of the word *Sprache* (language). The former takes with it the picture of the individual human speaker and of language as what he produces by his speech; and it is replaced by a picture of language as that out of which an individual speaker speaks and on which he depends in multiple ways that need describing.[105] This might seem to be a conventional enough picture; but any notion of language as a syntactic or semantic system that must be in place if individual speech-acts are to be performed falls far short of Heidegger's conception of language as the background against which the latter take place. Language understood as that on which discourse depends is described by him as a "showing" (*Zeige*) that "reaches into all regions of presence and lets what is in each case present appear and misappear (*verscheinen*) out of them."[106] This is in marked contrast to the view taken in *Being and Time* that discourse contributes to uncovering entities as entities, but only as a further articulation of an uncoveredness that has already been realized independently. On behalf of language as contrasted with discourse, Heidegger now makes the much stronger claim that it is "the word" that "first brings what is present into its presence" and that, even when unspoken, "proffers the thing to us as a thing." This conception of language as realizing our primary access to being is one that contemporary thought finds deeply congenial in the many contrasting versions in which it has been proposed. But this apparent consonance of Heidegger's position with our own predilections can prove very misleading, because the language that Heidegger characterizes in this way is not a language with a grammar and a vocabulary like English or Chinese; and it is not, therefore, to the constraining influence of such features of language that Heidegger attributes our apprehension of being. Instead, the enlarged significance that he now attributes to language is primarily due to the fact that, although he seems to be describing presence and thus being in terms that assimilate both to language, it is also and equally language itself that is being understood in terms of presence. He is thus claiming that the unitary presence of entities as entities is best understood as a kind of "saying" (*Sagen*), and that, as this "saying," language, in its unitary essence, is prior to all individual speakers and all natural (and artificial) languages in the same way that presence is prior to all particular perceptions and memories and choices and so on.[107]

Extravagant as such a claim will inevitably seem, it has in a way been anticipated by remarks made earlier about presence as having, not to be sure a propositional character, but something that might be called a proto-propositional character in the sense that it constitutes the milieu of truth within which what an entity *is* can eventually find expression in an assertion of some kind. At the same time, it must be conceded that the skepticism with which this dramatic expansion of the domain of

language meets is understandable. There have been so many naive theories of the identity of word and thing and of a natural language that
is somehow laid down in the order of creation that one inevitably approaches any theory that, like Heidegger's, may sound as if it were
invoking conceptions of this order with a good deal of caution. It will
be helpful to approach Heidegger's later treatment of language via theses
from the earlier period that prepare the ground for the much closer
association of presence with language of the later period. One such thesis
defended in *Being and Time* is that meaning is an essential character of
the world as presence and, as such, is prior to both discourse and language understood as deriving from discourse. If, independently of any
act of interpretation (in Heidegger's sense) or discourse, we understand
how to ride a bicycle or catch a fish, our world to that extent bears the
instrumental meaning that corresponds to these forms of understanding
and competence on our part. This meaningful character of the world
can then be expressed as its "saying" something to us. Such "saying" is
obviously silent, because there is no speaker in the ordinary sense and
no "act" of expression or communication. But if it is admissible to speak
of the meaningfulness of the world as a kind of silent "saying," then it
will also be appropriate to describe the relationship of human beings to
that "saying" as one of "hearing." In his later writings on language
Heidegger assigns great importance to this notion of hearing and goes
so far as to assert that the speaking of human beings is always and
necessarily preceded by a "hearing" in this sense.[108] This is a hearing of
the saying in which presence is realized; and because language in the
widest sense is just this presence and this saying, Heidegger can say not
only that "language itself speaks" but that "we hear the speaking of
language" (*das Sprechen der Sprache*).[109]

The difficulty for this way of understanding Heidegger's conception
of language as something that is in some radical way prior to expression
and communication on the part of human beings is that in the later
writings where the conception is put forward, the notion of *Zuhandenheit*
as the instrumental meaningfulness of the world is in abeyance. Indeed,
the notion of the world itself, on the rare occasions on which it is employed at all, is understood as only one element within what Heidegger
now calls "the Fourfold" (*das Geviert*) or "World-Fourfold," together with
"the earth," "man," and "the gods."[110] This conception is developed in
a way that can only be described as mythic, so its philosophical import
is far from clear. The pairing of world and earth would seem to correspond to the contrast between openness and hiddenness presented
earlier in this chapter; and "man" who defines himself as such in some
sort of contrast to the gods is, instead of being the ground of the world,
incorporated into the "play" of all these elements in the Fourfold with

one another. There is no reason to suppose that Heidegger no longer recognizes the kind of prior instrumental meaningfulness of the world that was so central to his account of *Dasein*; but it now appears to be encompassed within the wider "play" of the elements of the Fourfold. Heidegger also describes the latter as a *Gegeneinander-über*—a reciprocity of linkages in which "each of the regions of the World-Fourfold is open for the others—open as if hiding itself."[111] In the later writings, it is this play of reciprocity among the regions of the Fourfold that is understood as the "saying" by which man is addressed and to which any utterance of his must be understood as responding. This is really another way of saying that man is addressed not just by the world in the former sense in which he was its ground, but by being as that which lets what is present *be* present and, in the case of "the earth," present precisely as that which closes itself off from presence. It is as though man, instead of being spoken to only by the ontic (but implicitly ontological) instrumentalities of his world, were also being addressed by the explicitly ontological saying of being—the Fourfold—as such. In saying "explicitly ontological," I do not mean to suggest that this saying is a bit of philosophical ventriloquism in which man is the real speaker. It is rather that the elements of what is said themselves do the saying. It is what they say that man hears; and he can hear what they say because he can understand being as that which "lets-be-present." He does not organize the world as a Fourfold, any more than he constitutes the distinction between being and entities. Instead, because "we human beings have been admitted to the world of language (*das Sprachwesen*)" we cannot step out of it so as to view it from some other standpoint; as a result "we catch sight of (*erblicken*) language only insofar as we are regarded (*angeblickt*) by it."[112]

Although there is much in this notion of the Fourfold that is unclear and problematic, we will examine only the notion of language as prior to human utterance. There can be no doubt that in saying that our understanding of language must shift from language as something we do to language as something by which we are sustained and in some sense encompassed, Heidegger is expressing the sense that all students of language must have of the dependence of the individual speaker on the language he speaks. This dependence is usually associated with the rule-governed character of language; and our sense of submitting "blindly" to those rules can become so strong that it is as though our language were speaking us, rather than we, the language. That is an idiom that Heidegger himself uses, but not as a way of testifying to the rule-governed character of language. The language that itself speaks is not one that is ordered by syntactical and semantic rules; and it would be a serious mistake, as well as an encouragement to mystification, to apply what Heidegger says about language as the play of the Fourfold to natural languages. As he uses it, the notion of language as that out of which we speak expresses the fact that our utterance is possible only within a milieu of presence, and that the structure of presence as the Fourfold forms the indispensable context for every natural or constructed language and thus for the utterances of those who speak each such language. Heidegger is willing to go so far as to declare that "language is the house of being and it is by dwelling (in this house) that man ek-sists."[113] He adds that this house *of* being has also "come to pass (*ereignet*) and been fitted together (*gefügt*)" *by* being itself. Although the priority of language to man is thus asserted in the strongest possible form, it is noteworthy that in the same context man is spoken of as "the shepherd of being." It is also stated that as he dwells within language as the house of being, he "protects the truth of being to which he belongs."[114] Since the notion of protection immediately suggests a need— in this case, as before, a need on the part of being for man—it is evident once again that the relationship between being as presence and existence which, in the course of Heidegger's discussion of language may appear to be a one-sided dependence of the former on the latter, is a good deal more ambiguous than at first appeared.

The question is thus whether it follows that, if language is somehow prior to human utterance, language and its saying are independent of man. This in turn is really just a new version of the question that has been raised again and again in this book, especially in this chapter in the more general form of a question about the possible independence of presence from existence. In this new form that ties it to language, it sounds more than usually strange, because we tend to imagine that the language that might be prior to or independent of man is a language like English or French or some distillate of all such natural languages, and this idea of there being such a language independently of the existence of human beings seems just too incongruous to take seriously. But even when we are clear that the language we are talking about here is not a language in this sense, but rather the ontological context of presence that is required for language as more familiarly understood, the question remains. Fortunately, it is one to which Heidegger has addressed himself directly.

> And the saying itself? Is it something separated from our speaking (*Sprechen*) [and] which we could reach only by throwing a bridge over to it? Or is the saying rather the stream of silence that itself connects its banks—its saying and our re-saying—as it forms them? Our usual conceptions of language fall short here. Aren't we running the danger, if we try to conceive the nature of language (*das Sprachwesen*) on the basis of "saying," that we will raise language up into a fantastic being that exists in itself but that we can find nowhere as long as we reflect soberly on language? After all, language remains un-

mistakably bound to human speech. Certainly. But of what type is this bond? Whence and how does its binding character obtain? Language requires (*braucht*) human speech and it is nevertheless not the mere creature (*Gemächte*) of our speech-activity.[115]

This passage makes it clear that, although Heidegger's way of describing language often makes it sound as though some stronger kind of independence of language from human speech were intended, the kind that he is really talking about is consistent with language's being bound to human speech. In other words, we have here much the same patterns as before of an apparent assertion of a radical form of priority—in this case, of language; formerly, of being as presence—that is then qualified by an acknowledgment of a dependence on something human. It thus turns out that what is really important is the special character of the dependence that is only apparently being denied. This dependence is, in the first place, reciprocal, since without language man could not be man anymore than language could be language. It is also a dependence such that what is dependent—in this case, language—is nonetheless not created by that on which it is dependent and is not subject to any arbitrary form of control that the latter might like to assert over it. The fundamental articulation of the World-Fourfold is one that all speech and every natural language necessarily register and preserve, just as in *Being and Time* discourse and thus language presuppose the structure of being-in-the-world. How this independence within dependence is to be understood may not be altogether clear; but it is not to be explained by any notion of language as a thing in itself. It is interesting to note in this connection that Heidegger says that it is not just language as the silent play of the World-Fourfold, but language as what is uttered by human beings that can come to *look* as though it were separated from speaking and speakers and did not belong to them.[116] In both cases, however, the appearance is misleading, for there can no more be a language without speakers than there can be a Fourfold without man.

Communication does not figure at all prominently in the account of language in Heidegger's later writings. Nevertheless, at times that account comes very close to an acknowledgment of the commonness that characterizes what Heidegger calls *das Sprachwesen*. This is particularly obvious in the discussion of the reciprocal implication of the "regions" of the World-Fourfold in one another, and especially in the openness to one another that he claims is characteristic of this *Gegeneinander-über*. This kind of reciprocal openness is normally thought to obtain only with our fellow human beings, Heidegger notes, but he insists that we must expand our understanding of this fundamental mutuality to include things as well. Since he does not explain in which sense a chair is open to the wall against which it stands, to use the example from *Being and*

Time, where any such openness was categorically denied, these aspects of the mutual openness of the World-Fourfold must remain problematic. What is clear, however, is that no matter how much *more* it is supposed to include in the way of reciprocal openness, the *Gegeneinander-über* includes at least our reciprocal openness to our fellow human beings in the medium of language.[117] That openness itself presupposes that there are *things* that are open to us all, even though other things and we ourselves are not in any comparable sense open for them. In this non-reciprocal way, such things are drawn into the communication among human beings and in this way, too, they participate in the special kind of proximity that characterizes the relationships among the elements of the World-Fourfold. It is not necessary to require, as Heidegger apparently does, that things participate in that openness in just the way human beings do, in order to explain their role in such communication. Moreover, non-human animals appear to have a better claim to be included in the World-Fourfold than does the earth since there is undeniably a form of reciprocity and of what might be called quasi-presence between human beings and at least the higher mammals. It is therefore a little surprising that no mention of their participation in the World-Fourfold should be made when, in spite of its problematic character, that of the earth is so prominent.[118]

Although the theme of *Mitsein* can be shown to inform Heidegger's later treatment of language in the ways that have just been shown, he nowhere associates it with the peculiar independence-within-dependence of language in relation to its human speakers. This accords with his long-standing proclivities in these matters; but it does deny him an obvious and important resource for purposes of accounting for that independence in a way that does not effectively cancel out the associated element of dependence. The crucial fact about language, for anyone disposed to associate it with being as presence and thus with the unity and singularity of the latter, is that it is not egocentrically organized, and that the "space" that it opens up is one that is traversed by all possible lines of sight and reference, not just the ones running from the current speaker to the object with which he is concerned. It is also something that has come into being and that has a history, so that each new speaker in a very clear sense takes over and becomes responsible for what is handed on to him by those who precede him. It can thus be truly said to preexist in relation to each new speaker or generation of speakers and yet at the same time to depend on the latter, all this in a way that closely corresponds to the way in which independence and dependence are described by Heidegger as characterizing language. But if neither the fact that language opens a world that is common to an indefinitely extensive class of speakers nor the fact that it is taken over by successive generations of new speakers for each of which it is a prior reality is to be allowed to account for the special authority it has in relation to all speakers, then how can Heidegger provide an alternative explanation that does not transform language into the very "fantastic being that exists in itself" against which he warns? If he drew back from his assertion that being as such could obtain without entities and if the saying of language is identical with being, then surely he must adhere to his thesis that "language is unmistakably bound to human speech" and find a way within that bond to account for the priority and independence that nevertheless characterize it. I submit that only the social and historical character of language offers any real possibility of affording such an explanation.

CHAPTER NINE • BEING AS THE HISTORY OF BEING

It might well be thought that being as Heidegger conceives it is no more likely to have a history than is the being of Parmenides. But in fact, the idea of a history of being is of central importance in Heidegger's later thought. It must therefore be examined carefully so as to determine whether it has implications for the issue of the independence/dependence of being as presence vis-à-vis man or *Dasein*. Because this is such an unfamiliar notion, it will be helpful to begin by considering what Heidegger has to say about history in *Being and Time* and especially about the historicity of *Dasein*, so as to have a baseline from which to try to understand the historical character of being as such. In approaching the conception of a history of being, I will first distinguish two major senses that can be given to this notion. The contrast between the two is already familiar, at least in a preliminary way, as a result of the discussion in the last chapter of the ways in which being as presence can be hidden. I will argue that it is the notion of being as an unhiddenness that is typically also unthought that holds the key to an understanding of what Heidegger has in mind in speaking of a history of being. In the account that he gives of the actual course of the history of being, that history begins in ancient Greece and continues through what is at once the career of Western philosophy and that of Western civilization. The principal features of Heidegger's characterization of Greek and subsequent Western philosophy therefore require careful scrutiny. Of special interest in this connection is his characterization of the present stage of Western thought and civilization and of the objectifying tendencies that are endemic in it. These tendencies cast a good deal of light on a negative mode of *Mitsein* that has achieved dominance in what he views as the age of subjectivism. The chapter then concludes with a consideration of how the conception of a history of being impinges on the issue about the independence/dependence of being as presence.

I

In *Being and Time* a whole chapter in the second section of part I is devoted to "Temporality and Historicity," and it constitutes an important element in the discussion of time with which that section is concerned.[1] Historicity is presented there as an essential feature of *Dasein* that derives from the special character of its temporality, as described in chapter 7. Since for *Dasein* being in time is not a matter of simply being at one point in time—one Now—after another, but rather of being in the present in the mode of "having been" and "having to be," the movement of *Dasein* through its life is not one that can be described in a way that abstracts from these complexities of its temporal structure. This is a movement through the world as a space of possibilities, and it must be understood in a way that does justice to the implication in one another of the present, past, and future of *Dasein* and that presents the actions of *Dasein* as "a reciprocative rejoinder to the possibility of that existence which has-been-there."[2] *Dasein* is characterized by historicity in this sense under all conditions; but when the character of its own temporality is no longer obscured by misleading representations that assimilate it to world-time, the historicity that derives from it takes on a special quality of authenticity which, for all Heidegger's denials that this was his intention, assumes a distinctly normative character in *Being and Time*. In any case, it is clear that although what is distinctively historical in the life of *Dasein* essentially involves a relation to tradition as that which is handed down from the past, this relation also includes a response in the form of an action on the part of *Dasein*. Because historicity characterizes *Dasein* primarily in its character as belonging to social groupings like generations and communities, this action also has a shared character. Heidegger characterizes this aspect of historical life only very briefly, and it cannot be said that he presents any real theory of a distinctively historical process.[3] Nevertheless, he does emphasize the point that in its happening (*Geschehen*) history (*Geschichte*) is always a kind of destiny (*Geschick*). The use of the word *Geschick* does not imply a deterministic conception of the historical process; it seems to express rather the lack of any complete control over consequences that characterizes human agency and the resultant suffering or undergoing of those consequences that is inseparable from agency that is less than omnipotent. Overall, one can say that what appears to interest Heidegger is the historical character of human existence, rather than any particular theme—any substantive content or outcome—that human history may turn out to have.

It is not surprising, therefore, that he has a low opinion of empirical historiography. As in the case of the natural sciences, so in that of history as a form of knowledge, it appears that the instruments of inquiry that are designed to insure a measure of objectivity and sharable truth are, in Heidegger's eyes, so many ways in which the historian tries to conceal from himself the rootedness of his subject matter in the temporality of *Dasein*. Once again, this is a matter of relying on a context—in this case, that of *Dasein*'s temporality—that is not only never made explicit, but is actually obscured by the adoption of other conceptualizations of the historical process in which that context finds no place. For the average unphilosophical historian, things have historical characteristics just as unproblematically as they have other properties, physical or otherwise. What such a conception of history misses, in Heidegger's view, is the fact that it is *Dasein* alone that is historical in the primary sense and that historical descriptions accrue to entities other than *Dasein* only because they form a part of the latter's world.[4] Whether there have been, or could be, forms of empirical historiography that would acknowledge this fact, either explicitly or implicitly, and would not, therefore, be subject to the severe criticisms that Heidegger directs against historiography generally remains somewhat unclear.[5] In this connection it is perhaps significant that, although Heidegger was possessed of a vast historical erudition, especially in the history of philosophy, his often brilliant characterizations of thinkers and periods in that history are typically presented in a very high degree of abstraction from virtually everything but the internal dialectic of the theses under consideration.

These strictures on the procedures of empirical historiography should not lead one to suppose that any of the classical patterns of philosophical historiography were at all congenial to Heidegger. Of these, only the Hegelian theory of history, worked out in terms of concepts like those of substance and subject that are of profound importance in Heidegger's own thought, seems even to have been found worthy of his attention.[6] For Hegel, history is the process in the course of which natural consciousness—the finite subject—comes to understand itself as the infinite subject that it really has been all along; and in doing so, it overcomes and supersedes all the oppositions between subject and object and between subject and subject that appear so irrevocably fixed to common sense. As it turns out, they all prove to be internal to "experience," and the being of objects generally is subsumed in this "experience" which, as Heidegger puts it, becomes Hegel's word for being as such.[7] Plainly, the radical finiteness of *Dasein* as delineated in *Being and Time* makes any such movement from a natural to an absolute form of subjectivity quite out of the question for Heidegger, and with it any conception of history as the process in which such a movement takes place. In the writings of his later period he also states that, although being as such is "the matter of thought" (*die Sache des Denkens*) for him as for Hegel, the latter's identification of being with absolute thought is unacceptable to him for the further reason that it does not permit an acknowledgment of the difference between being as such and entities.[8] This statement is of special interest in light of the difficulties that this distinction generates for a concept of being as presence like the one of Heidegger's later period. But even if one accepts at face value Heidegger's way of contrasting his own conception of being with that of Hegel, one can hardly help noticing that, in other respects and especially in the case of the relationship between *Dasein* and being as presence, there are similarities between his position and Hegel's that would hardly have been imaginable in the period of *Being and Time*.[9] This is because Heidegger's later thought is so extensively concerned with the relationship between being as presence and man or *Dasein* as the deficient mode of presence as representation. To be sure, Heidegger energetically rejects the Hegelian thesis that the logic of the concept is the connecting tissue between finite and absolute thought. He does, however, postulate a process in which the relationship between being as presence and man or *Dasein* changes; and he holds that these changes determine the character of whole civilizations. Both these theses have an unmistakably Hegelian ring to them, even though Heidegger does not claim, as Hegel does, that there is any dialectic at work that will issue in the reconciliation of the finite and the infinite.[10] The more specific roles of the agency of being as presence and the agency of man or *Dasein*, if such there be, in this history of being will have to be determined carefully.

Because the theme of the hiddenness and unhiddenness of being as such is the central element in Heidegger's conception of the history of being, it is appropriate to notice the feature of the theory of *Dasein* that corresponds to it. This is the fact that *Dasein*, too, is in its own way both unhidden and hidden, both open (*erschlossen*) to itself and concealed (*verdeckt*) from itself.[11] This is because it both reveals to itself and conceals from itself the kind of entity it is. The reasons for this lie in the special kind of uncanniness and freedom with which *Dasein* would have to come face to face if it were to acknowledge explicitly its own mode of being as a clearing. As a result, *Dasein* represents itself and its mode of being to itself in terms of models that are drawn from the world and thus from entities whose mode of being is quite different from its own. It thereby covers up and hides from itself the kind of entity it really is. This covering-up, of course, can never succeed completely; it is always paired with an understanding of *Dasein* as the entity that uncovers. These paired understandings by *Dasein* of itself as *vorhanden*, an object among objects, and as opening upon entities that do not open upon it are inseparable, and even in authentic existence there can be no question of eliminating one in favor of the other. Nevertheless, in exposing the inappropriateness of these assimilations, as he does in *Being and Time*, Heidegger is also working out a concept of a *Dasein* that acknowledges its character as a clearing. It is evident, too, that although self-obscuration and self-disclosure are inseparable, Heidegger's effort to work out such a concept of *Dasein* implies some kind of preferred status for self-disclosure and the authenticity it mediates. There are strong indications that the grounds for this preferred status lie in the way the objectification of *Dasein* affects the life of decision and action.[12] As far as one can tell, then, self-disclosure and self-obscuration are functions of individual *Dasein* in *Being and Time*; and typically, such individuals will be in very different situations as regards self-disclosure and self-obscuration. The anonymous "They"—*das Man*—to which, in the mode of self-obscuration, the decisional functions of *Dasein* are assigned is understood in such a way as to make it a supra-individual constraint on individual responsibility; but the ability to pull away from this collective self (without thereby abolishing it) evidently resides in each *Dasein*.

In the later writings we hear nothing of this tendency of *Dasein* to misrepresent itself to itself. Self-disclosure and self-obscuration are now treated as functions of being as such—that is, of a unitary milieu of presence. Evidently, it is no longer in *Dasein*'s power to move away from self-obscuration and toward self-disclosure; instead it must await the self-disclosure of being and must do so together with the other members of the historical grouping to which it belongs. Whereas the self-disclosure of *Dasein* was reflexive in a double sense—disclosure of the self and disclosure to the self—that of being takes being itself as its direct object and *Dasein* or man as its indirect object. These are certainly momentous differences, but even so, they do not completely cancel out the affinity between the self-obscuration of *Dasein* in *Being and Time* and that of being as presence in the later period. Both, after all, issue in a comprehensive objectification of the world and of the self. The difference is that in the latter case the grounds of objectification are, if not altogether inaccessible to the individual self, then at least not of such a character as to be altered by decisional means—for example, by "the choosing of choice" as one's mode of personal existence, as Heidegger puts it in *Being and Time*.[13] Accordingly, it is important to determine what makes the one mode of self-obscuration so intractable that it can appear to be altogether independent of our decisions.

II

The notion of a history of being as such is so unfamiliar to most philosophers as to seem virtually unconstruable. A common reaction might be to suppose that by "being" Heidegger must mean whatever exists, and that a history of being is therefore history of the world or cosmos as the totality of what exists. If it is made clear that being is to be understood not as any such totality but in terms of presence, a likely second construal might be that Heidegger must be talking about something like a history of consciousness. The reasons why this conjecture, too, would be wide of the mark have been set forth already and need not be repeated. The central consideration here is simply that, for Heidegger, presence is not "consciousness" or "experience," but a clearing in which entities show themselves as entities; and so the question about the possibility of a history of being is a question about how such a clearing could have a history. But this is not to say that, when understood this way, the question can be answered unambiguously. It seems, first of all, that such a clearing either obtains or does not, and that if it does, its history could consist only in its coming about that there is such a clearing and subsequently, perhaps, that there is not. That would not be much of a history, and it can hardly be what Heidegger had in mind; but the obvious ways in which one might try to enrich such a history are just as clearly not germane to the notion of the history of being as he conceived it. One such effort would borrow again from Hegelian conceptions of history as the process in which subjectivity and objectivity are progressively brought into the right sort of equilibrium. It would then construe the history of being as presence as the emergence of the several domains of objectivity, including abstract and theoretical entities, and as the sorting-out of their relationships with one another within the matrix of the thought that has to be able to construct them conceptually if it is to affirm their existence. This would be the history of being as the history of objectivity—the conceptual history, in short, of the emergence of the different kinds of entities that make up the world understood as the totality of present entities. The difficulty with such an interpretation as this is simply that it provides no way of construing what Heidegger says about being hiding or obscuring itself. It has already been shown that this obscuration of being cannot be understood as a straightforward termination of being as presence so that there would be no clearing at all. But in that case being as presence must hide itself in the course of its "holding sway" as a clearing; and there does not seem to be any way in which this could be accounted for simply in terms of conceptual history as the emergence into presence of the several types of entities of which the world is made up. Even if one were to imagine a history in which there was a gradual erosion and loss of the conceptual articulation of the world, instead of the steady advance that is usually postulated, such a progressive simplification of the world-order would not by itself entail either an eclipse or even an obscuration of presence as such. If there is to be a history of being as presence in the course of which being itself is obscured and hidden, the character of that history must manifestly be defined in some way other than this.

Fortunately, an alternative interpretation is not hard to find, and its general character was indicated briefly in the last chapter. If one accepts the notion of being as a clearing at all, then one must also accept a distinction between the clearing as such and the entities that are cleared or uncovered within it. But if, following the qualifications that Heidegger appends to his initial assertion of the independence and priority of this clearing, we conclude that the entities so cleared must be cleared *for* someone, then it is quite possible that that someone could understand these entities as entities and yet not acknowledge or understand their presence as presence in its full distinctiveness. In that case, presence would remain invisible and hidden as presence, at the same time that it made possible the self-disclosure of entities. Since for Heidegger being is just this presence that makes possible seeing and being seen, being may "give" entities without thereby giving itself. If it gave itself as itself—that is, as presence—not only would the entity to which this disclosure was made dwell in a clearing—that is, a world—in which other entities are uncovered for it, but it would dwell in that clearing *as* a clearing or, as Heidegger says, "in the proximity of being" (*in der Nähe des Seins*).[14] But if, as is more typically the case, the human beings who are able to understand entities as entities are absorbed in the practical manipulation and use of these entities, they may simply take for granted this uncoveredness, and by not distinguishing it from the kinds of facts and events with which they are familiar, they may miss it altogether by just assimilating it to the latter. For such persons (or from such persons) being as presence would be appropriately described as "hidden," since even the fact that it has been missed—Heidegger would say "forgotten"—would itself be missed. The paradoxical result would be that the clearing in which all entities are cleared as such would not itself be cleared. It is just this possibility, in its multiple versions and with its full train of consequences, that constitutes the central event in a history of being. That history is thus one in the course of which being as presence at some point declares itself to some body of persons and at another hides itself from them, perhaps to emerge yet again at a later time.

On the interpretation just proposed, the history of being would be concerned with the openness of being as such, rather than with the uncoveredness of entities as entities, although it is being as presence that makes the latter possible even when it is not itself manifest. That there is such a distinction between the openness of being as such and the uncoveredness of entities as entities is not always fully clear in Heidegger's writings. Aristotle spoke of an inquiry into *to on he on*—that is, into entities, or what is as such; and in *Being and Time* and the lectures of that period the equivalence of being as such and entities showing themselves as entities seems to be accepted by Heidegger.[15] Later, however, this equivalence is no longer accepted, and it is laid down that to think entities as such is not to think being as being.[16] This is in keeping with the emphasis, already noted, on the fact that being or unhiddenness can be either thought or unthought, and that the latter is possible even when entities are grasped as entities. There is a difficulty here inasmuch as being as presence is a necessary condition that must be in place if entities are to show themselves as entities. From this it surely follows that to affirm entities as entities and at the same time to deny being as presence, whether implicitly or explicitly, must reflect a confusion of thought and, ultimately, an inconsistency. On the other hand, it does not seem that such an error would be a simple obliviousness to a logical implication, as though someone were to talk about "nephews" without admitting "uncles" to his universe of discourse. The distinction between being conversant with entities and being conversant with entities in their being—that is, presence—is of a different order, because what is missing in the first term of *this* distinction is not recognition of a conceptual linkage like the one between "nephew" and "uncle," but rather an understanding of the difference between an entity as a thing and an entity as embedded in a state of affairs—that is, as something that *is* such-and-such and that thus presupposes an order of truth.[17] In one sense, of course, anyone who is conversant with entities at all *must* understand this, or he would be unable to formulate propositions about such entities in which they are declared to *be* such-and-such. It is also a fact (and a momentous one at that), however, that people who do just this may altogether fail to recognize (and, if it is brought to their attention, pertinaciously deny) that there is a distinction between an entity and an entity taken (or showing itself) as something that *is* such-and-such. This is the distinction that Heidegger quite properly formulates as one between entities and being; and in this idiom it is being that is manifested *as* being when the distinction becomes clear. The same point can be made, however, by saying that on these occasions it is entities that are fully delineated in their character as entities—that is, in their relationship to truth—and this idiom would be quite consistent with the way Heidegger puts things in the period in which he accepted the equivalence of "being" with "entities as entities." In his later writings, however, he tends to reserve the latter phrase for the case in which the distinction elaborated above is *not* properly understood, and being as such remains unthought.[18]

Now if the distinction on which the notion of a history of being turns is along the lines just described, it is evident that it does not readily yield an empirical criterion for distinguishing epochs in which being is hidden from those in which it is not. What has just been said seems to imply that the only real criterion available for this purpose would be the emergence and use in some historical culture of a concept (and thus a word or set of words) that expresses the distinction noted above. Almost by definition, anyone who worked out such a concept would be a philosopher. It is hardly surprising, therefore, that Heidegger's account of the disclosure of being as such to the Greeks centers on the role of certain of their early philosophers like Parmenides and Heraclitus.[19] At the same time, it is evident that he thinks of being as having manifested itself not just to a handful of Greek philosophers, but somehow to the Greeks as a people; and the criteria that might serve to establish this claim are very much less clear. Even if it were to prove possible to establish that a given philosopher had worked out a concept of being that corresponds to the distinction of being from entities that Heidegger wants to make (and even this may prove far from easy), it would surely prove much more difficult to show that nonphilosophers in the same culture were conversant with that concept and that distinction. The difficulty is all the greater when one bears in mind that the criteria must also be able to show that being was not similarly revealed to other peoples or their philosophers, since this is evidently part of Heidegger's thesis of the unique role of the Greeks in the history of being. The evidence that he offers for both the narrower and the broader version of his thesis about the Greeks is literary and linguistic: the texts of the Greek poets and philosophers and the etymological structure of a number of Greek words. In both versions he attempts to bring out what would now be called the structure of the metaphors drawn from familiar life activities in terms of which some more abstract and "philosophical" term like "truth" or "existence" is grounded. It is not my purpose to try to determine who is right in the controversies to which Heidegger's construals have given rise, although it would seem that many of the interpretations advanced by Heidegger are, to say the least, profoundly suggestive. The relevant point here is to determine whether the results he obtains *could* confirm the conclusion he must establish. It is certainly hard to see how nonphilosophical literary texts could by themselves show that a distinction as unfamiliar to common sense as the one between entities and being was or was not understood by their authors and the audience they addressed. Superficially at least, these texts, moving as they do in the medium of the proposition and the "is" must *all* appear to be conversant with being as truth. But the same would hold for texts from all cultures; so, if further evidence is required to determine which ones *really* evince this understanding and which do not, it is once again unclear what that could be short of an explicit use of the right philosophical concept.

These considerations raise a more general methodological point about Heidegger's account of the history of being. The evidence for the claims he makes about this or that epoch in the history of being is mainly drawn from conceptual history. For example, he devotes a great deal of detailed attention to the different understandings of truth expressed in such Greek words as *aletheia* and in those that replaced it: *homoiosis* ("likeness" or "becoming like") and the Roman *veritas*.[20] What is involved here is a sequence of interpretations and translations of Greek terms that were evidently intended to preserve equivalence but, according to Heidegger, failed to do so. Now when someone misinterprets and mistranslates a word like *aletheia*, it would ordinarily be said that that person has *taken* the word in question in a certain way that happens to be mistaken. This way of describing the matter imputes an element of agency to the person responsible for misunderstanding the meaning of the original word. Normally, we would express what happens in such cases by saying that such a person is using the concept of *aletheia* as though it were equivalent to, say, *homoiosis*, although it really is not. But Heidegger is not at all willing to treat such erroneous renderings simply as matters of conceptual history understood as the takings and mis-takings of historical individuals. In his view, conceptual history is only the manifestation of a sequence of shifts that being itself brings about, not the historical thinkers whose names may be associated with them, as, for example, that of Cicero is with the passage of Greek philosophical concepts into the Roman world.[21] If such a thinker "mistranslates" a term like *aletheia*, it is because being (and thus truth) has disclosed itself to him and to his age differently, and his translation merely registers that change. At one point Heidegger imagines an objection being made to the claim that a "mere translation" could occasion an epochal change of this magnitude. He replies to the effect that we need to reconsider what can take place (*ereignen*) in a translation and adds that "the authentic, fateful encounter of historical languages is an unobtrusive (*stilles*) event, but in it speaks the destiny of being."[22] We are thus being told once again that we must abandon our subject-bound ways of understanding such shifts as these, just as we were previously admonished to call into question our understanding of something's being hidden in terms of what is not being noticed, rather than in terms of the state of being of that which is hidden. In the present case, however, conversion of the one idiom into the other would mean that what we think of as conceptual history is at most a registering of another kind of history—that of being itself—and that it is accordingly being itself (as well as truth and other related matters) that is changing.[23] It is this change that changes us, not the other way around.

As one would expect when such a thesis is being advanced, there is a strong emphasis on the inability of the individual human being to think independently of the conceptual ordering established in his time and place.[24] In the later writings, the picture suggested by *Being and Time* of individual human beings who at least have it in their power to detect the modes of self-misrepresentation they have employed and thus to resist the inauthenticity they entail is dropped. It thus appears that Heidegger became more willing to acknowledge the constraining character of language and conceptual systems and the impossibility of breaking with them once and for all at a single stroke. For many thinkers, such constraints are an important index of the social nature of human beings and of their close dependence on the conceptual configuration of the language they have learned as members of a particular historical community. To those who are impressed by this aspect of human life, any suggestion that this complex incorporation of individual human beings into communities of communication could be nullified by some decisional fiat has always seemed deeply implausible. It is just this emphasis on the social character of conceptual orderings, and thus of language, that is absent from Heidegger's way of portraying the constraints to which we are subject as individual thinkers. It is not our linguistically mediated interdependence that constitutes those constraints, but rather the fact that being has disclosed itself to us as a people or a community in a certain way which we therefore share with one another. Heidegger even goes so far as to say that "the concepts that form the essence of an historical people and thus its belonging to world history are antecedently impressed upon it."[25] It thus appears that it is not only entities and being as presence that are to be spoken of as being *given* to man or *Dasein*, but also the concepts he uses, or at least the most fundamental ones that mark out the ways in which his world is ordered. The contrast between the passivity that has traditionally been supposed to characterize sensibility and the activity peculiar to conceptual thought is thus set aside in favor of a construal of the latter as passive in the same sense as the former. Conceptual history is thereby being assimilated to the category of matters that we must be thought of as awaiting, rather than producing. It also follows that when Heidegger says that "no one can with one leap take himself out of the prevailing circle of representations (*Vorstellungskreis*) and especially not when it is a case of paths of prior thought that were entered upon long ago and run their course unnoticed," we are to understand him as speaking not of a difficulty that is susceptible of degree but of an impossibility.[26] Whether such a view is at all plausible to the extent that it goes beyond what can be justified in terms of what people historically have and have not been able to achieve—though not necessarily with one leap—in the way of moving beyond inherited ways of thought is something we will take up in the next chapter. In this connection it is also appropriate to ask how this thesis applies to Heidegger's own thought, which surely has not remained within any "prevailing circle of representations."

The history of being, as Heidegger presents it, begins in Greece, and its main subsequent stages are Rome, the Christian Middle Ages, and modern Europe. It is also part of his thesis that in the modern age, which for him is characterized primarily by its technology, the world as a whole has been drawn into the Western way of understanding being and has thus entered the history of being. But for the whole long stretch of time preceding the modern period, Heidegger's version of the history of being is Europocentric in the extreme. No attention is given to non-European cultures prior to their contact with Western European culture, and nothing beyond a few enigmatic remarks in *Being and Time* is said about primitive cultures.[27] Sometimes Heidegger seems to be prepared to defend this limitation of the history of being to Europe, as when he says that "there is no philosophy other than the Western" and that "there is only a Western technology (*Technik*)," since that technology is derivative from Western philosophy.[28] At other times he expresses a respectful interest in non-European cultures and their thought, as in his conversation with the Japanese in *On The Way To Language*, in which he expresses regret at the eagerness of Japanese students of philosophy to master Western ways of thought, apparently in the belief that they have in their own tradition something with which they would be wiser to concern themselves.[29] In any case, it is evident that, in Heidegger's view, something absolutely unique and unprecedented happened in Greece, and that human history from that point onward has to be understood as the working-out of the implications of that event (*Ereignis*) in which being as presence became manifest for the first time and, as Heidegger put it, drew man into a relation to itself. Whatever the truth of this thesis, it leaves us with no real indication of how we are to talk about perception and thought in non-Western cultures before there was any significant contact with the West (and for that matter, in Greece before the advent of being). What, for example, is the dividing line between animal life and human cultures to which being as presence has not yet announced itself? Can being be said to hide itself from cultures to which it has not yet announced itself? Is it possible that it has announced itself to other cultures and then hidden itself, in ways that Westerners are not well qualified to identify? Is there some element of plurality, through its relationships to many cultures, in being's self-disclosure and self-obscuration; and, if so, what justifies our treating all these varying modes of disclosure as deriving from some single and unitary being to which our concept of presence applies? Even within a single culture, is it the case that being announces itself to some—perhaps a very few thinkers— and not to others—the great mass of the population? It is not easy even to guess what Heidegger's answers to these questions might be. As long as the conception of a history of being remains undeveloped in these respects, however, it must be viewed as an interpretation of Western history, rather than of world history in any sense that would be inclusive of the entire history of mankind.

III

The thesis that the history of being begins in ancient Greece because it was in Greece that being for the first time disclosed itself as presence neatly reverses an interpretation of the role of the Greeks in the history of philosophy that was first argued by Hegel.[30] According to that interpretation, the Greeks had no adequate concept of subjectivity, and that concept first emerged as an achievement of Christian thought and modern, predominantly Cartesian philosophy. According to Heidegger, however, this was not a weakness of Greek thought, as Hegel supposed, but a strength inasmuch as the modern concept of subjectivity is merely a misconceived derivative of the original Greek concept of being as presence. The history of Western thought thus becomes the story of this first understanding of being as being and then of the gradual slipping away of the distinction between being as such and entities, as well as the resulting obliviousness to being as such and the progressive domination by the human subject that replaces it. With Hegel and Nietzsche this transformation of substance into subject reaches its climax and completes the history of Western metaphysics—the form of thought that understands being in terms of entities and remains blind to the distinction between the two. This blindness to being is the condition of our own time, in which presence has become invisible to us; and it is a condition that even Heidegger's own thought does not claim to be able to overcome. At best, it can try to make possible an understanding of that condition as one that has been reached through a certain course of thought, from the outcome of which we can at most draw back as we await another phase in the self-manifestation of being.

Since Heidegger's thesis about the Greeks rests not just on their philosophical doctrines, but on broad features of their culture as a whole, their art, their religious conceptions, and their language must somehow yield supporting evidence for it. The interpretation he offers of the Greek gods, not as supernatural personages, but as a shining and lighting-up of entities into which their "look" penetrates, has already been discussed. It is quite unclear, however, how widely Heidegger believes this understanding of the gods to have been shared among the Greeks themselves, and so the degree of evidential support it affords his thesis is indeterminate. Since the evidence for it is in any case linguistic in character, it seems best to concentrate on what he says about the Greek language. What he does in that regard is to draw attention to a set of words and expressions used by the Greeks to name what in modern Western languages would typically be described as mental acts and states. In Greece, at least before the time of Plato and Aristotle, the transition to this way of thinking had not begun, and so the language was full of expressions that characterized knowledge and truth in terms of the show- ing-itself of an entity. The Greeks' linguistic instruments for expressing the character of this event center on the word for light (*phos/phaos*) and its cognates, among which Heidegger emphasizes above all the verb *phaino*, of which the middle voice, *phainesthai*, gives the participle *phai- nomenon*, "showing itself " and "that which shows itself."[31] This word has had a long history in Western thought and has progressively moved away from the first "naive" use just described to one in which it serves mainly epistemic purposes and carries the disparaging implication of that which merely "appears." Heidegger views the increasing epistemic sophistication that is achieved in the course of that process mainly as a loss of understanding of the original "showing-itself," or *phainesthai*. Other families of words that serve to express this same notion are *aletheia* and those that fan out from "dēlos" and "dēlein"—"visible" and "to make visible"—from which derive a host of words for activities such as explanation. Perhaps the most controversial among the words Heidegger cites, because it is not cognate with words for light and making visible, is *ousia*, which he takes to be the Greek word for "the being-ness of entities" (*die Seiendheit des Seienden*) and thus for being as presence. Hei- degger's justification for attributing to this word a sense not listed in the lexicons is the way it figures in the related word *parousia*, which does mean something like presence.[32]

Quite apart from any judgment regarding the historical accuracy of these linguistic claims, it is not easy to know how Heidegger would have us appraise them. What he is most often criticized for is an arbitrary reading of his own philosophical ideas into Greek words, and to this he replies in effect that no interpretation that is not itself associated with a stand on the philosophical issues in question has any chance of getting at what the Greeks had in mind.[33] What this amounts to is an admission of circularity in his interpretations, together with a claim that this con- stitutes a virtue rather than a vice in them. One could argue, after all, that if one *begins* by accepting Heidegger's theses about being as presence, then it becomes perfectly reasonable to try to determine whether some understanding of presence found expression in the language and dis- course of a people such as the Greeks, and, if it did, what kinds of words may have served to express that understanding. An obvious answer to this question is that words for light and bringing to light would be a natural means for this purpose. The lighted-ness of the world and its corresponding hiddenness in darkness or night are familiar to everyone;

and though presence is not confined to visibility and being hidden in darkness is not equivalent to absence as the polar notion to presence, it is not unreasonable to suppose that the vocabulary of light and vision served the wider purpose of expressing a pre-philosophical understanding that the Greeks (or other early peoples) may have had of what Heidegger explicitly conceptualizes as presence. To object that light is really something physical and that the Greeks themselves were working out conceptions of light and vision that eventually led to a physical theory of light is beside the point. It is quite possible that notions derived from those of light and vision served in more than one capacity, and that in one such capacity they expressed the generalized notion of visibility that leads to the concept of presence. Indeed, even in our own day when, according to Heidegger, the primordial fact of presence has been split into mental states on the one hand and physical processes on the other, the notion of light can still serve this very different purpose.

But even if one is prepared to accept the requirement that such interpretations be informed by explicitly philosophical assumptions like those of Heidegger's philosophy, real difficulties remain. After all, the language of light is not uniquely privileged in comparison with other possible ways of testifying to the fact of presence; and if we, in our capacity as interpreters, are now entitled to postulate at least some implicit familiarity with presence on the part of all human beings, as Heidegger does, it seems that almost any set of words, and indeed the very fact of using words at all, would count as evidence for the kind of understanding he declares the Greeks to have had on the strength of their use of words like those cited above. In this way *all* cultures, not just Greek culture, would prove to be recipients of the gift of being. If, on the other hand, it is not just a question of an implicit understanding such as might be attributable to someone solely on the basis of his use of a word without his ever having thought about what the word means or tried to define it, and we require instead something approaching the definiteness of an explicit concept of being as presence, then even the Greek case may not be wholly unproblematic. Heidegger admits that the Greeks failed to achieve any understanding of certain essential features of presence as he defines it; and he declares that "we find the essential conception (*Wesensbegriff*) of the open nowhere among the Greeks."[34] This is simply a compact summing-up of what he says repeatedly about the failure of the Greeks to make the right kind of linkage between the notions of being and time and their tendency to understand time in terms of a kind of standing present that excludes both the past and the future and thereby misses the absence that is essential to presence as Heidegger conceives it.[35] Although he claims, nevertheless, that in the notion of *ousia* the Greeks had a concept of being as presence, a concept of presence that is not a concept of openness or of the ecstatic character of its temporality is surely something of a puzzle. Of course, even if the Greeks did not have a concept of the open as such, Heidegger would presumably still want to claim that they had a preconceptual understanding of the kind mediated by their use of the words cited above.[36] This would not only be a very much weaker thesis, but it would again call into question the uniqueness of the Greeks, since Heidegger is on record as imputing this kind of familiarity with being to *all* historical peoples.[37] In the absence of a fully articulated concept of presence that would bring into focus the implicit understanding that may be at work in the use of certain sets of words, it might turn out that the position of the Greeks in this regard was much more like that of other early peoples than Heidegger's uniqueness thesis can allow.

There are, in fact, scattered indications that the Greek case did not always seem wholly straightforward to Heidegger himself. In his essay on Anaximander he asks why, if the Greeks did have a concept of being as presence, they failed to develop further the understanding that that concept represented.[38] In this connection, he describes Greece as "the morning of the destiny as which being itself clears itself in entities and claims an essence of man which, as so destined, has its historical course in being sheltered in being and released from it but never separated from it."[39] He goes on to say that it is a "fundamental trait of being" and one that runs through all Western and now planetary history, that it hides "its essence and its essential origin."[40] This, in fact, is its way of clearing itself at first, and the result is that "thought does not follow it." "The unhiddenness of entities, the clarity that is accorded to them, darkens the light of being"; and "being withdraws as it dis-conceals itself in entities."[41] The history that follows this disclosure of being that is also a hiding of being is a process of error and mis-taking (*Versehen*). It thus appears that what was initiated in Greece was not so much a disclosure of being as such as an obscuration. But if that is really what Heidegger is saying, a number of highly paradoxical consequences have to be accepted along with it. It would follow, for example, that being as such was obscured without ever having been revealed to anyone, since such a revelation could hardly have been vouchsafed to a people that preceded the Greeks if it was denied to the latter. But even if we let this difficulty pass and agree that being was obscured in Greece rather than revealed, what will then count as the distinctive feature of Greek thought? If the passage above were taken literally, one would have to say that it was the fact that for the first time "being cleared itself in entities"; and this would mean that no prior people or culture was familiar with entities as entities. Not only would any such thesis be extraordinarily difficult to establish, but it would have a consequence that Heidegger would hardly welcome—

namely, that even the thought of Parmenides and Heraclitus, who, together with Anaximander, are always described by Heidegger as the authentic philosophers of being as such, did not really "follow (being)" and can have been conversant only with the unhiddenness of entities, and not with that of being itself. If that was indeed the case, it is not clear how it would have been possible for the Greeks even to confuse being with entities, since they would only have been familiar with the latter.

However it may have been initiated, the obscuration of being proceeded apace in the ancient world; and in Heidegger's view the philosophies of Plato and Aristotle played a major role in that process, as did the transmission of Greek thought to Rome and its subsequent Christianization in the Roman world. The concept of being as presence, which the Greeks must have had in some form or these subsequent developments could not have taken place at all, was first transformed by being treated as the notion of something present, with the result that it became itself an entity, although typically one of a superior order. According to Heidegger, this happened through Plato's separation of the "look" or *eidos* of things as present from *physis* as the wider process of the emergence of the entity that has this look into presence.[42] When this *eidos* is treated as an entity unto itself, as it is by Plato, philosophy becomes a set of questions about the relationships in which *these* entities—the "ideas"—stand to other entities, and the notions of *physis* and being as presence are lost. In general Heidegger seems to evaluate Aristotle more positively than Plato, especially for his elaboration of the concept of *physis*, which Heidegger treats as equivalent to that of being as presence. Indeed, a passage from *De Anima* which he had quoted approvingly in the introduction to *Being and Time* because it characterizes the soul as, in some sense, "all entities" and thus lays the foundation for his own concept of *Dasein* is quoted again in the lectures on Parmenides, although in this case the grounds for approval were apparently quite different.[43] The fact remains, however, that in the end Aristotle contributes to the loss of the concept of being as presence if only because he treats *physis* as only one kind of being—the kind that was later called "nature"—and the wider concept of being is not elaborated in a way that would preserve the original Greek understanding of *physis* as presence.[44]

Although medieval philosophy is discussed only in passing in Heidegger's mature works, it plays an important role in his conception of the history of being in the West.[45] It was through medieval philosophy and theology that the ancient understanding of being—an understanding of being *without* the distinction between being and entities—was transmitted to the modern world. It was a concept of that which is constantly present (*das beständig Anwesende*), but the presence by virtue of which entities are enabled to be present was not itself understood. As a result, being came to be thought of as an attribute of entities and most especially of the supreme entity, God, whose being is the ground of the being of all other entities. But entities that are treated as present independently of being as presence are thereby understood as *das Vorliegende*—Heidegger's translation of the Greek *upokeimenon*; and the concept of substance (*substantia*—the Latin translation of *upokeimenon*) thereby becomes the favored conceptual vehicle for representing the character of such entities.[46]

IV

The transmission to the modern world of the conceptualization of being as substance brings us back to the point at which Heidegger's critique of Descartes in *Being and Time* began. In his account of the history of being, Heidegger still regards Descartes's philosophy as setting the course of modern thought, but the grounds of the new critique are quite different. It is no accident, for example, that this critique forms part of Heidegger's interpretation of Nietzsche's thought. For Heidegger, Nietzsche represents the end point of the development that began with Plato and thus in some sense the end of Western metaphysics. In this development, Descartes plays a crucially important role in establishing the modern concept of the subject, and Heidegger sees an affinity between Descartes and Nietzsche that goes much deeper than the differences on which Nietzsche himself insisted. All this is rendered even more complex by the relationship of Heidegger's own thought to that of Nietzsche, both in the period of *Being and Time* and later.

In *Being and Time* the principal criticism directed against Descartes is that his concept of the subject as an immaterial substance within which knowing takes place misses the phenomenon of the world. This notion of the self and of the entities it aspires to know as substances was never subjected to any real criticism. The sole issue for Descartes was to determine what kind of knowledge can securely grasp the being of those entities that are constantly present at hand (*vorhanden*)—something that "mathematical knowledge is exceptionally well suited to grasp."[47] But this choice of mathematics was itself uncritical, since it is suited only to certain aspects of certain entities within the world; and when it is generalized, as it is by Descartes, to become an ontology of the world as such, the result can only be to obliterate the kind of being that belongs to sensory perception and to the entities that are encountered in such perception. It also assimilates *Dasein* itself to the inappropriate ontological type of substance and renders invisible its distinctive mode of being in-the-world; and it is on this fact that the primary emphasis of Heidegger's first critique falls.

In his later discussion of Descartes, little, if any, attention is given to this self-misrepresentation on the part of *Dasein*. Heidegger emphasizes instead what he takes to be the characteristic effort of modern thought to elevate the thinking self to the status of the preeminent and ultimately exclusive self for which all other entities that in medieval parlance were "subjects" on an equal footing with it become "objects."[48] Where the earlier critique concentrates on the loss of an adequate understanding of being-in-the-world entailed by Descartes's mode of conceptualization, the later critique concentrates on the positive aspirations that find expression in the establishment of the self as the preeminent entity. The latter are essentially concerned with the mastery and control over the domain of entities which thought in its representational activity (*Vorstellen*) places at the disposition of man. Thought, in fact, sets itself up as the measure of truth for all entities that are represented by it. Heidegger expresses this in the language of his later philosophy by saying that thought or representation in this new dispensation "decides about the presence (*Praesenz*) of each entity it represents, that is, about the presence (*Anwesenheit*) of what is meant in it, that is, about the being of the latter as an entity."[49] In his view, there is something presumptuous and even aggressive in this implicit claim of the *ego cogito* to be the supreme authority that determines what is present; and he is at pains to distinguish the Cartesian claim from the similar-sounding thesis of Protagoras about man as the measure of all things.[50] What he objects to is not so much the claim of scientific inquiry to render authoritative judgment about the matters with which it concerns itself as it is the thesis of Descartes and his successors that this representational activity itself gives rise to presence and thus to being. In a comment on Leibniz, in whose *Monadology* these tendencies move well beyond their Cartesian formulation, Heidegger says that as a result of these developments "*ousia* and presence (*Praesenz*) have been replaced by presence in the *representatio* with *veritas* as certitude as the intermediate term."[51] To this he adds that "presence has been expressly referred back to a monad, that is, in each case to a kind of ego and is really effected by the latter as its own distinctive ontological essence (*Seinswesen*)." In effect thought claims to produce presence and thus being, not, as Heidegger points out, in the sense of denying or casting doubt on the independent reality of what it represents as real, but in the sense of claiming to be itself the presence in which the being of the latter is validated.[52] In making this claim, the modern subject is motivated by a desire for power and mastery that ultimately has no object other than itself; and Heidegger sees this desire as distinctively modern, without any precedent in the ancient world. It is clear both that this desire for mastery constitutes a radical impiety in Heidegger's view and that it also affects our understanding of ourselves and of our way of being in the world with all kinds of other entities in ways of which he deeply disapproves.

The contrast between the two critiques of Descartes should now be reasonably clear. In the first, there is no suggestion that the *cogito* represents a disposition to substitute the representational activity of the self and the presence it effects for another kind of presence in relation to which the self would be passive. The criticism of the Cartesian doctrine of representation is rather that it substitutes a two-substance theory for the implicit understanding that *Dasein* has of itself as the entity that uncovers other entities in their being. Nor could one gather from anything Heidegger says in *Being and Time* that there is something objectionable about the functions of prediction and control by which *Dasein* orders its world in such a way as to facilitate the attainment of its ends, as long as these are not extended to *Dasein* itself.[53] Even the kind of objectification that effects the emergence of the merely *vorhanden* from the *zuhanden* for the purpose of simply observing what happens when we do not intervene is subject to criticism only if it is taken in by itself, so to speak, and forgets that *Dasein* is always active in maintaining the background conditions under which this pure observation is possible. What is new in the later critique is thus the claim that in laying down logical and epistemic conditions that have to be met if the reality of some object is to be treated as established, the modern subject is misrepresenting itself in a new way. It does so by failing (or refusing) to understand that all entities, including the most esoteric scientific objects, are present not as a result of the work of representative thought, but through the "giving" of being as presence itself.

Against this line of thought it might be objected that Heidegger fails to notice how much more stringent the criteria of truth become as a result of what he regards as the subject's determination to make itself the measure of all things. Especially when this characterization of the Cartesian project is made the basis for a supposed affinity between Descartes and Nietzsche, it might be thought that what is involved is some effort on the part of the subject to throw off all such constraints and to make its own will the final criterion of what is real, rather than subject itself to a more exacting discipline of truth. Nietzsche's name, after all, is associated with the view that a concern for objective truth typically serves as a cover for an aggressive determination to read the world in one's own way. There are Nietzschean overtones in Heidegger's account of modern subjectivism, as, for example, when he describes *Begreifen* (conceiving) as an *Angriff* (attack) and speaks of man as a subject as being "on the way to a limitless representing/calculating opening-up of entities."[54] It would be a mistake to suppose, however, that what he is charging the modern subject (or modern science) with is simply an effort to dictate on the basis of its own preferences what the actual contents of the world are. Although modern science does impose its own restrictive criteria of what is real, its distinctive procedures are also evident at a far more rarefied conceptual level than that of the fully determinate content of belief. In Heidegger's later writings and notably in his 1938 essay "The Age of the World-Picture," representational thought as such is said to be objectifying, and not because it postulates certain kinds of objects rather than others—for example, atoms rather than, say, feelings.[55] This greatly broadens the concept of objectification set forth in *Being and Time*, where it denoted a special kind of abstraction from the fact that the entities with which one is dealing belong to the world. In the later account, by contrast, representational thought turns the world into a picture and does so by transforming "things" into "objects" by treating them as its own conceptual constructions. When a thing becomes an object in this sense, it is tied to the subject that so constructs it; and, as the owner and operator of a conceptual system, the latter is accorded a special status as the "referential center" (*Bezugsmitte*) that "gives the measure and direction of all entities," which nevertheless count as entities only to the extent that they are drawn into this life of the subject and become its "experiences."[56] In becoming a subject in this sense, modern man has made everything an object and thus dependent on him for the "meaning and character of its presence."[57] In effect, the world is reduced to the status of a *Bild*—a picture, or representation—so that the only mode of presence it implies is the presence of the representation, which thus displaces and obscures the presence of being. Characteristically, however, Heidegger prefers to describe this whole evolution through which the modern subject acquires such an emphatic sense of its own sovereign conceptual agency as something that happens to it, not as something that it brings about by the very activity of thought on which it prides itself. Instead of saying that we come to understand ourselves as subjects, thus implying that we have been subjects all along and that our coming to think of ourselves as such is another act we perform in our capacity as subjects, he says that we have *become* subjects. The Greeks were not subjects, he insists, and they had no "experiences"; and if we are subjects and do have experiences, that is not to be attributed to the fact that we think of ourselves in this way any more than the fact that the Greeks were not subjects was due to their *not* thinking of themselves in that way.[58]

Heidegger's conception of the way in which the history of being as presence developed beyond Descartes to the present day treats Leibniz and Kant and then Hegel and Nietzsche as the philosophers of primary importance. In the case of Descartes, Heidegger's critique has been shown to proceed along quite different lines in *Being and Time* and in the Nietzsche lectures, but in both cases the attitude evinced is strongly negative.[59] With regard to Leibniz and Kant, there are strong indications in the period of *Being and Time* of a positive affinity with their thought on Heidegger's part; and the influence of Nietzsche on *Being and Time* has already been noted. But when Heidegger came to think in terms of a history of being as presence, all these philosophers were portrayed in a quite different and less favorable light.[60] This is so because, in Heidegger's view, each in his own way advances the domination of logic and the logical as the central business of philosophy at the expense of being as presence. The home ground of logic is representational or conceptual thought, of which it claims to be an authoritative formalization; and to assert the independence of logic from ontology is to try to establish the independence of representational thought from being, whether in the more traditional senses of that term or in Heidegger's sense. After this independence had been secured, as it was in some sense after Kant, it was Hegel's special role in the history of philosophy to restore the unity of logic and being, but this time on the terms set by the former—that is, by drawing being into the orbit of conceptual thought. But once being had been securely assimilated to the subject, as it was in Hegel's substance/subject identity thesis, it became possible for that subject to exhibit itself as desire and will and, in this new manifestation, to insist on its mastery over being. As will, the subject is not bound by any static and universal essence and is motivated only by the desire to maintain and extend the very dominance over all entities which it claims for itself on the strength of the identity between being and the will to power that it proclaims. This project of planetary domination is the reality of Western and world history in our time, according to Heidegger. This mastery over the earth is essentially mediated by the vast new forms of technological control that are the product of the scientific revolution and thus stand in the closest possible relationship to the metaphysics of the modern period.

The distinctive character of the modern Western world is defined for Heidegger by its peculiar coupling of objectivity and subjectivity along the lines just described and by the technology and technological mode of understanding that are the issue of that conjunction. Technological thought treats everything as being an object of one kind or another, and it does so because it is in this form that the world corresponds to the disposition to manipulate and control it. This disposition is observable in spheres of life as apparently remote from one another as philosophy and the technologics of management. What is common to these very different domains of thought is a growing determination to decide in terms of a kind of pragmatic a priori what kinds of entities are to be recognized as existing for the purposes of a given activity. This kind of advance laying-out of the object domain and of what will be acknowledged as present within it is a well-established procedure in the theoretical sciences, and we have already seen that Heidegger attributes to it the great achievements of the natural sciences in the modern period. But if it is true that such procedures could in principle remain confined to particular contexts of work and inquiry in which they have proved their value, it is not the temper of the modern mind to accept limitations of this kind. That would imply a limit to the applicability of a certain style of analysis and a corresponding lack of control over whatever is recognized as being unassimilable to the criteria of reality it deploys. It is true that an effort may be made to adapt these criteria in some ingenious way in an attempt to respond to complaints about what is being left out by these criteria in their normal mode of application. Thus, an economist may try to show that the concept of economic rationality that was originally abstracted from certain sectors of human conduct and refined into a concept of "economic man" can also serve to explain the value we attach to matters that are ostensibly quite removed from the economic domain. Even a willingness to do this is relatively rare, however, and for the most part whatever does not fit the categories in question is simply treated as nonexistent. As Heidegger remarks, "calculation does not allow anything except the calculable to appear," or to the extent that it does, it tickets what is not calculable in a way that indicates its insignificance for all public and serious purposes.[61] In the face of a disposition of this kind, as well as the extraordinary self-importance that is often associated with this sense of having assumed control over even these ontological decisions, it does seem appropriate to invoke, as Heidegger does, a certain modesty of thought and the need to acknowledge that we are not, for all our cleverness, the masters of what is.[62] A willful determination to make some thesis to which we are attached come out true is observable in many areas of life, from the scientific to the political, where it assumes its most sinister forms. Against it, there is surely a need to acknowledge a corresponding virtue, and this virtue is one that can hardly be described without appealing to notions of openness and modesty like those invoked by Heidegger.

Pan-objectivism in the service of a subjectivity determined to establish its sovereignty over nature and the world at large, achieves its ultimate philosophical formulation in physicalism—the thesis that everything that exists is a physical object of some kind. It is of interest to note that Heidegger nowhere discusses physicalism (or materialism) simply on its merits as a philosophical position. He was certainly no friend of the dualistic philosophies that draw a fundamental distinction between the mind and the body, but the effort to identify the one with the other as modern physicalism did evidently did not represent a serious philosophical alternative for him. One could argue, however, that the turn toward this kind of physicalism, which is so noticeable in philosophical life today, is really a continuation of the evolution sketched by Heidegger in his history of being. Physicalism projects a world of objects, among them human beings, into which nothing nonobjective like souls or consciousness is permitted to intrude. It thus represents the ultimate point to which a transcendental movement of thought can be taken, since it transforms everything it deals with into an object, thereby completely removing itself from the world it has so constituted. Because it claims to be simply the truth about this world, it does not feel any obligation to designate a place for itself as a theory and as an understanding of the world *within that same world*. Nor does the subject to which the world appears in this guise survive as the ultimate medium of thought in which the world is suspended, as in Hegel's idealism. This thought has suppressed itself in favor of the world it thinks and has thus removed itself as a possible counterinstance to its own thesis. Moreover, by comparison with Nietzsche's form of subjectivism especially, this physicalistic theory has a peculiarly anonymous character, since the project of dominating nature (and, indeed, society) that bases itself on this ontology is one that mankind as a whole, rather than any special elite of *Übermenschen*, has taken upon itself. On just this point Heidegger has made it quite clear that in his view a substitution of the "We" for "I" in no way alters the objectionable character of this modern subjectivism.[63]

Heidegger's wider characterization of the modern Western civilization in which such a philosophy as this expresses the prevailing understanding of being portrays it as an epoch that has become blind to being as presence. To speak of blindness here is clearly to say more than that we have failed to notice something that we could, and presumably should, have noticed. It is to say instead that being as presence has become invisible to us, and that this has happened not because it has mysteriously come to an end or because we have suddenly been deprived of a sense we formerly had. Rather, the unhiddenness of presence has come to be "unthought" through a series of substitutions in the course of which the concept of representation has replaced that of presence in so definitive a way that it is as though being as presence itself had been eclipsed. It no longer has a place within any shared discourse and is regularly assimilated to the only status that is available to it in the language of representational subjectivity. It is also an essential feature of this state of affairs that we are not able to escape it simply by retracing our steps and thereby finding our way back to an original understanding of being as presence under our own power, so to speak. The substitutions that have been made and by which we now live are such as to exclude the possibility that anything has been "lost" on their account, or that there *is* anything to which we could even try to reestablish an effective relation. But if it thus appears and must appear to us as if being as presence simply *were* not or had suffered a demise comparable to that of the God whose death Nietzsche announced, the case is really that this very unavailability has itself become a modality of presence.[64] It is distinctive in that the entities that are made present under this dispensation are present as "all there is," and thus in a way that effectively occludes their own presence insofar as it eludes the representational and causal models in terms of which our access to them is accounted for by an objectifying mode of thought. Those who inhabit this world of objects are thus in the strange position of relying for purposes of communication with one another on a unitary presence which they do not and in some sense cannot recognize for what it is, because it is allowed no place in their world and thus effectively does not exist *for* them. Heidegger does not characterize the peculiarities of this form of *Mitsein* that is a consequence of the occlusion of being as presence, but it seems clear from what he does say that a powerful conception of a negative—in the sense of self-diremptive—intersubjectivity is implicit in his account of this modality of presence.

It is from this occlusion of being as presence that all the most salient features of the modern age derive. Thus, the subject that replaces being as presence can only strive, so Heidegger thinks, to establish its own absolute dominance over all other entities. In such a world there is no place for gods, since in Heidegger's view these are associated with being as presence; and the earth itself is being progressively destroyed by the instrumentalities of technological exploitation of which we now dispose.[65] This is also the age in which mass man is paramount and a hatred of the exceptional and the creative has become the order of the day.[66] Even the life of the mind has been transformed into "culture"—something that Heidegger insists the Greeks knew nothing of—and self-development thus becomes the object of a new form of calculation and control.[67] The ultimate expression of all these tendencies seems, for Heidegger, to be nuclear weapons and the struggle for the mastery of the planet in which they are deployed. Any attempt made under these circumstances to devise an "ethic" by which the predatory tendencies of mankind might be held in check is contemptuously dismissed by him, as is any thought that the conjugation of subjectivities in a community or *Volk* of any kind could amount to more than an intensification of the planetary struggle for domination.[68] Such notions fall under the same condemnation as the whole notion of human culture as self-development and, in general, any tendency on the part of human beings to view themselves as autonomous.

But if human beings are to avoid this kind of presumptuousness and await the intimations of being—what Heidegger calls its "essential directives" (die wesentlichen Weisungen)—he says almost nothing about the latter. In a passage in his essay on the work of art, he states that the world is not simply "the open" or the clearing. "The world is rather the clearing of the pathways (Bahnen) of the essential directives to which all deciding conforms itself."[69] He adds that "every decision bases itself on something that has not been mastered, that is hidden and that leads one astray"; but the notion of the clearing as taking the form of "directives" is not clarified further. In Being and Time it was quite explicit that Dasein has a world in the mode of possibility—that is, the world presents itself in terms of what can and what cannot be done. This conception of possibility as an essential characteristic of the clearing is rarely touched on in the later writings; but even if it were understood to form part of Heidegger's later notion of presence, it would still be necessary to explain how a possibility becomes a directive. But Heidegger does not do that, and so, if being as presence can provide the guidance that human beings vainly seek from "ethics" of their own construction, those who depend on Heidegger for their understanding of how this might be accomplished remain unenlightened. What they do know, because this is something they are told repeatedly and emphatically, is that they must not think or speak of themselves as having any competence at all in such matters, and that any effort they make on their own can produce only a new form of objectification. Heidegger's doctrine on these matters is thus quite clear and definite on the negative point it makes about human incapacity and quite unclear about how "the essential directives" of being are "cleared," or how anything of this kind would even be imaginable in the degree of abstraction from the plurality of Mitsein that Heidegger effectively maintains.

In the picture that Heidegger presents of our time, it is not even possible to say how we might escape from the interlocking systems of objectifying thought and practice in which our lives are enclosed. The only hope he offers lies in the possibility that the danger by which man is threatened may come to be understood as a danger. This danger is that man will continue indefinitely in the managerial/manipulative mode of an occluded presence and "take all his measures from it"; and this is said to be a danger not just for human beings but for "all dis-concealing as such."[70] Here and elsewhere it almost sounds as though Heidegger fears that some final irreversible robotization of mankind may occur if the other possibility—that man "enters in a more primary way into the essence of the unhidden and of his own unhiddenness"—is not realized.[71] Indeed, the implication seems to be that presence itself may be somehow destroyed; and this is in keeping with the previously noted claim that being as presence stands in need of protection. Thus man is portrayed as being in a situation in which he must choose the one possibility or the other in terms of which this situation is defined. The danger posed by our technological civilization can become the occasion of a reversal, in which "the most intimate, indestructible belonging of man" to being will be revealed, "provided that we for our part begin to attend to the essence of technology."[72] This attending that is required of us is not an action in the ordinary sense; indeed, we are told that "human action can never directly meet this danger."[73] Nevertheless, the reflection (*Besinnung*) that is called for is an action at least in the negative sense of a stepping back from the course we would otherwise follow. As long as that is possible, the obscuration of being as presence cannot be thought of simply as a kind of fated event that we must undergo; it must also be understood as something in relation to which we retain at least some freedom and hence some responsibility.

V

It is now time to take up the question that was noted at the beginning of this chapter and that motivated the examination of the notion of the history of being. This is the question about the independence/dependence of being as presence vis-à-vis man or *Dasein* and about the bearing of the claim that being as such has a history on that issue. This issue is closely connected with the question about the agency involved in that history and especially with Heidegger's insistent denial that human agency in any of its familiar forms can account for the epochal movement that characterizes it. The connection between these two questions is supplied by the assumption that if man does not control the history of being, then whatever does—presumably being itself—must be somehow distinct from and thus independent of man. This assumption is open to doubt, however, for, as the last chapter made clear, the thesis of a strong independence of being as presence is not proved simply by establishing that the scope of individual human agency vis-à-vis presence is significantly limited. It is quite possible that man or *Dasein* participates in an openness that he does not control but that need not, for that or any other reason, be supposed to obtain independently of individual human beings. But even though these questions about independence and agency do not simply coincide, it is both natural and convenient to take them up in sequence as I will now do.

In the matter of the independence/dependence of being as presence, there cannot be much doubt that, whatever Heidegger's intentions may have been, the introduction of the notion of a history of being affords strong support to the second thesis—namely, that being as presence is essentially tied to and inseparable from man or *Dasein*. The reasoning that leads to this conclusion can be stated concisely. We have seen that the history of being, as Heidegger conceives it, is concerned, as it must be, with both presence as the presence of entities and presence as itself present and manifest, but that it is the vicissitudes of presence as presence that make up the central theme of that history. The presence of entities, by contrast, is not historical in any sense that appears to interest Heidegger; and his conception of being as having a history does not, therefore, have any significant implications for the independence/dependence of presence understood as the presence of entities. The conclusions of the last chapter point to a progressive qualification of the thesis of the independence of presence from man or *Dasein* and thus to a form of independence that is not separateness, although it is certainly not control by man or *Dasein* either. What this amounts to is something that can be equally well expressed as a qualified form of independence that excludes separateness and as a qualified form of dependence that excludes any such control.

When one turns to the history of being and to its special theme of presence as presence, which is also that of presence as misidentified with such disparate entities as Plato's forms, Hegel's *Geist*, and Nietzsche's will to power, the linkage of this history to thought and thus to man and *Dasein* is quite patent. Being is hidden when it is "unthought" and when, as a result, only entities are present and thus available for the kind of thought appropriate to them. When presence is itself manifest, it is because a very different kind of thought responds to it by "letting it be (*wesen*) as being itself" and by "no longer leaving it out but letting it in— in to the unhiddenness of the being that it itself is and that is thereby revealed for the first time."[74] But (and this is the capital point) both being as thought and being as "unthought" are modalities of being itself, which thus stands, both as absent and itself present, in an essential relationship to thought. It thus appears that the thesis of the dependence of being on man is one-sidedly vindicated by considerations deriving from the notion of a history of being, and that the epochs in the history of being are epochs in the history of thought. From this it would be just one further step to the claim that because it is, after all, man that thinks, the history of thought and thus the history of being must coincide with the history of man.

This last proposition would be most objectionable to Heidegger, however, and the reason for this suggests a qualification that needs to be made in the conclusion reached above. This qualification would take the form of a distinction between the history of man as it is understood when being as presence is occluded and even denied outright and a history of man that is understood in terms of presence as the necessary condition for everything that is characteristically human, even when its status as such is most energetically denied. If by thought we mean human thought, and by human thought a thought that is understood in abstraction from presence or that at most treats presence as one of its objects rather than as the milieu in which it is alone possible, then an identity between the history of being and the history of man cannot obtain. In Heidegger's view, the history of man has not only been understood in the latter way, but it could not have been understood in any other way in the absence of an understanding of presence as presence. He would presumably also want to say that this fact about human history is one that concerns not just the conceptual mode in which it is understood and narrated, but the substantive character of that history itself. Through the absence of presence, that history becomes, at least for the human beings who understand it and thus themselves in this way, something distinct and separate from the history of being as the presence they do not acknowledge. Even so, that does not alter the fact that the history of man as an entity among entities is itself possible only because it is embedded in a history that involves just that presence to which man is oblivious. It is this history of being that Heidegger has undertaken to characterize, if not actually relate; but again, it is not just a matter of a novel perspective from which history can be viewed, and thus of Heidegger's way of looking at what other historians look at from another angle. The history of being as presence is not an alternative historiographical mode for human history, but rather the vicissitudes themselves through which the milieu of presence in which human history becomes possible has itself passed. If Heidegger is right, moreover, then everything important in human history is really a consequence of what has taken place in the history of being, so there can be no question of treating the two as independent options for historians.

But if this much can be said on behalf of the notion of a history of being, it remains to ask *why* being as presence has passed through these epochal transformations—that is, why it emerged in the first place, if it did, and why it was subsequently eclipsed. Is this to be understood as the work of the thought with which being as presence is paired, or should it be imputed to being as presence itself? Heidegger habitually speaks as though the latter were the case; and in the language he uses, being becomes an agent that draws man to itself and then turns away from him. Such a way of speaking has the signal disadvantage of making it sound as though presence were itself an entity—*something* present—and it thereby violates a fundamental prohibition of Heidegger's philosophy. On occasion, he seems to warn against overly literal construals of such language and even denies that the ordinary distinctions that apply to a sequence of events, or *Geschehen*, are applicable to the history of being.[75]

Once again, it is unclear where such corrections that follow on the original attributions of agency to being really leave the question. Perhaps the upshot of the matter is that there is *no* explanation in terms of an agency of either being or human thought as ordinarily understood of why being as presence became manifest, if it did, or of why it was eclipsed, if it was. If so, all one can do is to register both these events and express them as facts about being as presence itself, and then try to fend off as best one can the mythological connotations that such a mode of statement inevitably suggests. Certainly, one could in this way at least acknowledge the fact that human thought depends on a milieu that it does not control and that it cannot even conceive properly without losing itself in its own erroneous renderings of what it may once have understood; and this may be all that Heidegger thinks it is possible to do.

At the same time, we can hardly forget that it is the philosopher Martin Heidegger who tells us about the hiddenness of being and about our own inability to do much more than point to what we have lost.[76] His doing so certainly seems to imply that, even in this unpropitious time, *he* at least has achieved an understanding of being as presence that we are in principle capable of sharing. After all, he does not claim to be the recipient of a private revelation of being; and his analysis traces our present condition back through Western conceptual history to early Greek philosophical texts that are accessible to us and that express insights into the nature of being as such. When he urges us to step back from the objectifying modes of thought of our time, he bases his appeal on considerations derived from philosophical argument and historical analysis. All this suggests that his thought (and ours) still counts for something, even in the difficult circumstances of our time, and that it is not necessary or even possible for the history of being to dispense completely with explanations drawn from the history of thought.

These thoughts about the place of Heidegger's own work in the history of being suggest wider reservations about the pervasively negative judgment he passes on almost every phase of the history of Western philosophy. If Western philosophy began, as Heidegger usually supposes it did, with an authentic apprehension of being as presence, then it is understandable that every subsequent movement of thought should have seemed to him to reflect a loss or a distortion of that original insight. If, on the other hand, it is accepted, as it is by Heidegger, that whatever the being of Parmenides may be held to represent, it is not a fully articulated concept of being as presence that would be comparable, for example, to the one that Heidegger himself has proposed, then the philosophical achievement of the centuries that separate these two thinkers may begin to look very different.[77] There is no reason to deny that there has been a great deal of misunderstanding of the thought of prior philosophers on the part of most, if not all, the great thinkers, not to speak of the lesser ones. There has also been much tendentious misreading of prior philosophical texts and even more inflated claims to originality, as well as a seemingly systematic lack of awareness of the channel in which one's own thought moves and which it often only digs a little deeper. Nevertheless, it is hardly possible to imagine a philosophical achievement like that of Heidegger otherwise than against the background of just this stretch of Western philosophical history; and to say this is not just to point to the Augean stables that he had to clean out. Whatever one thinks of Descartes or Kant or Hegel or Nietzsche, and even if one sees their philosophies primarily as intricate ways of missing the fact of being as presence, it remains the case that, if Heidegger had not been able to work both with and against the grain of their thought, his own would have been as lacking in conceptual articulation and thus in real philosophical power as that of Parmenides, for all its profundity, must unavoidably strike us as being. Heidegger may well be right in thinking that there is a special greatness that attaches to beginnings, in which some large theme of thought is enunciated for the first time, and that, by comparison, those who come later seem small and unworthy of the legacy of thought that has been left to them. Nevertheless, it is finally as impossible to separate those first founding intuitions from the later work of elaboration and criticism and amplification as it is to isolate the quintessential teaching of a great religious leader from the tradition he founds. It is the history of Western philosophy that made *Being and Time* possible; and it must therefore have been something more than just a great aberration from a truth that it did not want to understand.[78]

CHAPTER TEN • THE INTERDEPENDENCE OF EXISTENCE AND PRESENCE

The main thesis of Heidegger's later philosophy has now been set forth. It asserts that being as presence is the ground of existence, and it thereby reverses the order of priority between presence and existence that Heidegger established in the period of *Being and Time*, when it was understood that "there is being only as long as *Dasein* is." These theses appear to be in direct contradiction to one another, and yet the conclusions of the two preceding chapters indicate that this may not be the case. The picture that has emerged from an examination of the later writings is one in which a strong initial assertion of the priority of being as presence to existence is subsequently qualified in ways that suggest a complex interdependence of the two, rather than an unconditional independence of being as presence from existence. In this chapter, I will examine the more specific character of that interdependence, in the hope of amplifying the position taken by Heidegger in his later writings. In chapter 6 I argued that there was a clear need to revise the theses of *Being and Time* in such a way as to clarify the role of the agency of *Dasein*, which had been so strongly emphasized in the earlier conception of the clearing of entities as entities, and to safeguard the unity and commonness of being as the milieu of presence. It was also suggested that Heidegger's carrying-out of this task was substantially hampered by its being associated with a new, intensified critique of subjectivism, as well as by the fact that as a result of this critique the status of much of the conceptual apparatus of *Being and Time* became ambiguous in a way that made its role in any effort of reconstruction quite problematic. In this chapter, I will attempt to show how that effort might have gone, and also how perhaps it should have gone if the *données* of the problem had remained as they were at the end of *Being and Time*, without the preemptive and unexplained elimination of all but the most minimal forms of the agency of *Dasein* that took place in the thirties. The guiding assumption of this reconstruction is that Heidegger's identification of being with truth offers a way of construing both the independence of being as presence and its dependence on *Dasein* in such a way as to make them compatible with one another. I will also argue that a theory of truth along these lines will also afford a conception of the essentially shared character of being as presence. Such a theory would build on and amplify the conception of *Mitsein* that Heidegger introduced in the period of *Being and Time* but did not significantly develop further in a way that would have clarified its bearing on the issues with which his later writings deal.

I

The central paradox of Heidegger's philosophy stems from the fact that he wants to say that *Dasein* is the clearing and also that being is the clearing. If *Dasein* is inherently plural and being is just as inherently singular and unique, it is not apparent how both these assertions can be true. One way of dealing with this difficulty would be to argue that, if *Dasein* is taken generically and apart from any individuation it may involve, there will really be no difference between the concepts of being and of *Dasein*, and so the appearance of a contradiction will have been removed. The trouble with this idea is not only that it is impossible to abstract from the plurality of *Dasein*, but that, even when Heidegger seems most committed to being as the clearing, he continues to speak of *Dasein* not only as open and thus a clearing, but also as in some sense distinct from being. Thus, in the introduction that was added in 1949 to *What Is Metaphysics?* Heidegger states that when existence is properly understood, it permits us to conceive "the 'essence' (*Wesen*) of *Dasein* in whose openness being itself manifests itself . . . without its being the case that this truth of being exhausts itself in *Dasein* or can even be identified with it in the fashion of the metaphysical proposition: all objectivity is as such subjectivity."[1] This statement is followed by another in which existence is characterized as "the being of that entity that stands open for the openness of being." There is thus a continuing contrast between the openness of being and the openness of *Dasein*; and although it is made clear that the latter is in some sense dependent on the former, it is as itself open that *Dasein*, according to this passage, awaits the openness of being. In other words, it is as itself already open that *Dasein* is amplified by the openness of being. This passage is especially significant because, although it belongs to the later period, it uses the term *Dasein* rather than "man," and it is therefore clear that it cannot be the mere "presence in the representation" that constitutes the openness that is in question here, but rather a full-blown clearing of the kind characterized in *Being and Time*.

The difficulty here is to know how *Dasein* itself can be essentially open and yet require the kind of supplementation that the openness of being as such would provide. After all, it was made quite clear in the period of *Being and Time* that if "human *Dasein*" and thus the world exist at all, then entities as a totality are thereby open.[2] If that is the case, there does not appear to be any way in which a more complete form of openness could be supplied by being itself, especially when the latter is understood to be finite, as it explicitly was in the period of *Being and Time*. There is also a real difficulty about giving a sense to the notion of being "open for an openness." One such sense was proposed in the last chapter, where it was argued that presence or openness could remain hidden and thus not itself open as long as it was not thought *as* presence; one could therefore say that, when *Dasein* does think being, being is open to it as the openness it is. But this condition would not be satisfied in most cases, according to Heidegger, and the dependence of *Dasein* as a kind of secondary clearing on being as the primary clearing would by no means be limited to the cases in which it is satisfied. Heidegger uses many metaphorical constructions to try to suggest what this dependence relationship between primary and secondary clearings might be like; he even speaks of derivative forms of openness as "fiefs" of "that openness that holds sway in the essence of dis-concealing."[3] In spite of all these efforts, the notion of trying to move beyond the concept of *Dasein* by postulating *another* clearing or another openness to which the clearing that is *Dasein* is then somehow subjoined does not appear to be at all promising. The decisive objection to any claim that the openness of *Dasein* might be in some way deficient and therefore in need of such supplementation is the fact that *Dasein* is by definition familiar with being, at least in a pre-ontological sense; and if this is so, there cannot be, on the terms laid down by Heidegger's philosophy, anything more that *another* clearing could possibly impart to it. It is certainly true that a merely pre-ontological understanding of being makes *Dasein* susceptible to all the forms of blindness and obliviousness vis-à-vis being that were detailed in the last chapter. It would be pushing paradox beyond any tolerable limit, however, if *another* clearing had to be postulated in order to effect the openness of presence *as* presence. Such a clearing would be the openness of openness as openness; and if such a notion were to be invoked, one could surely speak with T. S. Eliot of a "superfetation" of *to on* with a vengeance.[4] Fortunately, the conclusions of the last two chapters with respect to the way in which the notions of hiddenness and unhiddenness can apply to being as presence and thus to openness indicate that this is not required. To this it may be added that if it is not *necessary* to speak in terms of a combining of clearings, it is also possible that by not doing so one could avoid a number of difficulties that arise when that idiom is introduced.

There is good reason to think that it is this notion of two forms of openness that is responsible for the paradoxes of agency that have been persistently associated with Heidegger's efforts to explain the subordination of *Dasein* or man to being as such. If being as such is the original clearing or milieu of presence, then it seems to follow that the proper relationship between that clearing and the clearing that is *Dasein* must be one that lets being be as being—that is, that does not supplant it or obscure it by assigning an undue prominence to any form of presence that is, as Heidegger puts it, the "handiwork" of man. The difficulty arises when one tries to specify what this normative posture would permit. There are unquestionably circumstances in which it would be natural to adopt Heidegger's idiom of "being giving itself" with respect to the presence of the entities that make up our world. These are circumstances in which those entities are so familiar to us and so well established within our world that they almost seem to announce their presence to us like old friends. This is especially true of the things with which common sense and ordinary language are conversant; and in the unproblematic presence of such entities we have no sense that we are doing anything or have done anything that in any way qualifies the independent and prior presence of what is there before us. There are other cases, however, that do not fit this picture of simply taking in the presence of some self-announcing and self-identifying entity. These are typically cases in which the presence of the entity in question is not apparent to the untutored eye. The moment a technical scientific term of reference to a common-sense object is involved and, most obviously, when even the existence of the entity in question has to be inferred in a way that involves reliance on some body of scientific theory, we can hardly remain unaware of a certain implicit conceptual activity on our part. This need not affect our acceptance of the reality of what we perceive; it may be that, as we become familiar with these new entities, our sense that they are "just there" returns and, with it, our obliviousness to any element of activity on our part. We are reminded of it again, however, whenever we have to explain to a neophyte what it is that we see and he does not. What we are reminded of is the fact that our perception of these entities and thus their presence to us is mediated by inquiry and by the knowledge that issues from such inquiry. In order to "take in" such objects, we have to be able to construct them conceptually. If we cannot do so, then we are in the position of the Aborigines who, when shown a book for the first time, could not understand what they saw and thus did not really see a *book*.

In such cases, is there any way in which the thesis of the priority of the original clearing in which conceptual construction has no place could be successfully reasserted? One way to attempt this would be to draw attention to the dependence of such construction on a prior commonsense familiarity with the entities on which these conceptual operations are performed, but which are not themselves so constructed.[5] This is an important point, especially insofar as it underscores the fact that all representational thought is ultimately dependent on something—that is, presence in its various forms, among them the perceptual, which it most certainly cannot constitute out of its own resources. What cannot be established in this way, however, is that the articulation of this presence into entities of certain kinds and with certain relations to one another involves no element of agency on the part of those for whom the world orders itself in these ways. In the first place, the world of commonsense objects is the domain of the *zuhanden*, which derives from the use that *Dasein* makes of the *pragmata* in its world; and although this domain is certainly not a conceptual construction, it involves human agency nevertheless and is therefore not assimilable to any understanding of presence from which such agency is excluded.

One can perhaps imagine other expedients by which such an understanding might be revised so as to make it capable of accommodating these facts about agency without yielding on the essential point. One such expedient to which Heidegger sometimes seems inclined would simply attribute everything that we think of as our own conceptual activity to being itself, thus leaving us only the quite passive role of receiving the product of such activity as something that is given to us. But apart from the fact that such an attribution could hardly avoid transforming being itself into an entity, it would produce multiple incongruities, as, for example, the need to say that when Cicero mistranslated various Greek terms for being, it was being itself that was mistaking itself for something quite different. But instead of exploring such unpromising options of thought any further, it seems more profitable to concentrate on the point that most deeply concerns Heidegger—namely, the question as to whether presence itself is to be understood as being somehow effected by representational thought and thus by human agency. It is evident that all the specific kinds of entities that are present might be correlated with human agency, conceptual or otherwise, as a necessary condition of their presence as just the entities they are, but that such conceptual agency would be in no sense a sufficient condition of such presence. In that case, a measure of independence from conceptual conditions would accrue to presence as such. It is worth noting that this conclusion would run counter to the previously noted disposition of contemporary philosophy to treat conceptual thought as enjoying an effective independence from, or even control over, perception as a primary mode of presence. To the extent that such a disposition exists, it is clear that in reserving this measure of independence for presence, Heidegger is at least not doing battle with a straw man of his own contriving. But the real issue is whether it is necessary or effective as a way of defending this claim to introduce the notion of an original or prior clearing to which the clearing that is *Dasein* is then described as being open. The disadvantage of such a strategy is that it concedes at the outset that one form of presence is indeed the "handiwork" of conceptual thought—namely, the kind Heidegger calls "presence in the representation"—and then attempts to compensate for this concession by insisting on the dependence of that clearing on another that is prior to all representation. But should that concession be made at all? Since the uncovering action of *Dasein* has been shown to be ontological and not ontic in nature, we must rule out the possibility that it could *create* presence as such. It has no control over the fact that entities are present to it as entities, even though what might be called the functional design of the constellation of entities that are so present *is* a function of its active concerns. The fact that we are now strongly inclined to suppose that thought creates its own milieu may define the character of our age, but it does not and cannot make it the case that the presence within which our thought moves is really created by it. Rather than invoke another form of presence, we should expose the falsity of the suppositions about representational presence that are currently entertained; and in that task the argumentation of *Being and Time* would be a major resource.

A case has now been made for the claim that a contrast between clearings as forms of openness or presence is misguided. The arguments that have been offered for this view are strengthened by the way Heidegger has been shown to qualify his own initial assertions of a strong independence of being as presence, as though he could not unequivocally espouse either an independence so conceived or an equally definite dependence of being on man or *Dasein*. In this connection it may be noted that his use of the verb *lassen* ("to let") in compound verbs like *begegnen-lassen* ("to let encounter")—a use that was common in the period of *Being and Time*—continues in the later period. When he speaks, for example, of *die Ankunft der Wahrheit* ("the arrival of truth") in the characteristic idiom of the later writings, he finds it necessary to supplement this description in which the agency of being itself is implicitly asserted by another description in which "the movement of the clearing as such" becomes a *Geschehen-lassen* (a "letting-happen") of that event.[6] The effect of this second description is to restore to *Dasein*, or to man at least, a shadow of the agency which it claims in a much stronger form when it describes its own relationship to truth as a *feststellen* ("an ascertaining" or "confirming"). The latter expression is objectionable in Heidegger's eyes, of course, because it "contains a willing that bars the arrival of truth," whereas the "letting-happen of the arrival of truth" is "a self-conforming (*sich-fügen*) and, so to speak, a not-willing that releases."[7] At the same time, Heidegger insists that this letting-happen is no mere passivity, as though *Dasein* simply stood by and did nothing. It is instead, the "highest doing (*höchstes Tun*) in the sense of *thesis*, the 'working and willing' that was (earlier) described as the ecstatic letting-oneself-into the unhiddenness of being on the part of the existing human being."[8] In these passages the complexity of the relationship between being as a clearing and *Dasein* as a clearing reaches a kind of climax in that the agency of being is continually reasserted in its very self-effacement. It is as though the effort to disqualify oneself as an agent and to make over one's powers of volition to being as such keeps alive precisely that which is ostensibly being repudiated. Such a failure is strongly reminiscent of the outcome of Hegel's dialectic of the finite and the infinite consciousnesses, in which the former has finally to acknowledge that, in spite of all its efforts to achieve identity with God, its own agency as expressed in that very effort remains distinct and unabsorbed into the infinite.[9]

II

The argument of the preceding section points to the conclusion that there can be only one clearing, and that the attempt to think in terms of two clearings leads to unresolvable tensions within Heidegger's account of these matters. At the same time, it is important to note that this conclusion in no way involves a dismissal of the considerations that motivated the attempt to emend the theory of *Dasein*. What it does mean is that these considerations will have to be given their due weight in a revised account of the single clearing to which the conclusion reached above points. Accordingly, they will be included in the attempt that will now be made to sketch in some of the main lines along which such a revision ought to proceed.

In chapter 6 it was argued that Heidegger's identification of being with truth offers the best clue to the direction in which an amplification of the account of *Dasein* in *Being and Time* should move. The aspect of truth that is relevant here is indicated in a passage from a work of Heidegger's later period that is distinguished by the extreme character of its repudiation of human agency as usually understood. This passage occurs in the context of a discussion of the notion of "region"—in German, *Gegend*, or *Gegnet*, as Heidegger prefers to call it, presumably because of its association with *begegnen* (encounter).[10] It is intended to serve as a new synonym for being and, like several others—for example, *Raum* and *Ort*—it is notable for its strong spatial connotations. At one point in this account Heidegger says that, for the sake of brevity, we can just as well say "truth" instead of "region." He then proceeds to use this equivalence as a key to understanding how truth (and thus region and being as presence) can be both independent of and dependent on man. "The human essence is made over to (*übereignet*) truth because truth needs man. But isn't the distinguishing character of truth, precisely in reference to its relation to man, the fact that it is what it is independently of man"?[11]

Heidegger seems to be appealing here to some established understanding about truth that everyone can be expected to acknowledge. In the form in which truth would be widely acknowledged as independent of man, it would typically be understood as something that cannot be changed by anyone and that is what it is whether we like it or not. That the sun will rise tomorrow morning or that Napoleon died on St. Helena would be examples of such truths. One notices immediately, however, that these are truths about entities—ontic truths—and it is doubtful that these are what Heidegger had in mind. Conceived in ontological rather than ontic terms, truth is a necessary condition for such ontic truths, but it is itself the unhiddenness or openness or presence with which being also has been identified. The sense in which unhiddenness as such might be independent of man is, of course, the question that has just been exhaustively examined, with largely negative results; and there is no special reason to think that the common sense understanding of truth as independent of man would array itself on Heidegger's side of that issue. Nevertheless, it may be that Heidegger's appeal to a standing conviction about truth that is principally associated with ontic truths points to an ontological feature of these truths that is relevant to this matter of the independence of truth.

It was pointed out in chapter 5 that when we make a true statement about some entity and say, for example, that the apple is red, or that there is an apple on the table, the entity we are talking about is in some sense broken up and then put together again. This is clearest in the case of a statement about a property like color, which has to be distinguished from the apple as such so that it can be designated as the color that the apple *is*. Again, when we say that there is an apple in a certain place, a distinction is made between the apple and the place in which it is located, even though place is not a property of the apple in the way that color is, and the two are then brought back into an articulated relationship that is expressed by the "is." The apple's being red or its being on the table is what is usually called a fact or a state of affairs; and it is quite clear that this is something quite different from the entity or thing itself—in this case, the apple. Even so, this distinction itself has given rise to many controversies and especially to the question as to whether the world itself is made up of entities or facts/states of affairs. For those who hold that the world is the totality of entities or things, facts, involving as they do the "is," are something that presupposes language; and it is therefore language and the existence of language-users that account for the distinction between entities and facts. On this view, a fact would be a true statement about something in the world; and the whole grammatical apparatus of distinctions that underlies such a statement has to be thought of as something that belongs to language, rather than to the world, and that is used as an instrument for accommodating entities to the logical form of a proposition. On this view, it is unintelligible to speak of apples as being red *in* the world. There are red apples in the world, but their *being* red is an artifact of language and language use.[12]

In chapter 2 it was emphasized that for Heidegger the world is the aggregate not of entities but of entities as present. He does not use the language of facts or states of affairs; but if he did, he would certainly include what goes by that name in the world understood as a milieu of presence. The world understood in terms of presence cannot be identified, of course, with the world that facts are *not* supposed to be in, according to the view just considered; and Heidegger would certainly not agree that facts or states of affairs—something being such-and-such—are artifacts of language. Nevertheless, insofar as correspondences are possible between such radically different modes of conceptualization, the distinction between things and facts roughly corresponds to Heidegger's distinction between entities and the being of entities. So understood, his fundamental thesis could be expressed as the claim that, prior to and independently of language, entities are present as embedded and articulated in states of affairs. The question about the independence/dependence of being thus corresponds to a question about the (ir)reducibility of states of affairs to entities. What complicates consideration of this question in either of these formulations is that, for Heidegger, presence itself is dependent on, or at least not independent of, *Dasein*. It is thus tempting to infer that being or states of affairs are simply projected on entities by *Dasein* when it exists, even though in *Being and Time* Heidegger strongly denies that this is the case. Nevertheless, this linkage of being to the existence of an entity, *Dasein*, sets limits to the kind of independence that can be attributed to it. The last two chapters have explored the senses in which an independence within a dependence or an interdependence of being and *Dasein* might still be defended. What can now be proposed as an answer to that question is simply the idea that the independence of being from man is like the independence of states of affairs when this is understood as both their irreducibility to entities and their not being created by human beings.

In this connection it is of great interest to find Heidegger discussing the distinction between being and entities in the period of *Being and*

Time in a way that underscores just the kind of independence that would meet the requirements of this situation.[13] The distinction is first placed in the closest possible relationship to what Heidegger calls "saying-'is'" (*"ist"-Sagen*)—that is, to saying that "this is such and such, (that) that is, (that) that is not so and that is."[14] This "is-saying" expressly includes both saying *what* something is and saying *that* it is; and the "is" that is common in both is therefore more fundamental than the distinction of essence and existence that emerges from it. We constantly make use of the distinction between being and entities, but without having any explicit representation of what this distinction involves. From this, Heidegger concludes that "it is not *we* (who) bring about (*vollziehen*) this distinction; instead *it* happens (*geschieht*) *with us* as the primal happening (*Grundgeschehen*) of our *Dasein*."

> If this distinction did not happen, then we could not even, in obliviousness to the distinction, devote ourselves, initially and for the most part, to entities alone. For precisely in order to experience *what* and *how* an entity in each case *is* in itself as the entity that it *is*, we have to understand already, even though not conceptually, matters like the What-ness (*Was-sein*) and the That-ness (*Dass-sein*) of entities. This distinction not only happens continuously; but it must (also) have *already* happened if we desire to experience entities in their being-such-and-such (*So-und-so-sein*). We do not learn—and certainly not subsequently—anything about being from entities; instead entities, wherever and however we come at them, stand *already in the light of being*. Taken metaphysically, the distinction thus stands at the beginning of *Dasein* itself. ...Man thus always stands in the possibility of asking: What is that? and Is it really or is it not?[15]

The essential point here is that being, in the distinction between being and entities, is coordinate and coeval with *Dasein*, and that *Dasein* is accordingly always already conversant with the What and the That as implicit articulations (*Gliederungen*) of entities and thus of its world. Plainly, being, so understood, is in no sense the *Gemächte*—either the creature or the handiwork—of *Dasein* or man; and in this sense being may be said to enjoy the independence vis-à-vis *Dasein* that Heidegger is so concerned to preserve. The status thus accorded to being, moreover, is one that does not require any doubling of the presence or clearing that is involved. It is also evident that within the one clearing—the one world—that is effected by the "happening" of this distinction between being and entities, the truth-character of being stands in an intimate relationship to the articulation that the "is" in all its modalities brings to entities. This is not because, as might ordinarily be supposed, truth is a property of propositions and thus presupposes the logical form of the latter; Heidegger's claim is rather that, in the world as the milieu of presence in which we have to do with them, entities always already *are*, in the several modalities of which the verb "to be" that eventually expresses them is susceptible. Truth as the presence of entities in what might appropriately be called their "be-ing" is thus both pre-predicative and pre-logical in the sense of being prior to language and judgment.[16] In other words, it is not as if, apart from language, presence could be only a beam of light playing over an unstructured entity or thing. What is present is always an entity as a such-and-such; and it is as be-ing such-and-such that it is understood— as, for example, this apple is understood as being here in front of me and not in the bag I left in the car, or this pencil as not making a dark enough mark. The difference between an entity and an entity's be-ing, whether in the mode of the What or the That, is not one that arises with the rendering of entities into propositions by language. It is one that is implicit in any form of presence as such. In presence something is *there*, and it is there *as* a such-and-such; and neither its being there nor its being such-and-such—that is, what will eventually be conceptualized as its existence and its essence—can be identified with the actual entity in question. The picture of a presence to which "logical form" would have to be added subsequently with the advent of language is therefore mistaken, at least in the sense that it treats such form as something wholly new for which there is no analogon in presence as such.

In the text quoted above, Heidegger states that being must always be articulated at least by a distinction between the fact that something exists and what that thing is.[17] The articulation of which being is susceptible is much more extensive than that distinction by itself, of course, and, as we have seen, the full articulation of being as presence can be given only in the context of temporality, with its contrasts of present, past, and future. In the account he gives in this same text of the principle of that fuller articulation of being, the notion of possibility as a modality of being is once again stressed; and possibility in turn is interpreted as "making-possible" (*Ermöglichung*) and is thereby connected to the notion of a project (*Entwurf*) and to action and choice.[18] Typically, it is at just this point that we are tempted to conclude that, as a result of these linkages, being itself must be somehow a product of human action. It is essential, therefore, to underscore once again the fact that being as well as truth as the be-ing of entities is *already* involved in the concept of project and thus of the action in which the project issues; it cannot therefore be understood as deriving from an ontic construal of project and action—that is, from one that itself makes no use of notions of being and truth. Once again, the independence of being and truth consists in their being coeval with possibility and project and choice in their ontological versions. They are thus prior to their ontic derivatives as long as the latter are isolated from the ontological matrix to which they in fact belong. In this sense the central role of possibility in articulating being as the milieu of presence and truth does not in any way prejudice the properly understood independence of being; and the eclipse that the notions of possibility and project underwent in Heidegger's later writings can be explained only on the assumption that for some reason—itself unexplained—it is only the ontic (and ontologically misconstrued) versions of these concepts that are at issue there.

There are two further points that need to be made about truth as the being of entities in presence. One concerns the status of animals as entities that are neither worldless (*weltlos*) in the manner of inanimate things nor world-building (*weltbildend*) as man is in the ontological sense that has just been discussed. The text we have been considering is unique among Heidegger's writings in that it subjects this whole matter to a lengthy consideration that draws extensively on the biology and the ecology of the period in which it was written.[19] It is remarkable, in the first place, because it explicitly uses the concept of openness to characterize animals and insists that "the connectedness (of the animals) with (their) environment, their opening upon the stimuli with which they encircle themselves (*Sich-umringen*), belongs to the inner essence of (their) behavior (*Benehmen*)."[20] In this respect, as he points out, animals stand with man and in contrast to things; and the basis for a radically non-behavioristic approach to the study of animals is sketched.[21] At the same time, Heidegger insists that this openness must not be confused with the openness of entities as entities that is characteristic of human beings. It is rather a mode of access (*Zugänglichkeit*) to entities in which they are not understood *as* entities. They are rather the occasions for the release of drives, but for just this reason they are never "something lasting that stands over against the animal as a possible object," never something that is just there (*vorhanden*).[22] They are, as Heidegger puts it, *beseitigt*—set aside—by the very urgency of the drive they release, with the result that the animal can never bring them into focus as what they *are*. That is what human beings *can* do, and entities that are understood as entities are thereby susceptible of all the articulations of temporality and modality that are systematized in the verb "to be." The somewhat perplexing feature of this account is that a criterion for making this distinction between the openness of which animals are capable and that of human beings is not provided. Normally, one would suppose this criterion to be the use of language; but it does not seem that it can be for Heidegger, because, in his view, being—entities manifesting themselves as entities—is not language-dependent even though it may always find expression in language. Thus the difference between animals and human beings could not be just a matter of the use of language by the latter and not the former, when language is understood as some form of overt behavior. (It might, however, coincide extensionally with a distinction made in these terms.) Openness in the case of human beings is informed by a system of distinctions—between the What and the That, between the actual and the possible—that is at once prior to and yet also equivalent to the system of modalities and tenses by which language is ordered. For many this will be hard to accept, not only because it may look as though the whole conception of such a system of distinctions has been borrowed from language, but also because this way of construing the difference between animals and human beings will seem to make the task of constructing some sort of transition from the one to the other much more difficult. In Heidegger's defense, however, it can be pointed out that we really should not make such decisions simply on the basis of our own conceptual convenience, and that, if the considerations relating to the ontological presuppositions of language set forth in earlier chapters are valid, then the discontinuity between animals and human beings will perforce have to be dealt with in the ontological terms that Heidegger has shown to be required. It must be admitted, nonetheless, that it will not be easy to distinguish between a form of openness that involves the presence of entities as entities and one that does not or between the kind of "setting aside" of entities as such that is characteristic of animals and the kind that goes with the dominant instrumental/functional understanding of entities as *zuhanden* that is characteristic of human beings.

The other observation that needs to be made concerns the relationship between truth as the be-ing of entities and the possibility of determining *what* the truth is in specific cases. To say that both being and truth must be understood in terms of what entities *are* may seem to be rather unhelpful as long as it is not amplified in a way that would show how this ontological conception of truth links up with an explanation of how ontic truths can be identified as such. The difficulty here is much the same as the one discussed in chapter 2 in connection with the topic of error and falsity; and the elaboration of Heidegger's position proposed in that discussion can be presupposed here. In both cases it is a question of showing that the identification of being and *Dasein* with openness or presence does not imply that what things are must therefore be immediately and incorrigibly evident. Any such inference has been shown to be invalid on the grounds of there being a contrast within presence between what is present in the sense of having already been uncovered and what is absent in the sense of having not yet been uncovered. But the point that needs to be made here is that the world as a whole, which includes both what is present in the narrower sense and what is absent, is made up of entities that *are* and that *are* such-and-such. To borrow a Kantian term that Heidegger also uses for his own purposes in this context, truth as the be-ing of entities as elements in states of affairs is the "form" of the world as a whole; and what we try to determine when we seek the truth is the determinate character of these states of affairs.[23] In his lectures entitled *The Basic Concepts of Metaphysics*, Heidegger acknowledges much more openly than he did in *Being and Time* that the modality of our relationship to this truth that we seek is that of uncertainty, and that the *logos* or proposition in which our best surmise is expressed is therefore necessarily "the possibility of 'either true or false.'"[24] To this claim he appends the further thesis that the truth as such has a binding character as that which "gives the measure" to our assertions.[25] "As a form of conduct, assertion must be in itself an acknowledging (*Zugeben*) of that which can be authoritative (*massgebend*) for assertion itself"; it thus presupposes a distinctive kind of freedom— a letting-oneself-be-bound (*Sich-binden-lassen*) that consists in "bringing itself as what is eligible for binding (*bindbar*) to that which is to be authoritative and binding in such and such a way."[26] That which binds is said to be "entities (*Seiendes*) that in each case are or are not such-and-such"; and it is on this pre-logical openness of entities as entities—that is, as be-ing whatever they are, that the *logos* as such and every assertion must rest.[27] This notion of binding, which, Heidegger says, presupposes that of freedom, is of great relevance to the public or common dimension of truth, the topic of the next section.

III

It is time now to return to the contrast between the singularity and uniqueness of being and the plurality of the entities that understand being—that is, human beings as *Dasein*. It may seem that the preceding discussion of being as truth has weighted the scales heavily in favor of the first term in this contrast, in the sense that it makes the plurality of the second term appear contingent and inessential to truth as the be-ing of entities. Truth so conceived is manifestly single and unique; and it now looks as though the entities—we ourselves—that apprehend it are in the position of having to presuppose that truth at every step and in a way that has nothing to do with the fact of their plurality.[28] It remains the case, of course, that if there were not such entities, there would be no truth as the be-ing of entities, but the character of this ontological dependence itself would seem to have nothing to do with the plurality of the entities in question. If so, the existence of one entity of the *Dasein* type would be enough to account for the "happening" (*Geschehen*) of the distinction between being and entities (and thus for the be-ing of entities); and the existence of every other such entity would independently do the same. *Mitsein* would still characterize the coexistence of these entities as their understanding that they are in the world together with one another; but their coexistence understood as the sum or aggregate of such entities would have no role in generating that distinction.

The trouble with this view is that it tends to call into question just the uniqueness of being from which it sets out. After all, if the existence of each *Dasein* realizes separately—in an ontological and not an ontic sense, of course—the "happening" of the distinction between being and entities, something like plurality must begin to characterize being itself, if only because there are many such "happenings." This immediately invites all the questions that Heidegger has declared inapplicable to being—questions as to whether one of these happenings is the same as or different from another and, if different, whether they are similar to one another, and so on.[29] The inadmissibility of these questions is enough to justify the conclusion that the happening Heidegger is talking about cannot be plural and cannot therefore be correlated with the existence of individual *Dasein*. But this conclusion can be misleading if it is taken to require the postulation of being as an event that is independent of the existence of *all* such entities; and this has been shown to be unacceptable to Heidegger, as well as fraught with very serious difficulties in its own right. The whole discussion thus appears to end in an impasse, since neither of the two alternatives is defensible.

It has already been suggested that an important and often neglected element in Heidegger's conception of being is its character as *to koinon*, the common.[30] It is common in the first instance because it is shared by *all* entities—stones, plants, animals, and human beings—but it is common to all these entities not as a *summum genus* but as an event (a *Geschehen* or *Ereignis*) that supervenes only on the condition that entities of the kind that have an understanding of being exist as well. There is reason to suppose that being is "the common" in a special sense in relation to entities of the latter kind, and that it is central to the *Mitsein* of which they are distinctively capable. A passage in Heidegger's lectures suggests the way in which this commonality of being for human beings works in the case of language and communication. In interpreting what Aristotle says about speech—the *logos*—as grounded in an agreement (*syntheke*) among human beings, Heidegger argues that this agreement cannot be treated as a mere convention about what certain sounds are to mean and that, instead, "words grow out of the *essential agreement (Übereinkunft)* of human beings with one another by which *they are open in their being-with-one-another for the entities that surround them* about which they can agree in detail and that is to say at the same time not agree."[31] The relationship among the parties to this "agreement" is further described in a discussion of false speech. The point Heidegger makes is that speech has to be antecedently understood as "showing forth" (*aufweisend*) what is in the world (which is to say in terms of a truth it is supposed to express), if it is to be capable of deceiving someone. "If I want to make false representations to another person, I must antecedently be in the posture of desiring to show something to him (and) he must quite generally take my speech in advance as intending such a showing-forth."[32] In these passages, being as truth is the shared presupposition of the communicative relationship in which human beings stand to one another; and it is this sense of the common that needs to be further explored.

One observation that immediately suggests itself in this connection is that the binding character that Heidegger attributes to the be-ing of entities and thus to truth must have a public or common character. In other words, it is not only something by which each of us lets himself be bound as a condition of grasping the truth himself, but also something that is implicit in our relationships to one another. Indeed, Heidegger confirms this surmise when he says, using the plural "we," although without specific emphasis on the element of reciprocity brought out in the previous passage, that "our ways of comporting ourselves (*Verhalten*) are always already pervaded by bindingness (*Verbindlichkeit*) insofar as we comport ourselves in relation to entities."[33] Now this "pervadedness" must be understood as very much including *us* as well as our modes of comportment, and there can therefore be no question of human beings, ontically understood, somehow jointly bringing about the be-ing of entities. But once again, Heidegger is careful to correct any inference that our dependence at every point on being as this "pre-logical openness" means that it is situated "outside man"; indeed, he states that it is man himself "in a deeper sense, he himself in his essence."[34] What this means is made still clearer in a discussion of the "original project" (*ursprünglicher Entwurf*) that defines the essence of man—"the *Dasein* in him"—and which "makes possible in a radical way (*von Grund aus*) all the familiar projecting in our everyday comportment."[35] The linkage of the notion of the project with transcendence and possibility has already been explained; and the project is here spoken of as an event and as an action—one of an arch-distinctive kind (*ureigener Art*) that "in a certain manner carries the projector away from and beyond himself" and "lifts him into the possible" that he is to make actual.[36] What is most striking in this account, however, is the bringing together of the notions of project and of the bindingness associated with being as truth. The project is said "to bind (one) to making-possible (*Ermöglichung*)"—that is, to what is required for the actualization of the possibility that has been projected.[37] Indeed, the project is said to be "the event that lets bindingness (*Verbindlichkeit*) as such emerge"; it is also "the authentic happening (*Geschehen*) of the distinction of being and entities."[38]

What all these passages point to is a conception of the essentially shared character of being as pre-logical openness. More specifically, if being is a unique and singular event that "builds" a world through a contrast between the actual and the possible that is to be made actual, and if this event is to be identified with the essence of man, then its uniqueness can be reconciled with the plurality of the entities—human beings—with whose essence it has been identified only if that essence is understood as encompassing their relatedness to one another. This is just what is effected by the association of the event that is the original project with the character of bindingness that has been described. It is true that when Heidegger speaks of this bindingness, it is usually in a way that does not acknowledge its public dimension explicitly; but in the light of the passages reviewed above, the latter can hardly be in doubt. There are other, even more emphatic statements in which Heidegger flatly declares that "insofar as a human being exists, he is transposed (*versetzt*) into other human beings.... The ability to transpose oneself into other human beings, understood as a going-with them and with the *Dasein* in them, has always already occurred (*geschieht*) on the basis of the *Dasein* in man—as *Dasein*.... For *Dasein* means: being-with (*Mitsein*) others and this in the mode of *Dasein*, that is, of existence."[39] To this he adds that *Mitsein* "belongs to the essence of the existence of man, that is, of each and every individual (human being)."[40] Given the prior identification of the project with this same essence of man, there can be no doubt that the bindingness that the project generates is one that must itself be understood in terms of *Mitsein* and thus in terms of a reciprocity between human beings in their relationship to the truth as the be-ing of entities. What this means is that the event that gives rise to the distinction between being and entities and to the bindingness inherent in a shared relation to the truth and to the interplay of possibility and actuality is not one that addresses human beings in their capacity as separate individuals, but as existing in the mode of *Mitsein*. In this sense, being as presence is inherently a "space" of communication based on a shared and symmetrical relationship to the truth.

It may well be asked what kind of event it is that brings it about that there is a world, as well as truth and a symmetrical relatedness to that truth and thereby to one another on the part of those entities *for* which entities *are* what they are. Since it is an event that separates human beings in the first instance from all inanimate material entities and secondly (and in a different way) from animals, we are tempted to conclude that it must be an event that has a place in cosmic or evolutionary history and that, accordingly, there was a particular time at which it took place. For Heidegger, however, the theory of evolution does not provide the kind of framework within which this event could be situated, because the ontological presuppositions on which that theory rests are faulty.[41] Interestingly enough, his reason for viewing it as unsatisfactory, at least

242 • PRESENCE AS THE GROUND OF EXISTENCE

for this purpose, is that its conception of animals is defective. This is because it fails to acknowledge the distinctive openness of animals to their environment and treats them simply as organisms abstracted from that openness. It makes the further mistake of treating animals as being simply *vorhanden* for us as physical objects of a distinctive kind. Against this view, Heidegger argues that "animals demand of us a quite specific mode of transposedness (*Versetztsein*)"—the same word he uses for human beings in their relation to one another—and within the animal kingdom there prevails "a peculiar transposedness of animals vis-à-vis one another."[42] He develops at some length this idea of the world as a totality of opennesses that are quite distinct from one another yet have a certain access to one another. At one point he even finds it necessary to deny that the conception he is outlining has anything to do with pantheism.[43] It is clear, in any case, that if there is a history in which the event that constitutes being as presence and as truth belongs, it would be one in which the world is understood as a totality of intersecting and yet, in some cases, incommensurate forms of openness, not one that is conceived in terms of the theory of evolution as currently understood.

Significant as this larger theme is within the context of Heidegger's thought, there is a good deal more that could be said about the distinctive modalities of the relationship of human beings to one another within a domain of truth than there is about the way in which radically different forms of openness are "transposed" into one another. It is disappointing, therefore, that, in spite of suggestive aperçus like the ones cited, Heidegger never worked out an account of the way in which the agreement among human beings of which he speaks—an agreement that presupposes truth as the be-ing of entities—implicitly orders the relationships of human beings to one another. Here, surely, is the locus of the "essential directives" that he speaks of but never explains; and here, too, would be the point at which one could show the grounding of ethical notions in a bindingness in our relations to one another that no one can do more than pretend to repudiate. Nevertheless, Heidegger made no such effort. Instead he was content to dismiss scornfully any effort to construct an ethical theory in abstraction from being as presence and to plot the disastrous course of the kind of thought that has progressively shut itself off from any understanding of being as "the common" as well as of whatever binding or normative character it may have. It is, therefore, of very great interest to note that there are passages in his lectures in which, in the course of explicating Kant's theory of moral freedom, he appears to espouse significant portions of that theory and to incorporate them into his own account of *Mitsein*.[44] In a discussion of the *personalitas moralis* as Kant conceives it, Heidegger speaks of the distinctive feeling of respect (*Achtung*) for the moral law as the making manifest of both the law as the determining ground of my action and of the self as an agent that is responsible to itself and for itself.[45] Although Kant's concept of the moral self—that is, the person—remains, in Heidegger's view, an ontic concept, it offers a clue to the ontological character of the concept of humanity (*Menschheit*) that Kant presupposes. That ontological character is identified with the second formulation of the categorical imperative, which enjoins each of us "to act in such a way that you always treat humanity, in your person as well as in that of any one else, as an end and never merely as a means." This principle is said to express what Heidegger, in his own language, describes as the authentic ontological obligation (*Seinsollen*) and the distinctive ontological capability (*Seinkönnen*) of human beings; and it thus connects with the notion of bindingness as a character of the human project that Heidegger develops out of his own mode of analysis.[46] It follows from this, Heidegger tells us, that as a moral agent and as his own end, man is in the kingdom of ends; and the latter is described as "the being with one-another, the commerce of persons as such and therefore the realm of freedom."[47] Very significantly, Heidegger adds that what is involved here is "the kingdom of persons existing with one another, and not a system of values, to which any 'I' that acts relates itself." This notion of a kingdom of ends is itself ontic as Kant employs it, but Heidegger argues that it lends itself to ontological interpretation as a principle of responsibility vis-à-vis oneself and thus of freedom. In this way, he indicates, "the unity of the theoretical and the practical 'I'" that Kant never succeeded in grasping can be understood in the proper ontological terms.[48] In this same vein, Heidegger claims in another series of lectures devoted largely to Kant that "the essence of the person is this self-responsibility (*Selbstverantwortlichkeit*)," which is described significantly as "binding oneself to one self, but not in an egoistic sense and not in relation to the I that one just happens to be."[49] The same formulation of the categorical imperative is cited, and Heidegger argues that it is only when the primordial character of the dimension of selfhood it represents is understood that we can comprehend the fact that "actual willing, i.e. essential willing, in and of itself and in a fundamental way, puts one into an agreement (*Einverständnis*) with others—a form of community that obtains only by virtue of the secret, the hidden actual will of the individual."[50]

At the very least, these passages show that Heidegger was quite at home with a concept of *Mitsein* that is prior to any distinction between knowledge and action and that has a distinctly normative character. It is this conception that he conspicuously failed to develop further in his later period, when, for the most part, the notion of the We is approached only in its negative aspect as an intensification of the misconceived subjectivity of the I. It is important to notice, however, that Heidegger nowhere repudiates anything that he said earlier about the bindingness of either the project or the distinction between being—the be-ing of entities—and entities. It is as though, instead of elaborating further in a positive sense these fundamental normative notions that underlie the character of being as *to koinon*, Heidegger had decided to explicate their negative variant as the defining feature of contemporary life. It must be remembered, though, that in doing this, he is dealing with a condition that is itself common and that, as such, presupposes the commonness of being and truth that it at the same time obscures. The strategy that thus replaces that of a direct characterization of being as presence is one that seeks to show how our present understanding of the world as a totality of entities is itself a permutation of being as presence to which it therefore testifies in its own enigmatic way. It is evident that the occlusion that this strategy seeks to exhibit as such is one that also encompasses the *Mitsein* of the entities—ourselves—that are capable of an understanding of being. There is every reason, therefore, to suppose that Heidegger continued to endorse what he said about the obscuration of *Mitsein* in his lectures two years after *Being and Time*:

> In the essential constitution of human *Dasein*, i.e. in the fact that the latter is, from the word go (*vom Hause aus*), a *Mitsein* with others, it is implicit that the factually existing human being in actual fact always and necessarily moves in some definite mode of *Mitsein* with . . . , i.e. in a Going-with (*Mitgehen*). But for various reasons, some of them essential in character, this Going-together-with-one-another is a Going-apart-from and a Going-against-one-another; in the first instance and for the most part, however, it is a Going-beside-one-another (*Nebeneinandergehen*). Precisely this unobtrusive, self-evident Going-beside-one-another as a determinate mode of the Together and of Being-transposed-into-one-another makes it appear as though this fact of Being-beside-one-another has to be, in the first instance, a matter of bridging over something, as though there were not, at that point, any transposedness into one another at all, and as though one person could reach the other only by way of empathy. This illusion has also stultified philosophy for a long time and to a degree that one would scarcely think possible. This same illusion is then maximally reinforced by philosophy through the latter's setting up the dogma that the single and separate human being is single and separate in his own eyes (*für sich*) and that the single and separate I is, with its first-personal domain (*Ichsphäre*), that which is initially and most certainly given to him. Thereby, the opinion is philosophically sanctioned that would make a state of Being-with-one-another something that had originally to be created out of this solipsistic isolation.[51]

What Heidegger is describing here is a *Mitsein* that, like being as presence generally, is for the most part "unthought" in its original character and is therefore typically misconceived in a way that turns it into a philosophical puzzle for which ingenious solutions must be devised. But if it were to prove possible to take the step back from these misconceptual-izations that Heidegger calls for, then the true plurality that is an essential modality of being and presence would also be freed from the occlusion in which these "solutions" confine it.

CONCLUSION

In the Introduction a claim was made regarding the significance of Heidegger's thought for contemporary philosophy; and it is time now that the basis for that claim be clarified. This requires a brief review of the present situation in the philosophy of mind, since it is as a distinctive alternative to positions currently held in that area of philosophy that Heidegger's thought has been presented in this book. There are, at present, two major positions in the philosophy of mind, both of which derive from a critique of Cartesian dualism, as does Heidegger's position, but which differ in the degree to which they reject its assignment of a distinct ontological status to mental acts and contents of various kinds. One of these is loosely affiliated with what is called "ordinary language philosophy"; and it approaches issues in the philosophy of mind primarily through questions about the kind of language—specifically, the kinds of predicates—that is needed to describe and explain those aspects of human conduct that have been traditionally thought of as "mental." The general disposition of this kind of philosophy of mind is anti-reductionist in the sense of holding that the locutions of ordinary language by which we describe ourselves and others as thinking, perceiving, and so on have a continuing validity and a significant measure of independence from the constructions of theoretical science. This independence is not to be interpreted in an ontological sense, however, since that would, it is thought, entail a rehabilitation of something like Cartesian dualism. The claim that this kind of philosophy makes is rather that there is a *via media* between dualism and a science-based physicalism. The latter is the second position with which I will be concerned, and it recognizes neither a special ontological status for the mental nor any inhibitions deriving from the priority of common sense and ordinary language in this domain against a wholesale annexation of the mental by the behavioral sciences and neuroscience. In recent years, as theoretical advances have been made in these sciences, and as the approach based on the integrity of the commonsense understanding of ourselves as "persons" has seemed to lose momentum, the physicalistic view has become more and more attractive, and its theses largely dominate current discussions.

What I will try to show first (and without too much unfairness, I hope, to the full complexity of the views under consideration) is that the positions I have just characterized are themselves still under the influence of Cartesian assumptions about the nature of the mental. For reasons that will be detailed and that reflect in good measure the way in which the successors of Descartes in the "way of ideas" reconstrued certain elements in his conception of the mind, "mental phenomena" came to be understood as, paradigmatically, certain elusive qualities or feelings—certain more or less anomalous items of "experience"—for which no secure domicile could be found in the public world. When "mind" became the repository of such heterogeneous bric-a-brac, a rather absurd dispute inevitably began between those who claimed that there really was no such thing and those who were sure that there was. It is hardly surprising that in that contest the negative thesis—that of physicalism—has gradually prevailed, if only because the conception of the "mental" that the other side was defending was too curious an affair to command much acceptance in the long run. A second point that I want to make in this connection has to do with the effort that some philosophers have made to avoid sliding all the way into physicalism after that conception was given up. They have tried to do this by defending the integrity of our ordinary—that is, pre-scientific—way of talking about thinking and perceiving, but this undertaking has little prospect of success, I will argue, as long as its ontological assumptions are at bottom the same as those of the physicalists. In a way, the triumph of physicalism has the advantage of ridding us of implausible conceptualizations of the mind and permitting us to bring into focus the way physicalism relies on understandings about itself as a form of thought to which it is not able to assign any status within the ontology it espouses. These are, I think, the very understandings that Heidegger has tried to formulate in a way that liberates them from the distorting Cartesian format with which they have been virtually identified for most of the modern period. It is therefore of great importance to see how this antithetical ontological position—physicalism—can paradoxically help to force these understandings into a new prominence.

I

Descartes's philosophy of mind was in a clear sense ontological. Consciousness and knowledge were the distinguishing features of one kind of entity—the mental substance that was radically differentiated from extended substance—the other principal ontological type that Descartes recognized. The criticism to which this ontology was subjected in the eighteenth century was primarily epistemological, however, and did not therefore address itself to the peculiarities of Descartes's ontological scheme as such or to the grounds on which it had been introduced. Berkeley and Hume raised no objection to describing experience as a collection of impressions and ideas, although it was the credentials of just this mode of description that most needed scrutinizing. For them, impressions and ideas were the very elements in the Cartesian scheme about which they had no real doubts at all on epistemological grounds, since they were so reassuringly and unmistakably present to the mind. What seemed dubious to them and probably quite unknowable were the substances they represented—things in the "external world"—and in Hume's case, those in which they were supposed to inhere—mental substances or minds. Hume's critique of the idea of the self as that to which ideas and impressions belong led to the kind of empiricism that analyzes both external objects and the thinking subject in terms of complex relationships among impressions, or, as they later came to be called, "sense-data." From that point onward, through J. S. Mill and Bertrand Russell and on up to the middle of this century, the philosophy of mind was mainly a matter of trying to construct perceptual objects and minds out of these basic entities. They had been designated as basic because they alone appeared to be invulnerable to epistemological objections. But if the ontology of such a philosophy of mind was one that posited sense-data as the basic entities, that ontology remained derivative in crucially important respects from the prior Cartesian ontology within which these entities were themselves rooted. It is true that attempts were made to portray sense-data, or *qualia*, as neutral with respect to the subject/object distinction, but this alleged neutrality could hardly remove the peculiarities of these entities that were the legacy of their origin as internal modifications of mental substances.

It was these peculiarities that became the focus of the critique of the concept of sense-data that was mounted by Wittgenstein and his followers from the 1930s onward. This critique had a logical character in the sense that it concentrated on the way sense-data could be described; and this way of coming at the matter was part of a more general linguistic turn that philosophy was taking at the time. Instead of talking about different kinds of entities and their putative relationships to one another, philosophers talked about the linguistic modalities for describing the latter and the logical relationships in which these stood to one another. The outcome of this logical examination of the language of sense-data was overwhelmingly negative; and in the fifties it was widely agreed that sense-data were totally unsuited to serve as the basic entities out of which the world was to be constructed, whether in the material or the formal mode. The broad anti-Cartesian implications of this conclusion were developed, and the definitive liquidation of the "ghost in the machine" was confidently announced. But if this attack on the Cartesian ontology of mind undoubtedly shared many of the epistemological objections that had earlier been made by Hume and others, its emphasis was different. What was now thought to be fundamentally wrong with the Cartesian picture was that it misinterpreted the actual ways of describing the "mental" element in human nature and conduct that are embedded in ordinary, nontechnical language. Indeed, it began to appear as though the role of philosophy in these matters were largely pernicious and consisted mainly in its misunderstandings of an otherwise sound commonsense ordering of similarities and differences laid down in ordinary language.

In one sense, this appeal to a pre-philosophical understanding that we supposedly had of the matters with which philosophies like that of Descartes dealt might have proved highly beneficial to philosophy itself. For the Cartesian domination of modern thought really to be terminated, it was essential that any prior understanding we have of the matters with which it dealt be accurately set forth, so that it could serve as the basis for a new effort of philosophical thought that might have a better chance of success. The likelihood that something of this kind might be achieved was considerably enhanced by the fact that among post-Wittgensteinian philosophers a far more Aristotelian than Cartesian conception of nature prevailed, in which middle-sized objects with their full complement of primary and secondary qualities supplied the familiar context of human acting and making. To this it should be added that among these philosophers an unusually strong emphasis on the public character of all characteristically human activities corrected any tendency to treat "consciousness" and "mind" as though they were the attributes of individual human beings taken singly. Nevertheless, and in spite of these advantages, the hold of Cartesian ways of thought proved to be stronger than these critics realized; and it made itself felt in ways that were detrimental to the prospects of their undertaking. In part this happened because the critics' historical understanding of the Cartesian tradition and its antecedents was superficial and treated it as simply a wayward episode in the history of modern thought, rather than the outcome of a long process of preparation extending back into ancient philosophy. More important, however, it was due to a failure to take the commonsense understanding of the world at a deep enough level and to ask questions about it that only philosophy, not common sense, can answer. This was especially true of the treatment of language, which had a very important place in these inquiries, but whose relationship to the world was for the most part simply taken for granted, without any examination of what was presupposed by the commonsense understanding of it. More generally, one can say that the concept of the world with which these philosophers of ordinary language worked was uncritical in the sense that it was simply that of a totality of entities, without any consideration of the kind of entity that can *have* a world. Since the mental was understood in good Cartesian fashion as a state or property of certain entities, there was no disposition to address the question of why it is that some entities— that is, those that are capable of perception and thought—are such that their "state" cannot be described without bringing in a reference to something that is distinct from them. This way of putting the matter itself bears the mark of the linguistic mode of formulating philosophical issues, but it is clear that it also raises the more fundamental question of why it is that some entities are such as to involve this very special kind of relationship to other entities. Moreover, this is not a question about "mental contents," so no amount of deflationary criticism directed against the notion of the sense-datum can turn it aside.

The limitations of this kind of approach can be illustrated by a brief consideration of a well-known theory developed by Peter Strawson.[1] This theory acknowledges the logical distinctness of the predicates that are used in describing typical episodes in our mental lives, such as perceiving something, feeling a pain, or believing in the existence of God; and it accordingly makes no attempt to reduce these predicates to some set of explicitly behavioral or physical predicates. At the same time, however, Strawson rejects all dualistic theories that postulate *two* substances—one physical and one mental—to which these different attributes would belong. Instead, he holds that both mental and physical predicates belong to a single logical subject, and that this subject is to be understood in terms of the concept of the person. At first blush, this idea of a single subject that bears both kinds of descriptions and is itself a primitive— in the sense of irreducible—entity-type within our conceptual scheme or ontology may sound promising. Nevertheless, the choice of the concept of the person for this purpose is questionable. Its prior associations are with ways of making the contrast between human beings and both things and animals in primarily ethical and legal contexts; and it is not apparent that it can cast much light on how these different kinds of predicates can belong to the same entity. The question about the person as a distinctive entity-type is simply whether it is a straightforwardly physical entity or one that is "primitive" in the sense of being *neither* physical *nor* mental, thereby eluding the conventional ontological alternatives in a way that might be comparable to what Heidegger attempts. Unfortunately, there does not seem to be much basis for construing Strawson's position along the lines of the second alternative. He tells us that the concept of consciousness is to be analyzed as "a secondary, nonprimitive concept" by derivation from the concept of the person.[2] The concept of body is not held to be secondary and derivative, however, in the way that consciousness is supposed to be. It has been antecedently declared to be the fundamental concept underlying our whole conceptual system, and so the possibility of the identification of particulars depends on it. It follows that identifying reference to individual consciousnesses can be achieved only via the identification of bodies, while the identification of bodies does not require "reference to particulars of other types and categories than their own"—that is, it does not require reference to any individual consciousness.[3] There is a further stipulation that mental predicates are by their nature such as to be attributable to other persons as well as oneself, and that the notion of "my" consciousness is, therefore, strictly correlative with that of "other" consciousnesses. Specifically, it cannot be abstracted from this web of mutual implication in which the concept of the bodies of these other persons is fundamental. About the concept of person itself we are told nothing more; it is apparently to be understood simply as a compound of the logically primitive concept of a body and the logically derivative concepts of various mental functions.

It is evident that Strawson's acknowledgment of the logical distinctness of mental predicates has only logical and linguistic applications. Thus, we may continue to use these predicates and do not need to worry about translating them into behavioral equivalents. But this thesis, together with the notion of person that it introduces, conceals only very imperfectly the ontological primacy of the concept of body on which it is premised. To say that the notion of consciousness is nonprimitive and derives from the concept of the person would represent a real alternative to an ontological behaviorism only if the latter concept were at once primitive and, in at least some respects, nonphysical in character. But what Strawson says about the concept of person does not assign it any ontological status at all other than that of being the subject of both mental and physical predicates—that is, something that one may *talk* about in two logically contrasting ways, but that evidently need not have any nonphysical characteristics in order to have mental predicates properly apply to it. How, one wonders, can the concept of individual consciousness be logically posterior to that of the person, as Strawson says it is, when the latter is just the concept of something to which both physical predicates and those that impute consciousness in the form of thinking or perceiving to their subjects apply? Surely, anyone who is able to understand what is involved in an attribution of thought or perception to another person or to himself already *has* the concept of consciousness. What is really at issue here is thus not the priority of the concept of person to that of consciousness, but the priority of the concept of body to that of consciousness. On that point, it might well have occurred to

Strawson, in light of the importance of the notion of identifying reference within his own philosophy, that, even if body and its spatial location play the central role within such identifications that he assigns to them, such references themselves are of equally fundamental importance to the concept of a human being (and thus of a person) and can hardly be treated as among the physical characteristics of the latter. In other words, in order to be able to make an identifying reference to another entity by means of the criteria of physical location that Strawson describes, a human being—a person—must already have a kind of consciousness— I waive for the moment the objections to the use of this term—that is certainly not in any readily specifiable sense a state of his body (or for that matter of his "mind"). It cannot be so understood because such references and the thinking and perception that are the context within which they are made essentially involve the existence of *another* entity; and there is no *physical* concept of the human body that would permit the latter to count as one of the states of that body. The only way in which one can avoid this conclusion is to treat such references, as well as mental functions generally, in "linguistic" terms, and this is to say in a way that either assigns them a wholly indeterminate status for ontological purposes or implicitly assimilates them to the functions of the organism and thus to a physicalistic ontology. Heidegger's reasons for viewing both these expedients as inadmissible have been set forth in detail in previous chapters; and they retain all their validity against a position like the one that has just been described.

II

In light of what has been said, it is hardly surprising that positions like Strawson's should have lost ground in recent years to another form of anti-Cartesianism that is not at all solicitous of ordinary language and makes no bones about espousing an explicitly physicalistic ontology. In one version or another, this sort of position is probably the dominant one in the philosophy of mind at the present time. As has already been noted, it is not a position to which Heidegger has devoted explicit attention, as he did to Cartesian dualism, but it does represent an extreme point reached by a line of development that he characterizes quite fully. This development is driven by a steadily intensifying disposition to reduce everything to the status of an object, an object, moreover, that, as law-governed, is in principle subject to one form or another of manipulation and control. The distinctive feature of contemporary physicalism, of course, is that the human beings who are the authors and proponents of this theory are treated as physical objects in just the way that the rest of nature is. The fact that physicalism is a theory about the world and that it is a theory formulated and held by human beings does not, in the view of its adherents, require any modification of what the theory says about their ontological status. And yet holding a theory is a form of thinking and of thinking about entities other than oneself; it appears, therefore, that it would not be possible to talk about the thought processes of the adherents of physicalism without bringing in that which they are thinking about—not in this case a particular object or event, but rather physical objects and events generally. But if thinking about a particular object or event cannot be treated as simply a state of the organism that does the thinking, then neither can thinking about other organisms as being, like oneself, physical systems. Since physicalism does not typically place much emphasis on the distinction between the logical as such (including itself considered as a set of propositions) and the physical milieu that is the only one recognized by its ontology, it seems to be even more directly confronted by the difficulty discussed in connection with ordinary language philosophy, for which this distinction has a good deal more weight. This difficulty may be described as the problem of characterizing the way physicalism itself, in its capacity as a posture of belief, is *in* the world for which it lays down ontological conditions.

The answer that would be given to this challenge to the thesis of an identity of, say, thought and brain-state is suggested by a recent defense of such a position by Arthur Danto.[4] He argues that it is one thing to consider a thought in terms of its content, or what it is *about*, and quite a different matter to consider what thought *is*. Danto's account of a thought's content is one that emphasizes heavily its referential or intentional character; and it seems clear that it would be impossible, in his view, to characterize a thought without talking about what it is a thought of, and thus about something other than the thought itself as an episode in my mental history. When he comes to his second question about what a thought itself is, however, there is no suggestion that the range of possible answers to this question might be narrowed by considerations deriving from the answer to the first one. The answer he in fact gives is that thought is a brain-event; and it is given in a manner that seems to suggest that one could hardly have imagined it to be anything else. In other words, the fact of "having a content" is not thought to be sufficiently curious in itself to raise questions about what *kind* of entity could properly be so characterized. And yet a little reflection reveals that we have no clear ideas regarding just what is entailed by "having a content," and so designating the brain as its ontological vehicle can hardly be said to amount to more than a way of not having to face up to any of the difficulties with which a careful scrutiny of this notion might confront us.

The underlying assumption in a form of physicalism like Danto's to which I have been trying to draw attention is that the relationship between the logical or functional state of some entity like a human being and its physical state raises no ontological problems; and my point is that this is a very large assumption, and that, if it is accepted without challenge, it will be difficult to resist the sequence of inferences that the physicalist is sure to draw from it. The assumption itself *seems* to receive a very significant measure of confirmation from the existence of very complex computing machines which, in respect of their own constitution, are undisputably "physical" if anything is, but which are also, just as indisputably, in a state that can only be described in logical or functional terms. Why, the physicalist may well ask, should we make more of a fuss about the ontological possibility of such an association in the case of human beings than we do in the case of computers? To mention computers is of course to come face to face with one of the master metaphors in which physicalism as a cultural ethos expresses its deepest intuitions. The central feature of this system of metaphors is the analogy between computers and human beings; and although at the more popular level the comparison is made in terms of performance—that is, in terms of what the one and the other can do in the way of computation within certain time constraints—what is more significant is the implication that it is in terms of the computer and *its* way of associating logical with physical states that human beings can come to understand themselves. It has always seemed to me that the most interesting feature of this parallel is the way in which the fact that computers are themselves human artifacts is not exactly denied or forgotten, but rather glossed over in a way that suggests that it is not of any great importance to an understanding of the philosophical issues at stake. Yet it does seem important to determine what degree and kind of independence from its creator the computer can realistically be said to have; and by "independence" here, I mean not just the kind that contrasts with the continuing requirement for physical maintenance by human beings, but the kind that has to do with the central task or function that these machines are said to perform. More specifically, are we to conceive the relationship of this artifact to its makers in such a way that its continuing dependence on them is merely contingent, something that may eventually be eliminable, or is it of a much deeper kind, involving a conceptual bond between the two by virtue of which it is only in its relationship to its makers or users that the computer can be said to be in a logical or functional state at all? At the very least, this second alternative deserves to be taken more seriously than it usually is, if only because it is obvious that, when the operations of the computer or, for that matter, those of the brain are consistently described in *purely* physicalistic terms, there will be no hint that any "task" is being performed or that the physical system so described is the domicile of any logical state at all.

How, then, *do* logical and functional descriptions accrue to the sequences of physical events in the computer or the brain? We can hardly answer that question without referring back to the larger partnership between the machine and its human user. The user, we remember, puts questions to the computer after he has succeeded in adapting them to a program that is so constructed that, when properly initiated, the purely physical sequences of the computer's operation will produce a result that is guaranteed to be the answer to that question. But if we have to bring in the human user of the computer in order to make sense of the latter's being in a logical as well as a physical state, we are asserting a conceptual bond between the computer and the human user in his unreduced state—that is, in the understanding we have of his state prior to the application to it of the computer-based model. It follows that the computer is not, as has been claimed, an independent and nonproblematic case of the association of a logical state with a purely physical state, and the nature of this association remains as unclear as ever. The illusion of such independence is possible only because, in describing the computer's operations, we make covert use of the knowledge we have of the larger system that includes both the computer and its (conceptually unreduced) human user; and although that may be perfectly unexceptionable in ordinary contexts, it clearly will not do when the issue at stake is the conceptual or ontological one that is begged by such covert use of knowledge whose source lies outside the domain to which we are claiming to limit ourselves.

From a Heideggerian standpoint, this covert, unacknowledged use of an understanding that is not accounted for in the theory that makes use of it takes on great significance. The understanding in question is one that we all have of the way we are in the world. That way has been described already, as existence in the sense of a standing-out into a milieu of presence in which we have to do with entities other than ourselves and with those entities as themselves existing or no longer existing or about to exist. This understanding is so fundamental to everything we do and are, including the philosophical and scientific theories about ourselves and the world that we construct, that it is only with great difficulty that we can even recognize it as an understanding that we have. Accordingly, nothing is easier than to rely on it, while not realizing that we are doing so, since whether acknowledged or not, it is the unspoken concomitant of everything we think and believe. Moreover, even when it is acknowledged, it typically has the sound of a barren truism, and we may wonder how anyone could regard this redundant "There is" as the foundation of philosophy. To this the answer must be that, if everything is so simple and straightforward, then this "truism" must already have found its appropriate mode of recognition within the theories that deal with such matters as "the mind and its place in nature." After all, what everyone knows must be equally well known to the architects of these theories, who would hardly omit such a universally shared piece of knowledge from their own comprehensive characterizations of the nature of mind.

The point that I have argued in this chapter and in the book as a whole is that this confident expectation is mistaken, and that it is precisely this understanding that finds no place within the philosophies of mind that have been reviewed. In one way or another, but most frequently on the grounds that commonsense views can hardly expect to be preserved and vindicated without major revisions in the kind of mature theory that in effect preempts their subject matter, this understanding is dismissed or reformulated out of existence by being expressed in the language of the new theory. In this way, the whole matter is assimilated to the status of a special case of the now familiar relationship of pretheoretical intuitions and well-substantiated theories. That relationship is typically a dialogue of the deaf, in which every claim that common sense advances has already been either disqualified or reinterpreted in such a way as to render it innocuous. In this case, the procedure has been so effective that it need not even become apparent that the understanding in question is in fact one on which the proponents of the superordinate theory themselves rely. That they rely on it in its original form is evident at every step, however, if we compare what is said in such a theory about "consciousness" or "thought" or about that theory itself as a *state* of a particular entity, with the "There is" that each of these essentially involves. In that "There is" a *world* is given, and even though that world is the one construed by the theory in question, the thought that carries the theory cannot be identified with one item or set of items *within* the world it claims to reveal. The illusion that this is the case is made possible by the theorist's failing to notice that he is constantly supplementing the account he has given of the ontological status of his own thought and thus of his own theory by his understanding of the theory itself as a particular mode of having a world. But it is just this implicit provision of a "There is" and thus of a world that must be made explicit within the theory itself.

The failure to take these considerations into account is responsible for some of the peculiar features that the philosophy of mind has taken on at the present time and especially for the way in which the theory of mind-body or mind-brain identity is defended. The acid test for any such identification might seem to be the question of whether the brain or the nervous system or the organism as a whole can be described, under a purely physical mode of conceptualization, as performing the functions that have traditionally been attributed to the "mind." If it were to turn out that this is not possible, then the theory would have cut the ground out from under itself as a way of having a world. As things stand, however, little, if any, attention is paid to this question. In order to address it, one would have to ask *how* it is possible for a neurophysiological process that is occurring at a given moment in time to *represent* something other than itself (or, for that matter, itself), and what the difference is, expressed in physical terms, between a physical process that carries such a representational function and one that does not. Because these questions are not asked, great freedom in attributing all manner of representational functions to the nervous system is claimed and exercised, although, if these theorists were really confining themselves to physical concepts, as they claim they are, there would be not the slightest reason deriving from descriptions of neurophysiological process in physicalistic terms for supposing that anything like perception or memory is taking place. It is evident that the source of the enriched "functional" or "mental" descriptions of the nervous system is an independent understanding that these theorists, like everyone else, have of themselves. It is this unavowed understanding that also explains why there is no apprehension on their part that it may not be possible to identify perception or memory with neurophysiological processes, or that, if neurophysiological processes are indeed the whole story, there may be no perception or memory or, for that matter, theory-construction at all. The reason is that, independently of their theories, they already understand perception and memory, and they understand them not as states of the organism or of the "mind," but as ways of having a world and as necessary conditions for a *theoretical* way of having a world. Since having a world is thus secured, but secured outside the structure of the theory that it makes possible, the proponents of the latter are left free to go ahead with the construction of a kind of physicalistic Cartesianism in which the nervous system takes over the representational functions once attributed to the mind. This way of proceeding is so well established that those who now speak so freely of physical processes in terms borrowed from the vocabulary of "mind" have no sense that what they are doing is parasitic on a prior understanding that has not been recognized as such. Indeed, one may say without exaggeration that the blindness to being as presence of which Heidegger speaks has been effectively realized in them, and that there is no realistic prospect of its even being recognized for what it is, much less overcome.

In the light of these paramount tendencies in the philosophy of mind, the suggestion I am making here about the contemporary relevance of Heidegger's thought may not seem very realistic. As I have already argued in the course of my discussion of the history of being, however, it is not possible simply to accept any such dispensation as a decree of fate, as long as one can point to what is invalid in the procedures on which it depends. However dark our time may be, the example of Heidegger proves that it is still possible to evoke the understanding we implicitly have of existence and presence and to attempt to find an adequate conceptual formulation for that understanding. It will probably be a long time before it is as evident as it should be that his has been the most radically conceived and the most deeply grounded effort to do that in this century. Nevertheless, it is clear already that his thought has a strong claim on the attention of anyone who seeks to make the contemporary philosophy of mind less oblivious than it has been recently to the understanding on which it draws, but which it does not and, as things stand, perhaps cannot acknowledge.

NOTES

INTRODUCTION

1. *SZ* 209. In *W* 58 Heidegger speaks of the need for a constant renewal of "an ontological interpretation of the subjectivity of the subject."
2. *ZSD* 9. See also Heidegger's comments on the continuing validity of the question posed in *SZ*, in his preface to William J. Richardson, *Heidegger: Through Phenomenology to Thought* (The Hague:Nijhoff, 1963), especially pp. xix–xx.
3. The *Gesamtausgabe*, for which the general editor is Friedrich-Wilhelm von Herrmann, began publication in 1975 and has so far published more than twenty volumes. Critical appraisals of this edition, which, in accordance with Heidegger's instructions has no critical apparatus, can be found in *Allgemeine Zeitschrift für Philosophie* 3 (1977):70–74, and *The New York Review of Books*, 4 December 1980, pp. 39–41.

I. THE CRITIQUE OF THE CARTESIAN TRADITION

1. *"Dasein* is an entity that I myself in each case am" (*SZ* 53). For Heidegger's account of our pre-ontological understanding of ourselves, see *SZ* 12–16 and 196–200, also *GP* 398.
2. For Heidegger's critique of Descartes, see *SZ* 89–101. An earlier version of this critique is presented in *PGZ* 231–51.
3. *SZ* 56.
4. For an account of this transformation, see *GP* 172–218.
5. *SZ* 202.
6. *SZ* 205.
7. Heidegger often quotes Descartes's definition of substance as the kind of thing *(res)* that exists in such a fashion *ut nulla alia re indigeat ad existendum*. See, e.g., *SZ* 92, where the Descartes reference is given, and *PGZ* 232.
8. *SZ* 206.
9. For Heidegger's critique of the concept of representation *(Vorstellung)*, see *SZ* 214–18 and 319–21.
10. *SZ* 163.
11. *SZ* 164.
12. *SZ* 164.
13. Heidegger speaks of "being true" *(Wahrsein)* as "subjective" only "in the sense of the properly understood concept of the subject as the *Dasein* that exists, i.e., that is in the world" (*GP* 308). See also *GP* 313.
14. See Maurice Merleau-Ponty, *Phenomenology of Perception*, trans. Colin Smith (London: Routledge and Kegan Paul, 1962) pp. 374ff.
15. *SZ* 206–08.

16. *SZ* 203–04. If Heidegger had wished to substantiate further his claim that Kant was deeply entangled in the assumptions of the Cartesian theory of mind, he could have quoted the passage below, in which Kant reduces matter to a set of representations and its apparent externality to an illusion.

"Matter, therefore, does not mean a kind of substance quite distinct and hetero-geneous from the object of inner sense (the soul), but only the distinctive nature of those appearances of objects—in themselves unknown to us—the representations of which we call outer as compared with those which we count as belonging to inner sense, although like all other thoughts these outer representations belong only to the thinking subject. They have indeed this deceptive property that, representing objects in space, they detach themselves as it were from the soul and appear to hover outside it." [*Critique of Pure Reason*, trans. N. K. Smith (London:Macmillan 1958), p. 355]

17. For a discussion of the uncritical use of the concept of the "in-itself," see *PGZ* 268–69 and 299–300, also *A* 202.

18. *SZ* 206.

19. For Heidegger's later comments on the abandonment of this word and its replacement by *Dasein*, see *W* 202–04.

20. See *Bewusstsein* in *Historisches Wörterbuch der Philosophie* (Basel/Stuttgart:Schwabe, 1971), vol. 1, p. 888, for a valuable discussion of the way the words for "consciousness" in the European languages have developed.

21. *The Oxford English Dictionary* offers many examples of such usages.

22. *SZ* 207.

23. For Heidegger's own account of his relationship to the phenomenological movement, see his essay entitled "Mein Weg in die Phänomenologie," in *ZSD* 81–90.

24. See especially *GP* 77ff. for examples of Heidegger's own employment of the term. These lectures were exactly contemporary with the publication of *SZ*; it is thus evident that he was still using the concept at that time.

25. See, e.g., *PGZ* 47 and *GP* 77–94.

26. *PGZ* 54–58.

27. *PGZ* 55–57.

28. *PGZ* 63.

29. *PGZ* 154–57.

30. *PGZ* 140–48. The passages in Husserl's *Ideen zu einer reinen Phänomenologie und phän-omenologischen Philosophie*, vol. 1, to which Heidegger refers can be found in *Husserliana* (The Hague:Nijhoff, 1950), vol. 33. pp. 115, 117, and 118.

31. *PGZ* 149–51. Other discussions of *Vereinzelung* can be found in *GP* 408 and *SZ* 188, 191, 263, and 336.

32. *Husserliana*, vol. 1, p. 139.

33. Husserl's discussion of transcendence-in-immanence can be found in his *Ideen*, vol. 1, p. 138.

34. *PGZ* 136. See also *GP* 29, where Heidegger explains that the purpose of the reduction is to make possible the understanding of being by distinguishing it from entities.

35. *PGZ* 138.

36. *PGZ* 139.

37. *PGZ* 147. Heidegger also remarks that, as such a region, "consciousness is not con-sidered in its concrete individuation and its attachment to animate beings *(Lebewesen)*," but only in terms of its generic intentional structures *(PGZ* 145–46).

38. *PGZ* 149.

39. *PGZ* 149. In the same context, the "entity in which consciousness and reason are concrete" is declared to be "man" *(PGZ* 148).

40. *GP* 64–67 and 77–107.
41. *GP* 79.
42. *PGZ* 156–57.
43. *PGZ* 146.
44. *PGZ* 151.
45. *PGZ* 147.
46. *PGZ* 161–62. The same point is made more briefly in *GP* 81.
47. *PGZ* 167–74.
48. *PGZ* 169.
49. *PGZ* 150.
50. *PGZ* 134. Heidegger has reservations, however, about both Husserl's interpretation of the natural attitude and the term *Einstellung* (attitude); for these, see *PGZ* 155–56.
51. *GP* 82.
52. *GP* 83.
53. *GP* 86.
54. These are available in *Husserliana*, vol. 9, *Phänomenologische Psychologie*, pp. 600–02.
55. Ibid., p. 601.
56. Ibid., pp. 601–02.
57. Ibid., p. 602.
58. Ibid., p. 602.
59. *PGZ* 144.
60. Husserl, *Phänomenologische Psychologie*, p. 602.
61. *PGZ* 152.
62. Husserl, *Phänomenologische Psychologie*, p. 602.
63. *GP* 89–90.
64. *GP* 91.
65. Statements declaring intentionality to be the "ontological condition" of transcendence can be found in *GP* 89 and 91; but the same volume also contains statements in which the relationship is reversed, e.g., *GP* 230. It is the latter view that ultimately prevailed, and a year later Heidegger stated in a lecture that intentionality "as ontic transcendence is itself possible only on the basis of the original transcendence: being-in-the-world" (*MAL* 170). But he retained the distinction between intentionality, properly understood, and intentionality as "directed inward." It is clear why the latter might be called "ontic" rather than "ontological"; but why the former, which was previously said to be "an ontological condition of transcendence," should be so described is not at all clear. In the absence of an explanation, one suspects that once again Heidegger is abandoning a term—"intentionality"—that has been misused to those who misuse it and transferring its proper sense to a new term.

2. THE WORLD AS PRESENCE

1. For the discussion of Kant's treatment of the concept of the world, see *W* 43ff.
2. *SZ* 48, 92; *KPM* 30; *MAL* 54–69.
3. *SZ* 63, 65, and 70; *PGZ* 265–66, 270–71, and 290–91.
4. *SZ* 106; *PGZ* 300 and 317–18. There are some indications that Heidegger considered a mode of expression in which the special character of the world as he understands it would have been conveyed adjectivally—as, for example, in phrases like "die nächstegegebene Welt" and "die primäre Umwelt" (*PGZ* 263, 265, and 269–71)—instead of by reserving the term "world" exclusively for this purpose. To those who object to his decision, it should be pointed out that there are many current uses of the term that are in fact closer to Heidegger's than to standard philosophical usage. Phrases

like "a doctor's world," "the seventeenth-century world," and so on denote the world not as "nature," but as the environment of certain human beings.

5. *HAD* 89.

6. Heidegger was notably allergic to the concept of value-properties, as he explains in some detail in *SZ* 99.

7. There is plenty of evidence of Heidegger's willingness to continue to use the concept of the subject in the exposition of his own position. In *GP* 103, for example, he speaks of the modern philosophical orientation toward "the subject, or what is fundamentally intended thereby, *Dasein*." Elsewhere in the same lectures he equates *Dasein* with "the subjective that exists" (107); and he says that his "leading problem is to determine what and how the subject is—what belongs to the subjectivity of the subject"—and that it is the concept of the world that forces him to "a more radical formulation (*Fassung*) of the subject-concept" (238). He also makes clear that "the traditional subject-concept" utterly fails to do justice to "what constitutes the authentic structure of *Dasein*, i.e. the structure of what *de facto* the subject-concept always intends" (*PGZ* 322). Other passages in which the positive sense of *subject* is referred to are *W* 34 and *GP* 90, 107, 147, 359, and 425. Of special interest in this connection is Heidegger's remark in *GP* 236 that he begins with the concept of the world in order to be able properly "to determine the ontological constitution of *Dasein*." "In so doing we go in a certain sense—roughly expressed—out from the object in order to get to the 'subject.' "

8. Heidegger observes that we are inclined to think of various characteristic features of the world such as something being far away or nearby as subjective because we use an objectified nature as our standard. He goes on to say, however, that this "subjectivity" is what is most objective with respect to *Dasein*, because "it belongs to the mode of being of *Dasein* itself and has nothing to do with 'subjective' arbitrariness (*Willkür*)" (*PGZ* 317–18). For Heidegger's view of the "objectivity" of the world, see *GP* 424–25.

9. Heidegger's treatment of this matter is found in *SZ* 52–59 and *PGZ* 210–15; see also *GP* 428.

10. For Heidegger's account of this feature of *Dasein*, see his discussion of *Jemeinigkeit* in *SZ* 42–43 and *PGZ* 204–07.

11. *SZ* 96–97; see also *L* 213–14.

12. Heidegger points out that this same tendency is at work in the kind of account given of intentionality. It is exemplified in Husserl's way of presenting intentionality as something "grasped" (*erfasst*) or "given" (*gegeben*), as though what is being so described were not identical with the very self that is giving the description, but were instead something from which the latter had managed to detach itself so as to be able *es in den Blick zu stellen*, rather like the hand in Descartes's example. It is almost as though it were being supposed that, through the right kind of objectification, intentionality itself could be envisaged as an object and then described, as objects typically are, in terms of its *Wesen* and its *Aussehen* even though, as Heidegger points out, such a procedure is in fact "alien" (*fremd*) to consciousness. See *PGZ* 146.

13. The word that Heidegger uses here to describe what happens in the case of my touching is *begegnen* ("to meet or encounter"). His use of this word is examined in chapter 3. The word *present* that I have used to render this notion corresponds to both *präsent* and *anwesend* in German. Only the latter is used in *SZ*, but in the lectures of the period *präsent* and *Praesenz* occur frequently. See, for example, *PGZ* 306, where *ist präsent* is equated with *begegnen*. On occasion Heidegger also uses the verb *apprä-sentieren* ("to make present"), and this verb takes "being-in-the-world" as its subject and "the world" as its object (*PGZ* 289). The fullest discussion of *Praesenz* is found in *GP* 431–45, where a distinction is made between "present" and "now," and where the

equivalence of *Praesenz* and *Anwesenheit* is also made clear (*GP* 436). The latter term remained in use throughout Heidegger's career, whereas the former largely drops out of use. Both terms are essentially equivalent to *Gegebenheit* ("givenness") as Heidegger uses this term.

14. *SZ* 55.

15. For Heidegger's reflections on the concept of relation and on the abuses to which it is subject, see *GP* 83–94 and 223–24. Other comments about relations can be found in *SZ* 77 and *L* 300. Of special interest is Heidegger's statement that "one of the principal preliminary tasks of *Being and Time* is to bring this 'relation' [that of subject and object] radically to light in its original essence" (*MAL* 164).

16. In one form or another the concept of the given (*das Gegebene*) was to maintain itself through all the periods of Heidegger's philosophical thought. For an early account of it and of its relationship to the concept of the world, see *L* 322–38.

17. *L* 323. Heidegger goes on to state that "I am that 'for' which something can be given"; to be this "for" is equated with "making possible the givability (*Gebbarkeit*) of a given for me" (*L* 330–31).

18. *SZ* 65 and 75; *PGZ* 266.

19. "Each entity that encounters is a Here and a There, even though in an indefinite and variable manner" (*L* 287). See also *SZ* 107, 119, and 132, and *PGZ* 308–12.

20. *SZ* 109–10.

21. *SZ* 369.

22. For Heidegger's introduction of this concept, see *SZ* 42 and 55–56. See *SZ* 318 for his equating of the concept of the *vorhanden* with that of substance. For the contrast between *Vorhandenheit* and both *Entdecktheit* (uncoveredness) and *Wahrgenommenheit* (perceivedness), see *GP* 68 and 95. These contrasts make it clear that *Vorhandenheit* is not to be confused with presence—either *Praesenz* or *Anwesenheit*—and this is the more important because Heidegger speaks of both "*ständige Vorhandenheit*" (*SZ* 96) and "*ständige Anwesenheit*" (*SZ* 423) in ways that might lead one to suppose that they are the same.

23. *SZ* 69ff.

24. *SZ* 75–76.

25. *SZ* 68–71.

26. For Heidegger's critique of the notion of property, see *L* 156–61 and *PGZ* 301.

27. For Heidegger's discussion of the pointing of the arrow, see *PGZ* 279–80 and *SZ* 78–79.

28. *PGZ* 272.

29. For Heidegger's treatment of possibility, see especially *SZ* 143ff. Also of value are the discussions in *GP* 389ff., *MAL* 55–58, 100–05, and *A* 161ff., in which the Aristotelian doctrine of potentiality is carefully analyzed.

30. Heidegger sometimes refers to such entities as *Weltdinge*, thereby conveying their embeddedness in the context of possibilities that is the world of *Dasein*.

31. *SZ* 71 and 149–50; *PGZ* 228; *GP* 107, 147, and 239.

32. It must be understood that a "subject-thing"—an expression applied by Heidegger to the subject as misconceived in terms of the category of substance—is not the same as what I occasionally refer to as a "subject-entity." The latter expression is a translation of *seiender Subjekt*, which Heidegger uses for *Dasein*; what it denotes is the subject not as substance but as a particular entity. For an example of Heidegger's use of this expression, see *SZ* 130.

33. *SZ* 73–74.

34. *SZ* 356–64.

35. *SZ* 68–69 and 86–88.

36. *SZ* 71; *PGZ* 261–62.
37. *PGZ* 339; *GP* 421.
38. In his earliest treatment of this theme Heidegger speaks of an *Eigenwelt*—a world of one's own—and implies a contrast between it and the *öffentliche Welt* (*PGZ* 261). But even here he insists on the essential character of the linkage between them; for a strong statement to this effect, see *PGZ* 339. It is interesting to note that the word for "public"—*öffentlich*— which took on a strongly negative connotation in *SZ* has no such connotation in these earlier uses.
39. The plural occurs only once in *SZ*, at p. 65 and in a context that makes clear that such a use, which has to do with "worlds" as subdomains of *the* world, is atypical. Where "world" is used with an indefinite article, this appears to be dictated by syntactical considerations and does not imply that pluralization is possible—e.g., *SZ* 109.
40. See, for example, *SZ* 118, where the complimentary character of such descriptions is emphasized; also *PGZ* 327.
41. *SZ* 123.
42. *SZ* 126–30. It is interesting to note that Heidegger's first account of *das Man* (*PGZ* 335–45) presents it in a much more neutral manner than the account in *SZ*, and it is identified with the "publicity" and "intersubjectivity" that are essential features of "the world." It is pointed out, however, that there is a need to determine "how the mutual understanding that always already obtains with *Dasein* can be distorted and misled in such a way that... understanding in the sense of understanding one another is always held down in a determinate average mode of being of *Dasein* itself" (*PGZ* 336).
43. For Heidegger's account of the relationship between the world and the entities within it, see *W* 52–55, where he states that the world is in a certain sense "subjective" because of its linkage to *Dasein* and that it is not "objective" if that means "belonging among existing objects" (54). See also *PGZ* 298, where it is stated that "the being of entities" does not consist in the "encountering" (*Begegnen*) with which the mode of being of the world is subsequently identified (300). The same point is made in many ways in *SZ*, beginning with the statement that "world" is ontologically not a determination of entities that are essentially other than *Dasein* but a character of *Dasein* itself (64). See also *MAL* 161 and *GP* 424 and 446.
44. Hardly any attention is given to error as such in *SZ* after the brief discussion in the introduction of the way things can "appear" other than they are (*SZ* 29–31). The lectures contain at least brief indications of the line Heidegger is disposed to take in the matter of error, however; see *GP* 84–85, 88–89, 295, and 448–49, and *L* 211. It is interesting to note that Heidegger appears to have been favorably impressed by the Aristotelian doctrine of perception as immune to error as long as it remains directed to its proper objects (*SZ* 33). There is no discussion in any of Heidegger's writings or lectures of the problem, so prominent in Anglo-American discussions of error and illusion, of how the "debris" of perception—e.g., after-images and the like—can be ontologically accommodated.
45. *SZ* 28–31.
46. *GP* 84–85; *L* 211.
47. *GP* 84.
48. *GP* 95.
49. *W* 55; *L* 250–51.
50. *L* 250–52.
51. *W* 52.
52. *SZ* 71; *PGZ* 270.
53. *W* 55; *L* 250–52.

54. *PGZ* 298–99; SZ 153 and 336.
55. *GP* 314–15.
56. *A* 202.
57. For a fuller discussion of this matter, see chap. 10.

3. EXISTENCE AND *DASEIN*

1. For a typical use of this expression, see *SZ* 130. That a *seiender Subjekt* is the equivalent of *Dasein* is made clear in *GP* 308.
2. For a good non-Heideggerian account of the way this concept of the body emerges, see John Cook, "Human Beings," in *Studies in the Philosophy of Wittgenstein*, P. Winch ed. (London: Routledge and Kegan Paul, 1969), pp. 117–51.
3. Heidegger does not characterize the relationship between the two concepts in these terms; sometimes he uses locutions like *das Dasein im Menschen* (*GM* 255) as a "material mode" way of expressing the nexus of the two concepts. Nevertheless, the alternative formulation I have chosen seems the one best suited to expressing the logical or conceptual character of that relationship as he conceives it. Heidegger occasionally touches on the logical aspect of the relationship, as, for example, in *SZ* 182, where he says that the "being" of *Dasein* cannot "be deduced from an idea of man." That the notion of extensional equivalence is appropriate here is shown conclusively by a passage in which, in a discussion of care as the essence of *Dasein*, Heidegger speaks of "the entity that we in each case are and that we *call* 'man,' " (*SZ* 196; my emphasis). This is made even more explicit in the lectures of this period, where it is stated that "we designate the entity that we also call 'man' as that which is itself its 'There' . . . (and) we thereby come to a rigorous formulation of the meaning of the term '*Dasein*' " (*PGZ* 349). There are many passages throughout Heidegger's writings and lectures of this period in which *Dasein* and *Mensch* are paired in a way that makes it clear that they denote the same entity; see, for example, *PGZ* 148 and *SZ* 198–99 and 212.
4. *SZ* 165.
5. A major attempt to bring the concept of *Dasein* as a particular openness into some definable relationship to our understanding of ourselves as bodies can be found in *GM* 274–396, and some aspects of this discussion will be taken up in chap. 10. In general, however, Heidegger leaves unexplored the whole topic of how the concept of the human body is to be understood within the context set by the concept of ourselves as *Dasein*. It may be that Maurice Merleau-Ponty's treatment of the concept of the body could significantly amplify Heidegger's thought in this area. See his *Phenomenologie de la perception* (Paris: Gallimard, 1945), part I, and *Le visible et l'invisible* (Paris: Gallimard, 1964), pp. 172–204.
6. *SZ* 42, 45, 122, and 143.
7. *SZ* 226.
8. An interesting example of a contemporary theory that equates perception with belief is George Pitcher, *A Theory of Perception* (Princeton:Princeton University Press, 1971), chap. 5. For a characteristically negative comment by Heidegger on the role of belief (*Glauben*), see *PGZ* 295.
9. "Not every knowing (*Erkennen*) is an intuiting (*Anschauen*) but intuiting is authentic knowing at which every other (kind of knowing) aims and has as an idea in the sense of an ideal" (*L* 113). See also *PGZ* 94.
10. J. Joyce, *Ulysses* (New York: Random House, 1934), p. 38. An informal survey of scientific works on the physiology of vision has turned up no descriptions of this seeing that everyone is familiar with; apparently, it has the kind of status that St. Augustine attributed to time.

11. This asymmetry is absent, of course, when I see a human being or an animal that also sees me; but this reciprocating vision is by no means a necessary condition of my seeing them.

12. "Uncoveredness (*Entdecktheit*) is not a property of what exists (the *vorhanden*); instead the latter encounters within the world of a *Dasein*, a world that is opened for the existing *Dasein*" (*GP* 312).

13. For an account of these ancient theories, see R. B. Onians, *The Origins of European Thought* (New York: Cambridge University Press, 1951), esp. pp. 76–78.

14. For Heidegger's use of the notion of light, see *SZ* 28, 133, and 350–51; see also *PGZ* 411–12.

15. Other verbs that Heidegger uses for this purpose are *frei-geben*, "to release," and *lichten*, "to clear or light up."

16. The distinction between the ontological and the ontic is never sharply formulated by Heidegger. It is coordinate with the distinction between being (*Sein*) and entities (*Seiendes*); but if questions about entities are normally to be regarded as ontic, any concern with the mode of being of entities is ontological. The distinction is further complicated by the fact that we are said by Heidegger to have a pre-ontological understanding of being. It thus appears that when the entity in question is *Dasein*, the distinction between the ontic and the ontological is primarily one between the levels at which that entity and its characteristic functions like understanding (*Verstehen*) can be approached. This understanding is spoken of by Heidegger as either *existentiell* or *existenzial*, depending on whether it has an ontic or an ontological character; but it seems that "in every *existenziell* understanding an ontological understanding (*Seinsverständnis*) of existence as such is included" (*GP* 395). For Heidegger's discussion of this distinction, see *SZ* 12–16, 43–44, 63–64, 181–82, and 199–200; also *GP* 395–96, 398–99, and 406.

17. For a discussion of the locutions that come to replace the verbs of action that take *Dasein* as their subject, see chap. 8.

18. These locutions occur at *SZ* 222 and *A* 206 respectively. Another striking example of this kind of language is the *Einbruch in den Raum* (breaking into space) of *Dasein* (*SZ* 369).

19. The actual occurrence of this Greek word in Heidegger's writing falls into the later period (*P* 215), but its identification with [*das*] *Durchsichtige des Lichtes* and with the closely affiliated notion of *die Lichtung* makes it clear that it could equally well have been used in the period of *SZ*. In this connection it is interesting to note that in his lectures on Hegel, Heidegger appears to endorse the latter's way of treating sensibility (*Sinnlichkeit*) "without the slightest mention of the senses or even of the organs of sense" (*HPG* 76). And Heidegger himself goes so far as to claim in connection with hearing that "it is pure accident that such things as ear-lobes and ear-drums exist at all" (*PGZ* 368).

20. I take this definition from *Funk and Wagnall's Standard College Dictionary* (New York: Funk and Wagnall, 1973), p. 1423.

21. In the English translation of *SZ*, *begegnen-lassen* is rendered as "to be encountered," but this passive construction obscures the complexity of the relationship between the two active verbs in the German expression.

22. *SZ* 147.

23. *N* 2. 219.

24. *A* 202.

25. *SZ* 133.

26. *PGZ* 169. For a discussion of Leibniz's variant of this conception of the soul, see *GP* 427–28.

27. *N* 2. 449.
28. See chap. 1, n. 7.
29. The German word that Heidegger uses for "entities" is *Seiendes*, which is a mass noun and thus adds obscurity to the whole issue of plurality and particularity that arises in connection with the concept of *Dasein*. It can be used with the indefinite article (*ein Seiendes*, *SZ* 6), however, and is then properly translated as "an entity." It is extremely important to understand that *Dasein* is "an entity" (*SZ* 7, *W* 63), since this has an immediate bearing on its being a particular.
30. Heidegger's most extended discussion of this concept of existence and its contrast with essence is in *GP*, chap. 2, esp. pp. 140ff. The specifically Heideggerian concept is introduced in *SZ* 12ff., 42ff., and 231ff.
31. *P* 208. This view of Greek thought appears to be explicitly stated only in the writings of the later period, but it is certainly implicit in discussions of Greek ontology like that in *GP*, chap. 2. For a fuller treatment of these matters, see chap. 9 of this book.
32. *GP* 155.
33. *W* 64.
34. The verb "to exist" takes as its subject, however, not only *Dasein* and "the world" (GP 422), but also "truth" (*GP* 313 and 317) and "being" (*GP* 318). In each case the association with "existence" connotes the linkage of the subject term to *Dasein* and the fact that, if *Dasein* did not exist, neither would the world (*GP* 420), truth (*SZ* 227–28, *GP* 317), or being (*SZ* 212, *GP* 25). For a fuller discussion of these matters, see chaps. 6 and 10.
35. *SZ* 120. There are a number of passages in the lectures in which Heidegger uses the indefinite article with *Dasein*. We thus get statements like *Wir sind jeweils ein Dasein* (*GP* 36) and *ein Dasein teilt sich aussprechend dem anderen mit* (GP 299), which are intelligible only on the assumption that *ein Dasein* denotes a particular entity which is one of many having the character of *Dasein*. Even more unmistakable constructions of this kind are *zu einem bestimmten, jeweiligen Dasein* (PGZ 373), and *das Ganze der Zeit eines Daseins* (GM 427–28); see also *MAL* 217. On occasion Heidegger even uses the indefinite article with *In-der-Welt-sein*, as at *MAL* 213.
36. Examples of the use of each of these phrases can be found in *SZ* 127, *MAL* 217, and *SZ* 124.
37. *SZ* 134 and 142.
38. *SZ* 133.
39. *SZ* 211–12. "It does not belong to the nature of *Dasein* as such that it as a matter of fact exists, but it is precisely its nature that it can in each case be nonexistent. The cosmos can be without human beings inhabiting an earth and presumably the cosmos was long before human beings existed" (*MAL* 216). See also *GP* 317.
40. *GP* 26.
41. *W* 55.
42. Heidegger's discussions of *Selbstheit* can be found in *SZ* 316ff. and *MAL* 238ff; see also *GP* 425–29.
43. *SZ* 84 and 194; *MAL* 246ff.
44. *MAL* 240–44.
45. *MAL* 244–45.
46. *MAL* 244.
47. *MAL* 231.
48. *MAL* 238; see also *MAL* 246.
49. *MAL* 238.
50. See chap. 2, n. 29.
51. There is an essential connection between possibility and *Entwerfen* as the self-projection

or transcendence of *Dasein* as agent. It is therefore proper to say, as Heidegger does, that "projection . . . throws possibility as possibility ahead of itself and lets it *be*" (*SZ* 145).

52. *SZ* 143–44.

53. Heidegger's most substantial discussions of transcendence are in *MAL* 203–80, *W* 48–71, and *SZ* 363–66.

54. *MAL* 204ff.

55. *SZ* 132; *GP* 310–11; *PGZ* 346–47.

56. *MAL* 211–13. It may be noted that Heidegger makes a distinction here between *Dasein* as this *Überschritt*, or transcendence, and *Dasein* as *faktisches*—that is, comprised, by virtue of its corporeality (*Leiblichkeit*), within nature, remaining *umschlungen* ("embraced," or "wound round") by nature even when transcendent and "free" *Dasein* is out beyond it. How this contrast comports with Heidegger's usual emphasis on the irremediable finitude of *Dasein* is not entirely clear.

57. *MAL* 212.

58. Heidegger's principal discussions of animals and their capacity for having a world, especially in the modality of perception, are found in *GM* 261–396. See also *GP* 270–71 and *P* 158–59.

59. Animals are, as Heidegger puts, it *weltarm* ("world-poor") rather than wholly *weltlos* ("worldless") as inanimate things are. For his exposition of this concept, see *GM* 289–377.

60. *MAL* 252. In this passage the world is said to be "a Nothing, not an entity—and yet something; not an entity—but being." This is reminiscent of Wittgenstein's famous statement in *Logical Investigations* (Oxford:Blackwell, 1953) that pain is "not something but not a nothing either" (p. 102). See also *MAL* 164 for another formulation of this type.

61. The concept of choice is explicitly invoked in connection with the account of transcendence in *MAL* 245–48. The freedom that characterizes transcendence and projection (*Entwerfen*) is said to be such that it "places *Dasein* in all the dimensions of its transcendence in a possible space (*Spielraum*) of choice" (248).

62. *SZ* 143–44.

63. Most of these choices are, of course, obscured in their character as choices by the "They" (*das Man*) in which each *Dasein* is deeply implicated. *Dasein* is thereby "relieved of the explicit *choice* of . . . possibilities," so that "it remains indeterminate who is 'really' (*eigentlich*) choosing" (*SZ* 268). It is clear, however, that insofar as choices are made, they are made by a particular *Dasein* that has "fetched itself back" from *das Man* and explicitly chosen "out of its own Self" what it has previously been "carried along with."

64. The term *welt-bildend* occurs as a characterization of *Dasein* in *W* 55, and its meaning is analyzed in considerable detail in *GM* 507–32.

65. *SZ* 124. Further discussion of *Mitsein* can be found in *PGZ* 326–35 and *GP* 393–95 and 421–23.

66. *SZ* 125.

67. *SZ* 125.

68. *SZ* 123.

69. *SZ* 123.

70. *SZ* 120.

71. Heidegger's discussion of death is in *SZ* 235ff. The connection between the concept of death as *Dasein*'s "ownmost possibility" and a negative attitude toward *Mitsein* is made plain in *SZ* 263.

72. One exception is the discussion of the Greek *polis* in *P* 132–34; but this can hardly be said to throw any new light on the concept of *Mitsein*. What is needed is an expansion

NOTES TO PAGES 72–84 • 271

of the statement in *GP* 421, where *Mitsein* is said to have to do with "the various factual possibilities of the intersubjective confirmation of what has been uncovered and of the intersubjective unanimity of world-understanding."

73. *PGZ* 276.

74. *MAL* 231.

75. *MAL* 252: "The world: a Nothing, a non-Entity—and yet something; not an entity—but being."

76. *W* 52.

77. *SZ* 36. Heidegger points out that the fact "that such and such an entity is uncovered in the There of its own existence is not decided by *Dasein*. Only *what*, in *what* direction, *how* far, and *how* it opens and uncovers is in each case the affair of its freedom although always within the limits of its thrownness" (*SZ* 366).

78. *SZ* 36.

4. TIME AND TEMPORALITY

1. The most important amplification in the lectures of Heidegger's account of time can be found in *GP*, part 2, and *L* 197–415. There is, by contrast, relatively little about time in *PGZ*, although these lectures are nominally about time.

2. See *SZ* 231ff.

3. *SZ* 192ff.

4. The discussion of death is in *SZ* 235ff.

5. *GP* 362ff.; *SZ* 370–72.

6. There is an extensive discussion in *L* 269ff. of Kant's struggle with the traditional view that the " 'I think' and all spontaneity lie outside time" (*L* 344)—a view that Kant only partially overcame.

7. *MAL* 54–62. The specifically temporal character of possibility remains implicit in this discussion.

8. Heidegger usually refers to this conception of world-time as "the vulgar understanding of time" (*SZ* 408), but his own use of the term "world-time" is almost always positive, since it reflects his own conception of the world in terms of presence. Another way of making this distinction would be to say that "the world" is being used here in an ontic sense and in the kind of abstraction from its ontological sense that is definitive for the whole "vulgar" treatment of *Dasein* as well as time. On this point see *SZ* 64–65, 420ff., and *GP* 383. For the connection between the concepts of the world and time, see *GP* 360.

9. *SZ* 419–20; *GP* 359–61.

10. *GP* 327–69; *SZ* 421ff.

11. *SZ* 423; *GP* 350.

12. *GP* 351–53.

13. *SZ* 417; *GP* 385.

14. B. Russell, *The Analysis of Mind* (London: Allen and Unwin, 1921), pp. 159–60.

15. "What is earlier, at the same time and later does not simply coincide with past, present, and future for what is past can itself (and as past) be earlier or later or at the same time and so can what is future" (*L* 238).

16. "Thus the Nows are in a certain manner *co-present-at-hand* (*mitvorhanden*); that is, entities are encountered and so too is the 'Now.' " Although it is not said explicitly that "Nows" are present-at-hand in the same way as things, they still get "seen" ontologically within the idea of presence at hand (*SZ* 423).

17. *SZ* 423–24; *GP* 372–74.

18. He does on occasion, however, use idioms of perception that might mislead one into supposing that he espouses some such view. He says, for example, that "understanding

must itself *somehow see that upon which it projects as what is uncovered (Enthülltes)" (GP* 402).

19. *GP* 370–71.
20. *GP* 370 and 381; *SZ* 412–14.
21. *GP* 431–45.
22. For Heidegger's very brief comments on Bergson's theory of time, see *SZ* 18, 26, 47, and 432n. and *GP* 328–29.
23. Heidegger's discussion of historicity (*Geschichtlichkeit*) is in *SZ* 372ff. I have given an interpretative account of this concept in my book *The Dialectic of Action: A Philosophical Interpretation of History and the Humanities* (Chicago: University of Chicago Press, 1979), chap. 3.
24. For typical uses of this expression, see *SZ* 365, 397, and 425.
25. The nonconceptual nature of time (and space) is explicitly stated by Heidegger in *L* 277 in the course of a discussion of Kant's views on the subject.
26. The concept of the *Augenblick* is introduced in *SZ* 338 and *GP* 407–12.
27. For a careful study of the contrasts between the roles of agent and spectator, although without reference to Heidegger, see L. W. Beck, *The Actor and the Spectator* (New Haven: Yale University Press, 1975).
28. "In resoluteness *Dasein* understands itself out of its ownmost potentiality-for-being (*Seinkönnen*). (This) understanding is primarily futural insofar as it comes back to itself out of the possibility of itself it has grasped ... In this coming back to itself out of its ownmost possibility, *Dasein* comes back to that which it is and takes itself over as the entity that it is. In coming back to itself it fetches itself with all that it is back to its ownmost potentiality for being which it has grasped" (*GP* 407). The choice-character that attaches to *Dasein*'s way of having a future is often conveyed by Heidegger's use of the phrase *zu sein haben* ("having to be"), as at *SZ* 12 and 134. Unfortunately the English translation carries just the opposite connotation, suggesting not possibility and thus choice, but rather "having to" in the sense of being compelled.
29. For a discussion of the "theoretical" attitude, see *SZ* 357ff.
30. Heidegger makes it clear in *SZ* 363–64 that objectification is possible only by virtue of the transcendence of *Dasein*. This transcendence is not canceled, therefore, by the objectification that it makes possible; and this would be true in the case of self-objectification as well. On this point, it should be noted that "*Dasein* can never in existing ascertain (*feststellen*) itself as a *vorhanden* fact ... it always 'finds itself' only as a *thrown* fact" (*SZ* 328). On this point, see *SZ* 276, where the *Faktizität* of *Dasein* is distinguished from the *Tatsächlichkeit* of the *vorhanden*; and it is stated that "existing *Dasein* does not encounter itself as something *vorhanden* within the world."
31. The entire second part of *L* is devoted to the discussion of time. For the treatment of spontaneity and receptivity, see *L* 338ff.
32. For Heidegger's discussion of Kant's doctrine of schematism, see *SZ* 23 and 365 and *KPM*, chap. 3. See also *L* 357ff.
33. *L* 400ff.
34. These phrases occur in *L* 341 and 345 and in *KPM* 71.
35. *L* 345.
36. *L* 339.
37. *L* 339.
38. *L* 406.
39. *L* 410.
40. *SZ* 421.
41. *L* 410.
42. *GP* 374; *L* 349.

43. *GP* 429–52; *L* 409–15.
44. *GP* 451; see also *VWF* 115.
45. *GP* 448.
46. *GP* 443.
47. *GP* 452–54 and 460.
48. "The resoluteness in which *Dasein* comes back to itself discloses current factical possibilities of authentic existing and discloses them *in terms of the heritage* which that resoluteness as thrown takes over" (*SZ* 383). See also *SZ* 326 and *GP* 375–76.
49. *GP* 382. For a discussion of the *Öffentlichkeit* of time, see also *GP* 373.
50. *SZ* 410–11.
51. *GP* 347.
52. *GP* 408; *VWF* 129–30.
53. *GP* 408.
54. *GP* 408.
55. "But if fateful *Dasein*, as Being-in-the-world, exists essentially in Being-with-others, its historizing (*Geschehen*) is a co-historizing and is determinative for it as *destiny*... Destiny is not something that puts itself together out of individual fates any more than Being-with-one-another can be conceived as the occurring together of several subjects" (*SZ* 384). For a similarly anti-individualistic statement, see *GP* 419–20.
56. For an account of *Dasein* as necessarily and properly understanding itself out of its world, see *GP* 419.
57. *GP* 410.
58. *SZ* 195.
59. Being "in time" is in fact equated with being *zeitlos* in this sense (*SZ* 382). The word *unzeitlich* is also used for such entities, as at *SZ* 420.
60. *GP* 370.
61. "If, therefore, we demonstrate that the 'time' which is accessible to *Dasein*'s common sense is *not* primordial, but arises rather from authentic temporality, then, in accordance with the principle, '*a potiori fit denominatio*,' we are justified in designating as '*primordial time*' the temporality which we have now laid bare" (*SZ* 329). An extensive discussion of the relationship between time and temporality can be found in *GP* 362–88.
62. The statement that "the subject does not first create time" occurs in *L* 339. The context is a discussion of Kant's conception of time as a condition of any possible objectivity and of the "self-affection" this entails. On this point, see the discussion earlier in this chapter.
63. The tensions that seem to underlie Heidegger's whole thought on this subject come out clearly in a passage in *EM* 64: "There was, after all, a time when man was not. But strictly speaking we cannot say: there was a time when man *was* not. Man was and is and will be at every *time* because time only temporalizes itself insofar as man is. There is no time when man was not, not because man has been from eternity and will be eternally, but because time is not eternity and time temporalizes itself at a particular time as human-historical *Dasein*." How Heidegger proposes to resolve the conflict between what he must say in order not to deny the reality of a pre-human past and what—"strictly speaking"—his conception of time permits him to say is not indicated. It seems clear, however, that he must find a way of saying both the one and the other; and that is what the emendation of his view that I am proposing would accomplish.
64. In this connection, see the discussion of entities as lying outside the world as a milieu of presence in chap. 8.
65. There is a notable contrast here between Heidegger and Sartre, whose ontology is

explicitly designed to make room for an *en-soi* defined so as to involve no reference to the *pour-soi* or to the world that the latter constitutes. For Sartre, the problem of being in general becomes a problem of somehow bringing the concepts of the *en-soi* and the *pour-soi* together under being as such as a *summum genus*; and this proves to be impossible. See Sartre's *Being and Nothingness*, trans. H. Barnes (New York: Philosophical Library, 1956), pp. lxiv–lxix and 617–25. This whole way of conceiving the character of being as such is utterly different from Heidegger's, as we will see in chap. 8.

5. FEELING, UNDERSTANDING, AND DISCOURSE

1. *SZ* 44–45.
2. For Heidegger's account of *Sorge*, see *SZ* 191–200; an earlier version is presented in *PGZ* 406–20.
3. *SZ* 139.
4. Husserl, *Ideen*, vol. 1, pp. 290–91.
5. There is also a detailed analysis of boredom (*Langeweile*) as a *Stimmung* in *GM*, part 1.
6. That one can "fear for" someone else, for example, without being afraid oneself is made clear in *SZ* 141–42.
7. *SZ* 134. The German phrase is *wie einem ist und wird*.
8. *SZ* 137.
9. "*Befindlichkeit* is a basic existential type (*Grundart*) of the equiprimordial disclosure (*Erschlossenheit*) of world, *Mitdasein*, and existence" (*SZ* 137).
10. Discussions of moods (*Stimmungen*) can be found in *SZ* 134–39 and 339–46 and *GM* 89–103.
11. *SZ* 186.
12. *SZ* 187.
13. *SZ* 188.
14. *SZ* 188.
15. *GM* 102.
16. *SZ* 190.
17. *SZ* 190.
18. "*Befindlichkeit* always has its understanding, even if it merely keeps it suppressed. Understanding always has its mood" (*SZ* 142).
19. "Understanding as self-projection is the basic species of the historizing (*Geschehen*) of *Dasein*. It is, as we can also say, the authentic meaning of action ... Understanding is not a kind of knowledge, but the fundamental determination of existing" (*GP* 393). See also *SZ* 144 and *PGZ* 286.
20. Heidegger's comments on Dilthey can be found in *SZ* 209–10 and 297–99 and in *PGZ* 161–64. For his critique of Dilthey's theory of understanding as empathy (*Einfühlung*), see *SZ* 123–25.
21. "(Other people) are encountered from out of the world in which concernfully circumspective *Dasein* essentially dwells" (*SZ* 119). See also *PGZ* 326–35 and *GP* 421–22.
22. For Heidegger's reflections on these capacities of the body, see *GM* 319–44.
23. For a contrasting view that has some affinities with Heidegger's position, see M. Polanyi, *Personal Knowledge* (New York:Harper and Row, 1964), pp. 78ff.
24. The concept of *Seinkönnen* is introduced in *SZ* 144–46 and is used extensively throughout the book.
25. All these facts about "things" belong to what Heidegger calls the *Bewandtnisstruktur* (the structure of involvements) in which they are embedded; and the "totality of

involvements" derives ultimately from the being of *Dasein* as *Seinkönnen* and as the
entity that "lets entities encounter as *zuhanden*" (*SZ* 84, 86).

26. See G. H. von Wright, *Explanation and Understanding* (Ithaca:Cornell University Press,
1971), pp. 71ff.

27. *SZ* 227.

28. Dewey repeatedly makes the point that traditional epistemology has been blind to the
element of active intervention that "knowledge" involves and has typically attempted
to interpret what emerges from such intervention as a prior structure of the object
of knowledge to which we as knowers stand in a passive or contemplative relationship.
See his book *The Quest for Certainty* (New York: Minton Balch, 1929), chap. 1.

29. For Heidegger's account of interpretation, see *SZ* 148–53.

30. *SZ* 149–51.

31. *SZ* 149–50.

32. *SZ* 145–46. See also the very full discussion of *Verstehen* as *Entwurf* in *GP* 389–418.

33. *SZ* 150.

34. *SZ* 100.

35. *SZ* 129 and 195.

36. *SZ* 356–64.

37. This view of science is stated more fully in Heidegger's essay "*Die Zeit des Weltbildes*,"
in *H* 69–104.

38. "All explanation, if we are speaking of explanations of natural phenomena, is distinguished by the fact that it maintains itself in the domain of what is not intelligible (*im
Unverständlichen*). One can in fact say: explanation is the interpretation of the unintelligible, but not in such a way that the unintelligible is understood through this
interpretation. It remains fundamentally unintelligible. Nature is that which is in
principle explainable and to-be-explained because it is in principle unintelligible" (*PGZ*
298). See also *SZ* 153 and 336.

39. The impossibility of such a purely spectatorial attitude is shown in *SZ* 357–58.

40. *SZ* 152–53 and 314–16.

41. *SZ* 152.

42. *SZ* 152.

43. The principal discussions of language in the period of *Being and Time* are in *SZ* 153–
70; *GP*, part 1, chap. 4; and *L* 127–61.

44. "In the last resort, philosophical research must resolve to ask what kind of being goes
with language. Is it a kind of equipment (*Zeug*) ready-to-hand within-the-world, or
has it *Dasein's* kind of being, or is it neither of these?" (*SZ* 166).

45. Throughout his career, Heidegger was strongly opposed to any conception of philosophy dominated by logic, such as that of the so-called Marburg school. For his
comments on the role of logic in philosophy, see *SZ* 155–60 and 165 and *GP* 252ff.

46. Heidegger's characteristic way of conceiving what is now called the semantic dimension
of language is clearly indicated by what he says in *SZ* 154: "The primary signification
of 'assertion' is 'pointing-out' (*Aufzeigung*). In this we adhere to the primordial meaning
of *logos* as *apophansis*—letting an entity be seen from itself." That the semantic and
referential dimension of language is possible only by virtue of the transcendence of
Dasein is explained in an interpretation of Aristotle's conception of the *logos semantikos*
in *GM* 442ff.

47. For a discussion of some of the issues that arise in connection with this concept, see
R. Rorty, "Realism and Reference," *The Monist* 59 (1976):321–40.

48. *SZ* 158.

49. Heidegger states that his "interpretation of language" in *SZ* was intended simply "to

indicate the ontological 'locus' for this phenomenon within *Dasein*'s state of being (*Seinsverfassung*)" (*SZ* 166). That locus—"the existential-ontological basis of language"—is explicitly identified as "discourse" (*Rede*) in *SZ* 160.

50. These distinctions are set forth in *SZ* 161–62 and in *GP* 297–99.
51. "The pointing-out that assertion does is performed on the basis of what has already been disclosed in understanding or discovered circumspectively" (*SZ* 156). "Assertion is not in a primary sense uncovering (*enthüllend*); instead it presupposes the uncoveredness of an entity" (*GP* 303).
52. *SZ* 154.
53. *L* 135–42; *GM* 456–60; *SZ* 159–60.
54. *GP* 300–04; *SZ* 159–60.
55. *GP* 300.
56. *GP* 300.
57. Heidegger's discussion of truth is in *SZ* 212–30. For the linkage between truth and discourse, see *SZ* 154.
58. "The upshot of our existential-ontological discussion of the phenomenon of truth is (1) that truth, in the most primordial sense, is *Dasein's* openness to which the uncoveredness of entities within-the-world belongs" (*SZ* 223).
59. *GP* 311.
60. *GP* 306; *GM* 496.
61. *GP* 308.
62. *GP* 314–15.
63. *GP* 314.
64. *GP* 317–18 and 310–11.
65. *GP* 318.
66. *SZ* 161.
67. *SZ* 224.
68. *SZ* 168–70.
69. *GP* 299.
70. *SZ* 163–64.
71. *SZ* 168.
72. *SZ* 169.
73. *GP* 244.

6. THE CONCEPT OF BEING

1. *SZ* 39.
2. *SZ* 327–61.
3. *SZ* 1.
4. *SZ* 6.
5. *SZ* 6–7.
6. *SZ* 3 and 38. A full discussion of the treatment of being as a property or attribute can be found in Heidegger's 1962 essay "*Kant's These über das Sein*," in *W* 271–307.
7. *SZ* 7.
8. *SZ* 8–11.
9. *SZ* 45.
10. This expectation may be influenced by the fact that this *is* the question that Sartre's *Being and Nothingness* attempts to answer. See chap. 4, n. 65.
11. The most extensive discussion of the unity of being in the period of *SZ* is in *A* 11–48, in the context of a discussion of Aristotle's views of the subject. It is important to note that Heidegger explicitly equates *to on*, which he refers to as *das Seiende*, with *to*

einai, which is rendered *das Sein*, and that both are contrasted emphatically with "this or that entity, the many entities—things, plants, animals, human beings, human works, gods—all entities together, the complete counted sum of particular entities" (*A* 20). Parmenides is also cited approvingly as the first to proclaim *to on* to be *to hen*—*das Eine* (*A* 7, 23). Another, briefer discussion of the unity of being can be found in *MAL* 192–93.

12. *SZ* 152. There are also important amplifications of this statement in *MAL* 186 and 195, where Heidegger says that "being gives itself *'in itself'* in an original sense; it is *proteron physei* and *pros hemas*, but, properly understood, it is not an entity (*ein Ontisches*) among others. Being is the unique and genuine 'In-itself.' " To this he adds that "because being is never something that accompanies entities as a property they have (*etwas am Seienden Mit-seiendes*), the question as to what being is as a property of that which is in itself has no meaning and no justification . . . There is being originally and in itself if it makes its entity (*sein Seiendes*) accessible. And with respect to this entity one cannot still in principle (*an sich*) inquire about its being in-itself" (195). For a statement to the same general effect from Heidegger's later period, see *W* 239.

13. *SZ* 183; *GP* 25.

14. *SZ* 183. See also *MAL* 179, where Heidegger characterizes the great achievement of Parmenides as the discovery that "being is related to the subject" (*subjektsbezogen*), and *MAL* 199, where it is stated that "the effecting of the distinction between being and entities lies in the understanding of being" by the entity "man." "There is being only if *Dasein* understands being."

15. *SZ* 212.

16. *SZ* 226.

17. See, for example, *MAL* 217, where Heidegger states that "the proposition: *Dasein* is, in its fundamental constitution, being-in-the-world, is not an ascertaining (*Konstatierung*) of its factual existence." A similar contrast is made in *MAL* 199, where "the factual existence of *Dasein*" is said to be a presupposition of the possibility of there being being in understanding, and an explicit parallel is made between this "factual existence" of *Dasein* and the factual existence (*Vorhandensein*) of nature, which the existence of *Dasein* presupposes. See also *MAL* 213.

18. *SZ* 230.

19. *A* 12ff. See also *L* 162ff.

20. Heidegger himself emphasizes the notion of touch as a way of expressing the nature of uncovering as *das durchhaltende Anwesendhaben des Worüber*; and he uses the Greek word for "to touch"—*thigein*—which he borrows from Aristotle. See *L* 181, 189.

21. *L* 191.

22. *L* 272–415.

23. *SZ* 233ff.

24. *L* 410.

25. *L* 414.

26. *L* 340.

27. *L* 339.

28. *L* 400.

29. That both being and truth are dependent on the existence of *Dasein* is made clear in *GP* 25 and 317–18. The finiteness of *Dasein* is asserted in *SZ* 384–85 and 424, and the finiteness of its temporality in *SZ* 330–31 and *GP* 386–87. The finiteness of being itself is acknowledged in *W* 17, where Heidegger states that "being itself is in its essence (*im Wesen*) finite (*endlich*) and reveals itself only in the transcendence of the *Dasein* that is held out into nothingness (*das Nichts*)." The finiteness of truth also emerges very

clearly from the discussion in *SZ* 226–28, where Heidegger says that "it will have been adequately proved that there are 'eternal truths' when it has been successfully established that *Dasein* has been and will be through all eternity." He calls this a fantastic assertion and declares that "all truth, in accordance with its essential mode of being which is of the type of *Dasein*, is relative to the being of *Dasein*."

30. See *SZ* 120.

31. See, for example, *SZ* 384–86, where the ideas of a communal destiny (*Geschick*) and tradition (*Überlieferung*) are discussed.

32. Backing for this claim, should it be thought to be necessary, is found in *GP* 392–94. Understanding as "self-projection" (*Sichentwerfen*) is there described as the fundamental mode of the "happening" (*Geschehen*) of *Dasein* and as "the authentic meaning of action." The project is further characterized as the way in which "I *am* my possibility, i.e. the way in which I exist freely." In the same context, the same "existing *Dasein*" that acts in this way is further described as projecting, in this understanding, " a *definite possible* being with others," so there cannot be any doubt that in its action it acts as an individual *Dasein*. For other comments by Heidegger on the relationship between the ontic and the ontological, see *GP* 406–07, 414–15, 419–20, esp. 454, and *KPM* 115.

33. The solitary character of resoluteness and of our relationship to our own death emerges clearly in *SZ* 297–301 and *SZ* 263, respectively.

34. For an interpretation of the difference between Heidegger's original intentions and the way the *Kehre* was actually carried out, see W. C. F. Gethmann, *Verstehen und Auslegung. Das Methodenproblem in der Philosophie Martin Heideggers* (Bonn:Bouvier Verlag, 1974), pp. 275ff.

7. THE TURNING

1. W. J. Richardson, *Heidegger: Through Phenomenology To Thought* (The Hague: Nijhoff, 1963), p. xxiii.

2. *W* 159.

3. *N* 2. 194.

4. The distinction between being and entities is clearly recognized in *SZ* 38, 94–95, 207, and 230. See also *GP* 454, where the distinction (*Unterschied*) between being and entities is explicitly declared to have "the mode of being (*Seinsart*) of *Dasein*" and to be generated in the temporalization of *Dasein*. On this last point, see also *W* 31.

5. The contrast between the understanding of *ousia* as presence (*Anwesenheit*) and as substance is clearly set forth in *SZ* 24–25 and 89–90. See also *GP* 153, *VWF* 50, and *MAL* 182–83 for further characterizations of the concept of *ousia*. For later criticism of the confusion of *ousia* with *substantia*, see *N* 2. 429–31.

6. Not only does *SZ* not interpret subjectivism this way; it associates action and choice positively with the rightly understood "subjectivity of the subject." This is especially evident in the treatment of *Gewärtigen* (expecting) as the inauthentic modality of the future of *Dasein*. This *Gewärtigen* is a kind of waiting for the future that *Dasein* authentically generates in the *Vorlaufen* ("running-forward") of its project. On this point see *SZ* 337 and 339 and *GP* 405–12.

7. The most emphatic expression of this activism remains the inaugural address, *Die Selbstbehauptung der deutschen Universität* (Frankfurt am Main:Klostermann, 1983), that Heidegger gave in 1934 as rector of the University of Freiburg. The 1983 edition also contains Heidegger's account of his period as rector under the Nazis. Heidegger's public statements from this period have been collected in *Nachlese zu Heidegger. Dokumente zu seinem Leben und Denken*, ed. G. Schneeberger (Bern:Helbing und Lichtenhahn, 1962).

8. *Die Selbstbehauptung*, p. 11. In this connection, it is worth noting that in *PGZ* 109

Heidegger explicitly identifies "philosophical inquiry" with "atheism" and associates himself on this point with Nietzsche. For another expression of similar sentiments at a somewhat later date, see *GM* 28–29.

9. This judgment is confirmed by Hannah Arendt in her *The Life of the Mind II: Willing* (New York:Harcourt, Brace, Jovanovich, 1978), pp. 172ff. It is interesting that Heidegger let stand through all subsequent editions a passage in *EM* 152 in which he refers to what apparently constituted in his eyes the "inner truth and greatness" of the National Socialist movement—that is, the encounter between a technology defined in planetary terms and modern man.

10. For a discussion of these texts, see chap. 8.

11. Thus, when the question "Why is there something (*Seiendes*) rather than nothing?" is asked at the beginning of *EM*, and Heidegger sets about answering it, he simply assumes, as a matter that does not require supporting argument, that what notions like *physis* and "being" signify is the emergence from hiddenness by virtue of which entities first become observable; and this, of course, is the notion of being that was developed in the period of *SZ*. See *EM* 11–12.

8. BEING AS PRESENCE IN THE LATER WRITINGS

1. *W* 91.
2. The expression *das Seiende im Ganzen* is used repeatedly in the essay on truth, from *W* 85 onward.
3. *W* 91.
4. *EM* 15.
5. *EM* 22 and 124.
6. *EM* 135.
7. *EM* 136 and 124.
8. The evolution of the relationship between "man" (*Mensch*) and "being" (*das Sein*) is discussed in *EM* 133–34.
9. See, for example, the discussion of representation in *EM* 90ff., which includes comments on man understood as a subject (104–07). A more extensive treatment of the same themes can be found in *N* 2. 141–68, in the context of a critique of Descartes. In this connection it is interesting to note that when Heidegger, in *EM* 22, denies that the "mineness" that had been declared in *SZ* to characterize *Dasein* means that *Dasein* is an "isolated (*vereinzeltes*) 'I'," he is not denying the plurality or the particularity of *Dasein*. The point is rather that *Dasein* is not separated from being and "is itself out of its essential reference to being as such." In other words, it is not a "worldless subject"; and this, of course, is just what Heidegger had denied in *SZ* as well.
10. *EM* 25.
11. *EM* 139–40.
12. *EM* 87.
13. *EM* 124–25.
14. *EM* 106.
15. *EM* 126–28.
16. *EM* 124.
17. *EM* 132.
18. *EM* 133.
19. *EM* 135.
20. *EM* 145.
21. *EM* 11. In spite of his identification of being with openness and presence, Heidegger continues to speak in a way that seems hardly compatible with this identification.

Thus he says that the essence of man has to be understood as "the place that being presses into service (*ernötigt*) for purposes of opening (*zur Eröffnung*)" (*EM* 156). If being itself is identified with openness, it does not seem that it should need any auxiliary in order to achieve it. In this same context *Dasein* is referred to as "the There that is in itself open"; its identification with openness thus appears to be closer than that of being.

22. *N* 2. 377 and 242.
23. *N* 2. 352–53.
24. *N* 2. 353ff.
25. *N* 2. 367.
26. *N* 2. 357.
27. *N* 2. 357–58.
28. *N* 2. 368.
29. *N* 2. 368. This passage seems to me to be of great significance for the resolution of the conflict between the treatment of being in *SZ* and that in the later period. For another statement to the same general effect, see *W* 383, where Heidegger says that "we are ourselves the source of the idea of being," provided, of course, that we understand ourselves in terms of "the transcendence of ecstatic *Dasein*." It is also worth noting that just as a kind of agency is involved in this notion of a "step back," so Heidegger also associates such agency with "the leaving-out of the staying-away of being." In *N* 2. 385 he says that "the will to overcome nihilism . . . locks itself out of the disclosure of the *essence* of nihilism . . . although without being allowed to know what it is doing."
30. *N* 2. 451.
31. What remains unclear, however, is whether Heidegger ever read anything by Sartre other than the short essay "Existentialism and Humanism" on which he comments in his *Letter on Humanism*. If he had read Sartre's *Being and Nothingness*, he could hardly have dismissed the possibility of an affinity between that work and *SZ* as unqualifiedly as he does in the *Letter*. To say this is not, of course, to deny that great differences of orientation separate *Being and Nothingness* and *SZ*. For an excellent comparison of the philosophies of these two thinkers, see Joseph Fell, *Heidegger and Sartre: An Essay on Being and Place* (New York:Columbia University Press, 1979).
32. *W* 157.
33. *W* 163, 165.
34. *W* 180–81; *SZ* 132.
35. *SZ* 212.
36. *W* 167.
37. The contrast between Heidegger's use of the terms *Dasein* and *Existenz* and the traditional philosophical uses of these terms is explicitly set forth in *SZ* 7 and 42.
38. *W* 163.
39. *W* 168.
40. *W* 168.
41. "The being of *Dasein* is care. It comprises in itself facticity (thrownness), existence (project) and falling (*Verfallen*). In its being *Dasein* is thrown; it is *not* brought into its There by itself. In its being it is determined as a potentiality for being which belongs to itself but which it has *not* in its own right (*als es selbst*) conferred upon itself" (*SZ* 284). My translation of this passage differs in important ways from the MacQuarrie-Robinson rendering. See also chap. 3, n. 77.
42. See, for example, the references to *Dasein* as choosing "its hero" (*SZ* 385).
43. *W* 163.
44. *W* 163.
45. *W* 163.

46. *W* 163.
47. *W* 163.
48. *P* 152 and 153.
49. *P* 153.
50. "The look (*der Blick*), *thea*, is not looking (*das Blicken*) as an activity or act of the 'subject,' but the aspect (*der Anblick*) as the arising coming-toward-one of the 'object' " (*P* 153).
51. *P* 154.
52. *P* 154. The interpretation of just what Heidegger is committing himself to in this introduction of the notion of gods presents many problems. On the one hand, he makes a very firm distinction between the Greek understanding of the divine (*to theion*) and anything that has to do with *religio* (*HAD* 14–15). He says that the Greeks did not have a "religion" or a "theology," since both religion and theology as they are now understood derive from Roman, rather than Greek, sources. On the other hand, although he had identified philosophy with atheism early in his career (*PGZ* 109–10), in *P* 166 he characterizes atheism as "godlessness" (*Götterlosigkeit*) and as the "forgetfulness of being" that has "overpowered Western history since the decline of Greece" and remains the "fundamental trait of this Western history itself." For another discussion of these matters, see *VA* 272ff.
53. *P* 154 and 158.
54. A very similar conception is developed by Maurice Merleau-Ponty in his posthumous *Le visible et l'invisible*, pp. 314–15. I have tried to explicate Merleau-Ponty's conception in my article "Merleau-Ponty's 'Ontology of the Visible,' " *Pacific Philosophical Quarterly* 61 (1980): 167–76.
55. *P* 160.
56. One very noticeable similarity between the two conceptions is the prominence in both of the imagery of light. Heidegger connects the notion of the gods as *daimones* with the Greek verb *daio*, which means "blaze" or "light up"; hence the gods are the *daiontes*, the ones who blaze or light up. This conception is then related to *aletheia* as the clearing of being. For his discussion of these matters, see *P* 157–58, 164–65, and 169. For his earlier use of the imagery of light, see chap. 3. n. 14.
57. In fact, Heidegger denies the personal character of the gods as the Greeks understood them. On this point, see *P* 161–65.
58. Heidegger's essay "Zeit und Sein" was published in *ZSD* 1–25.
59. *H* 364.
60. *ZSD* 5.
61. *ZSD* 12.
62. *ZSD* 12.
63. *ZSD* 12.
64. *ZSD* 6. An interesting passage in the conversation with "a Japanese" is included in *US* 85–155. Heidegger is asked why he used the word *Sein* for the quite different purposes that correspond to the two senses distinguished in this passage (110). Although his interlocutor seems to be suggesting that Heidegger is responsible at least in part for the resulting confusion, Heidegger claims to have kept the two senses clearly distinguished from one another.
65. *ZSD* 14.
66. *ZSD* 14–15. In *P* 226–40 there is an important discussion of the difference between Rilke's and Heidegger's understanding of *das Offene*.
67. *ZSD* 16.
68. *ZSD* 16.
69. *ZSD* 16.
70. *ZSD* 17.

71. *ZSD* 17.
72. *ZSD* 17.
73. *ZSD* 17.
74. *ZSD* 18. The concept of *das Ereignis* is introduced at *ZSD* 20–25.
75. *ZSD* 24 and 23.
76. *ZSD* 24.
77. *EM* 47.
78. *SZ* 226.
79. The only word in Heidegger's vocabulary that could really serve in this capacity would be *Lebewesen* ("living thing"), which he uses to translate the Greek word *zoon* ("animal") in the standard definitions of man as a "rational animal" (*SZ* 48, 165). I do not know of any passage in which Heidegger suggests that if man were to cease to be man—a possibility he frequently mentions—he would become a mere *Lebewesen*, but in *W* 334 a transition from the latter to the former is described.
80. *W* 102, n. 2, gives the original wording of this passage.
81. The concept of the world as the World-Fourfold is, of course, common in the later writings; but it is clearly quite different from the concept of the world that is an ontólogical character of *Dasein*.
82. Heidegger's principal discussion of the concept of *physis* is his essay "On the Essence and Concept of *Physis*. Aristotle's Physics, B, 1" (*W* 309–71). Other treatments of this topic can be found in *EM* 138ff. and *HAD* 141–81.
83. *EM* 139.
84. *EM* 139.
85. *EM* 139.
86. *EM* 139–40. The similarity of this conception to that of *Dasein* as "breaking into space" is striking. See chap. 3, n. 18.
87. *W* 342.
88. Heidegger's discussion of these Greek words is to be found in *P* 33–42 and 104ff. It would seem to follow that if hiddenness has this objective character, what is hidden would have to be hidden from everyone. But this is not always or necessarily the case.
89. *P* 40.
90. *P* 41 and 105.
91. *P* 47.
92. *P* 108.
93. *P* 91 and 105.
94. *P* 105.
95. *P* 123.
96. See chap. 3.
97. *HAD* 44ff. and *GB* 109–17.
98. Heidegger's fullest account of this difference is given in *ID*, but it does not resolve this question. In *SZ* it was unequivocally clear that entities (*Seiendes*) were independent of being (*Sein*); thus being was not what made entities entities. In *ID*, by contrast, Heidegger appears to deny this when he says that it is not as though "entities which were antecedently without being could only then be approached by being" (62). He goes on to speak of being as "passing over" entities, thereby "disconcealing" them; and the suggestion is that as a result they are enabled to *be* entities. This leaves unresolved the question of whether in the absence of being *das Seiende* could be distinguished from nothingness. In the afterword to *What Is Metaphysics?* published in 1943, Heidegger speaks of entities as remaining in "beingless-

ness" (*Seinslosigkeit*), which, he says, is not *ein nichtiges Nichts* (*W* 102). This seems to imply that entities do have some independence of being; but the whole matter is rendered problematic by the fact that in the same essay Heidegger speaks of entities as "descending from being" and claims that being itself is more primordial (*anfänglicher*) than entities (*W* 100).

99. *H* 40.
100. *H* 33.
101. *ZSD* 34. A similar statement was in fact made in *SZ* 17, where it is stated that the analysis of *Dasein* only displays the being of *Dasein* and does not interpret the meaning (*Sinn*) of this being. Heidegger adds that this repetition of the analysis of *Dasein* would take place on a higher ontological level. This can only mean that the further analysis of *Dasein* he proposes would be ontological in the sense of involving being as such, rather than just the being of the kind of entity that *Dasein* is. But if *Dasein* as that kind of entity is such as to involve a familiarity with being, and if being obtains only in the understanding of being that is peculiar to *Dasein*, this distinction between a higher and a lower kind of ontological treatment of *Dasein* does not seem to hold up.
102. *EM* 120.
103. The most important collection of essays on language is *US*, but there are also essays in *VA*. There is also Heidegger's extensive writing about Hölderlin's poetry, especially his *Erläuterungen zu Hölderlins Dichtung* (Frankfurt am Main:Klostermann,1944).
104. *US* 204.
105. For an extreme version of the view that the speaker in speaking creates the language he speaks, see Sartre, *Being and Nothingness* (New York:Philosophical Library, 1956), pp. 514ff.
106. *US* 255.
107. For Heidegger's account of *die Sage*, see *UD* 253ff.
108. *US* 254–55.
109. *US* 254.
110. *VA* 176ff.
111. *US* 211.
112. *US* 266.
113. *W* 164.
114. *W* 164.
115. *US* 255–56.
116. *US* 251.
117. *US* 215.
118. This is the more surprising since in *GM* Heidegger had fully acknowledged the distinctive mode of being of nonhuman animals. See chap. 10.

9. BEING AS THE HISTORY OF BEING

1. The reference is to chapter 5 of the second division.
2. *SZ* 386.
3. Perhaps the closest he comes to a statement of such a conception is in *GP* 39–43.
4. *SZ* 378–82.
5. The principal examination of the historiographical tradition under the aegis of Heideggerian views is H.-G. Gadamer's *Wahrheit und Methode: Grundzüge einer philosophischen Hermeneutik* (Tübingen:J. C. B. Mohr/Siebeck, 1960), translated as *Truth and Method* (New York:Seabury, 1975). This book is largely a critique of the conception of "method" under which empirical history has attempted to attain truth about the

past; and the judgment it implies on this whole undertaking does not seem to be very much more favorable than Heidegger's.

6. Heidegger's main discussions of Hegel can be found in *SZ* 428–36, *ID* 37–50ff., *W* 255–72, *H* 105–92, and *HPG* (entire).

7. *H* 166.

8. *ID* 43.

9. It is hard, e.g., to imagine Heidegger in the period of *SZ* speaking as he does in *GF* 129 of "the vocation for thought (*denkerische Bestimmung*) and mission (*Aufgabe*) of the Greeks," which is said to have been to "initiate thinking itself and to bring it to its ground." There is a strikingly Hegelian flavor to this whole discussion.

10. Heidegger remained resolutely opposed to all conceptions of dialectic during all phases of his philosophical career. See his comments in *SZ* 171 and *HPG* 104–06.

11. *SZ* 222.

12. See, e.g., *SZ* 294, where Heidegger claims that if the desire for "available and calculable possibilities of action" were met as it would be, for example, in a cognitivistic ethic, the existence of *Dasein* would be "forced under the idea of a business procedure that can be regulated" and would lose "the possibility of action."

13. *SZ* 268.

14. *W* 173.

15. In *SZ* 213 Heidegger quotes the Aristotelian definition of ontology as concerned with *to on he on*. Heidegger translates this as *das Seiende ... als Seiendes* and adds *das heiszt, hinsichtlich seines Seins* (that is, in respect of its being). In the period of *SZ* generally, this equivalence of "entities *as* entities" with "being" seems to be accepted; and earlier chapters have shown how closely Heidegger links his concept of being as presence with the concept of entities showing themselves as entities. Indeed there are clear indications that Heidegger himself accepts this equivalence as, for example, in *GM* 523, where a distinction is made between *to on hos on* and *to on he on*, and a concern with the latter is identified with "ontological truth." In another passage, the same distinction is made in the form of a contrast between two senses that can be given to "*to on he on*" (*GM* 467). In *GP*, he had stated that "entities can encounter us *as* entities only in the light of an understanding of being (390)"; he goes on to point out that in antiquity there was a pronounced tendency to construe *to on he on* ontically rather than ontologically, with the result that being is assimilated to the status of an entity (454). By contrast, in the later writings, this notion of an acceptable and an unacceptable version of the equivalence of being and *to on he on* yields to an insistence that what is truly ontological has to do with being as being (*N* 2. 346). Heidegger does not explain what the difference would be between a concern with being as being and one with *to on he on* in the acceptable sense that requires the kind of understanding of temporality that antiquity did not have (*GP* 454).

16. Passages from the later period in which the equivalence of "being" and "entities as entities" is denied include *W* 162, *EM* 77, *VA* 143, *H* 92–94, and *N* 2. 345–65. In this connection, it should be noted that during this period Heidegger continues to hold that even the sciences that deal with entities as entities and misunderstand being by assimilating it to entities are enabled by being itself "to see the entities they represent as such"—that is, as entities (*W* 248).

17. Heidegger insisted strongly on the nexus between being and truth throughout his career. For a full discussion of the issues involved, see chap. 10.

18. See, e.g., *W* 162.

19. There is no suggestion in Heidegger's writings that the distinctive role of the Greeks in the history of being is one that can be established only by a detailed philological comparison of the verb "to be" in Greek and in other languages. However, a com-

parison of this kind has been carried out by Johannes Lohmann, with results that he claims support Heidegger's general thesis about the Greeks. See his "M. Heidegger's 'Ontological Difference' and Language," in *On Heidegger and Language*, ed. J. Kockelmans (Evanston:Northwestern University Press, 1972).

20. For Heidegger's discussion of these shifts and their import, see *P* 57–79.
21. *N* 2. 483 and 489.
22. *H* 371.
23. "The history of being is being itself and this alone" (*N* 2. 489). More specifically, "the essence of nihilism is being itself in the staying-away of its unhiddenness which, as its own, is It itself and in staying away determines its 'is' " (*N* 2. 356).
24. Heidegger is not espousing cultural determinism in any of its familiar empirical forms, however; so the statement in chap. 8 about the distinction between Heidegger's theses about language and structuralist views of human thought can be allowed to stand.
25. *H* 62.
26. *US* 130.
27. *SZ* 50–51 and 81–82. See also Heidegger's review of *Das mythische Denken*, the second volume of Ernst Cassirer's *Die Philosophie der symbolischen Formen* (Berlin: 1925); English translation in *The Piety of Thinking: Essays by Martin Heidegger*, ed. J. G. Hart and J. C. Maraldo (Bloomington:Indiana University Press, 1976), pp. 32–45.
28. *HAD* 3.
29. *US* 86–88.
30. Heidegger discusses this claim in his essay "Hegel und die Griechen," in *W* 255–72.
31. *SZ* 28; *EM* 54.
32. See the discussion of these terms in *VWF* 60–62, where Heidegger defends his claim that the essential meaning of *ousia* is always that of *parousia*.
33. See, e.g., his comments on the interpretation of the fragments of Heraclitus in *HAD* 35–39.
34. *P* 208. For a rather unconvincing explanation of why the Greeks did not achieve a conceptual understanding of *aletheia*, see *GF* 108–33.
35. *EM* 147;*W* 336–42.
36. This is presumably what Heidegger has in mind when he says that for the Greeks *aletheia* was *das Fraglose*—"the unproblematic" (*GF* 118).
37. "Every human being in history knows (*kennt*) being immediately although without knowing about (*erkennen*) it" (*P* 222).
38. *H* 336. In his essay on Aristotle's concept of *physis*, Heidegger says that "the being of *physis* (and *physis* as being) remains unprovable because it does not need a proof; and it does not need it because wherever entities deriving from *physis* stand in the open, it has shown itself and stands in view" (*H* 333). This statement makes it hard to understand the statements in the Anaxagoras essay in which being is said to be hidden when entities are revealed by it.
39. *H* 336.
40. *H* 336.
41. *H* 337.
42. *EM* 137–38.
43. The relevant passages are *SZ* 14 and *P* 206. Heidegger discusses the well-known passage from Aristotle's *De Interpretatione* in which he appears to defend a correspondence conception of mental states (*ta pathemata tes psyches*) in *L* 167.
44. *W* 369–70.
45. Heidegger's knowledge of medieval philosophy was remarkably broad and deep, as can be seen from his early work *Die Kategorien- und Bedeutungslehre des Duns Scotus* (Tübingen:J. C. B. Mohr, 1916) and discussions like the ones in *GP* 108–40.

46. *N* 2. 429–36; *EM* 148.
47. *SZ* 96.
48. *N* 2. 141ff. and 387.
49. *N* 2. 162.
50. *N* 2. 135–41.
51. *N* 2. 449.
52. *N* 2. 169.
53. Nor does the long discussion in *GP* 389–418 of *Verstehen* as an existential modality of *Dasein* as being-in-the-world contain any hint of a suggestion that the active involvement of *Dasein* in the business of the world has anything to do with subjectivism.
54. *N* 2. 171.
55. *H* 86–92 and 109.
56. *H* 88 and 94.
57. *H* 110.
58. *H* 94 and 106.
59. That critique is developed further in *FD* 49–108 along the lines laid down in *N* 2.
60. See, for example, the discussion of Leibniz in *N* 2. 436–50 and of Kant in *W* 273–307.
61. *W* 104.
62. There is a passage of biting irony at the expense of the self-importance of the modern thinker in *HAD* 105–06.
63. See, for example, his statements on this subject in *P* 264 and *H* 111.
64. This is what Heidegger conveys by crossing out the word *das Sein* in his essay "Zur Seinsfrage," in *W* 213–53. In this context he also speaks of the "forgetfulness of being" as only "apparently separate from it" (243) and as really "belonging to the matter of being itself." He also observes that this crossing out of being, which expresses its paradoxical presence in absence, can help to fend off "the almost ineradicable habit of thinking of being as something out-there (*ein Gegenüber*) that stands on its own and then every once in a while approaches man" (*W* 239).
65. *EM* 29. Whether Heidegger can really be regarded as in some sense the philosopher of the environmental movement seems to me problematic, since, in spite of what now seems the remarkable prescience of his statements about "the destruction of the earth," there is little evidence of a concern on his part for the impact on living things of modern technologies and their by-products.
66. *EM* 29.
67. *EM* 34–38.
68. *P* 222.
69. *H* 42.
70. *VA* 33 and 40.
71. *VA* 33.
72. *VA* 40.
73. *VA* 42.
74. *N* 2. 389 and 371.
75. *N* 2. 485.
76. *VA* 135–36.
77. In *GF* 138 Heidegger seems to suggest that the Greeks somehow had to limit themselves to the acknowledgment of being as such without further conceptual elaboration of the notion of openness in order that "in the future thought might be initiated in the West and man as one who is (*als seiender*) could know himself as such in the midst of what is."
78. In a marginal note in his copy of *SZ* Heidegger annotates his own statement that

various earlier scientific inquiries had "aimed at *Dasein*" but failed to understand it properly. He says: "They absolutely did not aim at *Dasein*" (*SZ* 45).

10. THE INTERDEPENDENCE OF EXISTENCE AND PRESENCE

1. *W* 203.
2. *W* 52.
3. *P* 221.
4. T. S. Eliot, *Collected Poems* (New York:Harcourt, Brace, 1930), p. 63. In this poem "Mr. Eliot's Sunday Morning Service," the reference is, of course, to *to hen* rather than *to on*.
5. Heidegger appears to be developing some such point as this in *VA* 63ff., where he discusses what is unavoidably presupposed in each domain of inquiry.
6. *H* 70.
7. *H* 71.
8. *H* 71.
9. See J. Hoffmeister, ed., *Phänomenologie des Geistes* (Leipzig: Meiner, 1949), pp. 158–71.
10. *G* 63.
11. *G* 63.
12. There is presumably no way in which the attributive use of such property-terms as "red" can be disassociated from the predicative use; and if so, it follows that an "is" is implicit in the attributive use as well.
13. The reference is to the discussion in *GM* 435–532.
14. *GM* 518.
15. *GM* 519.
16. *GM* 494.
17. *GM* 519.
18. *GM* 524–32.
19. This discussion is in *GM* 272–396.
20. *GM* 375.
21. *GM* 368.
22. *GM* 372. There is a conspicuous irony in the fact that the contrast between animals and man is interpreted here in terms of the capacity of the latter for objectifying something in its environment as something *vorhanden*. One wonders whether in that case the notion of the *zuhanden* should not be applicable to the modality in which things are accessible to animals.
23. *GM* 413.
24. *GM* 489.
25. *GM* 496–97. This emendation by Heidegger of his own previous characterization of truth seems to go a long way toward meeting the criticism directed against the latter by E. Tugendhat in his *Der Wahrheitsbegriff bei Husserl und Heidegger* (Berlin:de Gruyter, 1967), pp. 331–48.
26. *GM* 497.
27. *GM* 497 and 505.
28. There is no evidence of a disposition on Heidegger's part to allow there to be *many* truths; and the singularity and uniqueness of truth follow in any case from the fact that being with which truth is in effect identified has these characteristics.
29. The singularity and incomparability of being are unambiguously asserted in *GM* 461 and *GB* 50–52.
30. Most of Heidegger's references to being as *to koinon* have a negative flavor since he is concerned to deny that the generality of being is that of a genus (*GB* 46, *GF* 62, *W*

207). Nevertheless, it is equally clear from *GB* 51 that being is in Heidegger's view "that which is common to all (entities) without exception and thus that which is most common (*das Gemeinste*)"; being thus qualifies in an affirmative sense as *to koinon*.

31. *GM* 447.
32. *GM* 450. For an unusual—for Heidegger—characterization of the antagonistic elements that are latent in this *Miteinandersein*, see *PGZ* 387.
33. *GM* 525 and 513.
34. *GM* 495.
35. *GM* 526.
36. *GM* 527–28.
37. *GM* 528.
38. *GM* 528–29.
39. *GM* 301.
40. *GM* 301. See also *GM* 408.
41. *GM* 402.
42. *GM* 402.
43. *GM* 515.
44. *GP* 185ff.
45. *GP* 192.
46. *GM* 196.
47. *GM* 197.
48. *GP* 207.
49. *VWF* 293.
50. *VWF* 294.
51. *GM* 302.

CONCLUSION

1. P. Strawson, *Individuals: An Essay in Descriptive Metaphysics* (London:Methuen, 1959).
2. Ibid., pp. 102–03. It is interesting that Strawson refers here to "pure consciousness" as "the ego-substance."
3. Ibid., p. 87.
4. A. Danto, *Analytical Philosophy of Action* (Cambridge: Cambridge University Press, 1973), chap. 3.

INDEX

Absence: element in being as presence, 85, 181, 221; in Greek thought, 208; in history of being, 222

Action: of *Dasein*, 58–60, 65–66, 89–93, 108–09, 114, 148; in later writings, 155–56, 220, 231, 235

Agency: of *Dasein*, 91–92, 148, 157, 171, 195, 225; in later writings, 168, 214, 220, 228–30

Anaximander, 4, 209, 210

Animals, their place in Heidegger's ontology, 68, 192, 205, 236–37, 241–42, 251

Appearing: as showing itself (*phainesthai*), 47, 57–58, 207; two meanings of, 164–65; as *physis*, 179; in language, 187. *See also* Error

Aristotle, 4, 79–80, 83, 111, 134, 135, 141, 207, 210

Assertion: as expressing being, 130, 187; and *Dasein*, 131–32

Authenticity: of temporality, 96–97; preferred status of, 197. *See also* Inauthenticity

Befindlichkeit: concept of, 102, 103, 104–11; ontological character of, 108–09; and knowledge, 109–11, 118, 119

Behaviorism, 252. *See also* Physicalism

Being: concept of, xv–xix passim, 135–41, 232–35; history of, xviii, 195–224, 259; of consciousness, 23, 24, 26, 102; relation of, to *Dasein* and man, 72, 145, 149, 158–60, 174, 177, 182, 186, 220, 233; of entities, 94–95, 145, 178–85, 201, 206, 209, 240; temporality of, 95, 143–44, 175–76, 235–36; and language, 130, 190, 193; as truth, 141–42, 144–45, 230–38; as presence, 143–48 passim, 158–60, 175, 180, 201, 209, 226–31; as giving,

168, 174–77, 200, 213, 228; in Greek thought, 172, 179–81, 202–10, 212; as *Ereignis*, 174–76, 186, 205; relation of, to world, 178; as finite, 181–82

Being-in-the-world: explained, 32–35; as entity, 52, 62; as *Befindlichkeit*, 107, 108; role of, in language, 123, 129; not understood by Descartes, 212

Belief, Heidegger's depreciation of, 13, 55

Bergson, Henri, 79, 86

Berkeley, George, 249

Body (human): concept of, 52–53; role of, in knowing how, 112; in dualism, 217; Strawson's view of, 252–53; identity of, with mind, 257

Brentano, Franz, 16, 23

Care (*Sorge*), as characterizing *Dasein*, 103–04

Causality: marginal status of, in concept of world, 59; role of *Dasein* in, 114–15

Choice: role of, in transcendence, 66–71 passim; role of, in temporality, 91–96 passim, role of, in *Befindlichkeit*, 108–09, 118, 119; in *Mitsein*, 148–49; choosing of, 198

Cicero, Marcus Tullius, 203, 209

Clearing (*Lichtung*): *Dasein* as, 63, 73–74, 168–69, 227, 231; being as, 164, 168–70, 171, 199–200, 227; entities in, 180, 182–83; as active, 230

Common sense: Heidegger's view of, 4; alleged naivete of, 12; about time, 85–86; not familiar with ontological difference, 202; role of, in theoretical knowledge, 228–29; and philosophy of mind, 250

Communication: as function of *Mitsein*, 132–33; in later writings on language, 191–92; communities of, 204; as involv-

Communication (*continued*)
ing presence, 218; in relationships among human beings, 240–242
Computers, as models of human being, 255–56
Consciousness: Heidegger's critique of, xiv, 8, 21–27; etymology, 14–15; picture theory of, 16; pure, 18; Husserl's concept of, 19–27 passim; Heidegger's ontological interpretation of, 102; nontheoretical, 105; contemporary treatments of, 250–252 passim, 257
Constitution: of objects, 19; as function of *Dasein*, 25–26

Danto, Arthur, 254–55
Dasein: concept of, xvi, 9–10, 62–74, 102–03, 197–98, 226–28; transcendence of, 67–70; individuation of, 70, 146, 226; temporality of, 75–76, 77, 78, 85, 89–92, 94–101 passim, 142–43; as *Befindlichkeit*, 105–10 passim; potentiality (*Seinkönnen*) of, 113–14; as understanding, 115–20 passim; and language, 129–33; and truth, 130–32; relation of, to being, 138–39, 144, 145, 164, 168, 169, 170, 227, 233; in later writings, 155–77 passim, 185–86; relation of, to concept of man, 163, 177, 183; historicity of, 194–98
Death, as distinctive possibility of *Dasein*, 72, 76, 149
Decision: implicit in temporality, 90, 96; in interpretation, 119, 120; anonymous, 198; directives for, 219
Descartes, René, xiii, xix, 3, 4, 5–15 passim, 34, 46, 60, 79, 134, 156, 211–13, 214, 215, 224, 248, 250
Dewey, John, 116
Dilthey, Wilhelm, 111–12
Discourse (*Rede*), as founding language, 102–04, 128, 185. *See also* Language, Speech

Earth: contrasted to world, 183–84; in World-Fourfold, 188–89; control over, 215
Entities (*Seiendes*): kinds of, xviii-xix, 137; relation of, to world, 32, 45–50 passim, 78, 135, 161–62, 227; presence as entities, 63, 68, 74, 75, 94–95, 146, 166, 176,
200–01, 225, 236–37, 238; independence of, from *Dasein*, 97–98; relation of, to being as presence, 135–41, 144, 160, 178–85, 189, 196, 209–10; as theme of metaphysics, 154, 210–11; contrasted to states of affairs, 232–35
Error: perceptual, 10; Heidegger's view of, 46–48
Essence: being as, xix; of consciousness, 26; as What contrasted to That, 137; of *Dasein*, 226
Ethics: as directives of being, 219; binding character of, 242–45; inherent in concept of person, 251
Evolution, theory of, 241–42
Existence: and presence, xvii-xviii, 74, 158–60, 225–45; as mode of being of *Dasein*, 39, 52, 60–62, 148–49, 164, 181, 226; as uncovering possibilities, 69–70; temporality of, 75, 76; active character of, 103, 198; of language, 124; of truth, 131, 144; and being, 137, 144, 169–70; as historical, 195

Facts. *See* States of Affairs
Feeling: subjective character of, 102, 104; intentionality of, 105; ontological interpretation of, 109; unconscious, 110; of pain and pleasure, 110–11, 118
Finiteness: of subject, 30; of temporality, 82; of being and truth, 181–82; of *Dasein*, 184, 196, 197; Hegel on, 197
Forgetting: of being, 162, 177, 200; Greek understanding of, 180
Freedom: of *Dasein*, 66, 94, 197; of man in being bound by truth, 238; Kant's view of, 242
Future: Heidegger's conception of, 84–87 passim; not a concept, 90; as involving choice, 91–92; unity with past and present, 94–99 passim; role of, in causality, 115; in Greek understanding of time, 208; as modality of being, 235

Given, Heidegger's concept of, 36; temporality as, 143–44
God: relation of, to world, 29, 68; his knowledge, 77–78, 93–94; and time, 98; as super-entity, 137; Greek, 172–73, 184–85; in World-Fourfold, 188; as ground, 211; death of, 218; Hegel on, 231
Goethe, J. W., 31

Greek thought: Heidegger's interpretation of, 202–03, 223; conception of being in, 206–10; as lacking idea of culture, 218

Hegel, G. W. F.: 95, 196–97, 199, 206, 214, 215, 217, 221, 224, 231
Heidegger, Martin: reputation, xiii; development of his thought, xiv; view of phenomenology, 15–16; revision of his thought, 153–60; contemporary significance of, 247–59
Heraclitus, 4, 202, 210
Hermeneutic circle, 121–22
Hiddenness (*Verborgenheit*): as "night," 83–85; of *Dasein*, 197; of presence, 200, 207–08, 222; of being, 209. *See also* Unhiddenness
Historicity of *Dasein*, 147, 194–98
Historiography: Heidegger's view of, 195–96; relation to history of being, 222
History: of being, 194–224; philosophy of, 196–97; of consciousness, 198–99; conceptual, 203–10, 223
Human Being(s): and being, 51, 154, 165, 168–70, 174, 177, 186, 200, 209, 222, 230; as rational animal, 53; difference from animals, 68; powers of, 69, 211–12, 220; relation of, to world and presence, 72, 74, 145, 188, 197; and time, 82, 176; and *Dasein*, 154, 159–60, 163–64, 177–78, 183, 226; and language, 190–191; and truth, 232; ethical character of, 241–45; as person, 251; computer models for, 255–56
Humanism, Heidegger's critique of, 168, 169, 171
Hume, David, 87, 249
Husserl, Edmund, xiii, xvi, 15–27, 104–05

Immanence: Husserl's conception of, 21–23; Heidegger's rejection of, 22–23, 67, 89, 102
Inauthenticity, 121, 123, 133, 147, 204. *See also* Authenticity
Indexicality: as feature of world, 37–38, 42, 43, 65; temporal, 83
Individuation: of consciousness, 20–22, 23, 24; of *Dasein*, 70, 146–47, 226; of temporality of *Dasein*, 96–97; of *Befindlichkeit*, 107–08; of potentiality of *Dasein*, 114

Intentionality: Heidegger's use of, xvi, 20, 22–27 passim, 28, 47, 67; Husserl's concept of, 16, 19, 105
Interpretation, 117–22
Intersubjectivity: Husserl's theory of, 20–21; as feature of world, 44–45, 70–71; of temporality, 95; of language, 132–33, 191–92; of being, 146–47; and subjectivism, 168, 218; in perception, 173–74; of truth, 238–45
Involvement (*Bewandtnis*): 43–44, 106

Joyce, James, 55

Kant, Immanuel, xiii, 3, 11, 29–30, 38, 93–94, 100, 134, 142–43, 214, 224, 237, 242–43
Knowing how and that, 112–13, 122
Knowledge: Heidegger's concept of, 12–13; consciousness as, 14; perceptual, 34; human k. not atemporal, 77–78; relation to *Befindlichkeit*, 104–05, 108–11; role in understanding, 111–12, 113, 116; scientific, 119–22; mathematical, 211

Language: relation of, to world, 42, 125–57; use of, for ontological purposes, 57; tense system of, 87–88; and knowing, 112; and interpretation, 117; ontological status of, 123–33; philosophy of, 123–24, 249–51, 254; Heidegger's later theory of, 185–93; translation, 203–04; Greek, 206–08; facts as artifacts of, 233; relation to human/animal contrast, 236–37
Leibniz, G. W., 212, 214, 215
Logic: Heidegger's attitude toward, 125, 215; logical states of computers and brains, 255–56

Man: *See* Human Being(s)
Meaning: as instrumental articulation of world, 41, 43–44, 50, 188; in interpretation, 118; absent from nature, 120; of being, 139
Memory, 80–81, 86–87, 258
Merleau-Ponty, Maurice, 10
Metaphysics: Heidegger's definition of, 154, 155; Western, 166, 171, 206, 215

Mill, John Stuart, 249

Mind: the philosophy of, xvi, 3, 75, 247–59; Heidegger's conception of, 50; and language, 124; dualistic view of, 217

Mitsein: Heidegger's conception of, 71–72; and temporality, 96–97; in understanding, 112; in communication, 132–33; relation of, to being as presence, 146, 148, 149, 157; in language, 192–93; negative forms of, 194, 218; directives for, 219; and truth, 226, 238–45

Moods (*Stimmungen*), 107, 110, 185

Natural attitude, 15, 16–17, 24–25

Nature: relation of, to world, 31, 36; as nontemporal, 98–99; as object of science, 120, 122; derivation of, from *physis*, 210

Newton, Isaac, 31, 115, 140, 182

Nietzsche, Friedrich, 206, 211, 213, 214, 215, 217, 218, 221, 224

Objectification: of self, 6; of world, 31–32, 36–37, 106; of the *zuhanden*, 43; of time, 91–92; in science, 121–22; of *Dasein*, 197–98; and subjectivism, 213–17 passim, 226, 253

Ontic/Ontological. *See* Ontological Difference

Ontological Difference: applied to actions, 57, 148, 230, 235–36; Heidegger's use of language to express, 59; in relation to temporality of *Dasein*, 98; as distinction of being and entities, 155, 234–35, 239; and truth, 232; applied to Kant's kingdom of ends, 243

Ontology: of subject, 12–13; entities defined in, 114; and language, 123–24; history of, 134; Heidegger's approach to, 137; ancient, 155; of Descartes, 211; and logic, 215; of Strawson, 254

Openness: of entities in world, 57, 60, 73; of *Dasein*, 64, 170, 226; of being, 162–67 passim, 200, 226; as gift, 174; temporal character of, 175; as *Ereignis*, 177; of World-Fourfold, 191–92; absence of concept of, among Greeks, 208–09; compounding of, 227; of animals, 236–37; pre-logical, 240; different forms of, 242

Parmenides, 4, 176, 194, 202, 210, 223, 224

Past: ontological status of, 80–81, 84, 85, 90; memories of, 86; in tense system, 87–88; of *Dasein*, 94, 98, 99; relation of, to being, 95, 235; Greek understanding of, 208

Perception: errors of, 10, 46–48; phenomenology of, 16; intentionality of, 22–23; Descartes's treatment of, 34, 211; Heidegger's analysis of, 54–60; temporality of, 95; and presence, 171, 184; not controlled by concepts, 229–30; our understanding of, 258

Persons, concept of, 247, 251–53

Phenomenology: Heidegger's relation to, 15–16, 28; as study of pure consciousness, 18; relation of, to feelings and emotions, 104–05, 110; linguistic, 124; of temporality, 142

Physicalism: influence of, on Heidegger's thought, 216–17; in contemporary philosophy, 247, 248, 253–55

Plato, 4, 77, 172, 210, 211, 221

Poetry, Heidegger's description of, 133

Possibility: as feature of world, 41–42, 219; of *Dasein*, 66–67, 69–70, 113; death as, 72; choice of, 91, 148–49; future, 92; temporality of, 95, 142; and care, 104; and being, 106, 107, 235–36; role of, in agency, 115, 118, 240–41; in understanding, 116; in historicity, 195

Potentiality (*Seinkönnen*): as "can" of *Dasein*, 113–14; and causality, 115–16

Predication, 130, 234–35

Presence: existence as ground of, xvii, xx, 69–70, 74, 113; as givenness, 35–36; world as milieu of, 45–46, 48–49, 51, 52, 138; and human being, 53, 220–21; in perception, 56, 59; and *Dasein*, 64, 67, 108, 184–85; temporality of, 76, 78, 87, 94, 95; as truth, 131; being as, 140–41, 142, 148–49, 194, 196; singularity of, 146; as ground of existence, 158–60, 164–65, 166, 178; commonness of, 173; and entities, 178–79, 183, 222; and absence, 181–82; in language, 187–88, 190; not consciousness, 199; obscuration of, 199–200, 210, 212–13, 214, 218, 219; as *ousia/parousia*, 207–09; as *physis*, 210; relation of, to history, 221–23; interdependence of, with existence, 225–45; nonconceptual, 230

Present: Heidegger's analysis of the Now, 82–86; relation to past and future, 87–99 passim; mutilation of, 142

Project: role of, in understanding, 118–19; Heidegger's revised view of, 170; and possibility, 235; as essence of man, 240

Properties: relational, 37; Heidegger's attitude to concept of, 40–41, 48, 54, 67, 104, 113, 135–36; and truth, 232

Protagoras, 212

Realism, Heidegger's criticism of, 10–12

Reduction, in Husserl's phenomenology, 17–18, 21; Heidegger's critique of, 22–23

Reference: as structure of world, 41–42; indexical, 45; temporal, 93, 126–27; linguistic, 126–27; of being to *Dasein*, 167; subject as center of, 214; identifying, 252

Representations: in mental substances, 7; Heidegger's critique of concept of, 9–11, 13, 102, 156; unknown to natural attitude, 15; in perception, 55; and presence, 60, 173, 197, 217, 229–30; of time, 82, 93; in linguistic reference, 126; role of, in concept of subject, 163, 165; Descartes's theory of, 212–13; role of, in logic, 215; as function of physical process, 258

Resoluteness (*Entschlossenheit*), 96, 149

Russell, Bertrand, 80–81, 127, 249

Santayana, George, 104

Sartre, Jean-Paul, 168

Schleiermacher, Friedrich, 111

Science: as objectification, 43–44, 119–21, 228; as basis for theories of language use, 123; as basis of modern civilization, 156; linked to modern subjectivism, 213, 214, 216; philosophies of mind based on, 247; application of computer s. to human beings, 256

Self: Cartesian concept of, 6–8, 211–13; empirical, 18, 19–20, 24, 25; transcendental, 18–20, 24, 30, 124; Heidegger's concept of, 65–67; in *Befindlichkeit*, 107; moral, 243–44; Hume's concept of, 249

Selfness (*Selbstheit*), 65–67

Sensation. *See* Sense-data

Sense-data: Heidegger's rejection of, 9–10; Husserl's use of concept of, 24; Descartes on, 34; as meaningless, 50; contrasted to feelings, 105; in the modern philosophy of mind, 249, 251

Space: as in world, 38; and involvements, 44; of *Dasein*, 82–83

Speech: Heidegger's account of, 129; and language, 131, 186–87, 191. *See also* Discourse

States of affairs, relation to being, 232–35, 237–38

Strawson, Peter, 251–53

Suarez, Franciscus, 6

Subject: role of, in Heidegger's thought, xiv, 12–13, 28, 52, 54, 102; in contemporary philosophy of mind, xix, 251, 252; Cartesian, 4, 7, 9, 14, 54, 154, 212; Heidegger's concept of, 25, 26, 50, 93, 168; as temporal, 84; in *Befindlichkeit*, 108; Heidegger's later critique of, 163–64, 171, 180, 214, 218; Hegel's conception of, 196, 215

Subjectivism: origins of, in Greek thought, 4; Heidegger's opposition to, 31–32, 50, 63; nonsubjective character of world, 44–45; later conception and critique of, 154, 155–57 passim, 159, 213, 217, 225; and objectivism, 169, 172, 196, 199, 215, 217, 226, 249

Substance: mental, 6–9, 108, 156, 249, 251; the *vorhanden* as, 39; self-sufficiency of, 60; confused with *ousia*, 154; as archetype for all entities, 211; Cartesian appropriation of, 211, 213, 215, 248

Technology, modern Western, 156, 205, 215, 218, 220

Temporality: in transcendence, 68, 70; Heidegger's theory of, 75–101; and being, 134, 141–44, 175–76, 235, 236; of presence and absence, 181; as historicity, 194–95

Time. *See* World-time

Transcendence: Husserl's concept of, 20–21; replaces intentionality, 27; realizes presence, 52; Heidegger's concept of, 67–70, 82; and choice, 71; and immanence, 89; as temporal, 90, 94–96 passim, 175; in *Befindlichkeit*, 109; project as, 240

Transcendental standpoint: Husserl's version of, 17; Heidegger's opposition to, 24, 77; temptations of, for philosophers, 63, 81–82, 103, 123–24, 127

Truth: correspondence theory of, 123, 132; and being, 130–31, 141–42, 168, 202–03, 225–26, 230, 231–38; as *aletheia*, 144; temporal range of, 182; and presence, 187; of history, 195; order of, 201; intersubjective, 238–45

Turning (*Die Kehre*) of Heidegger's thought, xv, xviii, xx, 144, 153–60

Understanding (*Verstehen*): average, 4–5; preontological, 12; implicit, 34; and indexicality, 38–39; in terms of the world, 97; philosophical use of the term, 102–04; of other people, 111–12; ontological character of, 111–22; and knowledge, 111–13; as project, 118–19; of being, 139–40, 165; as a "power," 185

Unhiddenness (*Unverborgenheit*): of being, 165–67, 194, 221, 227; attributed to gods, 172, 173; as *Ereignis*, 174; as *physis*, 179; as unthought, 209–10, 217; of man, 219; of truth, 232. *See also* Hiddenness

Values, concept not used by Heidegger, 105, 156

Vision: Heidegger's treatment of, 55–56; of animals, 68; as look, 171–73; of gods, 184–85, 206

Vorhanden (present-at-hand): concept of, 39, 40, 41, 42, 48–51, 61–62, 76; temporal form of, 83–84, 89, 94, 96, 99, 100; derivation of, 105; categories as, 113; in theoretical attitude, 121; words as, 126; contrasted to *Dasein*, 155; contrasted to *physis*, 179; mathematical objects as, 211; not applicable to animals, 242

Wittgenstein, Ludwig, 41, 128, 249

World: traditional concept of, 7–14 passim, 54, 249; Husserl's concept of, 17, 19; Heidegger's concept of, 28–51, 52, 200, 233, 257, 258; relation of, to *vorhanden*, 48–51, 179; as possibility, 67; role of, in transcendence, 67–68, relation of, to *Dasein*/man, 70–75 passim; singularity and commonness of, 70–74; relation of, to entities, 73, 75, 97–98, 125; as temporal, 76–78, 87, 89, 93, 97, 98, 99–100, 146; in *Befindlichkeit*, 107; in understanding, 113; as project, 118, 120; relation of, to being, 138; obscuration of, 156, 177, 178, 211; contrasted to earth, 183–84; as World-Fourfold, 188–90, 191, 192; objectified, 217

World-time, 75–98 passim, later conception of, 175–76

Wright, G. H. von, 115

Zuhanden (ready-to-hand): concept of, 39–43; not subjective, 44–45; *vorhanden* derived from, 48–50, 105; and *Dasein*, 65; as temporal, 87, 99; world as, 100, 188, 229; in understanding, 113, 237; language as, 125, 131